CHRISTOPHER COLUMBUS

HIS LIFE AND DISCOVERIES

Mario Di Giovanni

The Mentoris Project
Barbera Foundation, Inc.
P.O. Box 1019
Temple City, CA 91780

Copyright © 1991
Cover photo: ilbusca/istockphoto.com
Cover design: Suzanne Turpin

More information at www.mentorisproject.org

ISBN: 978-1-947431-08-9

Library of Congress Control Number: 2017960478

All rights reserved, which includes the right to reproduce this book or portions thereof in any form whatsoever except as provided by the U.S. Copyright Law. For information, address Barbera Foundation, Inc.

All net proceeds from the sale of this book will be donated to Barbera Foundation, Inc., whose mission is to support educational initiatives that foster an appreciation of history and culture to encourage and inspire young people to create a stronger future.

The Mentoris Project is a series of novels and biographies about the lives of great Italians and Italian-Americans: men and women who have changed history through their contributions as scientists, inventors, explorers, thinkers, and creators. The Barbera Foundation sponsors this series in the hope that, like a mentor, each book will inspire the reader to discover how she or he can make a positive contribution to society.

This book is dedicated to the loving grandchildren of Dr. Mario Di Giovanni: Lisa, Laura, Gina, Angela, and Annette. On behalf of my mother, sister, and myself, I also dedicate this book to all lovers of adventure.

My father did not live to see his work published, but I am sure he would have been overjoyed to know that his labor of love was finally in print.

The Di Giovanni family wishes to thank all those who worked so unselfishly to see this book published, especially Robert Barbera.

—Martin Di Giovanni

Contents

Preface   i

Part I
Of Intrepid Men & Sailing Ships

Chapter One: The American Aborigines   1
Chapter Two: The Pre-Columbian Visitors   5
Chapter Three: The Portuguese Naval Activity   15
Chapter Four: The Physical World of
    Christopher Columbus   29
Chapter Five: The Primary Causes for
    the Great Historical Events   51

Part II
Genoa: Columbus's Birthplace

Chapter Six: Genoa and the Colombos   65
Chapter Seven: Columbus's Early Years   75
Chapter Eight: The Portuguese Experience   85
Chapter Nine: Columbus and the King of Portugal   95

Part III
Columbus in Castile

Chapter Ten: Columbus in Castile   103
Chapter Eleven: Years of Agony; Days of Glory   111
Chapter Twelve: Capitulations and Royal Decrees   123

Part IV
The First Voyage to the Indies

Chapter Thirteen: The Ships and Crew for the First Voyage	133
Chapter Fourteen: Beginning of the Grand Enterprise to the Canaries	139
Chapter Fifteen: The Discovery of the West Indies	149
Chapter Sixteen: From San Salvador to Cuba	157
Chapter Seventeen: The Cuban Experience	171
Chapter Eighteen: Hispaniola	189
Chapter Nineteen: Shipwreck—La Navidad	201

Part V
Homeward Bound to Universal Acclamation

Chapter Twenty: Return Voyage, 1493	217
Chapter Twenty-One: Interlude in Portugal—Journey's End	233
Chapter Twenty-Two: Columbus's Letter—An Account of his Discovery	243
Chapter Twenty-Three: The Conquering Hero Returns Home	255

Part VI
The Second Voyage to the Indies

Chapter Twenty-Four: The Second Voyage of Discovery	269
Chapter Twenty-Five: A Litany of Saints	279
Chapter Twenty-Six: Return to Navidad	291
Chapter Twenty-Seven: Isabela and Cibao	305

Chapter Twenty-Eight: In Search of Terra Firma—
    The Explorations of Cuba, 1494   317
Chapter Twenty-Nine: Return To Isabela—
    June 13–September 19   327
Chapter Thirty: Discord in Isabela—
    Trouble with the Indians   337
Chapter Thirty-One: A Period of Discontent   349
Chapter Thirty-Two: Columbus Returns to Spain—
    March 10–June 11, 1496   359

Part VII

The Third Voyage to the Indies
June 11, 1496–May 25, 1498

Chapter Thirty-Three: Approval and Preparations for
    the Third Voyage   371
Chapter Thirty-Four: Third Voyage of Discovery—
    Landfall in Trinidad   383
Chapter Thirty-Five: Discovery of the Gulf of Paria and
    the New Continent   395
Chapter Thirty-Six: Rebellion in Hispaniola   407
Chapter Thirty-Seven: Columbus in Disgrace   421

Part VIII

The Fourth Voyage to the Indies
May 1502–November 1504

Chapter Thirty-Eight: Preparations for a Fourth Voyage   435
Chapter Thirty-Nine: Start of Fourth Voyage—
    Frightful Hurricane   447

Chapter Forty: Searching for a Passage to India	459
Chapter Forty-One: Adventure Along the Coast of Veragua and Panama	469
Chapter Forty-Two: Agony and Tragedy in Belén	483
Chapter Forty-Three: Homeward Bound from Belén	503
Chapter Forty-Four: Seeking Help in Hispaniola—Mutiny in Jamaica	519
Chapter Forty-Five: Home at Last	531

Part IX
The Death of Columbus
Epilogue 1505–1573

Chapter Forty-Six: Death of Columbus	541
Chapter Forty-Seven: Epilogue	557
Appendix A	573
Appendix B	575
Appendix C	581
Notes	583
About the Author	605

Preface

The life and voyages of Christopher Columbus are better documented than those of any other great navigator of his period. Many contemporaries who knew him personally and had the literary ability to portray his life and accomplishments wrote about him in great detail.

The first chronicler to report on Columbus was the Italian Peter Martyr (Pietro Martire), born in 1456 in Lombardy in the town of Anghiera on the south shore of Lake Maggiore. One of the most learned men of his age, he was the true Renaissance man. At the age of thirty he was invited by the Spanish ambassador in Rome to join the faculty at Salamanca and given the task of instructing the scions of the royal household. He was presented to the Sovereigns at Saragossa during the war with Granada and as a member of the military retinue kept a record, through his letter writing, of many campaigns against the Moors. He was sent as ambassador extraordinary by Ferdinand and Isabella to the sultan of Egypt to settle a very delicate problem: the sultan had threatened to put all Christians in his realm to death unless Spain put an end to the war with Granada. He discharged his duties with great ability and through clever diplomacy persuaded the sultan to retract his ultimatum.

Peter Martyr was with the court at Barcelona in April 1493, when Columbus returned from his first voyage to the New

World. He was able to obtain firsthand accounts from the Admiral and his shipmates—a practice he followed whenever the opportunity presented itself. Through these interviews, Martyr eventually wrote a history of the discoveries even though he himself never sailed on any of the voyages. His principal work is an account of the discoveries of the New World in eight parts, each containing ten chapters written in Latin but later translated into various languages. In many ways Peter Martyr may be considered the first news reporter in history, because in letters to distinguished contemporaries, he related current occurrences of the times. He was the Court's secretary and historian.

In one of his letters from Barcelona, dated May 1, 1493, and addressed to Count Borromeo, he gave the first brief account of Columbus's momentous discovery:

Within these last few days, a certain Christopher Columbus has arrived from the Western antipodes; a man of Liguria whom my Sovereigns reluctantly entrusted with three ships to reach that region, for they thought that what he said was fabulous. He has returned and brought specimens of many precious things, but particularly gold, which those countries naturally produce.[1]

Martyr's letters have the timely immediacy of a news wire to a metropolitan newspaper. In another letter to Cardinal Ascanio Sforza, dated September 13, 1493, he gave a more detailed account of the voyage:

The wonders of this terrestrial globe, around which the sun makes a circuit in the space of four and twenty hours, have until our time, as you are well aware, been known only in regard to one hemisphere, merely from the Golden Chersonese (the Malay

Peninsula) to our Spanish Gades (Cádiz). The rest has been given up as unknown by cosmographers and if any mention of it has been made, it has been slight and dubious. But now, Oh blessed enterprise! Under the auspices of our Sovereigns, what has hitherto lain hidden since the first origin of things, has at length been developed. The thing has thus occurred—attend illustrious Prince! A certain Christopher Columbus, a Ligurian, dispatched to those regions with three vessels by my Sovereigns, pursuing the western sun five thousand miles above Gades, achieved his way to the antipodes. Three and thirty successive days they navigated with nought but sky and water. At length from the masthead of the largest vessel in which Columbus sailed, those on the lookout proclaimed the sight of land. He coasted along six islands one of them, as all his followers declare beguiled perchance by the novelty of the scene, is larger than Spain.[2]

Peter Martyr was such an avid letter writer that a collection of them made up thirty-eight books, each containing the letters of one year. Published in 1530, they are of great historical interest because of their spontaneity and candor; however, for the same reasons, they suffer at times from inaccuracies and exaggerations. In 1524 he was appointed to the Counsel of the Indies and died in 1526 in Valladolid, having served the Spanish royalty for thirty-eight years.

One of the most important sources of information on the life of the discoverer of America is the biography written by his son, Ferdinand Columbus. This has been praised by Benjamin Keen as a "moving personal document that vividly recreates the moral and intellectual atmosphere of Columbus's world and the swirling passions of which he was the center."[3]

Ferdinand Columbus was born in August or September of 1488 in Córdoba, as a result of a love affair that the thirty-seven-year-old Columbus had with a young woman of Córdoba, Beatriz Enríquez de Arana. He lived the first few years of his life with his mother in Córdoba but was appointed a page to the king's son, Juan, after Columbus's first voyage. In May 1502, the boy accompanied his father on his fourth voyage: an adventurous, albeit disastrous, voyage that lasted two years and six months; he thus gained much experience and knowledge on all aspects of sailing. In 1509 he accompanied his older brother, Diego, to Hispaniola, but returned to Spain a few months later to resume his scholarly pursuits. He accompanied Emperor Charles V to Italy, Flanders, and Germany and later traveled all over Europe and to parts of Africa and Asia. Through his travels, he acquired much learning in geography, navigation, and natural history.

Very fond of books, he began to collect them at a rapid rate and formed a library of nearly twenty thousand books that he stored in a portion of the house he had built near the Guadalquivir River in Seville. Today this library, reduced to two thousand of Ferdinand's own books, is the renowned Biblioteca Colombina.

Ferdinand wrote the biography of his father during the last years of his life. He died in 1539 and because he had never married, he left the manuscript to Don Diego's widow, Doña María de Toledo. Eventually, the manuscript passed into the hands of her "playboy" son, Don Luis, who was hard-pressed for cash, sold it to the Genoese physician Baliano de Fornari. The work was translated into Italian by Alfonso Ulloa, an Italian of Spanish birth, and published in 1571. Unfortunately, the original Spanish manuscript was lost and never found. There is no doubt that some meaning and accuracy of detail have been lost in the translation, and there is evidence that Ulloa injected some personal conclusions to the narrative. However, in any translation of such magnitude, liberties are taken with idiomatic expressions that may modify the meaning of the original text. We thus face the anomaly of a Spanish manuscript translated first into Italian, then again into Spanish, English, and other foreign languages and that may have lost the spirit and flavor of the original.

In the present volume, I have quoted liberally from Ferdinand's biography of his father in Benjamin Keen's translation, entitled *The Life of the Admiral Christopher Columbus by His Son Ferdinand* (New Brunswick: Rutgers University Press, 1959).

Another contemporary who made use of Ferdinand's original manuscript was Bartolomé de Las Casas in his well-documented *Historia de las Indias* (Madrid, 1875–76). Besides the manuscript, he also had access to the journals and letters of Columbus and to those written by Christopher's brother, Don Bartolomé. He had a writing style which was perhaps even more vivid than that of the great explorer himself. De Las Casas's father had gone to Hispaniola with Columbus on his second voyage and had returned to Seville in 1498. Aroused by his father's account of the New World, Bartolomé, at the age of twenty-eight, went to Hispaniola in 1502 and witnessed Ovando's cruel treatment of the Indians. His zeal in the cause of the Indians, evidenced by his famous treatise of denunciation known as the "Brevisima Relación de la Destrucción de las Indias," lasted a lifetime and earned him the title of "the Apostle of the Indies."

Las Casas joined the Dominican order in 1510 and became a priest, the first to be ordained in the New World. Eventually, he became bishop of Chiapas, and lived in his newly conquered territory of Mexico from 1544 to 1547, after which he returned to Spain and resigned his bishopric in 1550. His *Historia de las*

Indias, consisting of three volumes, was started in 1527 and completed in 1559, when Las Casas was eighty-five years of age. It was not published, however, until 1875–76, because it described in detail the extremely cruel treatment of the Indians at the hands of the conquering Spaniards. A note written in Las Casas's handwriting begs the College of the Order of Preachers of St. Gregorio in Valladolid, to whom he left the first two volumes, not to let any secular person read his books until forty years after his death. The Historia is notable because it covers the history of Spanish discoveries from 1492 to 1520, encompassing not only Columbus's voyages but the aftermath of his discoveries and colonization, as actually seen and experienced by the author.

The source of some of the material in my book has been obtained from Las Casas's abstracts of the first and third voyages of Columbus translated by Milton Anastos and Samuel Eliot Morison for the Heritage Club Book, *Journals and Other Documents on the Life and Voyages of Christopher Columbus* (New York: The Heritage Press, 1963).

Another chronicler who, like Las Casas, served many years in the New World was Gonzalo Fernández de Oviedo y Valdés, commonly known as Oviedo. Born in Madrid in 1478, he was appointed at the age of twelve as one of the pages to the king's son, Juan. He was there as a member of the court when Columbus marched in his triumphant procession with the Indians from the discovered lands. King Ferdinand sent him to the Indies in 1513, where he served in various capacities: first as superintendent of the gold foundries and later, in 1535, as "Alcalde" (chief official) of the fortress of Santo Domingo in Hispaniola. He served in the colonies for thirty-four years, during which time he wrote several important works, the most important being the chronicle of Indies: *Historia General y Natural de Las Indias* (Salamanca,

1547). A monumental work, this history consists of fifty books, divided into three parts, of which only the first part of twenty books was ever printed. It is of particular importance because of his description of the customs of the inhabitants and of the fauna and flora of the New World, all illustrated with his own sketches. It also was instrumental in goading Ferdinand to complete his father's biography. Oviedo's startling claim, in Chapter 3 of Book 2, that the Indies already had belonged to Spain before Columbus's discovery, had to be countered. Thus, in Chapter 10 of his biography, Ferdinand challenges Oviedo's claim by stating:

I believe that Oviedo is led astray by faulty information, by the frailty of old age, or by blind prejudice when he argues that the story refers to the Indies that we possess today and not to the Azores.[4]

Except for this event relating to pre-Columbian visitors, Oviedo speaks well of Columbus both of his ability as a navigator and of his education and personality. In defense of Columbus when he was brought back in chains following Bobadilla's excursion, Oviedo wrote that to succeed in Hispaniola a governor had to have been "angelic indeed and superhuman." He died in Valladolid in 1557 at the age of seventy-nine.

A dear friend and sympathetic confidant with whom Columbus found much solace in his periods of despair was Andrés Bernáldez, curate of the town of Los Palacios from 1488 to 1513 and chaplain to Diego Deza, archbishop of Seville. Immediately following his second voyage, while waiting for an invitation from Sovereigns to pay his respects, Columbus stayed in the Bernáldez home. This gave Bernáldez an opportunity to talk with the Admiral about his recent voyage, the Cuban experience and the wonders of the New World. When Columbus left the Bernáldez household in 1496, after a five- to six-week stay, to meet with the Sovereigns who at that time were holding court at Almazan in the Upper Douro, north of Madrid, he entrusted the journals of the second voyage and other documents to Bernáldez, who found them useful for the *Historia de los Reyes Católicos*, which he was writing at the time. This unpublished manuscript is a highly reliable narrative of the voyages and life of Columbus as it contains many intimate details about the Admiral's experiences in the Indies. On this particular visit the Admiral had just returned from his second voyage and was accompanied by the retinue of Indians with parrots, gold jewelry, and priceless examples of Taino art. His account of the Admiral's sailing along the southern coast of Cuba is more detailed and more accurate than that of any other historian.

Additional contemporary information was disclosed through the correspondence of the voyagers themselves who shared their adventurous experiences with friends and noblemen. Most important of all the narratives, of course, are Columbus's journals of the first voyage, recently translated into English by Robert H. Fuson (*The Log of Christopher Columbus*, 1987) from which I quote extensively. Additional information is gleaned from the many letters he wrote to the Sovereigns, the most outstanding of which was the letter of 1493 known as the "Epistola de Insulis Nuper Inventis," reproduced in full in the present book. Dr. Chanca's letter, Michele de Cuneo's mirthful narrative, and the Scillacio tract constitute the best eyewitness information available for the second voyage. Bernáldez's and Ferdinand's narratives give a unique account of the second voyage, but it is secondhand information even though it was provided by the Admiral himself. Unfortunately, there is no existing journal written by Columbus on his second voyage.

PREFACE

On the third voyage, we have an abstract of Columbus's journal made by Las Casas, Columbus's "Letter to the Sovereigns" of October 18, 1498, and his letter to Doña Juana de Torres of October 1500. Las Casas's *Historia* lends additional coverage.

The Royal Instructions of March 14, 1502, the Roster and Payroll with the list of ships, Columbus's famous "Lettera Rarissima", and the narrative of Diego Méndez, together with Ferdinand's account of the voyage, are the most important sources for the fourth voyage.

By far the most exhaustive collection of documents on the life and voyages of Christopher Columbus is the monumental collection authorized by the Italian government for the fourth centennial of the discovery of America. A royal commission was appointed and delegated to locate all extant documents on the life and discoveries of Christopher Columbus and to collect them for future reference. The result of this investigation is the *Raccolta di Documenti e Studi pubblicati dalla R. Commissione Colombiana pel Quarto Centenario della Scoperta dell'America* (Rome, 1892–96). Edited by Cesare De Lollis, it consists of six parts divided into fourteen volumes and a supplement, and is available for research at Biblioteca Nazionale in Rome.

Another important collection of Columbian documents, this one motivated by the third centennial of the discovery of America, was prepared by Martín Fernández de Navarrete, secretary of the Spanish Royal Academy of History under the auspices of the Spanish government. It is entitled *Colección de los Viages y Descubrimientos que hicieron por mar los Españoles,* Vols. I–III (Madrid, 1825–29). Printed at about the time that Washington Irving was in Europe, it aroused enough curiosity in the famous American writer that he decided to write a book on Columbus based on some aspects of the data gathered by Navarrete.

With the Spaniard's encouragements, Irving later published a book entitled *The Life and Voyages of Christopher Columbus* (London, 1828), which at that time was the most complete and authoritative work of its kind in America. It remained for the distinguished historian Admiral Samuel Eliot Morison, with his two-volume biography of Columbus entitled *Admiral of the Ocean Sea* (Boston: Little & Brown, 1942), to reawaken in the American pubic an interest in the life and voyages of the great Genoese navigator. His one-volume edition, which lacked the valuable copious notes of the two-volume edition, was a best seller and was awarded the Pulitzer Prize for biography. Admiral Morison, an accomplished sailor in his own right, organized the Harvard Columbus Expedition consisting of the barkentine Capitana and the ketch Mary Otis, which in 1939–40 crossed the Atlantic from New England to Lisbon via the Azores, visited Huelva, Palos, Cádiz, Porto Santo, Madeira, and Grand Canary and jumped off Comera to follow as closely as possible the track of Columbus's third voyage. Later they continued sailing to many of the islands that Columbus had visited in the first, second, and third voyages. With this wealth of related nautical experience, Morison's appraisal of Columbus's skills as a seaman speaks volumes:

He had his faults and his defects, but they were largely the defects of the qualities that made him great....But there was no flaw, no dark side for the most outstanding and essential of all his qualities—his seamanship.[5]

Additionally, the exploratory voyages that Morison made on his own throughout the Caribbean allowed him to identify nearly all anchorages and landfalls that Columbus made in his four voyages. We are also indebted to Admiral Morison for the translation into English of many documents and journals heretofore available only in Spanish and Italian in his *Journals and Other Documents on the Life and Voyages of Christopher Columbus* (op. cit.), from which I have quoted liberally in this book.

I have attempted to bring to the attention of the reader many of the important documents identifying Christopher Columbus as the discoverer of the New World and establishing conclusively his national origin; yet, the scholarly Salvador de Madariaga in his controversial *Christopher Columbus* dares to ask:

Who is this mysterious man whose single spirit changed the course of history, deflected a mighty nation from its natural path, doubled the size of man's physical world, widened his mental horizon beyond the wildest expectations of the age, created, in fact, the setting for that bold, humanistic, conception, lured by which man, the super-monkey, has since then dreamt himself to be an undergod? ... Mystery surrounds him. Pride stiffens him up. A sense of mission entrusted to him from on high drives him. No one knows who he is, where he comes from, what he actually wishes to do.[6]

There were other skeptics such as Henry Vignaud, *Histoire critique de la grande entreprise de Christophe Colomb* (Paris: H. Water, 1911); and more recently Simon Wiesenthal in his *Sails of Hope: The Secret Mission of Christopher Columbus* (New York: Christopher Columbus Publishing, 1979) proposes that wealthy and influential Spanish Jews sent Columbus forth to find a new homeland for their brothers who had been chased out of Spain.

Their expectation was that Columbus might find the lost tribe of Israel in India or China.

The present book is in actuality not only a detailed account of the life and travels of Columbus—there are already many books on Columbus—but an attempt to describe the drama of an age that changed the course of the world and in which Columbus played a very important part. Great events are not caused by the efforts of a single individual. They are the result of less important but related events brought about through the years by individuals, technological advances, and socio-political conditions that reach fruition at a propitious time. Part I of this book consisting of the first five chapters deals exclusively with these events. I review those theories regarding pre-Columbian visitors to the Americas, the ancient theories and observations by Aristotle and other Greek philosophers, and the geographical concepts of Ptolemy and Strabo. Progress stood still through the millennium of the Dark Ages. Marco Polo revived the spirit of discovery; the Renaissance, which emphasized the development of man's natural gifts and the acquisition of knowledge about the physical world, created the atmosphere that culminated in the discovery of America. The learned men of that period—Roger Bacon, Cardinal Pierre d'Ailly, Aeneas Sylvius Piccolomini, and Paolo dal Pozzo Toscanelli—all had great influence on Columbus.

Improvements in sailing ships and navigational charts, and the invention of the magnetic compass and quadrant, encouraged oceanic sailing and exploration and prompted the Portuguese under the auspices of Prince Henry the Navigator to venture down the west coast of Africa. From 1419 to 1456, the Portuguese established a foothold on the Atlantic islands of the Azores and the Madeiras to the Rio Grande in Africa, south of the Cape Verde Islands. By 1487, Bartolomeu Dias had rounded the Cape of Good Hope.

PREFACE

Navigators had become increasingly more confident in their skills when Columbus made a proposal to King John II of Portugal for a western trip to the Indies, but was refused because of the previous success of Diaz. In Spain, Columbus found a more sympathetic ear in Queen Isabella, but the war with Granada had to take priority over any oceanic exploration. After the Moors' defeat, and with the various sections of the country united under one flag (with the exception of Navarre), the Catholic monarchs could start playing a role more fitting to their newly acquired status as a world power. Columbus's plan of exploration was finally accepted and he sailed into history.

This book was written in response to a concerted demand by many individuals who attended at least one of the approximately one hundred lectures I delivered in the United States to civic groups and various institutions of learning during 1970–80. The audiences confessed freely that they knew very little about Christopher Columbus, that they had learned much from the lectures and wondered why Columbus was such a famous unknown.

It is my opinion that historians, particularly those who wrote their histories before 1950, are to blame for the ignorance generally found in America regarding Columbus. Witness, for example, Charles A. Beard, who, in his *A Basic History of the United States*, begins Chapter I with the heading, "English Territorial Claims and Territorial Beginnings," completely disregarding Columbus and the Spanish occupations in the United States before the English settlements of Virginia.

It is my fond hope my *Christopher Columbus: His Life and Discoveries*, will be a primer for the delight and edification of all Americans in anticipation of the fifth centennial of the discovery of America.

—*Mario Di Giovanni*
Pacific Palisades, California

Part I

OF INTREPID MEN & SAILING SHIPS

Chapter One

THE AMERICAN ABORIGINES

When Christopher Columbus landed on the island of Guanahani (San Salvador) in the Bahamas on October 12, 1492, he met natives with perhaps thirty thousand years of culture behind them. In his journal Columbus reported:

All go as naked as their mothers bore them, and the women also although I did not see more than one very young girl. All those that I saw were young people, none of whom was more than thirty years old. They are very well-built people, with handsome bodies and very fine faces; though their appearance is marred somewhat by very broad heads and foreheads, more so than I have ever seen in any other race. Their eyes are large and very pretty and their skin is the color of Canary islanders or of the sunburned peasants, not at all black as would be expected because we are on the east-west line with Hierro in the Canaries…Many of the natives paint their faces; others paint their whole bodies; some only eyes and nose.[1]

Columbus erroneously assumed that he had reached the outer islands of Japan (Cipango), yet ironically he was describing the physiognomy of people who had originally come from

Asia perhaps twelve thousand to thirty-five thousand years earlier. Some archaeologists believe even in an earlier arrival of the first Americans and cite as evidence the skull of the Del Mar Man, found in a California coastal cliff and now in view at the San Diego Museum of Man. A new dating technique that analyzes amino acid changes shows the skull's age to be forty-eight thousand years old. Many artifacts discovered in America—both North and South—and verified by carbon-14 tests, have proven that man existed on this continent at least twelve thousand years ago. While scholars may disagree on the time of his appearance on the American continent, they all agree that the migration to America occurred by way of a land bridge that is now the Bering Strait. Who were these early inhabitants? It is agreed that the ancestors of the American Indians came from Asia, bearing with them the Mongolian traits such as skin of a copper color; straight black, coarse hair; and dark eyes and wide cheekbones.

The bulk of the early migration occurred during the last stages of the Pleistocene Glaciation, although carbon-14 tests suggest early-man sites in the Americas even before the end of the Ice Age. The northern half of North America lay beneath ice sheets two miles thick extending south to Kentucky. The ice sheets held so much water that ocean levels dropped several hundred feet, exposing continental shelves that in time became grasslands and forests. Mammoths and mastodons eventually grazed and died on these lands. The gap between Alaska and Siberia became an undulating plain one thousand miles wide, forming a land bridge for the migration of man and beast. Little or no moisture fell on this part of the Arctic, including the northern part of the Yukon, so that ice did not cover this area that became, by contrast, a huge grass-covered prairie called Beringia. From Beringia, many may have ventured south through an ice-free corridor along the eastern slope of the Rockies that existed at various periods of the Ice Age. This corridor separated the Cordilleran Ice Sheet on the Pacific Coast from the enormous Laurentide Ice Sheet that covered the northernmost section of North America to the Atlantic Ocean. It is also possible that many migrants ventured south along the Pacific Coast. Within a period of four thousand years, the migration of these Mongolian peoples had advanced to what is now Central America and by 9000 B.C. had reached the tip of South America.

At the time of Columbus's arrival in 1492, the American Indians in great part were still living in a Neolithic Age. They had invented polished stone tools but had not developed agriculture to the level practiced in the Old World. They did not cultivate cereals, nor had they begun to domesticate animals, except perhaps for the dog. Europeans introduced cattle, horses, and other domesticated animals. Some of the native Indians, however, particularly in Mexico and in regions of South America, had advanced beyond the Neolithic Age. These higher civilizations emerged nearly two thousand years ago in the Andean region of South America and in the highlands of Central America and Mexico. Here the Indians produced textiles, pottery, and magnificent ornaments of gold, silver, and cooper; their agriculture produced corn (maize), potatoes, and quinoa, a grain resembling rice. Social organizations were sophisticated with standing armies, priest emperors, schools, courts, and systemized religions. In Mexico, specifically Yucatan, the Indians used accurate calendars based on astronomical observations and hieroglyphic writing.

The Aztecs in Mexico, the Incas in Peru, and the Mayas in the intervening area of Yucatan attained the highest degree of culture. The Mayas are believed to have developed probably the optimal aboriginal civilization in the Western Hemisphere, although the Aztecs surpassed them in military proficiency and the Incas in the arts of weaving and dyeing. These civilizations had reached their apex before the Spanish Conquest. Simpler cultures such as the Pueblo Indians of the Southwest and the mound builders in the Mississippi Valley existed in the United States.

Specialized local cultures existed as well in the northeastern United States and Canada, in Alaska, and to a still lesser degree, in California. Yet, most North American Indians lived, at the time of Columbus's arrival, as they had lived in 10,000 B.C., a primitive cultural life built around hunting and fishing. The coming of the Spaniards and other Europeans quickly ended that way of life.

Chapter Two

THE PRE-COLUMBIAN VISITORS

The discovery of America by Christopher Columbus in 1492 was such a momentous event that many have tried to belittle it by claiming prior landfalls on the new continent. There is no doubt that many lost sailors chanced to land on the American shores before Columbus. No intelligent person will dispute that. After all, the American continent stretching from the North to the South Poles constitutes both a barrier and a haven to anyone sailing westward or eastward. A landfall, however, does not a discovery make. It was Columbus who generated an immediate and universal interest in his discovery and changed the course of history. Previous "discoveries" were just footprints in the sands that time erased. Nevertheless, such landfalls, some mythical, others merely hypothetical, and others completely without merit, need to be mentioned, if for no other reason than to be thorough in our methods.

THE PHOENICIAN VOYAGE, 531 B.C.

The greatest navigators of the ancient world were the Phoenicians, who lived in the coastal area of modern Lebanon, Israel, and Syria.

The Phoenicians knew every corner of the Mediterranean Sea one thousand years before Christ was born. Their skilled sailors ventured beyond the Strait of Gibraltar, reaching the farthest coasts of Western Europe. As early as 1130 B.C. they sailed up the coast of Spain, founding the city of Cádiz. They sailed north to England and as far south as the tip of Africa, around the Cape of Good Hope and north again to the Gulf of Aden; a feat that was not repeated until 1498 by the Portuguese navigator Vasco da Gama. It is possible that the Phoenicians reached America as well.

A theory that seafarers from the Mediterranean city of Sidon in Phoenicia landed on the coast of Brazil 2,023 years before Columbus has been advanced by some researchers, based on the discovery of a stone on the banks of the Paraíba River. In 1976, a team of scientists from Brandeis University examined the message carved on it and declared it of Sidonian derivation. The carving told of the venturesome voyage of ten Sidonian ships that circumnavigated Africa for two years to round Africa when they became separated. One of the ships with twelve men and three women aboard eventually made landfall on the coast of Brazil, leaving behind them the Sidonian tablet.

VISITORS FROM THE OLD WORLD

In recent years, archaeologists have also gathered a wealth of historical artifacts in Central and South America showing that many visitors from the Old World had landed in the Americas centuries before Columbus. Thus, from Guatemala has come an incense burner with the sculptured head of a man whose high-crowned nose, classically sculptured beard, and bemused, strangely serene expression decidedly identified him as a Semitic. This head was sculpted by Maya Indians during the period of

300–600 A.D. Even some sculptured heads of Negros have been found in Central America predating Columbian times.

There are also indications that the Greeks and Romans visited America. In 1961 archaeologists discovered a sculpted head from about 200 A.D., obviously Roman in origin, in a pyramid at Calixtlahuaca, Mexico. Iron artifacts and bronze cups similar to cups from the ruins of Pompeii have also aroused the curiosity of archaeologists, because the two metals had not yet been developed by the Stone Age Indians. It should be noted that the ships of the Roman period were as heavy as one thousand tons—ten times the size of Columbus's Santa Maria and fully capable of crossing the Atlantic.

ORIENTAL VISITORS

The Chinese also claim pre-Columbian visits to the West Coast of North America. Chinese-style stone anchors were found off of the California coast in 1976. The anchors, one found in shallow waters near the Palos Verdes Peninsula in Los Angeles County and another near Cape Mendocino in northern California, are about three thousand years old and Asian in origin. A UCLA anthropologist said at the time of the discovery that the anchors were not produced by California Indians. Chinese historian Fang Zhonapu identified them as being of Chinese origin, and this claim was substantiated by James R. Moriarty of the University of San Diego. Fang also claims that the first explorer of the American continent was a Buddhist monk named Huishen who sailed off to spread Buddhism in the year 452 and returned in 499 with an astonishing tale of a seven-thousand-mile voyage to a land called Fusang. By his description, this must have been Mexico. He described the cactus-like agave plant with its spiny margined leaves and flowers in tall spreading panicles whose fibers the Indians used for making garments.

Fang, a maritime historian, affirms that China had the naval technology and equipment to accomplish long oceanic voyages in ancient times. He states further that in the first century A.D., the Chinese already knew how to use the stern post rudder to keep ships on course. In the third century, Chinese sailors were able to calculate sailing speeds and the length of voyages. In the fifth century, there were frequent seaborne exchanges of envoys between China and other countries. So it would have been quite possible for Huishen to cross the Pacific in the fifth century and land in Mexico. China also had the ships to undertake long voyages. Fang notes that in the third century the kingdom of Emperor Wu had a navy of five thousand ships, the largest with several decks and enough berths for three thousand passengers! Voyages to the Philippines and other South China Sea ports were commonplace even before the birth of Christ. But the Chinese stone anchors found recently on the California coast are presumed to be three thousand years old. Nevertheless, because they represent an isolated case, it would be foolish to assume that there was friendly intercourse between China and the Americas during 1000 B.C.

The vast Pacific, it seems, was no barrier to sailors from the Japanese Islands either. Archaeologists have found five-thousand-year-old Japanese pottery in Ecuador, suggesting that both China and Japan had reached the shores of the American continent.

THE CELT MIGRATION

In his book *America B.C.* Barry Fell has advanced the theory that perhaps five hundred years before Christ, parts of North America were settled by Celts from Portugal. They clustered in

Vermont, New Hampshire, Connecticut, and in New York's Hudson Valley, where they built crude stone chambers that were used for religious ceremonies and for taking sun-sightings. These sun worshipers intermarried with the Algonquin Indians, and after many generations their identity was lost. The stone chambers—beehive-shaped structures—can still be found in the mountainous New England countryside. The origin of the chambers is surmised from the inscriptions found in the mounds surrounding the chambers; however, their dating is neither authentic nor reliable.

JEWISH SETTLEMENT AND POLISH CLAIMANTS

An additional artifact found in the American continent that has aroused the curiosity of archaeologists is the tombstone with Hebrew inscriptions and dated at about 200 A.D. It was found in the 1880s together with eight skeletons in a burial mound at Bat Creek, Tennessee. According to some Jewish proponents, this is poof of the presence on the American continent of the mythical lost tribe of Israel, which Columbus had been instructed to find by Spanish converts. This claim was made by Simon Wiesenthal in his book *Sails of Hope: The Secret Mission of Christopher Columbus* (New York: MacMillan, 1979).

Polish-Americans have attributed the discovery of America to Scolvus, whom they call Jan of Kolm, who supposedly came to America in 1476 in search of the Northwest Passage. There is absolutely no proof of his three voyages undertaken in the company of the Danish pirates Pining and Pothurst.

THE ST. BRENDAN LEGEND, 500–600 A.D.

Among the pre-Columbian explorers of the New World, no name is more popular or controversial than that of Ireland's

St. Brendan. His legend has been kept alive to this day in the form of a Christian "imram." Early Irish literature, both pagan and Christian, abounds in "imrama," as these Irish sagas are called. They deal primarily with the marvels and miracles of ocean voyages, and St. Brendan's is the most popular. Called "Navigatio Sancti Brendani Abbatis" (Voyage of Saint Brendan the Abbot), it describes Saint Brendan's legendary voyage to "Terra Repromissionis Sanctorum" (the Promised Land of the Saints), somewhere beyond the far reaches of the Western Atlantic. Sailing in a "currash," a skin-covered boat very common in those days, and accompanied by seventeen monks, St. Brendan left Ireland and headed northward, then westward. The voyage lasted seven years and introduced the monks to such wonders as demons who hurled fire upon them, a floating crystal column, and a sea creature as great as an island. Eventually, the adventurous crew reached the Promised Land, a huge, lush island divided by a mighty river. It was full of trees bearing ripe apples. They lived on this island that knew no night for forty days.

In exploring the island, they reached the mighty river that they hesitated to cross. A youth appeared, called each monk by name, kissed him, and sang the eighty-fourth Psalm. He informed them that this island was the place God left to them and their successors to own and inhabit until the end of the persecution of the Christians. He cautioned them not to explore any further but to return home laden with fruits and precious stones of the island.

Most of the events in the "Navigatio" abound in fantasies and marvels. More remarkable is the fact that St. Brendan was over seventy years old when he started his voyage in the middle of the sixth century. The significance of the voyage lies in the influence that it had on the cartographers and navigators of later periods. These mapmakers began to include the St. Brendan Isles in the wide expanse of the Atlantic Ocean, not knowing exactly at what latitude. Yet, subsequently some Irish writers wrote that St. Brendan journeyed as far north as Newfoundland and as far south as the West Indies and Mexico. Columbus, like other navigators, believed in the existence of the St. Brendan Isles. In fact, he makes reference to St. Brendan in the journal of his first voyage. As for the seafaring saint's presumed landfall on the New World, it is very doubtful that there was one at all. To date, not a single Irish artifact has been unearthed by archaeologists to substantiate it.

MADOC AND THE WELSH SETTLEMENT

According to a narrative told in the southeastern part of the United States, Madoc ab Owain Gwynedd, a Welsh prince, reached the shores of Florida in 1170, 322 years before Columbus's first voyage to the "Indies." Very much impressed with what he saw, he returned to Wales, recruited many Welsh men and women, and sailed back to America with the purpose of starting a Welsh colony. A tablet commemorating the reputed landing place in Alabama has been erected by the Daughters of the American Revolution at Fort Morgan, Mobile Bay, bearing these words: "In memory of Prince Madoc, a Welsh explorer, who landed on the shores of Mobile Bay in 1170 and left behind with the Indians the Welsh language."

This was the second Madoc memorial erected in the United States. The first one was put up by the state of Tennessee. Centuries later came "reports" of the existence of a mysterious tribe of "Welsh Indians" who actually spoke Welsh. An expedition in search of the reputed descendants of Madoc along the tributaries of the Missouri River ended a dismal failure.

THE NORSEMEN

All we know about the discovery of America by Norsemen is gathered from two important Norse sagas written down from oral sources around 1250 A.D. These sagas recount the travels of Eric the Red, father of Leif Ericson, who, to escape a manslaughter conviction in Norway, fled to Iceland and then went further west to a peninsula that he named "Greenland" to encourage settlement there. He returned to Iceland the next summer, in 985 A.D., to extol the advantages of settling in Greenland and was able to convince twelve shiploads of Icelanders to join him. The new immigrants set up farming and hunting communities; but because Greenland has no timber—the harsh environment precluding the growth of trees—they were hampered in building permanent shelters.

In the meantime, Biarni Heriulfson, sailing from Iceland to Greenland to visit his father, missed the island and eventually sighted unknown lands farther to the southwest that had an abundance of timber. Realizing he had sailed too far, he picked up a southwest wind and reached his destination in Greenland, where he told the settlers of the large area of timberland he had seen. Perhaps it was for that reason that Leif Ericson, second son of Eric the Red, set out with a crew of thirty-five in the summer of 1001 A.D. on a voyage of exploration to the west. His first landing was on Baffin Island (Canada), which he called Helluland (country of flat stones). He set out again due south and landed first on a land he called Vinland.

Several more attempts were made to colonize Vinland, one specifically by Thorfince Karisevni, Leif's brother-in-law, but the harsh environment forced the colonists to return in the summer of 1013. Another expedition in 1014 by a trader, Thorvard and his wife, Freydis, Eric the Red's illegitimate daughter, ended in bloodshed because of dissension among the colonists and harassment by the natives (1014–15). This episode ended the attempts of the colonization by the Norsemen, and the American adventures were reduced to a flame that gradually lost its luster and faded by about 1350 A.D. Before the close of the century, however, the greatest patron of cosmography and discovery, Prince Henry the Navigator, was born in 1394. An age of exploration and discovery that was to change the history of the world had dawned. With its advent, Columbus would fulfill his mission.

Chapter Three

THE PORTUGUESE NAVAL ACTIVITY

Following the Norsemen's oceanic wanderings, the Atlantic Ocean, especially its southern regions, would remain undisturbed for nearly three centuries except for some sporadic efforts by a few adventurous Italians. It should be noted that the influence of the Italians in their contribution to the age of exploration was incalculable. Through the commercial interests of the city states of Venice and Genoa, the Mediterranean had become the training ground for sailors and explorers. Additionally, the development of geographical and allied sciences in Italy, as evidenced by the works of Aeneas Sylvius Piccolomini and the letters of Paolo Toscanelli, evinced a distinct superiority over other countries. As early as 1291, the Vivaldi brothers had sailed from Genoa to find a route to India by rounding Africa. They were never heard from again.

The beginning of the Portuguese naval activity started with King Diniz (1277–1325) under Venetian and Genoese guidance. To build up his navy, King Diniz engaged a Genoese admiral, Emmanuele Pessagno. King Diniz's interest in the land and his exploration of pine forests to build ships earned him the name of "rei lavrador"—working king. In 1341, his son,

King Alfonso IV (1325–57), sent a fleet of three ships under the command of Nicholas de Recco down the south Atlantic—but with Genoese and Florentine advisors. Their discovery of the Canaries stirred the imagination of the Portuguese and made them aware that the future of their nation, with its advantageous location, depended on oceanic exploration and the discovery of new lands.

Portugal, which the Romans called Lusitania when they captured it in 100 B.C., is a small country, about the size of Maine. It occupies the westernmost point of continental Europe on the Iberian Peninsula, with the Atlantic Ocean forming its western and southern boundaries. The population at the beginning of the fifteenth century had reached one million.

The Moslem Arabs and Moors conquered the Iberian Peninsula in the 700s A.D. By the middle of the 1200s all the land of Portugal on the Iberian Peninsula had been won back from the Moors. Spain, on the other hand, did not expel the Moors until 1492. Thus, Portugal had peace and stability when other nations lacked it. England and France were both plunged in wars at home and abroad, and the Spaniards were attempting to rid themselves of the Moors and to unify the country under one ruler. The Italian city states, such as Genoa and Venice, did not have the resources to finance oceanic exploration because of constant wars among themselves and threats from foreign invaders.

Before the end of the fourteenth century, Portugal had established its complete independence from Castile. August 14, 1385, was a decisive date in the history of the country as King John I (João I) (1385–1433) of Portugal defeated the Castilians at the battle of Aljubarrota to establish the country's independence. King John I married Philippa of Lancaster, the daughter of John of Gaunt, in 1387. The dynasty thereby became part English—known in history as the Aviz Dynasty.

HENRY THE NAVIGATOR

The union resulted in the birth of five sons: Duarte, Pedro, Enrique (Henry), João, Alfonso, and one girl, Isabel. The third son, the Infante Dom Henrique (1394–1460), later called by English Historians "Henry the Navigator," initiated the voyages of exploration that established Portugal as the greatest maritime nation of the period. He was not a navigator, nor did he do much sailing. His historical role was to sponsor and promote the science of navigation to develop new sea routes, discover new lands, and try to unlock some of the mysteries of the oceans. To these ends he sought to help scientists, cartographers, astronomers, and navigation experts. These efforts resulted in the development of the caravel, and in improvements in the techniques of cartography and navigational instruments, which in turn stimulated oceanic commercial ventures. No less important was his desire to occupy lands and explore sea lanes to allow Christian Europe to triumph over the power of Islam. The days of the Crusaders were long gone, but the crusading spirit was to remain with Henry to his dying days.

Like any average medieval prince, Prince Henry was tutored early in the Greek and Roman classics, in the writings of the Church, and in the chivalric use of arms. King John I was reputed to have had the most complete library in Europe, according to the contemporary chronicler Zurara, and it is logical to assume that Prince Henry must have profited from it. This was the period, early in the Renaissance, when the works of Ptolemy, Cardinal d'Ailly, and Roger Bacon emerged to the delight and edification of students and scientists interested in the physical world. Later, Prince Henry was to be fascinated also by *The Travels of Marco Polo* that his brother Pedro brought back for him. It can be surmised that he received a good all-around education befitting a prince of that period.

The bachelor Prince Henry devoted his life mostly to the study of navigation, the pursuit of explorations, and to the propagation of Christianity. His career began in 1415, with the capture, by King John I, of the Moroccan city of Ceuta across the Strait of Gibraltar. Prince Henry, who had accompanied his father with two of his brothers, distinguished himself so that he was immediately appointed governor of the conquered territory with the responsibility of defending it against enemy attacks. His new position did not require him to remain in Ceuta and placed ships at his command. These he used to initiate his voyages of exploration.

In 1417 Prince Henry commissioned two young squires, João Gonçalves Zarco and Tristão Vaz Teixeira, to search for the land of Guinea. In heading south down the west cost of Africa in a small "barca" with a single square sail, they were driven by an easterly wind away from the coast, westward in the Atlantic. They made a landfall on a small island in the Madeira group that they called Port Santo, the Holy Haven. In 1420, Prince Henry moved with great dispatch to colonize the island. Several ships were sent out, one of which was under the command of Bartolomeo Perestrello, who was to become Christopher Columbus's father-in-law. Perestrello was the son of a noble Italian family of Piacenza that had emigrated to Lisbon in the previous century.

During this trip, the large island of Madeira in the Archipelago was discovered. Settlement of the islands was effected with great speed. The island of Madeira was divided between Teixeira, who received the northern part, and Zarco, who took the southern half. Perestrello was placed in command of the island of Porto Santo. Sugarcane shoots imported from Sicily were planted on the two islands. The crop flourished to the extent that the Madeira Islands became the principal source of sugar for Europe. Unfortunately, lack of manpower to harvest the sugar was responsible for the beginning of the slave trade from Africa.

In 1419, Prince Henry was made governor of the Algarve, the former Moorish province located in the southernmost part of Portugal. There on the rocky promontory of Sagres, near Cape St. Vincent, he built his main base of operation. This site, the extreme point of land of western Europe, which Strabo called the "Sacred Cape," was considered by the ancients the outer limit of the earth. It became a magnet for the ablest seamen of the period, which included cartographers, shipbuilders, astronomers, and instrument makers. From the harbor of Lagos, a few miles down the coast, Prince Henry's ships were dispatched to the south and southwest to unknown destinations.

In 1420, Prince Henry was appointed Grand Master of the Order of Christ—a continuation order of the Knights of Templars that had been instituted by St. Bernard of Clairvaux in the twelfth century for the defense of Jerusalem. That was the event that was to change his life. As a member of the order, the prince took a vow of celibacy and excluded himself from worldly and dynastic ambitions. The crusading spirit was evident in all of his undertakings, going as far as displaying a red cross on the sails of all his ships. His appointment was important in another way: it gave him access to the extensive financial support of his order for exploration and crusading efforts.

EXCURSIONS TO ATLANTIC ISLANDS

Prince Henry's immediate goal was to sail to Guinea and perhaps circumnavigate Africa. Strategically, it was also necessary to gain control of all the important islands located in the Atlantic, west of the African coast. Some of them, such as the

Canary Islands, had already been discovered, and others were known to exist. Henry's objectives were to rediscover and colonize them. As already noted, the Canaries had been visited by the Portuguese in 1341 but in 1344 the pope had assigned them to Castile.

Prince Henry considered these islands a threat to his plan of discovery and expansion, and prepared to take them by force of arms. A fleet of 50 ships with 2,500 men and 150 horses, under the command of João de Castro, was organized and then stormed the islands in 1425. The invasion failed, partly because of the tenacity of the native Guanches and partly because of the rugged terrain, which offset de Castro's advantage in horses and arms. Additional efforts were made in later years to wrest control of the islands from Castile and all were equally unsuccessful. They were finally confirmed as possessions of Castile by the Treaty of Alcacovas in 1480. Henry's failure proved to be providential, for under Spanish control they became ports of haven for Columbus's trips to America. He continued his exploration, and his persistence finally paid off through the discovery and colonization of the Azores Archipelago: a group of nine islands located in the north Atlantic, roughly eight hundred miles west of Lisbon.

In 1427, Prince Henry had sent Goncalo Velho Cabral with two ships in search of some islands that were thought to exist in the Atlantic Ocean. They had sailed from Lagos, heading directly west, but had turned back just as they were within sight of the eastern outpost of the Azores. The following year, Cabral had sailed again and, on the Feast of the Assumption, had discovered an island he called Santa Maria. Additional expeditions were to discover more islands. In 1432, sixteen ships had been dispatched to the islands, establishing a permanent settlement there. Situated farther from the mainland than any other group of islands, these became very important for the exploration of the African coast. Thus, ships heading north to Portugal would find it easier to sail directly north to the Azores, then head east on the prevailing favorable winds to the mother country.

EXPLORATIONS OF THE AFRICAN COAST

The Portuguese voyages down the coast of Africa at first proceeded slowly and cautiously. Ancient legends told of the terrors of a tropical sea where the hot sun turned men black and made the ocean boil, and the Canaries' current that supposedly accelerated so that it swept ships over the edge of the world. Understandably such stories struck fear in the hearts of sailors. Prince Henry's first objective was to find out what lay beyond Cape Nun. Many ships were dispatched to round the Cape but all returned without success. Eventually Gil Eannes passed Cape Nun and, in 1433, reached Cape Bojador without encountering any of the legendary terrors. The advance to the south became more rapid after that. The expeditions began to bring back gold and African natives. The slave trade had begun. King John I died in 1433 and Duarte I, Henry's oldest brother, ruled only from 1433 to 1438.

As the fear of the unknown abated, each successive voyage was accomplished with more ease. Gil Eannes with Afonso Gonçalves Baldaia in 1436 sailed one hundred leagues beyond Bojador to Río de Oro and proceeded another fifty leagues to a port they called Port of the Galley. In three seasons the combined efforts of Eannes and Baldaia had added more to man's knowledge than the cumulative lore from the fourteen voyages that had preceded them. For the next five years the exploration of the African coast was suspended because of the Tangier military campaign that had ended in total disaster for the Portuguese in 1437. Prince Fernando, Henry's youngest brother, was taken prisoner in the campaign and held for ransom by the Moors. He died after five years in captivity. King Duarte was spared the knowledge of Fernando's death because he, himself, died of the plague in 1438, four years before his son.

Exploration was resumed in earnest in 1441 as Gonçalves reached the Rio de Oro without difficulty. Nuno Tristão, in a new type of ship called a caravel, went as far south as Cape Branco—the White Cape (1443)—and Dinis Diaz in 1445 reached the mouth of the Senegal River. In 1446, Nuno Tristão began his third but fateful voyage. He passed Cape Verde and the Gambia River, eventually reaching the Rio Grande. He went upstream with two of the ship's boats and twenty-two men but they were attacked by natives in a dozen primitive crafts. Poisoned arrows killed Tristão and nineteen of his crew; four others were seriously injured. In one of the bravest exploits of the voyages, five crew men—all young boys—sailed the ship home two thousand miles away.

In 1448, the first European trading post overseas was established on Arguin Island. The extensive trade in slaves and African goods made this necessary. These posts, which were also forts and warehouses, became the trademark of the Portuguese commercial interests.

Alfonso V was only six years old when he became heir to King Duarte's throne in 1438 with his uncle, Prince Pedro, acting as regent. Alfonso V attained his legal majority at the age of fourteen, but Pedro was reluctant to turn full power over to the young king. Armed conflict ensued between the two and Pedro was killed in a skirmish at Alfarrobeira in 1449.

PRINCE HENRY—LATER YEARS

Very much saddened by the tragedy of Alfarrobeira, Prince Henry spent most of his late years at Sagres, concentrating not only on sponsoring more voyages to Guinea but on developing trade with territories already discovered. In 1454 a Venetian sailor and merchant by the name of Alvise Ca de Mosto, known as "Cadamosto," was driven by foul weather to take refuge at Sagres. This fortuitous event was to have great significance in the Portuguese exploration of the African coast. Prince Henry invited him to be his house guest and then enlisted him to sail to Guinea with the promise that they would share in the profits.

Cadamosto's fame in the Portuguese adventure was due not only to his successful expeditions but to the excellent written account of his voyages. A keen observer, he studied the African flora and fauna and the African scene and customs. His book *Paesi Nuovamente Ritrovati* is a valuable textbook on an emerging Africa and the Portuguese events of that period. On his first voyage in 1455, he sailed to the Madeiras, then to the Canaries, and finally to Cape Branco. On his second voyage in 1456, Cadamosto sailed directly to Cape Branco and in the process discovered the Cape Verde Islands.

In 1458, Prince Henry accompanied King Alfonso V on his crusade in Morocco, where they defeated the Moors at Ksar es Seghie. He lived two more years after his return to Sagres and died on November 13, 1460.

During his lifetime, Prince Henry's ships had ventured two thousand miles south of Lagos, past the Tropic of Cancer and headed for Sierra Leone, only ten degrees above the equator. Before the end of the fifteenth century, the whole world was opened to European shipping, primarily because of Prince Henry's efforts. The Spanish, the English, the French, and the Dutch became the beneficiaries of the Portuguese contribution.

PRINCE HENRY'S CONTRIBUTIONS

Prince Henry planted the seeds of future oceanic explorations. His systematic and scientific approach initiated a period of intensive exploration, which led eventually to the discovery of America by Christopher Columbus and the circumnavigation of the earth by Magellan. However, Prince Henry considered himself a failure for not having reached India and not having found a Christian king who could have helped him in a crusade against the Moors.

As a Christian ruler, Prince Henry had hoped to find the mythical Prester John (Priest John)—a Christian monarch of immense power whose realm was located in "Nearer India."[1] He was the man whose aid as an ally against the Infidel was sought by many rulers of the period. Prince Henry had hoped to seek his help in a pincer attack against the Moors.

Following Prince Henry's death, the West African voyages were discontinued for nearly ten years, as King Alfonso was concentrating his efforts on a crusade against the Moors. The crusades were unsuccessful since King Alfonso had spent his energies and finances in other areas. Fernão Gomes, a wealthy merchant of Lisbon, made a commercial deal with the king to take over the rights to the Guinea venture at a cost of two hundred milreis per year. Gomes also made a commitment to explore one hundred leagues of African coast per year. Actually, he nearly doubled that distance, for in a five-year period his captains discovered two thousand miles of new coast from Sierra Leone to the Borque de Santa Maria, more than Prince Henry's captains had accomplished in forty-two years. In the first attempt, Sociro da Costa sailed to Axem on the Gold Coast. In the second attempt (1470–71), João de Santarem and Pedro de Escolar reached Mina, farther down on the Gold Coast in the present territory of Nigeria. The bulge of Africa had been rounded. Lopo Gonçalves now was able to head due south, reach the equator, and cross it (1472). Ruy de Sequeira sailed past Cape Lopez and anchored at Cape St. Catherine, two degrees south of the equator, to establish a foothold in the southern hemisphere.

JOHN II'S CONTRIBUTION

When Prince João, the heir apparent to the throne of Portugal, was invested with the responsibility of supervising the African maritime efforts, he did not renew Gomes's contract, deciding instead to accept the challenge of future explorations himself.

João (John) II, son of Alfonso V, ascended to the throne in 1481. In 1474, his father had entrusted him with the "trade of Guinea" and the African explorations. As a result, the work of exploration was continued with much enthusiasm and energy, aided in part by the new group of advisors as competent as Prince Henry's. His sea captains were now better prepared and scientifically more knowledgeable than Prince Henry's because of the technological advances made in cartography, seamanship, and instruments for navigation. Moreover, in order to solidify Portugal's African discoveries, in December of 1481, he sent Diogo de Azambuja to build the Fortress of St. George at Mina (São Jorge da Mina) near Benin, in the territory of modern Nigeria. Construction of this fortress was deemed necessary because the African trade had now doubled the royal revenues. Christopher Columbus either took part in the de Azambuja expedition or made the voyage shortly after.

Under orders from King John to push the African explorations farther, Diogo Cao in 1482 laid a course direct to Cape Lopo Gonçalves—850 miles across open sea—and then continued past Cape St. Catherine to the Congo River, adding 1,000 miles of new coast to the map.

At about this time, Christopher Columbus requested King João II's sponsorship for a voyage of discovery. His plan was to reach Cipango and Cathay by sailing west, but it was rejected by a Royal Commission.

On a second voyage down the coast of Africa (1485–86) Diogo Cao advanced to Cape Cross and Cape Negro. Subsequently, in August 1487, Bartolomeu Dias, who had been at Mina with Diogo de Azambuja, set sail down the African Coast. Accompanied by a state ship for the long sea voyage, he rounded the Cape of Good Hope—the southernmost tip of Africa. He then headed a few miles northward on the east coast of Africa. He had sailed six thousand miles from Portugal and three thousand miles below Mina. He returned in December of 1488—sixteen and a half months after his departure. He had proved that the continent of Africa was a peninsula and that, contrary to what was generally believed at that time, there was no land connection of Africa with Asia below the equator. The Indian Ocean separated the two continents and thus a sea route to India was possible.

Following Dias's historic voyage, the attempt to reach India was delayed for nine years because of internal troubles in Portugal with disputes with Castile. Christopher Columbus had discovered the "Indies" by sailing the Atlantic. A great feeling of excitement and anticipation spread throughout the major countries of western Europe. King John II reacted by ordering the preparation of an expedition to India by way of the Cape of Good Hope and by contesting the Spanish claims to all lands west of the Atlantic. By the Treaty of Tordesillas (June 7, 1494), a line of demarcation on a meridian 370 leagues west of the Cape Verde Islands was established with Spain—a decision that eventually secured most of Brazil for Portugal, for west of that line all discoveries would belong to Spain.

VASCO DA GAMA REACHES INDIA

After King John II died of uremia in 1495, his successor, King Dom Manuel, dispatched in July 1497 four vessels commanded by Vasco da Gama to make discoveries and search for spices.

The expedition to India was finally on its way. The total crew for the expedition consisted of about 170 men. Vasco da Gama's navigational equipment, the most advanced of that period, consisted of the latest "portolani" maps, compasses, an astrolabe, and astronomical charts. Da Gama sailed from Lisbon on July 8, 1497, headed for the Cape Verde Islands and then directly south, swinging over two thousand miles away from the African coast. Then he headed eastward to St. Helena Bay, rounding the Cape of Good Hope on November 22. He then sailed northward along the east coast of Africa, stopping at trading centers in Mozambique (March 1498) and Mombasa. Arab traders at these centers were suspicious of the Portuguese and attempted to seize their ships. After much difficulty, the expedition sailed northward to Malindi, where they found the king more friendly and willing to furnish a pilot to cross the Indian Ocean. On Tuesday, the April 24, 1498, they set sail for a city called Qualecut. A month later, on May 22, the fleet reached Qualecut on the Malabar coast of India. The reception of the local Indian ruler was a cool one as the gifts da Gama brought him were of little value. The Muslim traders were even more aloof and refused to do much trading with the Portuguese. In August 1498, da Gama sailed home with only a small sample of Indian goods. On the return trip, he sailed nearer to the west coast of Africa to the Cape Verde Islands and then directly north to the Azores to take advantage of the westerly winds. Da Gama arrived in Lisbon in September 1499. The trip had taken a terrible toll on his crew, with many of the sailors dying of scurvy and other diseases. Only fifty-five survived. In spite of Vasco da Gama's failure to establish trade relations with India, Portugal became an important trading and naval power in the Indian Ocean.

The survival of Prince Henry the Navigator's vision even after his death is a clear measure of his contribution to the age of exploration.

Chapter Four

THE PHYSICAL WORLD OF CHRISTOPHER COLUMBUS

When Christopher Columbus was born, knowledge of the physical world was a combination of fact and fancy, of myth and suppositions, that had evolved from the writings of ancient scholars from Greece and Egypt and reinterpreted by medieval and Renaissance thinkers.

It was the world as seen by Aristotle, Strabo, Eratosthenes, Ptolemy, Pliny the Elder, Roger Bacon, Marco Polo, Pierre Cardinal d'Ailly, Aeneas Sylvius (Pope Pius II), and Paolo Dal Pozzo Toscanelli, a contemporary of Columbus.

ANCIENT THEORIES

The Greeks were the first to study geography in the scientific manner. Early in the Renaissance, observations of Aristotle, Strabo, Ptolemy, and others originally stored in the library at Alexandria were rediscovered, translated, and printed, thus becoming influential sources of information for exploration. The Greeks were also the first to believe that the earth was spherical in shape and actually made calculations to determine its circumference.

Early philosophers had advanced conflicting theories concerning the shape of the earth. One theory claimed that it was disk-shaped and floated on water; another insisted that it was a cylinder on top of which rested the habitable world. Anaximenes even conceived the idea that the earth was a flat rectangular plate held in place by compressed air. Pythagoras, Plato, and Aristotle concluded that the earth was spherical by observing celestial bodies. Pythagoras assumed that because the moon and sun were spherical, the earth must also be of the same shape. Plato stated that the highest type of motion is the uniform revolution of a sphere on its own axis and in the same spot. This was gleaned from Plato's description of the process of creation when his intention, apparently, was to explain the heavenly bodies, their periods and revolutions. His was a philosophical approach. Aristotle looked to the heavens for his clue and observed that the earth's shadow on the moon during a lunar eclipse was curved and he deduced that the earth was spherical in shape. In his treatise *On the Heavens (De Caelo)*, he wrote:

Our observations of the stars make it evident, not only that the earth is circular, but also that it is a circle of no great size. Also, those mathematicians who try to calculate the size of the earth's circumference arrive at the figure of four hundred thousand stades. This indicates not only that the earth's mass is spherical in shape, but also that as compared with the stars it is not of great size.[1]

THE LIBRARIAN FROM ALEXANDRIA CALLED ERATOSTHENES

It remained for a scholar of many talents, the chief librarian of the Alexandria Museum, by the name Eratosthenes, to prove not only the sphericity of the earth but to calculate its circumference with amazing accuracy as well. Eratosthenes lived between 276 and 196 B.C. after the death of Alexander the Great and before the rise of Rome as a great power. Founded by Alexander in 332 B.C. at the mouth of the Nile, the city of Alexandria had become an important center of culture and commerce in the Hellenic world. Its museum was a research center that attracted philosophers, geographers, astronomers, mathematicians, physicians, writers, and seamen from all over the Hellenic world. Its library was the repository of most of the world's recorded knowledge, the equivalent in papyrus rolls of about one hundred thousand books. By the time of Julius Caesar, it is estimated that the count of manuscripts alone had risen to seven hundred thousand.

The rulers of Alexandria were the Ptolemies. In about 240 B.C., Ptolemy III appointed Eratosthenes chief of the museums library. With the library at his disposal, Eratosthenes immersed himself in philosophy, science, mathematics, and every subject that stimulated his imagination. His versatility served him well in discovering a simple method to prove the earth was round and to calculate its circumference.

On June 21, when the sun was shining down a well in Syene (Aswan) casting no shadow, Eratosthenes measured the length of the shadow cast by an obelisk in Alexandria located five hundred miles to the north. Because the shadow is one side of a right triangle and the length of the obelisk the other side, the angle that the rays of the sun make with the earth can be easily calculated by trigonometry. This angle was found to be 7°12', nearly one fiftieth ($\frac{1}{50}$) of a complete circle. As Eratosthenes knew that the distance between Syene and Alexandria was approximately 500 miles, the circumference of the earth must then be 50 x 500 = 25,000 miles. And because the circumference of the earth at the equator is actually 24,902 miles, Eratosthenes's estimate came surprisingly close.

THE FIRST GEOGRAPHER

Many Greek and Roman historians occasionally digressed from their favorite subject to describe geographical situations or aspects of geography to provide background material for their accounts. Strabo (64 B.C.–4 A.D.) was the first to write a comprehensive geography of the known world. A native of Amasia in Asia Minor, of Asiatic and Greek descent, he received an exceptional education in literature, geography, and philosophy. His main interests were history and geography, and he learned from and was much influenced by reading the works of Homer, Herodotus, Eratosthenes, Polybius, Pytheas, Hipparchus, and Posidonius. He also studied in Rome and made that city his home, following his many travels.

Strabo derived the plan for his voluminous *Geography* from Eratosthenes but substantiated the source of his material from his many travels. He had traveled from Armenia in the East to Italy in the West; he had been in Greece and Egypt, where he had sailed up to the Nile and as far as Ethiopia; and he spent at least five years in Alexandria, consulting the Alexandria library for much of his material.

Strabo's *Geography* consists of seventeen books. Book Seven, however, has never been found. The first two review the history of geography from the earliest times to Strabo's day. The remaining fifteen books describe the geography of various continents, countries, and regions, beginning with Spain and continuing with Britain, Western and Eastern Europe, Asia Minor, India, Persia, Mesopotamia, the Ethiopian coast, and Egypt. Strabo, in his *Geography*, speculated on the possibility of new continents still undiscovered. He reasoned that beyond what was then known and discovered, there must have been other lands inhabited by different races of people. After all, the width of the inhabited world as determined by him was only about 8,400 miles while its height from north to south was about 3,450 miles.

Strabo's work is regarded by some historians as the most important geographical work to have come down from antiquity. Since the first printed edition of the *Geography* appeared in Rome in 1469, it is possible that Columbus may have seen and read it.

PTOLEMY'S GEOGRAPHY

Ptolemy (Claudius Ptolemeus, ca. 100–170 A.D.), of Greco-Egyptian heritage, was a celebrated astronomer, geographer, and mathematician whose work had a profound influence on subsequent generations up to the sixteenth century. He wrote his major work *The Almagest* in Alexandria between 127 and 160 A.D. This was an encyclopedic work that included a "Guide to Geography," containing descriptions and maps of the three known continents. In the *Almagest*, Ptolemy described the solar system based on the idea that the immovable earth was at the center of the universe and all the planets and stars rotated around it. This system, which came to be known as Geocentric or Ptolemaic, was universally accepted until the sixteenth century, when Copernicus and Galileo advanced the heliocentric system.

In the *Geography*, Ptolemy described in great detail, and showing maps, the world as it existed in the middle of the second century. The *Geography* consists of eight books, six of which outline the boundaries of the known countries, listing for the first time even parallels of latitude and meridians of longitude superimposed on nearly eight thousand localities. The first book deals with the principles of mathematical geography and map projection, while the last book deals with astronomy.

Ptolemy rejected the Eratosthenes measurement of the earth and accepted Posidonius's original calculations showing the earth to be thirty percent smaller. He also made the assumption that the world at the time covered 180° longitude from the Canaries in the west to the easternmost coast of Asia, an error that would have put the shores of Asia in the middle of the Pacific, not too far from the present Wake Island. These errors, which shortened the distance between Europe and Asia, actually encouraged Columbus, 1,300 years later, to risk the unknown seas with confidence.

Despite these serious errors, Ptolemy's reputation rests secure, for he laid down the basic principles of cartography, which include drawing maps exactly to scale and using a system of coordinates called parallels of latitude to locate places on the maps. He also devised methods of drawing the spherical earth on a flat sheet by using the proper projection. The result was a projected surface in which the meridians were straight lines equidistant at the equator and converging at the poles in circular arcs. Perhaps most important for navigation, Ptolemy's most impressive contribution was his collection of maps: twenty-six regional maps and a world map—all drawn to scale with parallels and meridians of latitude and longitude locating all places.

He also originated the practice of orienting maps so that the "north" is at the top and the "east" is to the right, a practice that has become standard procedure for map-making. For his development of map-making on a scientific basis, Ptolemy may correctly be called the father of cartography. His *Geography* was very influential up to the Middle Ages and beyond, until its theories were disproved by the discoveries of the Renaissance.

The boundaries of the world as outlined by Ptolemy on his map of the world are: on the north, the British Isles and the northern part of Europe, including the adjoining oceans; on the east, he shows the northern Asian continent; the Indian Ocean to the south is depicted as an inland sea because of the land connection with the southern tip of Africa. According to this map, it would have been impossible to reach India by sailing in an easterly direction.

No doubt, the lack of proper tools for measurement, the difficulties of journeying from one land to another, and the almost complete ignorance about remote lands such as China—*terra incognita* for many centuries to come—contributed to his miscalculations.

Despite these errors, Ptolemy had enormous influence on the science of geography and on exploration. His *Geography* was translated into Latin in 1410. It appeared in print in 1475 in Vicenza, Italy, and the knowledge that the earth was spherical in shape quickly spread among Italian scientific circles.

PLINY THE ELDER, 23–79 A.D. (GAIUS PLINIUS SECUNDUS)

Pliny the Elder—not to be confused with his nephew by the same name—was born in Novum Comum, modern Como, in Northern Italy, in 23 A.D. In his early twenties, he began an active military and governmental career that occupied him for the rest of his life. On official missions he traveled to Germany, Spain, Gaul, Africa, and the Middle East. He served as governor of provinces and advisor to the Roman Court. Very active in the Roman public life, Pliny was also a prolific writer and is best known for his monumental *Historia Naturalis (Natural History)*.

The work consists of twenty-seven books and was completed in 77 A.D. It is a comprehensive survey of all contemporary knowledge of the physical universe dealing with astronomy, meteorology, geography, mineralogy, zoology, and botany. It also includes sections on fine arts, painting, sculpture, human inventions and institutions, religion, ethics, and literature. A treasure of data on the natural sciences, the work was highly authoritative despite a number of inaccuracies discovered by Renaissance investigators.

Pliny's *Natural History* was the first scientific work published in Venice in 1469, only twenty-one years after Gutenberg and Fust had set up their printing shop in Mainz. It became an important source of reference and general education to the scientists and navigators of the Renaissance. It gave Columbus a broad foundation on geography and, more important, it made him dream of discovering the mythical islands that Pliny said were in the Atlantic. The islands of Antilla, or Brazil, or the Seven Cities were believed to be somewhere in the Atlantic. Many early maps located at various places in the Atlantic islands such as St. Brendan's Isle, visited by St. Brendan, the Irish monk, and St. Ursula's Island, the place where St. Ursula and her virgins were supposed to have fled before the ravaging of the Huns.

ROGER BACON AND THE *OPUS MAJUS*

Roger Bacon, considered to be one of the greatest thinkers of the medieval world, if not of all ages, was born near Ilchester, Somersetshire, England, in 1214. After taking holy orders at Oxford University in 1233, Bacon attended the University of Paris, where he earned a Doctor of Theology degree. In 1240 he joined the Franciscan Order. In 1250 he returned to Oxford to lecture and carry on his scientific studies and experiments.

His Franciscan superiors followed his scientific pronouncements with apprehension and eventually curbed his freedom to write. The Church looked with suspicion on Friar Bacon because his teachings dealt with education and science rather than with religious matters. The mysterious experiments he carried out in his laboratory eventually alarmed his superiors, and he was banished to Paris, where he was denied all opportunity to write and perform experiments. However, his fame as a scientist had already reached the ear of the new pope, Clement IV, who in 1265 sent a letter to Bacon instructing him to write a general treatise on the sciences. Accepting the Pope's secret mandate, Bacon immediately began writing his greatest work, the *Opus Majus* (Major Work), which he completed in eighteen months and sent to Pope Clement in 1267.

The *Opus Majus* is primarily an encyclopedia of medieval knowledge and, in part, a criticism of existing scholarship and scientific methodology. He believed strongly in the scientific method and concluded that experimental methods alone produce truth in science. He believed that without experiment nothing can be adequately known and that experimental science is the queen of sciences and the goal of all speculation.

Bacon's insatiable curiosity led him to the discovery of many practical facts. He knew more about optics than any man of his time; he suggested the practicability of eyeglasses to correct vision and built a primitive type of telescope he used to observe a spiral nebula; he peered at cells and microorganisms through a crude, primitive microscope. He conceived ideas for the design of airplanes, armored cars, mechanically propelled boats, and even gunpowder. He even speculated on the possibility of reaching India by sailing west across the Atlantic. In this respect, he was in agreement with the size of the world as envisioned by Aristotle, Ptolemy, and Seneca.

Because Ptolemy's book was not available in Europe, it is possible that Bacon may have obtained this information from Arab sources.

MARCO POLO—1254–1324

The Travels of Marco Polo the Venetian, written by Rusticano as dictated by Marco Polo (while both were sharing a Genoese prison cell) was studied assiduously by Columbus, who made many marginal notes on his copy. He prized his copy so much that he carried it with him on his first voyage. There is no doubt that Columbus was enthralled by Marco Polo's exotic report, accepting perhaps as true even some of the Venetian's exaggerated stories. He must have concluded that the three-year-long land trip could have been made faster with less peril by traveling west across the Atlantic, instead of east across the mountains, deserts, and rivers.

Marco Polo was a young man of seventeen when he accompanied his father, Niccolò, and uncle Maffeo Polo, both of whom had already been to the Orient and to the court of Kublai Khan several years before. The city of Venice at that time was the maritime center of the West. Traders would bring all eastern imports to Venice, from which they would be distributed to the rest of Europe at a very high profit. Spices and silks came from China, gold and pearls from Japan, diamonds and sapphires from India, carpets from the Near East, and ermines and sables from Siberia.

The Travels of Marco Polo describes in vivid details the trip back to Kublai Khan's capital. The Polo party wandered through what is now Turkey, Iraq, Persia (Iran), Afghanistan, the Pamir

Mountains, the Gobi Desert, the frontiers of the great Steppes of Mongolia, and northwest China to Peking.

A friendly reception awaited the travelers in Kublai Khan's palace. Marco Polo, then twenty-one, was immediately enrolled among the emperor's attendants. He was to travel far and wide and was to record accurately the habits of the peoples of China, Japan, Tibet, Mongolia, Korea, Burma, Siam, Ceylon, India, Sumatra, Java, Borneo, and a hundred other hitherto unexplored regions. Marco Polo was also fascinated by the advanced civilization existing in China in the thirteenth century: the high degree of sophistication in literature and philosophy, the arts, architecture, landscaping, transportation, streets and roads, canals, mechanical devices, the use of paper money, block printing, all of which represented a culture far superior to that of medieval Europe.

The Polos remained in China for seventeen years. The return journey lasted from 1292 to 1295. Following the accounts of their visit, a growing number of merchants and missionaries traveled eastward by land and sea to China.

PIERRE CARDINAL D'AILLY (1350–1420) AND THE IMAGO MUNDI

The French cardinal Pierre d'Ailly wrote a famous geographical treatise in 1410 called *Imago Mundi* (Image of the World). In it, he described the habitable earth and, in keeping with the opinions of ancient writers, suggested that Asia could be reached by a westward passage from Spain. A copy of the *Imago Mundi* preserved in the Columbian Library at Seville contains hundreds of marginal notes written by Columbus.

Cardinal d'Ailly was born in 1350 at Compiègne and studied at the College of Navarre in Paris, obtaining a Doctor of

Theology degree in 1381. In 1389 he was appointed Chancellor of the University of Paris and became successively Bishop of Puy (1395) and of Cambrai (1397) and then was elected cardinal in 1411. A rigorous promoter of church unity and reform, he dominated the early sessions of the Council of Constance (1414–18) that ended the Schism, the split in Christianity that had seen the creation of popes and antipopes between 1378 and 1417. While most of his writings were theological in nature, his most renowned work, *Imago Mundi*, dealt with secular matters and had great influence on Christopher Columbus.

Ferdinand Columbus, in *The Life of the Admiral Christopher Columbus*, observes: "Pierre d'Ailly says that India and Spain are near each other in the west."[2] Columbus first became familiar with the *Imago Mundi* in Portugal, as Prince Henry had used it in its manuscript form. After it was printed in 1483 in Louvain, Belgium, Columbus bought his own copy from his own stock as for a short period in that era he had taken on the job of selling printed books. It should be noted that Ptolemy's *Geography* had not as yet been rediscovered by Western Europe and that its reference in the *Imago Mundi* did not motivate Columbus as much as d'Ailly's account. Many of d'Ailly's references to earlier authors are misleading. These include references to Ptolemy, Aristotle, and Seneca. The following excerpt is taken from the 1927 edition published by the Massachusetts Historical Society of the *Imago Mundi* (1930), which contains Columbus's 848 marginal notations.[3]

OF THE EXTENT OF THE HABITABLE EARTH

Ptolemy holds that about a sixth part of the earth is habitable with respect to water, and all of the rest is covered by water. Also, in his second book, the Almagest, *he states that habitation is known only in a quarter of the earth, or that which we inhabit, the length of which from east to west is half that of the equatorial line, and its breadth is from the equator to the pole and covering a fourth of a great circle. Aristotle also says towards the end of his book of the sky and the earth that the habitable area is greater than a quarter, which Averroes confirms. Aristotle says that the sea is small between the western extremity of Spain and the eastern part of India. Moreover, Seneca in the fifth book of things of nature says that this sea is navigable in a few days if the wind be favorable.[4] And Pliny teaches in the second book of the natural history that one can navigate from the Arabian Gulf to the Columns of Hercules in no very great time. For these and many other reasons, on which I shall have to enlarge when I speak of the ocean, some conclude that apparently the sea is not so great that it can cover three-quarters of the earth. We can call on the authority of Esdras in his fourth book to support this, who says that six parts of the earth are inhabited and the seventh is covered with the waters.[5]…From what we have said, and from what is to be said below, it appears that the habitable earth is not round like a disc (ad modum circuli), as Aristotle says, but is the fourth part of the surface of a sphere, of which a fourth and two outermost parts are to some extent cut off, namely those which are not inhabited by reason of too-great heat or cold.*

AENEAS SYLVIUS
(ENEA SILVIO DE PICCOLOMINI, 1405–1464)
HISTORIA RERUM UBIQUE GESTARUM

Aeneas Sylvius can be considered a true Renaissance man—a man for all seasons. The *Commentaries*, an autobiography, reflects a person of great erudition in history and literature. He has been called a humanist, scientist, geographer, poet, satirist, scholar, and politician. The historian Burkhardt in his *The*

Civilization of the Renaissance in Italy makes reference to Aeneas Sylvius on many diverse subjects no less than thirty times. Commenting on the development of geographical and allied sciences among the Italians, he states: "Where, in the middle of the fifteenth century, was there, anywhere but in Italy, such a union of geographical, statistical, and historical knowledge as there was in Aeneas Sylvius? Where such harmonies exposition? Not only in his great geographical work, but in his letters and commentaries, he described with equal mastery landscapes, cities, manners, industries and products, political conditions, and constitutions, wherever he draws from his own observations at the evidence of eyewitnesses."[6] Again commenting from Book I of *The Commentaries of Pius II:* "…In geography as in other matters, it is vain to attempt to distinguish how much is to be attributed to this study of the ancients, and how much to the special genius of the Italians. They saw and treated the things of this world from an objective point of view, even before they were familiar with ancient literature…but they would not have attained such perfection so rapidly had not the old geographers shown them the way."[7]

Enea Silvio Piccolomini, known to the world by the Latin name of Aeneas Silvius, was born near Siena, Italy, on October 18, 1405. He attended the University of Siena studying law, poetry, and the classics. He distinguished himself early in his career at the Council of Basel in 1432, which began to consider reforms of the church, as a lay person assistant to Cardinal Domenico Capranica. He was a leading spokesman for counciliarism. Later he was appointed secretary to the antipope Felix V in 1439. In 1442, the Habsburg ruler Frederick III made him imperial poet. His talents were recognized early, and his rise in the church was dazzling. He was ordained in 1446, became Bishop of Trieste in 1447 and of Siena in 1450, was made Cardinal in 1456 by Callistus III, and was elected pope in 1458. His pontificate was short lived. He made efforts to reassert the papal authority over the clergy and sponsored a general program to reform the church. He also tried, without success, to start a crusade against the Turks in 1463. (Constantinople had fallen to the Turks in 1453.) His appeals were largely ignored by the preoccupied Europe. Nevertheless, he took the leadership himself and called for the mustering of the Christian troops at Ancona on the Adriatic coast. He died there on the night of August 14–15, 1464. Pope Pius II is considered a brilliant and versatile pope, but his reputation rests on his literary achievements.

Pius II's major literary work is the *Historia Rerum Ubique Gestarum*, published in Venice in 1477. Following Aristotle and d'Ailly, Pius II stated that a narrow ocean lay between Europe and Asia, a reassuring opinion for Columbus, who owned a copy of the book. The Admiral, in fact, took his copy amply underlined and glossed to the New World.

PAOLO DAL POZZO TOSCANELLI, 1397–1482

What Columbus had learned from the works of Pius II, Cardinal d'Ailly, and Roger Bacon convinced him that the Indies could be reached without too much difficulty by sailing westward from Spain. His mind was now made up. Yet, he felt that he would be more secure if he could strengthen his proposal with an opinion from a contemporary authority. He was able to get this reassurance from a Florentine physician named Paolo dal Pozzo Toscanelli, who was also a well-known geographer, astronomer, and man of science. Florence in the fifteenth century, under Medici, was the most brilliant center of culture in Europe. Cosimo de Medici, a dominant figure in the city from 1434 to 1464, was an enthusiastic collector of classical manuscripts and established the Library of San Marco and the Medici Library. Under his direction, Greek classics, particularly the works of Plato, were translated; and a Platonic Academy was founded where seminars and lectures were given by eminent Greek intellectuals brought to Florence for the revival of the ancient Hellenic classics.

Lorenzo de Medici, the Magnificent (1428–92), continued his grandfather's cultural patronage by surrounding himself with a brilliant group of intellectuals, artists, political figures, humanists, and scientists. In a comparatively short period of time, easily the zenith of the Renaissance, Florence gave the world the greatest collection of individuals whose intellectual and artistic achievements have been unsurpassed in history. These included Botticelli (1444–1510), painting; Leonardo da Vinci (1452–1519), painting and invention; Brunelleschi (1377–1446), architecture; Donatello (1386–1466), Ghiberti (1378–1455) and Verrocchio (1435–88), sculpture; Michelangelo (1475–1564), painter, sculpture, architect; Machiavelli (1469–1527) and Guicciardini (1485–1540), political theory; Pulci (1432–87), poetry; Vespucci (1451–1512), navigation; Toscanelli (1397–1482) cosmography; and many other important figures.

Paolo dal Pozzo Toscanelli was born in Florence in 1397, studied at the University of Padua, and became a physician. He was an intellectual of many talents who possessed an avid interest in cosmography, astronomy, mathematics, and fine arts. Some historians believe he taught the principles of perspective drawing to the famous architect Brunelleschi. But his fame rests primarily with having reinforced Columbus's determination to undertake his westward voyage to India. This came about in an indirect way. Toscanelli took part in the Church Council of

Florence, 1438–45, where he met Canon Martins, a delegate from Lisbon. Years later, when news of the Portuguese efforts in rounding the African continent reached Toscanelli, he wrote a letter to Martins in 1474 to influence King Alfonso V to consider the western route to the Indies instead of going around Africa. Unfortunately, following the death of Prince Henry in 1469, there had been a slackening of activity on the part of Alfonso V, who for financial reasons resulting possibly from his wars against the Moors and Castile had leased the Guinea trade to Fernão Gomes for five years. Alfonso took no action on Toscanelli's letter. Columbus learned of the existence of the letter and through the efforts of Lorenzo Giradi, a Florentine residing in Lisbon, he hastened to write to Toscanelli, including with his letter a small globe. The Florentine replied by sending Columbus a copy of the letter he had sent to Canon Martins in 1474, including a sea chart "like the one I sent him, that your demands may be satisfied." In the Canon Martins letter, Toscanelli had stated: "From the city of Lisbon due west there are twenty-six spaces marked on the map, both of which contain two hundred and fifty miles, as far as the very great and noble city of Quinsay" (Hangchow, China). China, then, was only 6,500 miles from Lisbon—a very short distance indeed! Moreover, the letter stated "…from the island of Antillia…to the very noble island of Cipango (Japan), there are ten spaces which make 2,500 miles." Because the mythical island of Antillia was thought to be in the Atlantic at about the same parallel as Cape St. Vincent, Japan was also at a comparatively short distance, easily navigable from Portugal.

The Toscanelli letter to the Portuguese was copied by Columbus on the back of his copy of Aeneas Sylvius's *Historia Rerum*, now in the Biblioteca Columbina, Seville. Toscanelli sent another letter to Columbus, written possibly a year before his death in which he declared with confidence that, "…the voyage has become not only possible, but certain." Then he explained the advantages to be gained by the voyage.[8]

THE PHYSICAL WORLD DEFINED BY COLUMBUS

Columbus's diligent research in assessing the size of the earth and the shortest distance to India had concluded that the circumference of the earth was much smaller than it really was. Additionally, Toscanelli's letters had confirmed what he really suspected all the time—that the earth was small enough and that the Atlantic could be crossed without much difficulty. All the cosmographers consulted by Columbus had arrived at the westward distance to the Indies from Europe by deduction. That is, the result was arrived at by estimating the distance to the Indies in the eastward direction in degrees of latitude and subtracting this angular distance from the established total of 360. Then, knowing the net distance in degrees, it was easy to multiply it by the length of the degree to obtain the distance. It is obvious that this method is valid only if the factors are correct; that is, both the angular eastward distance and the equivalent linear distance of a degree must be true.

Another factor to be taken into consideration is the units to be used in calculating the distance to be traversed. Thus, while the current mile referred to as the statute mile is 5,280 feet, the nautical mile, defined as the distance traveled by the earth in one minute of latitude, is about fifteen percent longer, depending on the sphericity of the earth. On the other hand, the Roman or the Italian mile is 432 feet shorter than the statute mile. The Arab mile used by Alfraganus is the longest, being twenty-two percent longer than the statute mile. The league is usually assumed to be four Roman miles although it may vary considerably from the equivalent of 2.4 to 4.6 statute miles, depending on whose standards are adopted. For this reason, it is used to approximate distances, never for scientific measurements. In attempting an estimation of the angular distance of the Eurasian land mass, Columbus was confronted not only with diverse opinions and conflicting statements from all the authorities he consulted, but he himself made gross errors in the units used to determine the length of the degree.

In estimating the length of his voyage, Columbus could have resorted to the following sources:

1. The second book of the prophet Esdras had stated with the authority of the Apocrypha that God had dried up six-sevenths of the globe and left one-seventh of the globe for the ocean. One-seventh of the 360° is 51.43°.
2. Pierre d'Ailly in the *Imago Mundi* had stated that the Atlantic "was of no great width."
3. Toscanelli had stated that the distance to Quinsay (Hangchow) was a mere 6,500 miles due west from the city of Lisbon.
4. Ptolemy taught that the known world from the meridian of Cape St. Vincent to Catigara in Asia was 180°.
5. Eratosthenes had calculated that the degree of the earth at the equator covered 59.5 nautical miles.
6. Marinus of Tyre had estimated that the land mass of the known world covered 225° of the globe.
7. Alfraganus had arrived at the figure of fifty-six and two-thirds miles for a degree at the equator.
8. Marco Polo's discoveries estimated at 28° for the Chinese mainland and another 30° for the reputed distance to Cipango.

In calculating the distance across the ocean to Cipango, Columbus considered the already inflated angular displacement of 180° for the Eurasian land mass estimated by Ptolemy but accepted instead the value of 225° proposed by Marinus of Tyre as being more realistic. To this he added Marco Polo's estimates, as reported by d'Ailly, of 28° for the Chinese mainland and 30° for the reputed distance to Cipango across the present Sea of Japan. Because he was planning to sail across the ocean from the Canary Islands situated 9° west of Cape St. Vincent at a latitude of 28° north, he arrived at a total of 292°, which when subtracted from 360° gave him the remarkably short angular distance of 68°. In converting the 68° into a linear distance, he used the figure of Alfraganus of fifty-six and two-thirds miles, thus giving him a distance at the equator of 3,853 miles. Unfortunately, Columbus made still another error by assuming this distance to be in Roman (Italian) miles instead of Arabic miles.

The length of a degree at any latitude is a cosine function. Thus, the length of a degree at 28°, which is equivalent to 0.8829, multiplied by the length of the degree at the equator of fifty-six and two-thirds miles, giving a product of fifty miles, making the total distance to Cipango 3,400 miles. Because he assumed this to be in Roman miles, its equivalent in nautical miles came out to 2,712 miles. This was even shorter than the Toscanelli estimate. Measuring this distance on today's globe, Columbus placed his Cipango in the vicinity of the Virgin Islands in the West Indies.

With an average sailing speed of one hundred knots, his goal could be reached in twenty-eight days. (It took him thirty-three days out of Ferro in the Canaries on his longer first trip.) This was well within the range of the sailing vessels of his day. Indeed, he himself had already sailed only recently on an equivalent distance to the fortress of São Jorge de Mina on the Gold Coast. This, however, had been a voyage within sight of the African coast with the intermediate landing at the Canaries, along a well-known route. A westward voyage to Cipango would be a new experience to unknown areas with the possibility of encountering weak and possibly contrary winds preventing his safe return. Columbus, however, was not concerned about hitting the doldrums for he had devised the unique plan of sailing westward below the zone of doldrums, known to later sailors as the "horse latitudes," and returning home above it.

Columbus had noticed on his trips along the African coast to the Canaries that the prevailing winds became northeasterly at that point and continued blowing towards the southwest all the way to the Cape Verde Islands. Also, in returning to Lisbon in the latitude of the Azores and northward, the prevailing westerlies would help vessels sail eastward to Lisbon. In short, Columbus, always observant of the weather conditions, had noted wind patterns in the latitude of the Canaries that would aid him on his westward voyage and another in the higher latitudes that would help him sail back to Lisbon. This knowledge of wind patterns would prove to be one of the most valuable contributions to his success. Columbus was well prepared for his historical event. He was also aware that while many cosmographers had known that India could be reached by westward ocean voyage, he would be first to put the idea to the test. In this respect, the words of Roger Bacon, that without experiment nothing can be adequately known, became a motivating force in his quest, which would eventually initiate a new era in the history of the world.

Chapter Five

THE PRIMARY CAUSES FOR THE GREAT HISTORICAL EVENTS

Great historical events are usually the result of several compelling factors among which may be listed technological advances, socio-political conditions, personal commitment, and propitious timing—this last factor being a very important catalyst. For example, when the Soviet Union launched the first artificial satellite, the Sputnik I, in early October 1957, America immediately set the course to explore the universe. By 1961 President Kennedy had committed the nation to a moon landing "before the decade is out." On July 16, 1969, Apollo II was launched into outer space. Four days later the lunar module landed on the moon and Neil A. Armstrong walked on its forbidding surface as billions of people watched in fascination.

The compelling factors for this great historical event—the first of its kind—are self-evident. Without the technological advances made in astronautics, rocket propulsion, telecommunications, and instrumentation, the moon landing could not have succeeded; neither could it have succeeded without the resolute commitment of the President. The element of timing was indeed an important catalyst as the Sputnik launching signaled that the Soviets had arrived as a world power with the capability of challenging American technology, not only in space but in strategic weaponry as well.

The parallel of America's discovery by Christopher Columbus nearly five hundred years earlier with the moon landing is not far-fetched. The technological advances made in sailing ships, instrumentation, and navigation, immensely accelerated by a half century of Portuguese activity along the African coast, made a westward oceanic voyage to the Indies a distinct possibility. The time was propitious, for with the fall of Constantinople to the Turks in 1453, the usual channels of direct communication to the land of spices had been shut off. And there was Christopher Columbus—not merely committed to the idea of reaching India by a westward route, but actually obsessed with it. There were also socio-political and religious reasons for a westward trip, but at the time these were less important.

What were the technological advances that led to the discovery of America? By comparison, they were not as sophisticated nor as precise as those that put the men on the moon, but they were advanced enough for a man such as Columbus to take the chance. His great skills as a navigator made up for the lack of highly sophisticated instruments. Twentieth-century technology had the tools to predict the results with certainty, barring unforeseen malfunctions. The course of Apollo II to the moon was monitored and every phase of the operation was tracked by mission control on earth. Columbus, on the other hand, was on his own as soon as he left port—his destination unpredictable and entirely up to chance.

SAILING SHIPS COME OF AGE

Whereas the ships of the northern European sailors had hardly changed for three hundred years after the Viking exploits, those in the Mediterranean had been steadily improved. In northern countries the single central-masted, square-rigged, clinker-built ship was a durable work horse of the Middle Ages. In clinker-built hulls, the planks were overlapped (lapstraked) and riveted to each other. A notched rib on the inside of the hull provided the structural support.

In the Mediterranean a different type of ship, designed primarily for commerce, had evolved. These ships were called lateeners after the Latin countries where they were used; they could sail closer to windward than ships rigged with square sails. Lateeners built for the Crusades were eighty-six feet in length and carried one hundred men plus a crew of thirty and their equipment on their two decks. When the ninth Crusade was being planned in 1286, its leader, King Louis IX of France, ordered his transports built by Genoese and Venetian shipwrights.

It was not long after the beginning of the fifteenth century that elements of the northern and Mediterranean ships were incorporated into one design. The result was a ship possessing the best qualities of both: the sturdy construction of the north Atlantic sailing ships and the superior performance of the lateeners, with few of the undesirable characteristics of either. During the latter part of the fifteenth century, the basic design was to spawn ships of many different names such as carrack, nao, caravel, barca, fusta, gale, and verinel, each of which was employed for a specialized function.

The deployment of cannons on these ships was begun to protect them from pirates. At first when guns were small, they were mounted on the superstructure and no alterations to the structure of the hull were required; but larger and heavier guns could be carried only below deck and gun-ports had to be incorporated in the side of the hull.

THE NIMBLE CARAVEL

Portuguese legend has exalted the caravel as the most famous sailing ship in the age of exploration. It was easy to handle thanks to its lateen sail, inexpensive to build, and capable of performing exceptionally well to windward. Because of its low draft—less than ten feet—it could sail upstream inland to city ports as much as two hundred miles from the coast.

Prince Henry the Navigator liked the caravel and contributed to its refinement to the point where it was regarded as the most reliable sailing vessel of the middle of the fifteenth century. Indeed, according to Cadamosto, Prince Henry credits the caravel for conquering Cape Nun. But its most important achievement was Dias's rounding of the Cape of Good Hope since it opened routes to the Indian Ocean.

Columbus's two ships, the Niña and the Pinta, were caravels. His favorite, the Niña, was a "caravela latina," all of sixty tons, and of approximately seventy feet in length. Eventually re-rigged in the Canaries on his first trip to America as a "caravel redonda," its lateen sails were replaced with square sails and thus it was made very effective in sailing west before the trade winds.[1] Columbus also used the Niña during the exploration of Cuba on his second trip in 1494.

As voyages of exploration became longer, the ships were made larger. The caravel came to be regarded as a coast-wise vessel. Despite Columbus's Atlantic crossings, it became obsolete when long ocean travels became more commonplace. Oceanic travels were made in naos or carracks. The same Dias who rounded the Cape of Good Hope in a caravel, when given the responsibility of planning the expedition to take Vasco da Gama across the Indian Ocean to Calicut, discarded the caravel and chose instead the nao.

ADVANCES IN THE TECHNOLOGY OF NAVIGATION CHARTS, INSTRUMENTS, AND METHODOLOGY

The earliest practical charts for navigation, the "portolani," were simply the graphic representations of the log books of early-day Italian sailors. Hence, these charts were maps that contained sailing instructions. There were no parallels or meridians on them and the sphericity of the earth was not taken into account. The charts were made by establishing a succession of base points in the sea and then drawing from these base points straight lines corresponding to the points of the compass. The distance along these straight lines, known as "bearings," radiating from the base points like sun rays, were measured in miles, not degrees, and ships could find their ways to shore points or other base points with remarkable accuracy. All charts were drawn with the magnetic north as the vertical.

Genoa, Pisa, Venice, Majorca, Barcelona, and Lisbon had skilled chart-makers who drew charts from information garnered from their pilots and captains.[2] These charts were revised and updated as new information became available. Bartholomew Columbus, Christopher's younger brother, and Columbus himself worked in Lisbon as chart-makers. Other Genoese and Venetian expatriates worked in Portugal, where João II, following in the footsteps of Henry the Navigator, encouraged the mapping and charting of the African coast.

The centers of chart-making spread soon beyond Italy to Majorca, Barcelona, and Lisbon, where the contact with Arabs and Jews brought new refinements to the art. Abraham Cresques, a Jew of Palma, on an assignment from Charles V of France, produced in 1375 the famous Catalan Atlas, a beautiful portolan map in six colors, showing in great detail all that was known about the world. It was the highest point reached by the portolan technique in the Middle Ages.

These maps evolved with the invention of the magnetic compass. Their most distinctive feature was the maze of rhumb lines (lines of constant course) that radiated from a number of wind roses placed at many intervals on the chart. To get to a known destination, the mariner set his course with the aid of the magnetic compass on the required rhumb line until he reached his destination.

Columbus carried a number of sea charts showing the coasts of Spain, Portugal, Africa, and the Atlantic Islands on his historical voyages. He also included on his sea charts Cipango and Cathay drawn in a location estimated by him from the information gathered from mariners of Tyre, Marco Polo, and Toscanelli. These charts were drawn on sheepskins. Their surfaces were crisscrossed by rhumb lines in the typical portolan fashion. It is possible that Columbus may also have had charts with latitude grids on them. We must remember that Columbus had sailed down the African coast under Portuguese patronage.

King João II, the great-nephew of Henry, after his ascendancy to the throne of Portugal in 1481, had geographers and mapmakers at his personal retinue. By the last quarter of the fifteenth century, Portuguese captains had already acquired the technique of "shooting" the sun and the North Star to determine latitude. Every time they returned from their African voyages, their charts contained additional information of the coast with reasonably accurate latitude grids.

Stated simply, the art of navigation is the science or ability of conducting a vessel from a given place to another in the best way possible. The navigator must establish his starting position then lay out the route along which the vessel will travel. Once the direction has been set, the speed must be estimated to establish how long it will take to reach a given destination.

Planning the voyage is simple enough. The problems arise along the voyage, for the navigator has to move in the correct direction and must know at all times the speed of the vessel. Because speed is a function of distance and time, the distance traveled and the time taken must be calculated, taking into account the vagaries of the wind. The navigator of the fifteenth century used the magnetic compass for direction. To check his position at sea, he would determine his latitude by sighting the Pole Star with the cross staff or the quadrant. With the developments in the design and rigging of sailing ships, improvements in navigational instruments and charts were made as well. The mariners' compass reappeared in the same period that the carrack was being developed and became invaluable in Portugal's conquest of the African coast.

The early compass was a primitive instrument in which a magnetized piece of iron was made to float on a straw in a bowl of water. It is difficult to imagine how any accurate readings could have been made aboard a moving vessel. The sailors of Amalfi in 1100 A.D. placed the magnetic needle on a brass dart located in the center of the bowl, thus allowing the needle to rotate. Sicilian and Arab sailors were using this type of primitive compass around 1200 A.D. Later, in 1300–20, Flavio Gioia, a native of Amalfi, improved the compass further by mounting the needle under the compass card marked with thirty-two points of direction and then installing the card assembly on the center pivot. This card assembly, known as the "compass rose" remained essentially the same for centuries thereafter. A later addition was the incorporation of the 3,600 graduations for more accurate reading. A clue to the Italian origin of the compass rose is the emblem that indicates north—an embellishment of the letter "T" that stands for "tramontana"—Italian for "north wind" and used to this day.

The compass was to be an invaluable instrument to the Portuguese in their African explorations. They made further improvements on it, especially in the suspension of the compass rose. Columbus's compass was typical of his age. It is possible that Columbus's compass may have been mounted on gimbals in order to keep it essentially level with the pitch and roll of the vessel. The first recorded evidence of gimbal-mounted magnetic compasses dates back to 1515. But it is difficult to imagine that it would have taken the Italians and the Portuguese over a century to find a solution to the compass rose's jamming on its pivot in heavy seas.

The emergence of the magnetic compass revolutionized the science of navigation and brought important changes in cartography. It was now possible for a captain to determine the location of any coastal features, islands, and other points of interest by taking compass bearings in relation to the magnetic north. It made the portolan charts more useful. At the end of the fifteenth century, the compass had an easterly deviation all over Europe and most likely in the African waters frequented by the Portuguese. In fact, Columbus was the first navigator to notice a westerly deviation.

At regular intervals on long trips, pilots of his day used to check the ship's compasses against the Pole Star, which, at that time rotated around the true pole with a radius of approximately 3 ½°. This required instruments for celestial observations. The compass was very useful in establishing the vessel's direction; but for determining the exact location on the globe, the pilot looked to the heavenly bodies—the sun, the Pole Star, and the galaxies—for guidance.

The instruments used for astronomical observations were the astrolabe, the quadrant, and the cross-staff. The astrolabe, used primarily by scientists and astronomers, was beyond the comprehension of the average pilot and very difficult to use on ships.

The mariner's quadrant was so simple in construction that nearly every sailor could make one. The cross-staff consisted of a graduated staff, with a transom cross piece free to slide along its length. With one end of the staff held to his eye, the observer looked along the staff to the heavenly body and slid the cross piece along the length of the staff until it fit exactly between the heavenly body and the horizon. The angle of altitude was then read on the staff.

Unfortunately, there were no chronometers to measure time accurately in those days. The early navigators relied on the sundial and later on the sandglass to measure time, but with woefully inaccurate results. Determining longitude by celestial navigation was thus practiced only by men of learning: by astrologers, scientists, and physicians. In fact, when Magellan undertook his historic circumnavigation of the earth, he enlisted the aid of the Italian pilot Antonio Pigafetta, a man of great learning and skilled in the art of celestial navigation.

Columbus sailed by dead reckoning, as did many navigators of his day. He calculated his longitude by estimating the number of miles sailed every day. Speed was estimated by the expert eye of the beholder as he watched the water and bubbles go by the side of the ship. Another method was to toss a chip of wood at the bow of the ship and time how long it took to travel the length of the ship. A still more accurate method was to toss a log tied to a knotted rope from the stern of the ship and then count the number of knots passing through the hand of the holder in a given time. This method gave birth to the "knot," the unit indicating the speed of ships.

The traverse board, a carryover from the medieval navigators, but still used by mariners of the fifteenth century, was used to plot the direction of a ship's course by inserting pegs into holes on the board. The ship's position would be placed at the center and pegs would be inserted into holes located concentrically at various distances from the center; eight holes were bored along each point of the compass. From the center outward, each hole stood for one half-hour of the watch timed by the half-hour sandglass. If the course for the first half-hour was due west, a peg was put into the first hole west of the center. If the direction changed to west by south in the next half-hour, a peg would be put in the second hole on the west by south, and so on.

The traverse board dramatized the need for a more accurate method of measuring time. Watching the sand run down the sandglass and turning it to call out the half-hour could hardly be construed as a scientific method. Because the watches at sea lasted four hours, the grommet had to turn the sandglass eight times. Yet, the sandglass had to be used for several more centuries before the marine chronometer came aboard late in the eighteenth century. This accurate timepiece eventually made possible tracking the meridians of longitude. But the basic tools for navigation, greatly improved by Portuguese exploits, were now available. The magnetic compass, the stern post rudder, the three-masted ship with lateen rigging to sail against the wind, the improved sea charts, and instruments for sighting celestial bodies could now be depended upon for long voyages in all seasons away from the visible coast. The time was now propitious for Columbus to sail westward into a new world. A little later Magellan would circumnavigate the earth.

Part II

GENOA: COLUMBUS'S BIRTHPLACE

Chapter Six

GENOA AND THE COLOMBOS

Like a jewel-studded crown, the region of Liguria borders with France to the west and with the Tuscan city of Massa Carrara to the east. In the middle of the crown lies its scintillating jewel: Genoa—"La Superba" (the Proud). At its base, the Gulf of Genoa mirrors the city and the hillsides. The Apennine mountains, backbone of the Italian peninsula, rise northward and swing westward to embrace Liguria. The Ligurian Alps to the west complete the embrace and shelter the region, thus enabling it to enjoy mild weather throughout the winter—a boon to navigation and maritime pursuits. With the mountains stacked behind her, Genoa's natural transportation outlet—throughout the centuries—has been the sea.

Genoa attained its greatest power and prosperity toward the end of the thirteenth century. By that time, the city had established possessions and commercial lanes not only in the eastern Mediterranean and Black Seas, but in the North Sea as well. Its possessions included Corsica and Sardinia in the Mediterranean; Samos, Chios, and Lesbos in the Aegean Sea; the city of Pera near Constantinople; Amisus and Kaffa in the Black Sea; and Azov past the Kerch Strait in the Azov Sea. The lanes opened to Genoese commerce extended through the Mediterranean to Tunis, Rhodes, Acre, Tyre, and Constantinople through the Black Sea to Crimea and Trepizand. They also extended westward through Gibraltar and the Atlantic to Rowen, Bruges, and ports on the North Sea.

In spite of its power and wealth, Genoa was beset for centuries with discord and civil strife between commoners and the nobility. It waged, also, several wars against neighbors and against Venice with varying outcomes. During the battle against Venice, at Curzola in 1298, Marco Polo was taken prisoner. In the course of his four-year captivity in Genoa, he dictated *Il Milione*, a book that had enormous influence on Christopher Columbus and on the age of exploration.

To relieve the constant tension, a new form of government was instituted in 1339 after Simone Boccanegra had led the sailors and other workers in a revolution that culminated with his becoming the first Doge of a dynasty that ruled Genoa until Napoleon took over the city in 1797. Incidentally, Giuseppe Verdi was to commemorate Simone Boccanegra in a famous opera. In 1378 the Genoese, under Admiral Luciano Doria, won an overwhelming victory over the Venetians in the North Adriatic Sea near Pola, capturing fifteen galleys and two thousand men. Under siege for over a year, the Venetians regrouped and counterattacked in 1379, using, for the first time in history, cannons firing stone projectiles weighing nearly 150 pounds. They forced the Genoese to retreat and eventually sue for peace in 1381. Genoa never recouped from the war. In 1393, a revolution forced all the nobles out of office. In five years (1390–94) Genoa had ten revolutions and, to prevent Milan from gaining control, sought the protection of France. In 1398, the French were expelled, but civil strife continued under local rule. Bloody battles were fought in the streets and property was destroyed. In desperation, the Genoese surrendered to Milan in 1421. However, the despotic rule of the Milanese became unbearable and another revolution brought back the republic in 1435.

In 1453, the Ottoman Turks, under the leadership of Sultan Mohammed II, conquered Constantinople. This was a serious blow to Genoa's commerce. The city lost not only control of Pera on the Bosphorus, but access to the Black Sea as well. The French took advantage of Genoa's vulnerability and occupied the city in 1458, but the Milanese under Francesco Sforza regained control of it in 1464. A minor revolution in Milan in 1476, in which Galleazzo Maria Sforza was assassinated, brought a period of freedom and independence to Genoa. This lasted until the end of the century, at which time Louis VII occupied Genoa after seizing Milan in 1499. It was the famous Genoese Admiral Andrea Doria who commanded the large fleet that drove the French out of Genoa. He established a new government with a new constitution in 1528 and brought peace to Genoa until the coming of Napoleon in 1797.

Because of the constant wars and internal disorders, Genoa contributed very little to the arts and humanities. It was too busy fighting wars and exploring the seas to contribute to the Renaissance movement. Its main contributions were to the science of shipbuilding and navigation, which early in the fifteenth century proved invaluable to the Portuguese efforts. However, enterprising Genoese businessmen developed accounting and financing and marine insurance to a degree unsurpassed in the fourteenth and fifteenth centuries. The development of double-entry bookkeeping, marine insurance, and high-level banking is attributed to the Bank of St. George. This institution was the financial backbone of the Genoese Republic in war and peace. It was the amalgam that held the republic together after the fall of Constantinople and it seemed to become stronger and more stable with each calamitous event. The bank of St. George became the clearinghouse of Europe through a modern system of banking where all currencies could be accepted and exchanged on the basis of their worth in gold, thus establishing, in fact, the gold standard. The most powerful mercantile and rich families of Genoa—the Dorias, the Spinolas, the Feischis, the Di Negros, and the Grimaldis—were deeply involved in the operation of the Bank.

By the end of the fifteenth century, Genoa was considered one of the richest cities in Italy, second only to Rome and Venice. Ironically, the merchants were too busy making money trading with all of Europe, and the nobles too involved in politics, to notice that one of Genoa's own sons, Christopher Columbus, was begging the Spanish monarchs for a chance to find a new route to the land of spices.

THE COLOMBO DYNASTY

What we know about Columbus and the Colombo family of Genoa has been garnered from diverse sources: from legal documents, especially notarial deeds; from biographical articles written by contemporary authors and his son, Ferdinand Columbus, who accompanied his father on his fourth voyage; from letters and dispatches written by Columbus; and from sailors who sailed with him.

Columbus's four voyages of discovery to America have been well recorded by Italians Peter Martyr, news writer and correspondent to the great; by the royal historian Captain Gonzalo Fernández de Oviedo; and by Bishop de Las Casas.

However, the best sources of information on the Colombos of Genoa are the notarial deeds of which about twenty are extant. These documents list dates and ages of individuals involved, their jobs and professions, places where they lived, and other personal data and events. They were all written in Latin, the legal language of the day throughout Europe.

It is from one of these deeds (by Notary Quilico of Albenga, dated at Genoa on February 21, 1429[1]) that we learn that Columbus's grandfather, Giovanni Colombo, who lived in the village of Moconesi and had settled in Quinto, placed "Dominicus eius filius" (his son Domenico) in the care of William Brabanta, a German who lived in Genoa, to learn the trade of wool weaver. We further learn that the boy was eleven years old at that time in 1429 and that his apprenticeship would last six years.

Giovanni, in addition to Domenico, had another son, Antonio, and a daughter, Battistina. Antonio was the father of three, and possibly four, sons, all weavers. One of these, Giannetto by name joined his cousin Christopher on his third trip to America in 1497. Domenico had four sons and one daughter, Bianchinetta. His eldest son was Christopher. The others were Bartolomeo (Bartholomew), Giacomo (Diego), and Giovanni Pellegrino—the first two becoming eventually governors of Hispaniola. Not much is known about Giovanni Pellegrino except that on August 7, 1473, he cosigned a notarial deed with his brother Christopher and his parents to sell the house near the Olivella Gate in Genoa. An earlier deed, dated 1440, notes that Domenico Colombo leased a house and land in Vico dell'Olivella, a lively street at that time, in the Portoria district, not too far from the Gate of Sant'Andrea. The landlords were the monks of the Monastery of Sant'Andrea.

In 1445, Domenico married Susanne Fontanarossa, daughter of one Giacomo, a weaver who lived in the valley of the Bisogno River. In 1447, at the age of 29, Domenico was appointed by the Doge of Genoa to the wardship of the tower and Gate to Olivella Street. This was a supplementary job paying a mere seven pounds (13 dollars in gold) per month and lasting until the end of 1451.

Christopher Columbus was born in 1451, between August 26 and October 31—the exact date is unknown, as no record of his birth has been found in Genoa. A couple of years later, Bartolomeo, Columbus's devoted brother, was born. The other brother, who also made history with Columbus, was Giacomo (Diego), who must have been at least seventeen years younger than Christopher.

In 1470, Domenico was sent by his fellow weavers to the city of Savona, west of Genoa, on business relating to the establishment of a "common tariff." On returning to Genoa, Domenico was involved in a lawsuit that resulted in a one-year jail sentence for him and a fine of thirty Genoese pounds, which he could not pay without the help of his nineteen-year-old son, Christopher. This indicates that Christopher was already working as a seaman and earning enough money to help his father out of trouble. After serving his jail term, Domenico moved his family to Savona, where he added to his income by becoming a tavern keeper: "*...Domenico de Columbo, civis Ianue...panorum et tabernarius*," as stated in the notarial deed we have examined. Domenico's efforts at augmenting his income from other sources must have not been too successful, for according to the notarial deeds, Christopher had to guaranty payments for his father's purchases of wine and cloth. By 1484 the family had moved back to Genoa, where Giacomo began his apprenticeship in the craft of wool weaving. Still in financial difficulty, Domenico signed a deed, consigning his shop on the ground floor to a shoemaker, and occupying the top floor with his enlarged family. By 1489, Christopher, Bartolomeo, and Giacomo were already listed in the deeds as living in Spain, and Domenico, now a widower, claimed to be the legitimate administrator of his three sons. His fourth son, Giovanni Pellegrino, had died and Bianchinetta had taken up residence in the Gate of Sant'Andrea house.

One of the most important notarial deeds was filed in 1501 by Genoese citizens who swore on oath that the three Colombo brothers had "been absent from the city and far from the jurisdiction of Savona for a long time, beyond Pisa and Nice in Provence and that they were living in the country of Spain as was and is well known."[2]

The notarial deeds cited in this chapter are important because they establish first of all that the Colombos were not of noble birth, as Ferdinand Columbus suggested in his father's biography, nor peasants, but productive artisans. The deeds indicate that Columbus's father was not only a master weaver, belonging to a monopolistic guild, but also important enough to be appointed by the Doge to supervise the Olivella Gate. Additionally, in becoming a "tabernarius" (tavern keeper), he rose to the loftier station of merchant and financial speculator. Taverns in those days were miniature stock exchanges where financial speculators gathered to discuss business and financial transactions.

The notarial deeds also pinpoint within several months the birth date of Christopher Columbus, which Washington Irving and other nineteenth century authors had put at the earlier date of 1435 to 1436 in agreement with the evidence supplied by Bernáldez. Muñoz, in his *Historia del Nuevo Mundo*, concluded that Columbus was born in 1446. But most importantly the notarial deeds prove once and for all that Christopher—the "Christ-Bearer"—was born in Genoa between August and September 1451.

HIS NATIONAL ORIGIN

A number of writers have attempted to prove that Columbus was actually a Spaniard, a Portuguese, a Catalan Jew, an Armenian, a Greek, and a Swiss. Such claims fly in the face of history and should be put to rest.

No contemporary of Columbus had any doubts about his Genoese nationality. Indeed, throughout the centuries and up to the end of the nineteenth century, no one questioned the fact that Columbus was Genoese. As for Columbus, he always regarded himself as Genoese. In the "mayorazgo," or provisions, for the succession to his estate executed on February 22, 1498, before embarking on his third voyage, he directed that part of the revenue of his estate be deposited with the Bank of St. George for the relief of the overtaxed citizens of Genoa, "where I was born," and for the maintenance of a house where members of the Colombo family might live honorably.[3] Later, on April 2, 1502, to be exact, he wrote a letter to the directors of the Bank of St. George stating with obvious sentimental attachment to his native city that, "…although my body wanders here, my heart is continually in Genoa."[4] His son Ferdinand stated:

Some say that he was from Nervi, others from Cugureo, and still others from Bugiasco, all of which are little places near Genoa and situated on the same coast…others that he was Genoese.[5]

Ferdinand wrote his father's biography about thirty years after the Admiral's death; hence, his confusion about his father's exact place of birth.

Captain Gonzalo Fernández de Oviedo, royal historian, and Bishop Bartolomé de Las Casas both knew the Indies well and both wrote famous histories about Columbus and his discoveries.

Oviedo, in his *Historia General y Natural de Las Indias*, published in 1547, accepted Columbus as a Genoese. Concerning his origin, he states in Chapter 3:

I will say that Christopher Columbus, as I have heard from men of his nation, was a native of the province of Liguria, which lies in the city and lordship of Genoa. Some give his birthplace as Savona, or a small town or village called Nervi, on the Levant coast, two leagues from Genoa, but the most reliable story is that he came from Cugureo, which is also near Genoa.

Las Casas, whose *Historia de las Indias* covers the whole history of American exploration up to 1520, believed that Columbus was of Genoese extraction.

Peter Martyr, Italian correspondent and reporter, who met Columbus at Barcelona on his return from the first voyage of discovery in April 1493, refers to Columbus as "Colonus Ligur."[6]

The list of contemporary writers, be they Spaniard, Portuguese, or Italian, who wrote about Columbus and his discoveries and referred to him as a Genoese is endless. Thus, it would be pointless to continue. I am satisfied that modern scholarship has conclusively established that Christopher Columbus was indeed Genoese.[7]

Chapter Seven

COLUMBUS'S EARLY YEARS

Not much is known about Columbus's education. Most historians agree that he never had a formal education. There are no extant records to substantiate it. His son, Ferdinand, however, maintained that Columbus:

Learned his letters at a tender age and studied enough at the University of Pavia to understand the geographers of whose teaching he was very fond; for this reason, he also gave himself to the study of astronomy and geometry, since these sciences are so closely related that one depends upon the other.[1]

Because there is no record of Columbus attending the University of Pavia, most historians dismiss his claims as fiction. It is possible that Ferdinand was referring to the school in the Vico di Pavia (Pavia Alley) that was kept by the woolworkers' guild for their children. Columbus, as the son of a woolworker, may have attended that school. Giustiniani, in his edition of the *Psalterium,* writes that Christopher Columbus learned the rudiments of letters as a child and navigation in his young manhood, but he does not explain the circumstnaces.[2] It is possible that he acquired reading skills at the school in Vico di Pavia. He may have also been tutored by relatives or friends. But we simply do not have the answers to many of the questions regarding Columbus's education. We do know, however, that a bright, inquisitive young mind can overcome the barriers of illiteracy without a formal education.

Columbus himself gives us a clue to his education in a letter he sent in 1502 to the King and Queen of Spain. He is quoted by Las Casas as having said:

All the seas and coasts that have been sailed to the present I have sailed. I have talked and lived with the learned—churchmen and laymen, Latins and Greeks, Jews and Moors, and many others of other creeds—and to this design of mine I found Our Lord very favorable, and for its sake He gave me the spirit of understanding: in sea-faring He over-endowed me; of astronomy He taught me sufficient as of geometry and arithmetic, with invention in my soul and as a draftsman's hands. Over the years I have seen and studied books on every science: cosmography, history, chronicles, and philosophy and other arts, whereby Our Lord opened my understanding with this manifest hand that it was possible to navigate from here to the Indies.[3]

This is a confession of a self-educated man. Columbus was a person of great intellect, quick to learn what interested him—the art of sailing and navigation, and related subjects. "In sea-faring He over-endowed me," he stated. No one will argue that point.

"Over the years have I seen and studied books on every science," he boasted, perhaps with good reason. Columbus must have learned how to read and write Latin because most of the books of that period were written in Latin. But we do not know how and when he did so.

It is also likely that he had a reading knowledge of Italian, the idiom used by Dante, Petrarch, and Boccaccio that existed only, at that time and well into the nineteenth century, as a literary language. His native tongue, of course, was Genoese, which is primarily used for oral communication and not as a written language. It is interesting to note on this point that the imperfections found in Columbus's use of Spanish—which were cited by Las Casas on several occasions and which have been attributed by scholars to the interference of the Portuguese language—were due to the linguistic interference of the Genoese dialect. A study by Virgil I. Milani proves rather conclusively that those unfamiliar terms and those spelling errors that one encounters in the *Diario* derive from the Genoese dialect and not Portuguese, as many claim.[4]

Christopher Columbus began sailing at the age of ten and started a sailor's life at fourteen. At twenty-one he was already a sea captain. An illiterate person could not have risen to a rank of authority and importance so rapidly. And because the sea was his inspiration, the sea also provided him with intellectual nourishment.

Christopher Columbus was born and lived at the zenith of the Renaissance. This movement was distinguished by a renewed interest in the world of letters, arts, and scholarship. It left its imprint on most Italian cities, but strangely it bypassed Genoa. The intellectual fervor present in Italian cities was not matched by an equal zeal for unity against foreign invaders. Soon French, Spanish, and German armies began to occupy Italian territories. There was no united resistance against the invaders as each Italian city-state strove to survive by making alliances with foreigners against its neighbors. As a result, the French were quick to capitalize on the inherent weaknesses of the Italian cities. Genoa, engaged primarily in commerce, was not militarily prepared to offer serious resistance to foreign invaders. Milan, however, under the despotic rule of the Sforzas (1450–1500), following the dynasty of the Viscontis, was an efficient military machine capable of defending itself and even on occasions of succoring its neighbors.

This was the climate in which Christopher Columbus lived in his early years. This also explains why Columbus sailed on his historic voyages under the patronage of Spain. Within the first eight years of his life, he would see Genoa dominated successively by France, Aragon, and France again. Hapless Genoa was an unwilling victim in the war between René I of Anjou and Alfonso V of Aragon for the conquest of the Kingdom of Naples. Alfonso V (1385–1458) already ruled Sicily as Alfonso I when in 1420 he assisted Queen Joanna (Giovanna) II of Naples in defeating Louis III of Anjou, her rival for the Neapolitan throne. As a reward, Joanna promised to make Alfonso her heir. Later, however, she suspected him of an attempt to usurp her power and she disowned him; she died in 1445, leaving her throne to René I of Anjou. War followed as Alfonso attempted to seize the throne. Unfortunately, while besieging the port of Gaeta immediately north of Naples, he was captured by a Genoese fleet and brought north before Filippo Maria Visconti in Milan. Alfonso was able to convince his captors that French power, already pushing from the north on Milan and upon Genoa from the west, would constitute a serious threat to the Italian cities and to Italy itself. Filippo accepted Alfonso's logic and released him to continue his quest for the throne. A few years later, Alfonso attacked René, and captured Naples in 1442; in 1443 he was crowned King Alfonso I of Naples by Pope Felix V. Alfonso reunited the crowns of Naples and of Sicily and made Naples the current center of the Argonese empire in the Mediterranean.

THE MAKING OF A NAVIGATOR

Columbus was only seven years old when King Charles VII of France appointed Jean d'Anjou, son of René, to Governor of Genoa. At about the same time (1458) Alfonso died and his illegitimate son, Ferrante (Ferdinand I), laid claim to the throne. Charles too cast his eye on the crown of Naples. However, Ferrante triumphed thanks to the support of Francesco Sforza of Milan and Cosimo de' Medici of Florence, both of whom feared a French occupation of Genoa. The struggle between the Aragonese and the Angevins, who occupied Genoa, continued for many years. And it was during this period that Columbus, at the age of fourteen, went to sea, perhaps as a privateer for René and Jean d'Anjou.

This period must have been financially rewarding for Columbus. At the age of nineteen he was able to get his father, Domenico, out of difficulties by paying a judgment of thirty Genoese pounds imposed on him by the courts.

This was also an intense period of learning for Columbus. He learned his craft by doing it. He learned it so well that, as recorded by his son Ferdinand, by the age of twenty-one he was already in command of a ship. From a letter written by Columbus to Ferdinand and Isabella from the island of Hispaniola, we learn that he was quite adept with the instruments of his trade:

King René (whom God has taken) sent me to Tunis to capture the galleass Fernandina; and when I was off the island of San Pietro, near Sardinia, a vessel informed me there were two ships and a carrack with the said galleass, which frightened my people and they resolved to go no further but to return to Marseilles to pick up another ship and more men. I, seeing that I could do nothing against their will without some ruse, agreed to their demand and, changing the point of the compass, made sail at nightfall; and at sunrise the next day we found ourselves off Cape Carthage, while all aboard were certain we were bound for Marseilles.[5]

In Cuba, during his voyage to America, Columbus, who was still in quest of the Grand Khan, was shown by the boatswain of the Niña some resin from local shrubs he identified erroneously as resin similar to the mastic he had seen on the island of Chios on an earlier voyage. He assumed that this was the mastic resin from the lentisk shrub (Pistacia Lentiscus) that was particularly esteemed in the Middle Ages for use in medicine. The Giustiniani family of Genoa obtained a monopoly of the mastic trade and became the chief European supplier for over two hundred years. While the Giustinianis, as owners of the island, supplied the mastic, the Spinolas had the responsibility for shipping it, not only in Genoa, but as far north as Bristol. In 1474, Gioffredo Spinola fitted out a four-masted ship named "Roxana" for trade with Chios with a number of workers, seamen, and soldiers from Savona. And among them was Christopher Columbus.

This voyage, perhaps the longest he had taken up to that time, was to be the most rewarding venture of his life. Chios, at the eastern end of the Aegean Sea, lies only a few miles off the west coast of Turkey near Smyrna. From Genoa the shortest route to Chios is south through the Strait of Messina, then eastward through the many Greek Islands and straits, to the west coast of Turkey—nearly 1,150 nautical miles, the last third of the distance requiring seamanship of the highest order.

The similarity of sailing in the Aegean to the Caribbean Sea must not have gone unnoticed to Columbus in later voyages. There is no doubt that he learned valuable lessons from this Chios experience—the ability to sail between narrow passages, avoiding shoals and the violent squalls that can fall on a ship when she is on the lee side of hills and mountains, and the sudden currents generated by the wind in narrow passageways between islands. It is not known in what capacity Columbus sailed on the Roxana—whether as a seaman or a worker. But he was a keen observer and already an accomplished sailor, and must have treasured the opportunity to learn.

He had experienced sailing nearly the whole length of the Mediterranean Sea when the opportunity finally came to Columbus to discover the pleasures and perils of the Atlantic Ocean. Unfortunately, 1476 was a dangerous year to sail the Atlantic for most of the Mediterranean nations were at war. For that reason, Genoa organized a large convoy in order to deliver mastic from Chios to Portugal and England. The convoy was composed of ships belonging to the Spinolas and the Di Negros. One of the vessels, named *Bechalla*, was manned mostly by men from Savona, including Columbus. The convoy left on May 31, sailed northward along the Spanish coast, headed towards Gibraltar, and reached the southern coast of Portugal on August 13. Not far from Cape St. Vincent, in the maritime realm that Prince Henry the Navigator had made famous, they were attacked by a Franco-Prussian fleet of thirteen ships under the command of Guillaume de Casenove, the famous French Admiral under Louis XI. The Genoese put up a terrific fight and gave a good account of themselves. Using Ferdinand's words:

Here they came to blows fighting with great fury and approaching each other until the ships grappled and the men crossed from boat to boat, killing and wounding each other without mercy, using not only hand arms but also fire pots and other devices...they fought from morning to the hour of the vespers with many dead and wounded on both sides.[6]

Three Genoese ships and four of the enemy's ships went down. Columbus fought bravely from the *Bechalla*, which eventually caught fire and began to list. Columbus leaped overboard and, again, according to Ferdinand:

The Admiral being an excellent swimmer, and seeing land only a little more than two leagues away [over six miles] seized an oar which fate offered him and on which he could rest at times; and so it pleased God, who was preserving him for greater things, to give him strength to reach the shore. However, he was so fatigued by his experience that it took him many days to recover. Finding himself near Lisbon, and knowing that many of his Genoese countrymen lived in that city, he went there as soon as he could.[7]

From a moment of near disaster, on the midsummer night of 1476, Columbus suddenly found himself on the shores of Lagos near Sagres and Cape St. Vincent—*the Sacred Cape*—the outer limit of the earth—immortalized by Prince Henry the Navigator. There is an aura of mysticism about the whole incident. A person destined to discover a new world could not have landed on a more propitious location for the realization of his dream. The Portuguese were deeply committed to exploring the western coast of Africa and had already sailed past the equator. The western bulge of Africa had been rounded, Guinea had been taken, and the concept of a sea route to India had been formulated. This was an exciting period in which the art and science of navigation had advanced immeasurably, and the twenty-five-year-old Columbus had every opportunity to learn and to dream. This was a paradoxical event in which a human tragedy became an act of providence. Portugal would become the stage for a dream in which the protagonist, through a succession of fortunate events, and despite great odds, would achieve greatness.

Chapter Eight

THE PORTUGUESE EXPERIENCE

Columbus's foundering on the shores of Prince Henry's territory in Sagres has many overtones of destiny. It was the turning point in his life. The nine years he spent in Portugal were to have considerable bearing on his future. They elevated him socially, intellectually, and professionally. Later through an advantageous marriage he made contacts and received favors from important personages. Through personal sacrifices and hard work, he improved his ability to read and write Latin so as to study cosmology and geography, which in those days were always written in Latin. The works of Ptolemy, Roger Bacon, Pierre d'Ailly, Aeneas Sylvius Piccolomini, and others became very familiar to him.

In addition to book learning, Columbus gained practical experience in sailing the Atlantic Ocean northward, westward, and southward, and he acquired valuable information for his ultimate goal of discovery. There is no doubt that the "Great Enterprise of the Indies," as he called it, was born during this period and grew to such importance as to seem an obsession.

But, on that summer night of 1476, on the shores of Portugal, Columbus was merely a shipwrecked sailor, forlorn and destitute, somewhat confused but with high hopes. Similarly, the political fortunes of Portugal were at a very low ebb—confused but aspiring to better times. Only a few months before, King Alfonso V, aided by his son João, had suffered a crushing defeat at Toro at the hands of Isabella and Ferdinand of Castile. Alfonso had invaded Spain to dispute Isabella's succession to the throne of Castile but he had been turned back with terrible losses, both militarily and psychologically. He suffered a mental breakdown and lost his title of King of Portugal. Finally, he had to exchange his royal robes for the brown habit of a Franciscan friar. The war succession, however, did not affect the maritime activities of the Portuguese, nor did it reduce their dominance in the exploration of the African coast. Indeed, under the leadership of Prince João, later King João II, such activities were pursued with renewed vigor.

From Cape St. Vincent, Columbus headed for Lisbon, over one hundred miles to the north, where he found solace and compassion among his many compatriots, some with the familiar names of Di Negro, Spinola, Centurione, Vazo, and others. He was also greeted by his brother Bartolomeo, who had emigrated to Portugal a few years earlier and who was currently engaged in mapmaking. According to Antonio Gallo, the chronicler, Christopher was taken into partnership by his brother and promptly learned the art of cartography—a skill that was to serve him well on his voyages to the New World. He did well at it too, judging by a map he made of a portion of the coast of Haiti—the only extant sample of his draftsmanship. Andrés Bernáldez, in his *Historia de los Reyes Católicos,* stated that Columbus was very skilled in cosmography and in making maps of the world. Bernáldez also stated that Columbus sold books to augment his income when he was not going to sea. No doubt being a bookseller gave him an excellent opportunity to read, to learn, and to meet people of more than average curiosity and intellect.

EARLY ATLANTIC VOYAGES

In the month of February 1477, Columbus embarked on a voyage to Thule from Lisbon. Ferdinand's account reads:

I sailed one hundred leagues beyond the island of Tile whose northern part is latitude 73 degrees N and not 63 degrees as some affirm; nor does it lie upon the meridian where Ptolemy says the West begins, but much further west. And to this island, which is as big as England, the English come with their wares, especially from Bristol. When I was there, the sea was not frozen, but the tides were so great that in some places they rose twenty-six fathoms and fell as much in depth.[1]

Tile was another name for Thule—today's Iceland. A brisk trade had been established between Lisbon and Bristol with the Icelanders. Manufactured goods, woolens, wines, and special foods not available in the far north would be exchanged for salted cod and other fish. Therefore, there is no reason to doubt Ferdinand's claim that his father went to Iceland. What is questionable, however, is Ferdinand's assertion that Columbus sailed one hundred leagues beyond the island of Tile. One hundred leagues is approximately three hundred miles and due northwest would have brought him above the Arctic Circle.

In that region, the sea might have been frozen at that time of the year and naval activities curtailed by the diminished daylight. It is also difficult to explain two other errors in Ferdinand's quotation regarding his father. Iceland is located approximately at latitude 630° N, as Ptolemy had indicated and not 730° N, as challenged by Ferdinand. The tides rising twenty-six fathoms is conceivably not only an error in units (*bracci*, not fathoms) but an error of observation as well. Twenty-six Genoese *bracci* is fifty feet, and tides of such magnitude have never been recorded in Iceland. At any rate, Columbus's trip to Iceland is of historical importance because he may have learned from the people of Iceland about the Norse voyages to Vinland.

It's possible that he may have heard about remote lands to the north or west of Iceland or even Ireland, where the story of St. Brendan and his legendary voyage was well known. But mysterious lands and islands west into the Atlantic were suspected in every port from Lisbon, Bristol, and Galway. Columbus himself believed in the existence of exotic lands to the west, for in the company of Aeneas Sylvius's *Historia Rerum* he wrote:

Men have come hither from Cathay in the Orient. Many remarkable things have we seen, particularly at Galway in Ireland, a man and a woman of most unusual appearance adrift in two boats.[2]

Columbus immediately imagined that the two bodies he saw came from the Orient, which is hardly possible in the vicinity of Ireland. But it does indicate that he was already convinced that the Cathay of Marco Polo lay out there to the west in the Atlantic Ocean. Columbus returned to Lisbon by the end of spring 1477, stopping on the way at Galway and Bristol to refurbish his ship and pick up deliveries for Lisbon. He worked with his brother for some months and before long, in July 1478, he went back to sea to buy sugar in Madeira for the Centurione family, whose Genoese branch, as already stated, were important merchants. In 1420, Prince Henry had colonized the Madeira Islands, and the Madeira Islands had become the principal sugar source of Europe. Columbus's instructions were to buy the sugar mostly on credit and deliver it to Genoa. Apparently, some confusion arose between the supplier and consignee as to how payments had to be made. As a result, Columbus sailed back to Genoa with far less sugar than ordered. This turned out to be his last time in Genoa, because he returned to Lisbon late in August or early September of 1479. He was just shy of being twenty-eight years old—tall, handsome, and eager for more adventurous exploits. Indeed, he was on the threshold of momentous achievements that would affect his entire life.

COLUMBUS'S MARRIAGE, HIS APPEARANCE, AND BEARING

First, there was an adventure of the heart. He courted and eventually married Doña Felipa Perestrello y Moniz of an illustrious Portuguese family of Italian descent. Historians and students of Columbus have often wondered how it was possible—during a period in which class distinctions and social status were extremely important—for a stranger, a seaman, part-time mapmaker, and bookseller to win the hand of a woman of nobility (on both sides of her family). The logical answer is appearance, perhaps circumstances, and possibly the romantic demeanor of the suitor.

What did Columbus look like? What were his personal traits? What were the circumstances that brought the two young people together? Once again, for our answers we must rely on the chroniclers of the period: his son Ferdinand, Oviedo, and Bartolomé de Las Casas. According to Ferdinand the admiral was:

A well-built man of more than average stature, the face long, the cheeks somewhat high, his body neither fat nor lean. He had an aquiline nose and light-colored eyes; his complexion was too light and tending to bright red. In youth his hair was blonde, but when he reached the age of thirty it all turned white. In eating and drinking and in adornment of his person, he was very moderate and modest. He was affable in conversation with strangers and very pleasant to the members of his household, though with a certain gravity. He was so strict in matters of religion that except for fasting and saying prayers he might have been taken for a member of a religious order. He was so great an enemy of swearing and blasphemy that I give my word I never heard him utter any other oath than "By St. Ferdinand!" And when he grew very angry with someone, his rebuke was to say: "God take you!" for doing or saying that. If he had to write anything, he always began by writing these words: "Iesus cum María sit nobis in via." And so fine was his handwriting that he might have earned his bread by that skill alone.[3]

Just how did he meet Doña Felipa? According to Ferdinand's iconic explanation:

A lady named Doña Felipa Moniz, of noble birth and superior of the Covenant of the Saints, where the Admiral used to attend the Mass, had such conversation and friendship with him that she became his wife.[4]

Surely this must be the shortest love story on record! The Covenant of the Saints was actually a convent belonging to the nuns of the Military Order of St. James established for the purpose of providing a home for the wives and daughters of the knights of St. James while they were away fighting the Crusades. Though the resident ladies had to take a vow of chastity, poverty, and obedience, they were not there necessarily to become nuns. In actuality, it was a fashionable boarding school attended by young women of nobility. The practice of sending young ladies to convents for schooling in manners and morals was quite common in many Catholic countries of the day.

Doña Felipa was the daughter of Bartholomew Perestrello, whose father came from the Italian city of Piacenza and settled in Portugal during the reign of King João I. Bartholomew Perestrello (as we saw in Chapter 3) participated in the second expedition to colonize the Madeira Islands in 1425 and was made hereditary governor of Port Santo by Prince Henry. Her mother, Doña Isabel Moniz, Perestrello's third wife, was the daughter of Gil Ayers Moniz, who had fought with Prince Henry at Ceuta. Thus, Columbus's wife was noble on both sides of her family. After the death of her husband in 1457, Doña Isabel ceded the captaincy of Porto Santo to Pedro da Cunha, a son-in-law by an earlier marriage.

In 1473, her son, Bartholomew Perestrello II, took over the captaincy of Porto Santa and was still governing the island when his sister Felipa married Columbus. Doña Felipa, the older of two sisters, was twenty-five years old when she married Columbus.

Much has been said about this historic union of a woman of noble birth and a handsome stranger in town. It is not unusual for two young people from different social levels to fall in love. Many romantic novels have been written about the poor, handsome, but ambitious boy falling in love with the rich patrician girl. In this instance, the girl may not have been rich, thus the marriage may very well have been one of convenience for both. Doña Isabel had already been a widow for twenty-two years supporting two daughters, perhaps with some financial drain on her limited resources. Her older daughter, at twenty-five, was considered an "old maid" by that period's standards. Moreover, she had no available means of providing a suitable dowry to entice eligible noblemen. Suddenly, a solution was at hand. The Genoese suitor was handsome, intelligent, and ambitious; he came highly recommended by the Centuriones in Lisbon; and because he was a stranger, no one could really prove or disprove his nobility. Why not consent to the marriage? In turn, Columbus may have seen this marriage as a means for furthering his career. To bring to fruition his plan for a trip to China through the west, contacts with sponsors—possibly with Prince João himself—were required. Marrying a lady of nobility would certainly improve his social status and open channels to the aristocracy, which were not usually available to mapmakers and booksellers. Rewards were quick to follow. Columbus and his bride went to live with Doña Isabel, who, according to Ferdinand, recognized the Admiral's great interest in geography and gave him her husband's writings and sea charts.

Columbus continued to live in Lisbon for a while in Doña Isabel's home. Later he and his bride moved to Porto Santo, which at that time was governed by Doña Felipa's brother, Bartholomew Perestrello II. Their first son, Diego, was born there late in 1480. Columbus had been to the Madeira Islands only a few years earlier to buy sugar for the Centurione interests. But this time he began to experience a feeling of closeness to the exotic lands of his dreams. The way to the Indies was westward, he felt, not southward along the African continent as believed by Prince João. The islands of Antilia would perhaps lie further out; some maps of the period had already indicated their mid-Atlantic position. Cipango must certainly lie perhaps a few hundred miles further out. His fantasies were reinforced by the account of tales told by the natives about strange objects, including unrecognizable tree trunks, tropical seeds, and other vegetation washed ashore after prolonged westerly gales. There was even a report that two bodies had washed ashore at a nearby island, those of men who were very broad-faced and differed in every aspect from Christians.

In 1481 Columbus returned to Lisbon with his wife and infant son. In the same year, King Alfonso V died and was succeeded by his twenty-five-year-old son, King João II. King Alfonso had not taken much personal interest in the voyages of exploration along the African coast, preferring instead to reap the financial rewards from the exploration so vigorously advanced by Prince Henry, his uncle, by selling some of the rights to the Guinea coast to Fernão Gomez, a wealthy merchant of Lisbon. King João had concluded that business deal a few years before and now had begun to pursue the African coast explorations even more vigorously than Prince Henry, intending ultimately to reach the Indies by rounding Africa. In fact, to protect the Portuguese rights to the Gold Coast against interlopers and emerging European powers, King João decided to build a fortress on the Gold Coast at São Jorge da Mina, a region where gold mines were known to exist. Diego de Azambuja was put in charge of the expedition. On December 13, 1481, he left Lisbon with a fleet of twelve vessels, two of which were urcas—cargo vessels—the remainder caravels. There were five hundred soldiers in the expedition and one hundred artisans.

The expedition reached the site by the end of January. Construction began almost immediately, and in twenty days, the outer wall of the fortress had risen to the first floor. By the end of spring, most of the structural work had been completed, and the caravels had headed for home. There is good reason to believe that Columbus was part of that expedition and that he might have made another trip to São Jorge da Mina the following year, according to marginal notes he jotted down in several of his books. In these notes, he commented on the torrid zone, and specified some navigational sights he had taken with his instruments.

Following these voyages to the Gold Coast, Columbus's reputation was greatly enhanced and he was widely accepted as a first-class sailor and navigator. Prior to his Portuguese residence, he had sailed mostly on the Mediterranean, an inland sea. Now, he had gained valuable experience on the Atlantic Ocean by sailing north to Thule, west to the Madeira archipelago, and south past the equator. He had taken particular notice of the ocean currents, of the vagaries of the Atlantic winds, and of the flora and fauna of the places he had visited.

Portugal had provided him with the opportunity to study and to acquire first-hand knowledge of that body of lore that would be crucial to the success of his future enterprises. He learned Portuguese and perfected his Latin. He read avidly all the available books on geography, including the old classics and the more recent *Opus Majus* by Roger Bacon, *The Travels of Marco Polo*, *Imago Mundi* by Pierre D'Ailly, and the *Historia Rerum Ubique Gestarum* by Aenas Sylvius. He sought help and received valuable assistance from the Florentine cosmographer Paolo dal Pozzo Toscanelli. He became more and more convinced that his plan to cross the Atlantic to reach the Indies was sound, and his conviction was so strong that it was misinterpreted as arrogance by many. He studied intensively to accumulate geographic data in preparation for the presentation of his project to King João.

Chapter Nine

COLUMBUS AND THE KING OF PORTUGAL

King João II of Portugal, known as *The Perfect*, pursued the exploration of the African coast with the same energy as his great uncle, Prince Henry. He was proclaimed king in 1481 when the tragic King Alfonso abdicated following the debacle at Toro, but stepped down while still retaining control when his father returned to Lisbon from his self-imposed exile in France. Four years later, Alfonso died, and João resumed his reign, which lasted until 1495. Despite having had to quell a revolt of the nobles led by Ferdinand of Braganza and supported by the Catholic monarchs of Castile and Aragon, he initiated a far-reaching program to consolidate the Guinea holdings and accelerate the efforts to reach India by rounding Africa.

Following the example set by Prince Henry, King João had assembled an advisory group of high-powered individuals, consisting of Master Rodrigo, Royal Physician and Mathematician; Bishop Ortiz, the Royal Chaplain; José Vizinho, a Jew, disciple of Zacuto of Salamanca; and later Zacuto himself. By 1482 they had completed a very important navigational manual entitled *Regiment do Astrolabio e do Quadrante.* The manual consisted of tables for the observation of the North Star, noting in particular that the star ceased to be visible as one approached the equator; it proposed the "rule of the Sun," which listed the "Alturas" (elevations) from the equator northward. In 1482, King João ordered Diogo Cão to sail down the coast of Africa. Cão passed São Jorge da Mina and reached the mouth of the Congo River in 1483. He had added the Congo and nearly one thousand miles more of African coast to the map. Upon his return, the people greeted him with great enthusiasm and the king knighted him. It was during that wave of Portuguese enthusiasm that Christopher Columbus petitioned the Court for ships and support for a voyage to discover "islands and mainland in the ocean sea."

Columbus had spent years preparing for such a presentation to the king. He had studied all available information on geography and, following d'Ailly's description in the *Imago Mundi*, had reached the conclusion that the Atlantic was actually not very wide between Africa and the Indies. Furthermore, Marco Polo's exaggeration of the width of the Asian land mass led Columbus to underestimate even more the expanse of the Atlantic Ocean. He could even bolster that conviction with a reference to the Bible. Had the prophet Esdras not stated with the authority of the Apocrypha that God had dried up six-sevenths of the globe, leaving only the remaining seventh for ocean?

Columbus made still another critical error in estimating the length of a degree at the latitude involved. Disregarding Eratosthenes's accurate figure of approximately sixty miles, he had adopted Alfragan's figure of a little under fifty-seven Arabic miles—approximately sixty-six nautical miles. He compounded that error by interpreting the Alfragan figure to be in Roman miles, which is even shorter—about forty-five nautical miles. Thus, he came up with a figure of just under 2,400 miles to reach Cipango (Japan), a figure not much out of line with Toscanelli's estimate. Columbus had already sailed an equivalent distance down the African cost to Mina; Cão had already done better than that by sailing further south to Santa María, a distance of 3,500 miles down the south Atlantic. Columbus felt that his proposal was reasonable and well within the range of the equipment available at that time.

Ferdinand described his father's meeting with King João in Chapter 11 of his biography:

Although King João listened attentively to the Admiral, he appeared cool toward the project, because the discovery and conquest of the west coast of Africa, called Guinea, had put the prince to great expanse and trouble without the least return. At that time, the Portuguese had not yet sailed beyond the Cape of Good Hope, which name according to some was given that cape in place of its proper one, Agesingua, because it marked the end of those fine hopes of conquest and discovery; others claim it got that name because it gave promise of the discovery of richer lands and of more prosperous voyages.

Be that as it may, the King was very little inclined to spend more money on discovery, and if he paid some attention to the Admiral it was because of the strong arguments that the latter advanced. These arguments so impressed the King that the launching of the enterprise waited only upon his acceptance of the conditions laid down by the Admiral. The latter, being a man of noble and lofty ambitions, would not covenant, save on such terms as would bring him great honor and advantage, in order that he might leave a title and estate benefiting the grandeur of his works and his merits.[1]

What were Columbus's inflexible claims? Basically, they were the same demands for honors and privileges that he would eventually present to the Sovereigns of Spain, namely, a knighthood to be passed on to his heirs, the title of Grand Admiral of the Ocean Sea, and Viceroy and Governor of the islands and terra firma that he would discover. In addition, he expected one-tenth of all the income accruing to the king from all things of gold, silver, pearls, precious stones, metals, spices, and other profitable objects found in the new territories.

If these demands seem inordinately extravagant, it is important to stress that in the feudalistic society of that period, a person of low social rank could elevate himself by performing a great deed benefiting his country, such as becoming a military or maritime hero. The son of a blacksmith could hardly ever rise above the level of a blacksmith; similarly, the son of a wool weaver was destined to be a wool weaver too. Nearly everyone tacitly accepted that tradition.

Another thing to consider is the old adage that compensation must be comparable with the job done. Needless to say, a voyage in the uncharted waters of the Atlantic was fraught with many dangers, real and imagined. His chances of coming back alive were at best fifty-fifty. Then even if he were to survive, if he returned empty handed, he would be disgraced for the rest of his life. Diogo Cão, who had returned triumphantly to Lisbon from Guinea (and was knighted by King João), made another voyage to pursue his African exploration further south but never made it back.

João II received the proposal with interest despite the fact that it did not fit in with his plans. He submitted Columbus's plan to his learned and skeptical advisory group. The Commission rejected it primarily because the members did not believe that the distance to Cipango was as short as Columbus had indicated. Ferdinand says that his father left Portugal in anger when he learned that King João had sent a caravel to check out Columbus's claim and thus forestalled his plan. Ferdinand wrote that the operation had been a failure because of the ineptitude of the people sent by the king, lacking:

…the knowledge, steadfastness, and ability of the Admiral, they wandered about on the sea for many days and returned to Cape Verde and thence to Lisbon, making fun of the enterprise and declaring that no land could be found in those waters. When he learned of this, the Admiral, whose wife had meantime died, formed such a hatred for that city and nation that he resolved to depart for Castile with his little son Diego.²

Ferdinand's accusation against King João may not have been founded on fact. There is no evidence in any Columbian documents to support Ferdinand's claim. It is possible that Ferdinand may have confused this event with Fernão Dulmo's voyage of 1487.³

Ferdinand was also unusually severe in his condemnation of Lisbon and Portugal. Actually, Columbus and the king parted friends. A letter that the king sent to Columbus in 1488 shows no trace of malice.

It is also strange that Ferdinand should refer to the death of his stepmother Felipa with such indifference. The Portuguese experience had been an invaluable period in Columbus's life. While his marriage to Felipa indeed may have been a stepping-stone for his career, Columbus seems to have felt genuine love, admiration, and respect for his wife. It was her family that provided him with the political connections that made it possible for his enterprise to be even considered. Yet Felipa has no epitaph other than Las Casas's statement that the Lord had taken her away for good reasons.

We really do not know too much about Columbus's married life with Felipa. We do not even know exactly when she died. Diego was born in 1480, and Columbus was an acknowledged widower when he made his appeal to King João II in the late months of 1484. Because Las Casas indicated that Doña Felipa had passed away when the meeting with the king took place, we may presume that she died in the early part of 1484.

In the summer of 1485, Columbus left his brother behind in Lisbon to take care of the chart-making business and with his five-year-old son sailed southward to the port of Palos in Andalusia. At the age of thirty-four, he was a somewhat disillusioned, poverty-stricken, and unemployed explorer, who was not ready, however, to give up his quest. He would try his luck in Spain.

Part III

COLUMBUS IN CASTILE

Chapter Ten

COLUMBUS IN CASTILE

Columbus could not have landed in a more advantageous place than in Palos de la Frontera on the Río Tinto in Andalusia. The region, also known as the Niebla, consists of mostly lowlands and coastal bluffs traversed by the Río Odiel and the Río Tinto, whose waters join at the apex of marshes south of Huevla, at the monastery of La Rábida; there they form the Río Saltes, which empties into the sea two miles away. The city of Huelva is situated on the east bank of the Río Odiel, about three miles north of the apex of the marshes. Huelva, La Rábida, and Palos were to play important roles in Columbus's life. The whole region close to the southeasternmost borders of Portugal was involved in commercial maritime pursuits and had acquired the reputation of being a "little Lisbon." Because of its proximity to Cape St. Vincent and to Portugal, it was a frequent point of departure for sailors on their way to Madeira and southward along the African coast to the Canaries, the Cape Verde Islands, the "Mine," and Guinea.

Columbus was then in a familiar environment—amid the spirit and vibrancy of maritime activities, and it seems reasonable to assume that he met and exchanged views with some of the important sailors of the area.

Columbus had two brothers-in-law living in Huelva: Pedro Correa, Isen Perestrello's husband, and Miguel de Mulejart, the husband of Violante Muniz. There is some reason to believe that Columbus may have had ideas of leaving his son Diego with the child's aunts but may have changed his mind after he learned about La Rábida, the Franciscan monastery he had seen on the high bluff as he was sailing up the Río Tinto on his way to Palos. It occurred to him that the Franciscans might be able to provide lodging and schooling for little Diego. It was not long after landing in Palos that father and son hiked the three miles on the dusty road to the monastery and asked for food and lodging, which Fray Juan Perez, guardian of La Rábida, granted them. Seeing that Columbus was interested in astronomy and cosmography, Fray Juan introduced him to Fray Antonio de Marchena, "custodio" of the Franciscan sub-province of Seville and a man of great intelligence who had acquired a reputation in the area as a worthy astronomer.

They immediately developed an excellent rapport. The erudite monk was greatly impressed with the knowledge and exuberance of his visitor, who in turn felt great respect for his host. Fray Antonio believed very much in Columbus's plans for the great enterprise and decided to help him find a sponsor. Application was made to the most powerful of Spanish Magnates, the wealthy Don Enrique de Guzman, Duke of Medina Sidonia, whose large estates in Andalusia included miles of the sea coast below Cádiz, including the harbor of Sanlucar. Owning a fleet of caravels, which he used for his commercial and sometimes military pursuits, the Duke could easily have financed the enterprise. However, his freedom of action had been restricted by Queen Isabella as a result of a quarrel between the Duke and another grandee, the Marquis of Cádiz. Isabella's efforts for establishing permanent peace and tranquility in Seville in 1477 were frustrated by a long-standing feud between the great families of Guzman and Ponce de Leon, headed by the Duke of Medina Sidonia and the Marquis of Cádiz, respectively.

Medina Sidonia had been a loyal supporter of Isabella in the War of Succession, while the Marquis of Cádiz had temporized, cautiously withholding his allegiance. The two rivals had systematically occupied royal towns and fortresses as well as territories belonging to local cities. A war of attrition had existed between these barons to the detriment of the peace and security of the region. The queen was momentarily at a loss on how to handle the situation, especially with the Marquis, who had remained out of touch in his fortified castle in Zeroz. She was surprised when she received a visit from him, offering allegiance in exchange for her pardon for his past indiscretions. The queen complied with his request, but not without exacting restitution of fortresses and domains he had usurped from the Crown and the city of Seville. Similar concessions were demanded of the Duke of Medina Sidonia. In addition to keeping peace between these great and powerful dynasties, she ordered a cooling-off period for an indefinite time by confining them to their country estates. The Duke of Medina Sidonia was therefore not free to accept Columbus's proposal, despite his willingness to do so. Hence, he had to reject the project.

Having had no luck with the Duke of Medina Sidonia, Columbus applied to Don Luis de La Cerda, fifth Count and later first Duke of Medinaceli, who was interested enough in his plan to offer him hospitality in his palatial estate and to help him with a stipend for a period of almost one and a half years.

The Duke of Medinaceli was not as rich as the Duke of Medina Sidonia, but he possessed a more noble heritage and large land and seashore holdings in Andalusia. Las Casas reports that the Duke actually ordered that ships be prepared for Columbus at his El Puerto shipyards; however, he thought better to notify the queen about Columbus's plan because of its great importance. He wrote to the sovereign from Rota, and she replied, requesting further particulars, which were sent to her. The queen passed the information on to Alfonso de Quintanilla, Chief Treasurer and Accountant to the Sovereigns. Columbus was ordered to come to Court; and on January 20, 1486, he arrived at Córdoba but found that the royal party had left the city for Madrid. It should be mentioned that at the time the royal court was an itinerant court, continuously moving from city to city to bring the government directly to the people. They were not due back in Córdoba until the end of April.

A LOVE AFFAIR IN CÓRDOBA

While waiting for the monarchs to return to Córdoba, Columbus met a young woman of that city named Beatriz Enriques de Harana, with whom he had a love affair. Columbus was almost thirty-five years old at that time while Beatrice was only twenty or twenty-one. Beatriz was the daughter of a peasant named Pedro de Torquemada, a distant relative of the famous grand inquisitor and of Ana Nuñez de Harana. The fact that she did not use her father's surname—unusual for a Spaniard, as both a father's and mother's names are used—would indicate her feeling shame or fear in adopting the de Torquemada surname. She became an orphan at a tender age and, with her elder brother Pedro, went to live in Córdoba with her mother's cousin, Rodrigo Enriquez de Harana. The Haranas were well known in Córdoba, having been residents there for a long time. Rodrigo, a wine presser by trade, had a son, Diego de Harana, second cousin to Beatriz, who eventually became marshal of the fleet on Columbus's first voyage. Columbus met Beatriz through Diego, whom he got to know in a local apothecary shop owned by a Genoese named Leonardo de Esbarraia. The apothecary shops of those days were meeting places for physicians, intellectuals, scientists, and curious individuals who had some leisure time to relax and spin yarns. Columbus, of course, also enjoyed going there because the owner was a "paesano."

He met Diego de Harana there, became friendly with him, and was eventually invited to his father's house, where he met Beatriz. He was smitten by her youth and sensual beauty and she became his mistress. Columbus never married her—a fact that proved to be a load on his conscience. He felt that he had not done the right thing by not marrying her, although he did not seem to have had a choice in the matter. Spanish law forbade marriage between persons of high rank and commoners.

So for the present time, she remained his mistress. It was an accepted practice in those days among men of high rank to have such mistresses, but it was considered immoral if practiced by common people. An advantageous marriage would still be open to him should a lady of rank come along. In the meantime, Beatriz's family was pleased and proud of their relationship with Columbus. The Admiral reciprocated by appointing her brother and cousin to important positions in his fleets. Strangely, Ferdinand, born of this union on August 15, 1488, did not ever mention their relationship.

Diego Columbus, to whom the Admiral entrusted her care, was equally discreet. Columbus loved and esteemed her and tried to discharge his obligations towards her by providing her with a modest pension of ten thousand maravedis a year. Eventually, he gave precise instruction in his will to his son Diego to "Take care of Beatriz Enriquez, mother of Dona Hernando, my son, that she be provided for so that she can live honestly, as someone towards whom I have many obligations. And this is to relieve my conscience, for it is something that weighs heavily on my spirit."[1]

COLUMBUS MEETS QUEEN ISABELLA

In the spring of 1486 Queen Isabella and King Ferdinand returned to Córdoba, taking up residence in the Alcazar. On May 1, Columbus, eager to present his great plans for discovery, was admitted into the audience chamber to meet the Sovereigns.

Columbus's contention that he could reach the Indies by sailing due west must have struck a response chord in Queen Isabella. The queen, who was the same age as Columbus, was probably inspired by the eloquence and self-assurance of the man standing before her and offering her a glimpse into the unknown. The rapport that was developed between the queen and Columbus lasted through the years that followed, in spite of the many setbacks suffered by the latter. At any rate, Isabella was a very pragmatic and intelligent woman who glimpsed through the words of the would-be Admiral and saw possible rewards in supporting his plan to find a route to the Indies. By the Treaty of Alcacovas, the Portuguese had already been granted the southward route around Africa. Columbus's western route could be shorter, and therefore worth investigating further. Apparently, she thought enough of the idea to refer Columbus to her Comptroller of Finances, Alonso de Quintanilla, who put him on the royal payroll. Additionally, Fray Hernando de Talavera, the queen's confessor and subsequently Archbishop of Granada, was delegated to form a commission to examine the feasibility of

Columbus's project. The Talavera Commission, which included men of letters, scientists, and seamen, met for the first time in Córdoba in the summer of 1486; and, when the court moved to Salamanca late in December, it held meetings in the College of St. Stephen at the University of Salamanca. The Commission's deliberations were probably concluded in the spring of 1487. However, they were not published officially until 1490.[2] In the meantime, the Sovereigns' reply to Columbus's petition was vague enough to allow him to hope that it might be reconsidered again at a more opportune time. The war against Granada was a much more pressing problem for Ferdinand and Isabella and they would not promise anything until that conflict was resolved satisfactorily. All Columbus could do at this point was to hope that the war would be concluded quickly. Sadly, for him it was not.

The campaign to drive the Moors out of Spain, which was to last until early in 1492, engaged the entire country in one common action. In fact, one shrewd contemporary historian, Niccolò Machiavelli, regarded Ferdinand's actions especially worthy of being imitated because he was able to overcome the jealousies that existed among the powerful princes of the Iberian peninsula by offering them a common foe: the Moors.[3] In liberating Spain from the Moors, Ferdinand and Isabella made themselves monarchs of a larger nation, bringing the various sections of the country (except for Navarre) under their rule, making Spain a more powerful presence in the European context. Once the country was united, the Catholic kings were ready to project their newly acquired power beyond their boundaries. The financing of Columbus's voyage may be considered, among other things, a way of asserting Spain's importance in the council of nations.

Chapter Eleven

YEARS OF AGONY; DAYS OF GLORY

While it was clear to everyone that the members of the Talavera Commission had serious and substantive objections to Columbus's plan of discovery, the fact that they did not publish their findings until late in 1490 allowed Columbus to continue to hope on a reversal of his fortunes. It was also clear that the Sovereigns, or at least Isabella, did not want to reject Columbus's proposal outright. Their reply held out the hope that under more serene circumstances they would reevaluate his plan. In the meantime, Columbus was put on the royal payroll. He received small sums of money from the royal treasuring (three thousand maravedis on May 4, 1487, and on July 3; four thousand on August 27, 1487, to go to the royal encampment at Malaga; four thousand maravedis on October 15, 1487; and three thousand maravedis on June 16, 1488). Nevertheless, those were bitter years for Columbus.

But he did not remain idle; he used the time at his disposal to prepare himself for the next meeting with the Commission or the Sovereigns. He would be ready to answer any questions with assurance and authority. He read assiduously, writing notes in the margins and on the backs of his books. He read, among other books, a 1485 Latin translation of the *Book of Ser Marco Polo* and a new Italian translation of Pliny's *Natural History*, at the same time as he reread his favorite ancient books, and especially Ptolemy's *Guide to Geography*.

Columbus spent most of his time in Córdoba with his mistress, Beatriz, and with his infant son, Fernando, and some time with his elder son, Diego. Not much is known about his financial situation, but there is good reason to believe that he was earning a precarious living as a bookseller—at least after his royal allowance had been discontinued.

Early in 1488, in a period of complete dejection, he wrote to King João II of Portugal to offer to return to Lisbon to reopen the negotiations of 1484–85 and to ask for a safe conduct into Portugal. The king replied on March 20, 1488, inviting him to return to his court and assuring him of protection from any suits, civil or criminal, that might be pending against him. Columbus delayed his decision to return to Portugal for many months, probably still hoping that the Talavera Commission would report favorably on his plan. The delay was costly. When he finally went to Lisbon in December of 1488, he was just in time to witness the triumphant return of Bartolomeu Dias from his rounding of the Cape of Good Hope and his discovery of an eastern route to the Indies. Obviously, a western route would now be of little interest to Portugal. There is no record that Columbus's plan was ever presented again to King João. Undaunted by this additional setback, Columbus met with his brother, Bartholomew, who was still working in Lisbon and made plans to send him to England to seek the backing of King Henry VII. If English backing were not forthcoming, Bartholomew was to petition Charles VIII of France. Both Oviedo and Ferdinand Columbus stated that Bartholomew did go to England and did obtain an audience with the English monarch, but their accounts of the outcomes are completely at variance with each other.

Ferdinand's account of his uncle's trip to England is dramatic and a bit implausible. According to his version, his uncle was captured by pirates and held captive for a long time. When he finally was allowed to continue his mission, he obtained an interview with the parsimonious Henry VII, to whom he presented a map of the world, perhaps a copy similar to the one sent by Toscanelli to Columbus. As for the outcome of the mission, Ferdinand wrote:

After the King of England had seen that map and informed himself of the Admiral's offer, he gladly accepted his proposal and summoned him to his court. But God had reserved that prize for Castile, for by that time the Admiral had successfully completed his enterprise and returned home again, as shall be told at the proper place.[1]

Oviedo's account tells a different story. According to him, the English royal advisers convinced the king to turn down Columbus's proposal as being totally impractical. The events that followed seem to lend more credence to this than to Ferdinand's version, for we find Bartholomew in France next, attempting to interest the French king in his brother's plans of exploration. Charles VIII, who was perhaps too busy with his meddling into Italian political affairs (he was to invade Italy in 1494), was not interested either. Bartholomew, however, made the acquaintance of Ann de Beaujeu, the king's older sister, who became interested enough to retain him for a few years on her own payroll as a cartographer, until news of Columbus's great discovery reached him.

THE ITALIAN CONTRIBUTIONS TO THE EXPLORATION OF THE NEW WORLD

Interestingly, England, Portugal, and France, following the discovery of America by Columbus, all sought and used Italian navigators for American adventures and explorations. This eventually resulted in their respective territorial claims to the New World. Thus, John Cabot (Giovanni Caboto), who came to England from Venice in 1495 with his wife and three sons, was chosen by Henry VII, after he had learned of Columbus's discovery, to undertake a north Atlantic crossing to discover a short ocean route to the Indies. Departing from Bristol in a small ship of barely fifty tons, the *Matthew*, on or about May 20, 1497, Cabot and a crew of only eighteen reached Newfoundland on June 24, 1497. Henry VII rewarded Cabot with a miserly gift of ten pounds for his discovery, as recorded in the royal household books of August 11, 1497. Later, perhaps as an afterthought, or finally realizing the importance of Cabot's discovery, the king increased the annuity to twenty pounds. John Cabot's voyage heralded the English empire in North America.

In Portugal, four years later, King Dom Manuel invited the Florentine pilot Amerigo Vespucci to accompany Gonçalo Coelho in an exploration of the land to the west that under the Treaty of Tordesillas had been granted to Portugal. The first Coelho-Vespucci fleet sailed from Lisbon on May 10, 1501, and made landfall in Brazil on August 17, 1501. The expedition spent roughly six months exploring the coast. Vespucci made important notes on the fauna and flora and the primitive customs of the natives. The fleet departed from Brazil on February 13,

1502. A second Coelho-Vespucci trip left Lisbon on May 10, 1503, charged with the task of exploring of the Brazilian coast and discovering goods that might be exported. The fleet returned to Lisbon on June 8, 1504. Vespucci, in several letters to his compatriots, notably the one written to his Florentine friend, Pier Soderini, gave an exceptionally vivid account of the New World. Martin Waldseemüller, a young professor of geography at the college of Saint-Die in Lorraine, printed a Latin translation of Vespucci's letter to Soderini in a new edition of a Ptolemy book on cosmography in which he proposed that the new lands be called "Amerige" or "land of Americus" or "America." So, the name "America" printed on a map of the continent that lay between Europe and Asia eventually was accepted as the name for the whole continent. The proper name of the new lands should have been "Columbia" in honor of its true discoverer.

France's claim to North American territories was based on the explorations of the Florentine navigator Giovanni Verrazzano. Francis I of France had a strong, almost biased affinity for Italians. He invited great artists, such as Leonardo da Vinci and Benvenuto Cellini, to work in France. He enticed Italian generals into his army and Italian statesmen into his government. A recognized bon vivant, he loved Italian food and imported Italian chefs-de-cuisine and even Italian mistresses. It was inevitable that he too should also turn to an Italian navigator for his voyages of exploration.

In choosing Verrazzano, who at that time was living in Dieppe, he chose perhaps one of the finest navigators of his age. He was well born, well educated, and well trained. In his career, he had sailed in the north Atlantic possibly to Newfoundland, and in the Levant. In 1523, at the age of thirty-eight, this gentleman navigator left Dieppe aboard *La Dauphine*, a one-hundred-ton ship of the French Navy, with a crew of fifty and headed for the Madeira Islands to seek a northern route to the Indies and Japan. Verrazzano left the Madeiras on January 17, 1524, on a course well above the range of the easterlies and on March 1 made landfall on North Carolina's southernmost cape, Cape Fear. After sailing south for about fifty leagues, he turned around so as not to come into contact with Spanish ships and headed north. He explored the east Atlantic coast as far north as Newfoundland, halting his northward advance to avoid intruding on the English. In the period of approximately six months, he explored the east coast thoroughly, writing copious notes on the country and the natives and naming each sight in Italian or French. On April 17, 1524, *La Dauphine* anchored in the narrows of New York Bay, which he had named "Bay of St. Marguerite," almost the present site of the Verrazzano Bridge.[2] Continuing northward, he made anchorage in Narragansett Bay, rounded Cape Cod—which he called Capo Pallavicino"—and made another anchorage on the coast of Maine, where he made contacts with the Maine Indians, who unlike other Indians proved to be so hostile to him that he named the coast "Terra di Mal Gente," Italian for "Land of Bad People." According to his records, he sailed as far north on the Atlantic coast as 50°N off Newfoundland, at which point he replenished his supplies and then made a speedy passage back to Dieppe, anchoring there on June 8, 1524.

Verrazzano did not find the Northern Strait to Cipango, but he did discover a vast new empire for France.

COLUMBUS WINS APPROVAL FOR HIS PLAN

Despite the negative report of the Talavera Commission, Ferdinand and Isabella did not announce their decision. They sent word to Columbus, probably on Isabella's insistence, that once the Moors were finally defeated they would be prepared to reconsider his proposal. Because of the nation's geographical position, Isabella was convinced that the future of Spain lay in her maritime conquests. Spanish naval activities had already reached a level of eminence in the Mediterranean and to some degree in Africa. Don Jayme Perrer, a Catalan navigator, had reached the Río de Oro, five degrees below Cape Nun, in August 1346, well ahead of Prince Henry the Navigator's effort of 1419. James the Great (1213–76) raised the efficiency of the Catalan-Aragonese navy to a level until then unknown in those seas. His conquest of the Balearic Islands (1229–35) was the beginning of the creation of an Aragonese Mediterranean empire.

During the same period, Ferdinand III, King of Castile, 1217–52, and León, 1230–52, captured Córdoba and Seville from the Moors with the assistance of his navy. A center of naval and cosmography studies similar to Prince Henry's center at Sagres was established on the island of Majorca. Thus, reliance on the sea and familiarity with it were part of the Spanish tradition for a long time. The marriage of Isabella and Ferdinand in 1469 brought together monarchs with a great naval heritage. In a campaign begun in 1479, they had conquered the Canary Islands that became the domain of the Spanish crown, according to the Treaty of Alcacovas of 1479–80. By the conditions of the same treaty, the Azores, the Madeiras, and the Cabo Verde Islands became the domain of Portugal. That treaty, confirmed by the papal bull "Aeterni Regis" in 1481, gave Spain the right to explore the western oceans above the latitude of the Canaries. That is why Columbus's plan of exploration of the western oceans appealed to Queen Isabella. The Portuguese had already made great advances along the southern coast of Africa in an attempt to find a southern route to the Indies. Columbus's plan seemed to Isabella a logical alternative. For these reasons Isabella chose not to reject Columbus's plan outright and kept him on the royal payroll. The total annual stipend was equivalent to the stipend of an able seaman. Unfortunately, the stipend was abruptly cut off, possibly because with the fall of Malaga, the queen's attention was entirely concentrated on the war. It is possible at this stage that the Duke of Medinaceli picked up responsibility for supporting Columbus all over again. In May of 1489, the queen summoned Columbus again and provided him with an open letter to all municipal and local officials, ordering them to furnish free board and lodging as he journeyed to the royal court encamped at Baza. The reason for the invitation is not clear. The Talavera Commission had not yet announced its decision and Columbus may have asked for another audience out of impatience.

Columbus followed the queen to the fields of Baza, and he was there when Baza capitulated on December 4, 1489. Then he returned to Córdoba to await the report from the Talavera Commission, which was finally made public in Seville late in 1490. Columbus, of course, was disappointed with the outcome. His only ray of hope was the queen's message that his plan of discovery might again be brought to her attention at the conclusion of the war with Granada. Columbus waited in Spain for another eight, possibly nine, months, until he decided to join his brother Bartholomew in France, in the hope of offering his plan to Charles VIII. In the summer of 1491, Columbus set off for La Rábida to call for his son Diego, who was boarding there with the Franciscan friars. Before departing for France, he had planned to leave his eleven-year-old boy at Huelva with his aunt. Fray Juan Perez, head of the monastery, was disappointed at Columbus's intention of leaving Spain. After consulting with Dr. Fernandez, the local authority on astronomy, and possibly with Martín Alsonso Pizón, a well-known ship owner from Palos, he promised to obtain another audience with the queen if only Columbus would stay. Fray Juan, who had been confessor to the queen, was still a firm believer in the success of Columbus's enterprise, and was confident that he could arrange another audience with Isabella, whose court was in Santa Fé during the siege of Granada. Fray Juan sent a letter to the queen, and in barely two weeks' time received a favorable reply. Isabella commanded Fray Juan to come to court immediately and to tell Columbus to await a royal summons of his own. A short time later, the queen wrote directly to Columbus, including with that letter the sum of twenty thousand maravedis for him so he could acquire proper clothing and a mule.

In the early summer of 1491, Columbus appeared before the queen in Santa Fé. The queen set up an ad hoc committee to review and report on the plan. Columbus made a very interesting presentation to the committee and discussed his narrow-ocean concept with a world map. However, his plan was rejected again. Undoubtedly, the demands in honors and titles that Columbus made seemed extraordinary. They might have been the very same that he had proposed to the King of Portugal in the negotiations of 1484–85. Possibly out of sheer frustration and resentment for the treatment he had received, Columbus indeed may have made additional demands for a coat of arms and appropriate hereditary titles. While most of the experts seemed opposed to Columbus's venture, the final decision rested with Queen Isabella and King Ferdinand.

Granada surrendered on January 2, 1492, but the triumphant entry into the city by the sovereigns was not made until January 6, 1492. As a measure of Columbus's stature, he was allowed to take part in the triumphant procession into the city. Unfortunately, his expectations did not materialize. The sovereigns had been shocked by Columbus's demands and in private audience announced that his project was finally and absolutely rejected.

It is possible that more moderate rewards were offered to Columbus, but he would not accept compromise. He had spent the best part of his life in fruitless solicitations; had endured poverty, ridicule, repeated disappointments, and mental anguish. He was about to risk his life and that of his crew in the service of Spain and he felt that the enormous risks involved deserved commensurate rewards.

Neither Columbus nor the monarchs could have imagined at that time the magnitude of his eventual discovery. Columbus stubbornly stood his ground. If Spain were unwilling to grant his requirements, he would seek patronage for his enterprise elsewhere, in France and possibly in England. He took leave of his friends, gathered his worldly goods, mounted his mule, and left Santa Fé on a dreary morning, early in February of 1492, heading for Córdoba on his way to meet Bartholomew in France. The same day he left, one of his "friends," the powerful Don Louis De Santangel, Minister of the Budget to King Ferdinand, went to see Queen Isabella and, according to Ferdinand Columbus:

Told her he was surprised that her Highness, who had always shown a resolute spirit in matters of great weight and consequence, should lack it now for an enterprise that offered so little risk yet could prove of such great service to God and the exaltation of His Church, not to speak of the very great increase and glory of her realms and kingdoms. The enterprise, moreover, was of such nature that if any other ruler should accomplish what the Admiral offered to do, it would be a great injury to her estate and a cause of just reproach by her friends and of censure by her enemies.[3]

Santangel then suggested that if the Sovereigns were hard-pressed for funds, because the war had taken its financial toll, he would undertake the financing of the enterprise. There was no need for the queen to pawn her jewels.

As it turned out, of the two million maravedis borrowed for the enterprise, 1,400,000 came from the Santa Hermandad endowment fund (which was eventually repaid by the Crown), 250,000 maravedis from Columbus's Italian friends in Seville, and the balance from Santangel himself.

Isabella, much impressed by Santangel's logic and sincerity, immediately ordered that Columbus be overtaken and brought back to Santa Fé. Columbus had already pursued his lonely journey across the plains and crossed the bridge of Pinos, about four miles out of Granada, when overtaken by the queen's "Alguazil." He returned to Santa Fé—and to everlasting fame.

Chapter Twelve

CAPITULATIONS AND ROYAL DECREES

The fall of Granada in 1492 brought about two significant but unrelated events in the history of Spain: the expulsion of the Jews and the discovery of America. For many centuries, Spain had been split into Moorish and Christian kingdoms, both of which tolerated each other's minority populations and the Jews. Both kingdoms practiced proselytism. In the Christian kingdom, there were many Moors who had converted to Christianity and many Jews who had become "conversos" (converts to Christianity). The Jews were an important factor in the development of Spanish civilization. They contributed immensely to the industrial, commercial, and cultural heritage of the nation. Exceptionally industrious and intelligent, the Jews easily scaled the social ladder; those who had become "conversos" occupied positions of great prestige and responsibility in the government, in the military, and in the Catholic hierarchy. For these advantageous reasons nearly all monarchs of Christian Spain considered themselves the natural protectors of the Jews.

With the fall of Granada, an opportunity presented itself to the Catholic Sovereigns to eliminate once and forever the religious conflicts that had been plaguing Spain for centuries and that were exacerbated even further by the Inquisition. Therefore, a royal order was issued on March 30, 1492. All unbaptized Jews were ordered to leave Spain within three months, never to return on pain of death. This order did not apply to "conversos." Indeed, it had been hoped that the order might encourage conversion of many Jews, but such was not the case. The exodus of the Jews, thousands of them, must have provoked heartrending scenes throughout the land. Swarms of refugees who had lived in Spain for many generations were forced to sell their properties for a pittance and forbidden to take money along with them.

It was under those circumstances that the Columbus agreement was signed on April 17, 1492. Known as the Articles of Capitulation, they consisted of five articles, drawn by Columbus himself and signed after each article by Juan de Coloma and by the Sovereigns. Juan Perez acted as Columbus's representative, while Coloma, King Ferdinand's Secretary, represented the Sovereigns.

The main documents of the great enterprise are the Capitulations or Articles of Agreement of April 17; the "Titulo" or the Title of April 30; the Letter of Credence to foreign potentates dated April 30; the Passport; and three orders by the monarchs, dated April 30, for fitting out the fleet.[1]

A. *The Articles of Agreement, April 17, 1492*

The things requested and which Your Highnesses give and grant to Don Christóval Colón in some satisfaction for what he has discovered in the Ocean Seas for the voyage which with the help of God he is now about to make therein, in the Service of Your Highnesses are the following:

First, that Your Highnesses as actual Sovereigns of the said Ocean Seas from henceforth appoint the said Christóval Colón their Admiral in all those islands and mainland which by his labor and industry shall be discovered or acquired in the said Ocean Seas during his life and, after his death, his heirs and successors from one to the other perpetually to that office and just as Don Alonso Enriques, High Admiral of Castile and his predecessors in the said office, held their jurisdictions.

Further, that your Highnesses appoint said Don Christóval Colón their Viceroy and Governor-General in all said islands and mainlands which…he may discover…and that for the Government of each and every one of them he may name three persons for each office so that your Highnesses may take and choose the one most suitable to your service and thus the lands…will be better governed;

That all merchandise whatsoever, whether pearls, precious stones, gold, silver, spices, and other things and merchandise…of whatever kind…which may be obtained within the limits of said Admiralty, Your Highnesses grant from henceforth said Don Christóval Colón and decree that he take and keep for himself the tenth part of the whole after all expenses have been deducted;

Further, that, if an account of the goods that he brings from the said islands and lands which, as has been said, may be acquired or discovered will be adjudicated by him or his deputy;

That in all the vessels which shall be equipped for the said traffic and business…the said Don Christóval Colón may, if he wish, pay and contribute the eighth part of the total expenses of the equip-

ment and that also he may take and also keep for himself of the profit of the eighth part of all that may result from such equipment.

*It so pleases Their Highnesses
Juan de Coloma*

B. The Título or Conditional Grant of Titles and Honors

The confirmation of titles and honors to be bestowed upon Columbus and his heirs is expressed in detail in the Título or Conditional Grant of Titles and Honors of April 30, 1492, given in the city of Granada.

Whereas you, Christóval Colón, are setting forth by our command to discover and acquire...certain islands and mainland in the Ocean Sea; it is just and reasonable that, since you are exposing yourself to the said danger in our service, you be rewarded for it. And in desiring to honor and favor you on account of the aforesaid, it is our will and pleasure that you, the said Christóval Colón, after you have discovered and acquired the said islands and mainland in the said Ocean Sea, or any of them, shall be our Admiral and said islands and mainland which you thus shall have discovered and acquired and shall be our Admiral and Viceroy and Governor therein, and shall be empowered thenceforward to call and entitle yourself, Don Christóval Colón. And likewise, your sons and successors in the said office and charge shall be empowered to entitle and call themselves Don, and Admiral, and Viceroy, and Governor thereof. And that you shall have the right to exercise and enjoy said office of Admiralty of the said islands and mainland that you may so discover and acquire...and to hear and decide all suits and cases, civil and criminal, appertaining to the said office...and shall have the power to punish and chastise delinquents...

C. Letter of Credence

The next document to be prepared for Columbus was a letter of introduction or Letter of Credence to be presented to the sovereign of the islands or mainlands he might visit. Several copies were carried by Columbus with the salutation left blank so as to insert the proper name and title of the host potentate or sovereign. It is dated April 30, 1492, from the city of Granada.

To the Most Serene Prince _____ our very dear friend, Ferdinand and Isabella, King and Queen of Castile, Aragon, León, Sicily, etc. greetings and increase of good fortune. We have learned with joy of your esteem high regard for us and our nation and of your great eagerness to be informed about things with us. Wherefore, we have resolved to send you our noble Captain, Christophorus Colón, bearer of these, from whom you may learn of our good health and our prosperity, and other matters which we ordered him to tell you on our part. We therefore pray you to give good faith to his report as you would to ourselves, which will be most grateful to us; and on our part, we declare ourselves ready and eager to please you.

> *From our city of Granada, 30 April A.D. 1492.*
> *I the King, I the Queen*
> *Done in triplicate, Coloma, Secretary*

D. The Passport

The Sovereigns also provided Columbus with a passport briefly written in Latin and undated, translated as follows:

By these presents we send the nobleman Christóval Colón with three equipped caravels over the ocean seas toward the regions of India for certain reasons and purposes.

E. Royal Decree Requiring People of Palos to Provide Caravels

A royal decree was issued requiring the people of Palos to provide Columbus with the caravels Pinta and Niña on April 30, 1492.

Recruiting volunteers for a journey into the unknown was a difficult enterprise. Therefore, a royal decree ordering the suspension of judicial proceedings against criminals, provided they ship with Columbus, was also issued on April 30, 1492.

...So by these presents we grant safe conduct to all and whatsoever persons who sail on the said caravels with the said Christóval Colón on the said voyage which he is making at our command...so that they may suffer no harm, damage, or injury to their persons or property or to any of their interests by reason of any crime they may have committed or perpetrated prior to the date of this our decree and during the time of their journey thither, their sojourn in that place and return to their homes, and two months thereafter.

It was this document that created the myth that Columbus's crew consisted almost entirely of jailbirds. According to Columbian scholars, only four men in the entire crew took advantage of the royal decree.[2] These men had been jailed as accessories to the crime of having helped a friend escape from jail. Columbus had no problem with them during the voyage.

Two additional royal decrees were issued. One ordered that Columbus be given every facility to report his vessels and obtain supplies at reasonable prices. The other demanded that no taxes be assessed by suppliers on provisions, ship chandlery, and other things necessary for the fleet.

It is incredible that a sailor who had already been dismissed on several occasions as a dreamer full of "fancy and imagination" by the cosmographers and savants of his day for his preposterous ideas should suddenly be entrusted with a fleet, with the promise that if he made good on his offer to discover, colonize, and Christianize new lands, he would be granted honors, titles, and wealth beyond belief. No sea captain or delegated explorer in Portugal or Spain had ever received such a remarkable offer. Perhaps it was because of his unswerving belief in his own ability—self confidence that bordered on paranoia. Perhaps it might have been his sense of mission—his charismatic personality. Obviously, Columbus made an offer that the sovereigns could not refuse! He had offered them a New World, perhaps a New Empire, on an investment of less than $50,000. It was worthwhile taking such a chance. The Sovereigns authorized the "converso," Juan de Coloma, Ferdinand's Secretary of State, to draw up the documents and Articles of Agreement between themselves and Columbus. Less than three weeks before, Coloma had signed the royal order banishing the Jews from Spain.

The royal decrees in his pocket, and his fortunes for once shining brighter than ever, Columbus left Granada on May 12, heading for Palos, the little harbor where he had first set foot in Spain seven years before and that he was to immortalize.

Part IV

THE FIRST VOYAGE TO THE INDIES

Chapter Thirteen

THE SHIPS AND CREW FOR THE FIRST VOYAGE

A few days before Columbus's departure from Granada, Queen Isabella issued a letter-patent appointing Diego, Columbus's son, about twelve years old, page of Prince Juan, the heir apparent, and authorized an allowance for his support. Henceforth, young Diego would have a home in the magnificent halls of the royal court, a remarkable improvement to the barren walls of the monastery of La Rábida, where he had lived for the past seven years. With his younger son Ferdinand living with his mother, Beatriz de Harana, in Córdoba, Columbus was now free of fatherly responsibilities and better able to concentrate on his quest.

Columbus arrived in Palos on May 22 and proceeded immediately to the nearby monastery of La Rábida to meet Fray Juan Pérez. The following day the two of them went to the Church of St. George in Palos, where, in the presence of the Alcalde and many interested citizens of the community, the royal decrees relating to Columbus's voyage were made public. The decree dated April 30, 1492, was addressed to Diego Rodriguez Prieto and to other citizens of Palos and required them to provide Columbus with completely equipped caravels for a twelve-month period.

The order also stipulated that the caravels had to be made ready within ten days. The other decrees of April 30, described in the previous of this book, were also read, but it was specifically this decree that embittered the citizens of Palos and made them react with grumbling and even hostility. It was necessary to exert more pressure on them with another reading of the orders at a later date. As it turned out, it took ten weeks and not ten days—which, of course, had been unrealistic—to comply with the royal commands. Discounting the ill feelings, the Sovereigns could not have chosen a better port from which to launch the expedition. The Niebla region, of which Palos, Moguer, Huelva, and Crepe are a part, effectively was an extension of the Portuguese Algarve ruled by Prince Henry. Its people were cut of the same fabric, and its ships were very similar in design to the Portuguese caravels. The ships from Niebla had been involved in unlawful raids against the African coast. It was probably in reparation for these crimes that the Sovereigns demanded the use of two caravels for Columbus. Note that in the same decree, quoted in the last chapter, the Sovereigns warned the sailors not to irritate the Portuguese by stopping at St. George of the Mine.

THE NIÑA, THE PINTA, AND THE SANTA MARÍA

To pay the penalty for their offenses against the Crown, the town of Palos chartered two caravels, the Niña and the Pinta—the Santa María, Columbus's flagship, was classified as a "nao" and was chartered by the Crown. The three ships were relatively small. The Santa María was roughly one hundred tons, had a big castle aft and a smaller one at the prow, and at eighty-two feet, was slightly longer than the caravels. The Niña and the Pinta have been estimated at sixty tons each and seventy to eighty feet long, with beams of about twenty-five feet and drafts of about seven. The beam and draft dimensions of the Santa María can only be surmised. We simply do not know what she looked like. Comparing her to similar ships of that period her beam was probably twenty-eight to thirty feet, with a draft only slightly longer than the caravels.

Columbus was not pleased with the performance of the Santa María. He found her too slow and unwieldy and unsuitable for coastal explorations. It belonged to Juan de la Cosa, had been built in Galicia, and was appropriately called "La Gallega." Columbus had to settle for the Santa María because there were no better ships available. The exodus of the Jews from Spain at that time caused a shortage of vessels of any type. The Niña belonged to Juan Niño and the nearby town of Moguer and was called la "Niña," meaning "the child," the feminine of Niño.

Related to the Niños, and also from Moguer, were the Quinteros. Cristóbal Quintero was the owner of the Pinta, but relinquished her command to Martín Alonzo Pinzón. There were three Pinzóns on the Pinta: Martín, her captain; Francisco, his younger brother, her master; and Diego, a cousin who was a seaman. In addition to Cristóbal Quintero, who also became master of Columbus's flagship on the third voyage, there was Juan Quintero, the Pinta's boatswain, who sailed on all four of Columbus's voyages.

Ninety men sailed on these three vessels: forty men aboard the Santa María, twenty-six aboard the Pinta, and twenty-four on the Niña. Apart from Columbus, only four were foreigners: a Portuguese, a Genoese, a Venetian, and a Calabrian. Louis de Torres, a converted Jew, was chosen as the official interpreter because he knew Hebrew and Arabic, the latter language thought to be understood on Cipango and the Indies. Most of the complement consisted of local sailors, the majority of whom knew each other. They joined the crew not for the adventure, but primarily for the promise of personal gain. One exception was Diego de Harana of Córdoba, cousin of Beatriz de Harana, Columbus's mistress, whom the navigator appointed marshal of the fleet. The most remarkable thing about the crews was the high level of competence among the officers and sailors. They were very well prepared and organized for discovery and exploration—but not for military activities. There were no soldiers onboard—just seasoned and eager sailors.

How was it possible for a foreigner, Christopher Columbus, to attract a top-notch crew? No doubt, the royal decree played an important part. Enlisting for a long ocean voyage across the Atlantic Ocean to a place nobody had ever visited—a place that may not even have existed—was not an easy choice. The odds of arriving at the unknown destination and returning alive were at best fifty-fifty. The wages were not exceptional—just the going rate. The captains were promised 2,500 maravedis per month; the masters and pilots, 2,000; seamen, 1,000; and grommets (ships' boys) 666. (At that time, a pig cost four hundred maravedis and a bushel of wheat cost seventy-three maravedis.) The crown allowed twelve maravedis a day for feeding a seaman in the navy.

The success of enlisting sailors and procuring vessels was due in great measure to Martín Alonso Pinzón and his brother Vicente Yañez Pinzón. Renowned navigators and ship owners, they were highly thought of and had great influence on the inhabitants of Palos and nearby Moguer. They offered their services and one of their vessels, setting an example for the rest of the ship owners and mariners. Martín Alonso Pinzón had a powerful reason for supporting the enterprise, and it came to be revealed at the inquest held in Seville in 1515 in which the hereditary privileges of Columbus's descendants were questioned by the Pinzón family. It was brought out that Martín Alonso Pinzón had obtained certain information in Rome in 1491, in the library of the Queen of Sheba. Martín had planned to rediscover the passage himself. However, when he learned that Columbus's plan had already been sanctioned by the Sovereigns, he decided to join his expedition. This may explain Pinzón's disappearance and unusual behavior during Columbus's first voyage.

The three ships were provisioned for at least one year. The provisions usually carried on ships of that era were dried fish, salt meat, salt pork, biscuits, beans, peas, rice, olive oil, honey, syrup, and plenty of water. Live animals to be slaughtered at sea, such as pigs and poultry, were also taken as "fresh" provisions. Salt, flour, nuts, and dry cheese were other standard provisions of the day. In other words, all edibles that would not spoil with time were included. The exclusion of all fresh fruits and vegetables, sources of vitamin C, was the chief cause of scurvy among sailors of that era.

In addition to the usual naval tools and instruments, Columbus also carried—for trading with the natives—glass beads, hawks' bells, brass rings, and western clothing. These had been found very attractive items in trading with African natives.

It is reasonable to assume that the exodus of the Jews may have delayed preparations and actually put off the departure date. The number of Jews leaving Spain has been estimated by some sources from a low of 160,000 to a high of 600,000. When Columbus learned that the final date of their expulsion had been set by the Crown for August 2, he adjusted his own departure for August 3, 1492.

Chapter Fourteen

BEGINNING OF THE GRAND
ENTERPRISE TO THE CANARIES

On the second of August, 1492, the fleet anchored in the Río Tinto near Palos de La Frontera, and was all set to start its historic voyage. Every member of the crew had made his confession, received communion, and boarded the ships for the night. On Friday, August 3, Columbus, whose title now was Captain-General, received his communion in the Church of St. George at Palos, boarded the Santa María before sunrise, and gave orders to weigh anchors and set sails. There was not enough wind and the sails hung limp, as the graceful ships rode the ebb tide down the Río Tinto. Approximately a mile and a half downstream from Palos, on the port side, they passed the monastery of La Rábida. The chants from the friars could be heard as they sang in their canonical hour of Prime an ancient liturgical hymn, familiar to the Captain-General. The island of Saltes was immediately ahead. Using the sweeps for steerage, the fleet altered its course to port into the Río Saltes (today known as the Río Odiel) and floated past the island, then turned fifty degrees to starboard and crossed the bar (Banco de Umbria) at eight in the morning. Once they were on the ocean, the stiff breeze inflated the sails, which bore the fleur-de-lis cross of the Spanish Order of St. James, a symbol of the crusading zeal of the expedition. But the winds were variable and by sunset the ships had managed to sail only fifteen leagues. During the night, however, the direction of the wind became favorable and the Captain-General set the course for the Canaries—south by southeast.

Columbus wrote a daily journal of the first voyage. The prologue of the journal is herewith reproduced in full:

In the Name of Our Lord Jesus Christ. Most Christian, exalted excellent, and powerful princes, King and Queen of the Spains, and of the islands of the sea, our Sovereigns: It was in this year of 1492 that Your Highnesses concluded the war with the Moors who reigned in Europe. On the second day of January, in the great city of Granada, I saw the royal banners of Your Highnesses placed by force of arms on the towers of the Alhambra, which is the fortress of the city, and I saw the Moorish king going to the city gates and kissing the royal hands of Your Highnesses, and those of the Prince, my Lord. Afterwards, in that same month, based on the information that I had given Your Highnesses, about the land of India and about a Prince who is called the "Great Khan," which in our language means "King of Kings," Your Highnesses decided to send Christopher Columbus to the regions of India, to see Princes there and the peoples and the lands, and to learn their disposition, and of everything and the measures which could be taken for their conversion to our Holy Faith.

I informed Your Highnesses how this Great Khan and predecessors had sent to Rome many times to beg for learned men in our Holy Faith so that his people might be instructed therein, and that the

Holy Father had never furnished them, and therefore, many peoples believing in idolatries and receiving among themselves sects of perdition were lost.

Your Highnesses, as Catholic Christians and Princes devoted to the Holy Christian faith and to the spreading of it, and as enemies of the Muslim sect and of all idolatries and heresies, has ordered that I should go to the east, but not by land as customary. I was to go by way of the west, whence until today we do not know with certainly that anyone has gone.

Therefore, after having banished all the Jews from all your Kingdoms and realms, during this same month of January Your Highnesses ordered me to go with a sufficient fleet to the said regions of India. For that purpose, I was granted great favors and ennobled; from then henceforward I might entitle myself Don and be High Admiral of the Ocean Sea and Viceroy and perpetual Governor of all the islands and continental land that I might discover and acquire, as well as any other future discoveries in the Ocean Sea. Further, my eldest son shall succeed to the same position, and so on from generation to generation for ever after.

I left Granada on Saturday, the 12th day of the month of May in the same year of 1492 and went to the town of Palos, which is a seaport. There I fitted out three vessels, very suited to such an undertaking. I left the said port well supplied with a large quantity of provisions and with many seamen on the third day of the month of August in the said year, on a Friday, half an hour before sunrise. I set my course for the Canary Islands of Your Highnesses, which are in the Ocean Sea, from there to embark on a voyage that will last until I arrive in the Indies and delver the letter of Your Highnesses to those Princes, and do all that Your Highnesses have commanded me to do.

To this end, I decided to write down everything I might do and see and experience on this voyage, from day to day and very carefully. Also, Sovereign Princes, besides describing each night what takes place during the day, and during the day the sailings of the night, I propose to make a new chart for navigation on which I will set down all the sea and lands of the Ocean Sea, in their correct locations and with their correct bearings. Further, I shall compile a book and shall map everything by latitude and longitude. And above all, it is fitting that I forget about sleeping and devote much attention to navigation in order to accomplish this. And these things will be a great task.[1]

Columbus states in this prologue that the Jews had been expelled from Spain in January. The royal decree that ordered the expulsion was dated March 30, 1492.

SOUTH BY SOUTHWEST TO THE CANARIES

There were several important reasons for Columbus's choice to sail south by southwest to the Canary Islands, nearly seven hundred miles away. Always observant of wind conditions, he had noticed that on his previous voyages, in the latitudes of the Canaries, the wind always blew mostly from the northeast, thus aiding him in his westward voyage. He had also learned that in the latitudes of the Azores the prevailing westerlies would take over, aiding vessels in sailing eastward to Lisbon. Columbus's navigational strategy was simple: to go west, pick up the easterlies in the latitude of the Canaries; to return to Lisbon, pick up the westerlies in the latitude of the Azores. This was his "secret weapon" that gave him great confidence in his ability to get back when most sailors despaired of ever returning to their homeland. Sailing westward from the Canaries also established a latitude reference point, for Cipango lay roughly in the same latitude. In theory, to reach his destination the Captain-General needed to maintain a constant latitude.

Still another reason for going west by the way of the Canaries was one of precaution and safety. The stretch of ocean between Spain and the Canaries is usually very rough—a condition useful in proof-testing the structural integrity of his vessels. Any malfunction or structural failure that occurred could be fixed in the Canaries before facing the perils of an unknown ocean. Columbus's precautions saved the day as it turned out, for only three days after leaving Spain the rudder of the Pinta snapped out of its gudgeons, forcing the crew to strike sails. The sea was too rough for help to be given. Columbus came up to the Pinta to hearten the crew and relied on Pinzón to repair the damage temporarily. They bound the rudder with rope so that the ship could proceed on her course. However, this makeshift repair lasted only a day because the wind increased, putting more pressure on the rudder. It was at this time that Pinzón suggested to Columbus the possibility of sabotage by Cristóbal Quintero, the grumbling ship's owner who resented having had his ship commandeered for the voyage. They secured the rudder again as best they could, and headed for Lanzarote, the closest of the Canary Islands. However, the rudder gave trouble again and the Pinta began to take water. The gravity of the problem convinced Columbus to head directly for the Grand Canary Island, where there was a better chance of exchanging the crippled Pinta for another vessel or repairing her damage.

At dawn on August 9, within sight of the Grand Canary, the fleet ran into contrary winds and then calms, which held it at sea for two more days. Because of the delay, when the breeze sprang up again, Columbus ordered Pinzón to take the Pinta to Las Palmas on the Grand Canary while he headed for Gomera with the Santa María and the Niña. Columbus hoped to save time in chartering or buying another vessel. On Sunday evening, August 12, Columbus reached San Sebastian in Gomera only to learn that no ship was available for chartering. He was told, however, that the mistress of the island, Doña Beatriz de Peraza y Bobadilla, had gone to the Grand Canary in a forty-ton ship belonging to one Grajeda of Seville and was on the way back home and that the ship might be available. The Captain-General decided to wait in Gomera; but after two days with no sign of the ship, he sent Pinzón a message explaining his delay with a brig bound for Grand Canary. As he remained without news for a long time after the brig's departure, Columbus decided on August 24 to head back to Grand Canary with his two ships. On his way, he overtook the brig, which had spent ten days becalmed between Gomera and Tenerife. He took the messenger aboard. During the night they passed Tenerife, whose lofty volcano was erupting with flames. Columbus, observing the astonishment of the crew, explained to them the cause of the phenomenon, citing the example of Mount Etna in Sicily.

The fleet arrived at the Grand Canary the following afternoon and found that Pinzón had arrived there only the previous day after many difficulties with the Pinta. Columbus also learned that Doña Beatriz had left five days earlier with the ship he had hoped to get. Convinced now that no suitable replacement was available for the faltering Pinta, he decided to repair her in Las Palmas, where blacksmith facilities for forging iron and ship repair were available. They caked all leaks, forged a new rudder with new bolts and straps, and installed new gudgeons and pintles. By retrimming the ballast, they lifted the stern higher above the water line and gave the ship better stability. At the same time, they changed the Niña's rigging from lateen to square for more speed under the strong easterlies, which Columbus anticipated from the Canaries westward. Her aftermost mast was moved into the bow to serve as a foremast. They installed a bowsprit on her, and her sails were cut and resewn to make her a square rigger like the Pinta and the Santa María. They completed the repairs in six days, so that by September 1, the fleet was on its way westward to Gomera, roughly one hundred nautical miles away. The next day they reached Gomera, where Columbus finally met Beatriz de Peraza.

DOÑA BEATRIZ DE PERAZA Y BOBADILLA

Who was this Doña Beatriz so eagerly sought after by Columbus? Born Beatriz de Bobadilla, she was first cousin, once removed, of the eminent Marquess De Moya. An exceptionally beautiful woman, she was appointed maid of honor to Queen Isabella and attracted the amorous attention of King Ferdinand who, though he loved his wife dearly, was not known to be an overly faithful husband. Aware that the king had a more than platonic interest in Beatriz, Isabella cleverly contrived to get her married to Hernan Peraza, Captain of Gomera. Peraza had been ordered to appear at Court to answer charges of having murdered a rival conquistador in the Canaries. The queen promised Peraza full pardon for his crime, on condition that he marry Beatriz and take her back with him to Gomera. Marrying a beautiful and aristocratic lady of Castile to obtain a pardon for murder was indeed a good bargain, and Peraza did not hesitate.

Later, Peraza was killed in Gomera for having seduced a native girl, leaving Beatriz to rule the island as guardian of her minor son Guillen, later the first Count of Gomera.

Under thirty years of age, Beatriz was still in the flower of her womanhood when Columbus, at forty-one, arrived in Gomera. Because he sought her out, it is reasonable to assume that he had met her before, possibly at Spanish Court in Córdoba. Columbus, if we are to believe Michele de Cuneo, a Genoese "gentleman volunteer" who accompanied him on his second voyage, was smitten by her beauty and became infatuated with her. The reception given to Columbus when he stopped at Gomera, before setting sail on his second voyage, was memorable, according to Cuneo: "If I should tell you what we did in that place (Gomera) with salvos, Lombard shots, and fireworks, it would take too long. This we did because of the Lady of that place with whom our Lord Admiral in other times had fallen in love."[2]

It may have been an ardent lover's desire that brought Columbus back to Gomera on September 2. He could have made his departure for the Indies directly from Las Palmas but chose instead to go back to Gomera to spend the last night ashore with a "beautiful widow." He was delighted to find that Doña Beatriz had come back from Lanzarote and that she was in residence in her castle. He sought her out and was suitably entertained by the lovely lady. She, in turn, found in the tall handsome Genoese a sexually attractive, amorously disposed, and eager lover.

Columbus was to meet Doña Beatriz again early in October of the following year when, during his second voyage, his huge Grand Fleet sailed to Gomera. This has been already disclosed in Michele de Cuneo's letter. It may very well be that Columbus in his new role of Admiral might have proposed marriage to

Doña Beatriz only to be told that if he married her he would have to settle down on the islands, as she had been banished from Castile by the queen. This situation Columbus, whose star was now rising, could never accept, and they parted never to see each other again. It was just as well that this illicit union did not continue for Doña Beatriz, so highly desirable to Columbus for her beauty, could also be extremely cruel when provoked. The story is told that when a local inhabitant of San Sebastian spread the rumor that Doña Beatriz had not been chaste during her widowhood, she invited him to her castle for a social visit. A discussion followed with the scandalmonger, after which she signaled to her servants to seize the slanderer and immediately hang him on a rafter in the castle hall. She then had his body hanged again outside the castle walls as a warning to all gossipers. She eventually found a suitable partner when she married Alonso de Lugo, Mayor of the Grand Canary.

Following the tryst with Doña Beatriz, Columbus was eager to depart. A month had already elapsed since leaving Palos. His ships had been repaired and properly conditioned; fresh provisions had been taken aboard; and best of all the crews were in good spirits and intact, as not one member had jumped ship in the Canaries, possibly due to their loyalty to the Pinzóns.

Chapter Fifteen

THE DISCOVERY OF THE WEST INDIES

On Thursday, September 6, Columbus departed from Gomera. However, the wind was not cooperative and the fleet lay becalmed in the channel between Gomera and Tenerife all day Thursday and Friday. At about 3:00 a.m. on Saturday, September 8, the northeast trade wind began to blow and the course was set to the west. The fleet was on its way on a thirty-three-day excursion that proved to be, aside from psychological considerations, surprisingly uneventful. There were no storms or prolonged calms on the way, no encounters with the Portuguese, no shortages of food or water, and no serious illnesses. The only concerns were psychological. Foremost on the sailors' minds was the fear, as the wind blew swiftly from the west, that they would never be able to get back home. How could they buck such strong trade winds on the return trip? The fleet's encounter with the Sargasso Sea and the premature land sightings caused some concern and lowered the crew's morale. Weighing most heavily on their minds was the uncertainty of what they might find along their route, the fear of the unknown.

The Captain-General spoke of Cipango and the Indies, but his words sounded less reassuring to the sailors with each passing day. From the moment the fleet passed Ferro, Columbus logged distances that were less than those actually covered, a deliberate deception intended not to frighten the sailors if the voyage should be lengthy. Thus, from the very beginning Columbus had anticipated a problem of morale, which would increase in direct proportion to the distance sailed westward. From September 9 to 18, inclusive, the fleet held a steady course at approximately 28° latitude and made 12,160 nautical miles under a steady trade wind. Runs of 60 to 174 actual nautical miles per day were logged, indicating a maximum speed of 7¼ miles per hour on the fastest day! Things were going so well and so pleasurably that the Captain-General's log entry for September 16 declared that "era plazer grande el gusto de las mañanas" (the taste of the mornings was a great delight). The weather, he remarked, "was like April in Andalusia."[1] The only thing missing was the nightingale's songs.

On the same day, they crossed the 33° west longitude and began noticing gulfweeds. They were entering the huge Sargasso Sea. At first the sailors were alarmed lest they be stuck in the thick half-inch carpet of weeds, but they observed that it parted easily, allowing the boats full freedom of passage.[2]

Another phenomenon that concerned the crew was the apparent variation of the compass needle, reported by Columbus on September 13, with Polaris as the pole star. He found that the needle varied to the northwest a full point (11¼°). Columbus reasoned that perhaps the Polaris moved and not the needle. The phenomenon known as "Precision of the Equinoxes" had been described by the Greek astronomer Hipparchus as early as 125 B.C. and finally explained by Sir Isaac Newton eighteen centuries later.[3] Columbus was the first navigator to report a westerly variation of the compass. All navigators had assumed for centuries that the North Star was immovable and could be depended upon to mark a true north position. His discovery of the diurnal rotation of Polaris was a major contribution to navigation.

By September 19, the northeast trade winds had died down and, according to Columbus's log, "between day and night the fleet made only twenty-five leagues" (eighty miles). By Thursday, September 20, there was practically no wind at all and, as a result, the fleet changed its direction to the W by N and WNW logging all told but seven or eight leagues (seventeen miles). This was the wrong direction to take. Columbus was sailing almost on the northern boundary of the northeast trade winds, which is about 28° latitude N at that time of the year. The belts of wind move farther poleward during the summer, and conversely with the northeast trade wind, closer towards the equator at the approach of the winter. Had Columbus sailed a few degrees of latitude farther south, he may very well have hit the region of the northeast trade winds all the way to his destination. By heading WNW, the fleet sailed to 29°N outside the northeast trade winds and on Monday, September 24, it traveled only fourteen and one half leagues (thirty-two miles) all day. On the evening of September 25, Martín Alonso came up on the stern of his ship and joyfully shouted to the Admiral, claiming the prize for sighting land. When the Admiral heard this, he went down on his knees to give thanks to the Lord, and Martín Alonso said the Gloria in Excelsis Deo with his crew. They sailed on this course to the W thence to the SW until the afternoon of September 26, but what they had thought was land was only sky.

Once again at sunrise on Sunday, October 7, the caravel Niña, which was in the lead because of her superior speed, raised a flag and fired a lombard to signal land ahead. The fleet kept going westward but by evening the sailors' hopes had been dashed. There was no sign of land. A great flock of birds passed over, going from N to SW; for this reason, the admiral decided to abandon his W course and turned the prow WSW.

On Wednesday, October 10, the crew began to complain of the long voyage, but the Admiral cheered them, assuring them that land was not far off. He added that it was useless to complain as he had set out for the Indies and would continue until he found them, with the help of the Lord.

The momentous events of October 11 and October 12, which would change the history of the world, are best described by the Admiral of the Ocean Sea himself in Las Casas's transcription and in Robert H. Fuson's English translation. We thank Professor Fuson for the use of his translation:

THE DISCOVERY OF THE BAHAMAS
Long Entry for Thursday, 11 October 1492

I sailed to the WSW, and we took more water aboard than at any other time on the voyage. I saw several things that were indications of land. At one time, a large flock of sea birds flew overhead, and a green reed was found floating near the ship. The crew of the Pinta spotted some of the same reeds and some other plants. They also saw what looked like a small board or plank. A stick was recovered and looked man-made, perhaps carved with an iron tool. Those on the Niña saw a little stick covered with barnacles. I am certain that many things were overlooked because of the heavy sea, but even these few made the crew breathe easier; in fact, the men have even become cheerful. I sailed eighty-one miles from sunset yesterday to sunset today. As is our custom, vespers were said in the late afternoon, and a special thanksgiving was offered to God for giving us renewed hope through the many signs of land He has provided.

After sunset, I ordered the pilot to return to my original westerly course, and I urged the crew to be over-vigilant. I took the added precaution of doubling the number of lookouts, and I reminded the men that the first to sight land would be give a silk doublet as a personal token from me. Further, he would be given an annuity of ten thousand maravedis from the Sovereigns.

About ten o'clock at night, while standing on the stern castle, I thought I saw a light to the west. It looked like a little wax candle bobbing up and down. It had the same appearance as a light or torch belonging to fisherman or travelers who alternately raised and lowered it, or perhaps were going from house to house. I am the first to admit that I was so eager to find land that I did not trust my own senses, so I called for Pedro Gutierrez, the representative of the king's household, and asked him to watch for the light. After a few moments, he too saw it. I then summoned Rodrigo Sánchez of Segovia, the comptroller of the fleet, and asked him to watch for the light. He saw nothing, nor did any other members of the crew. It was such an uncertain thing that I did not feel it was adequate proof of land.

The moon, in its third quarter, rose in the east shortly before midnight. I estimate that we were making about nine knots and had gone some sixty-seven and a half miles between the beginning of the night and two o'clock in the morning. Then, at two hours after midnight, the Pinta fired a cannon, my prearranged signal for the sighting of land.

I now believe that the light I saw earlier was a sign from God and that it was truly the first positive indication of land. When we caught up with the Pinta, which was always running ahead because she was a swift sailer, I learned that the first man to sight land was Rodriguo de Triana, a seaman from Lepe. I hauled in all sails but the mainsail and lay-to till daylight. The land is about six miles to the west.

Friday, 12 October, 1492

At dawn we saw naked people and I went ashore in the ship's boat, armed, followed by Martín Alonso Pinzón, captain of the Pinta, and his brother, Vicente Yañez Pinzón, captain of the Niña. I unfurled the royal banner and the captains brought the flags, which displayed a large green cross with the letters F and Y at the left and right side of the cross. Over each letter was the appropriate crown of that Sovereign. These flags were carried as a standard on all of the ships. After a prayer of thanksgiving I ordered the captains of the Pinta and the Niña together with Rodrigo de Escobedo [secretary of the fleet], and Rodrigo Sánchez of Segovia [comptroller of the fleet] to bear faith and witness that I was taking possession of this island for the King and Queen. I made all the necessary declarations and had these testimonies carefully written down by the secretary. In addition to those named above, the entire company of the fleet bore witness to this act. To this island I gave the name "San Salvador," in honor of our Blessed Lord…

The people here called this island "Guanahani" in their language, and their speech is very fluent, although I do not understand any of it. They are friendly and well-dispositioned people who bear no arms except for small spears and they have no iron. I showed one of my swords, and through ignorance he grabbed it by the blade and cut himself. Their spears are made of wood, to which they attach a fish tooth at one end or some other sharp thing.

I want the natives to develop a friendly attitude toward us because I know that they are a people who can be made free and converted to our Holy Faith more by love than by force. I therefore gave red caps to some and glass beads to others. They hung the beads around their necks, along with some other things of slight value that I gave them. And they took great pleasure in this and became so friendly that it was a marvel. They traded and gave everything they had with goodwill but it seems to me that they have very little and are poor in everything. I wanted my men to take nothing from the people without giving something in exchange.

This afternoon the people of San Salvador came swimming to our ships and in boats made from one log. They brought parrots, balls of cotton thread, spears, and many other things including a kind of dry leaf that they hold in great esteem. For these items, we swapped them little glass beads and hawks' bells.

Many of the men I have seen have scars on their bodies, and when I made signs to them to find out how this happened they indicated that people from other nearby islands come to San Salvador to capture them; they defend themselves the best they can. I believe that people from the mainland come here to take them as slaves. They ought to make good and skilled servants, for they repeat very quickly whatever we say to them. I think they can easily be made Christians, for they seem to have no religion. If it pleases Our Lord, I will take six of them to Your Highness when I depart, in order that they may learn our language.[4]

Chapter Sixteen

FROM SAN SALVADOR TO CUBA

Columbus's account of his landing on San Salvador as noted in his journal is terse: "At dawn we saw naked people and I went ashore in the ship's boat, armed, followed by Martín Alonso Pinzón, captain of the Pinta, and his brother, Vicente Yañez Pinzón, captain of the Niña."[1] This landing was the result of a dramatic excursion that set the pattern for the future and established Columbus's reputation as the greatest sailor of reefs and shoals in history. Columbus had approached the island from the east or windward coast and because he had been fighting heavy seas on October 11, it would have been foolhardy to land at night—if not impossible. Columbus never got too close to an unfamiliar coast without taking soundings. On this occasion he noticed, at daybreak of October 12, that the island was isolated by reefs on the east side. He, therefore, began to sail around the southern part of it, seeking a clear passage to shore on the western or leeward side. Proceeding northward he found a stretch of about two miles unobstructed by reefs between two points known today as Riding Rock and Gardiner's Reef. Columbus sailed into the bay without incident and anchored off a curved beach of gleaming coral sand. He went ashore, followed by his officers, and touched a new world: the greatest discovery in the history of mankind. He was richly attired in scarlet befitting a Viceroy. Holding the royal standard, he stepped off his boat, fell to his knees, kissed the ground, and gratefully gave thanks to God with a solemn Latin prayer, which was to be repeated by other explorers such as Balboa, Cortez, and Pizarro upon their discoveries of new lands:

O Lord, Almighty and Everlasting God, by Thy holy Word Thou hast created the heaven and the earth and the sea; blessed and glorified by Thy Name, and praised be Thy Majesty, which hath deigned to use us, Thy humble servants, that Thy holy Name may be known and proclaimed in this other part of the earth.[2]

Rising to his feet, Columbus drew his sword, displaying the royal standard, and took possession in the name of the Castilian Sovereigns. He was surrounded by two captains, Martín Alonso Pinzón and Vicente Yañez Pinzón, with the Sovereigns' representatives, Rodrigo de Escobedo, "Escribano de toda la Aramada" (Secretary of the Fleet), and Rodrigo Sanchez, "veedor real" (Royal Comptroller), and the rest of the officers, i.e., masters and pilots. He then asked all present to swear allegiance and obedience to him.

The natives had watched with fear as the boats landed, wondering who the strange beings encased in steel and wearing fancy and multicolored clothes might be. At first, they had scattered and had run into the woods in fear. But seeing that the Spaniards had no intention of harming them, they came out of the woods and, driven by curiosity, approached the men who must have appeared to them as creatures from heaven.

THE BAHAMA ISLANDS

Columbus landed on one of the islands of the huge Bahama archipelago. Because he believed he had landed on one of the outer islands of India, he called the natives Indians, a name that has remained as a designation for the indigenous populations of the New World.

The natives of Guanahani (the name means "iguana") and of all the other islands whom Columbus met on his first voyage were Taino Indians who spoke a common language known as "Arawak." These Indians had migrated from the South American mainland, settling in the Bahamas, Cuba, Jamaica, and Haiti.

The total habitable area of the Bahamas is small, but the extent of the archipelago, including reefs and cays rising from the banks near the surface of the water, is very large—nearly six degrees in latitude and more than six degrees in longitude. Stretching through a total distance of 780 miles, these islands, about 3,000 in number, form a barrier before the eastern entrance to the Gulf of Mexico.

Consisting of windblown piles of shell and coral sand, the Bahamas are different in geographical formation from the Greater and Lesser Antilles. The islands, usually level, are merely the exposed tips of a great submerged ridge. Their total area is roughly 4,400 square miles. San Salvador is sixteen nautical miles long and seven wide. Though some of these islands were the first to be discovered, they were the last to be settled. Spain paid little attention to them and the English colonized them. The English were the first to come, establishing a settlement on

New Providence in 1629; however, Spain reasserted her claim of discovery, and the English were expelled, only to return in 1680. The islands did not become a possession of the British crown until 1787. Today, Nassau on New Providence Island is the most populated city and Andros the largest island in the archipelago.

The location of Columbus's landfall—San Salvador Island—remained a mystery for many centuries, partially because the Spaniards never occupied it.[3] Ironically, when the English took over the Bahamas, it was renamed Watling Island, after a notorious pirate. When later in the middle of the twentieth century the island was identified, the British government officially renamed it "San Salvador."

RESPITE IN SAN SALVADOR

At daybreak, following the day of discovery there came to the beach many young men all naked and "…all of good stature, very handsome people….They came to the ship in dugouts [canoes] that were fashioned like a long boat, [made] from the trunk of a tree, all in one piece….They row with a thing like a baker's peel."[4] These canoes made from tree trunks were the common means of transportation in the ocean and waterways. They came in all sizes—some of them capable of transporting as many as fifty people or more.

Columbus became interested in the gold pieces hanging from the noses of some of the Indians. Using sign language, he inquired about the source of the gold. The Indians replied that there was a king there who had great vessels of it in the southern part of the island. The possibility of having found mines of the precious metal excited the Admiral, who probably recalled the rich lands described by Marco Polo. The Venetian had never been to Cipango (Japan) but he had reported that its sovereign had a palace even richer than the Khan's, his lord host. Columbus may also have remembered John de Mandeville's *Travels*, in which the opulence of the Great Khan of Cathay was described. As Mandeville reported, at one of the Khan's banquets there sat as many as four thousand guests. Columbus wrote in a log, "I intend to go and see if I can find the island of Cipango,"[5] a brief notation that announced a program of discovery. In its terseness, we are given merely a hint of Columbus's determination to reach the Indies, a determination bordering on obsession. Because Marco Polo had reported that Cipango lay 1,500 miles from the continent of Asia, he had reason to believe that he was very close to it.

The natives' lack of clothes was clearly indicative of a lack of civilization to Columbus. It also suggested a lack of religion, and hence, the possibility of conversion to Christianity, which was one of the avowed reasons for undertaking the journey. Columbus was confident that the Indians' docility was congenial to Christianity and that they could easily be converted to Christianity.

Columbus also reported, in great detail, the manners and customs of the natives and the beauty of the new continent. He described the fauna and flora of the islands he discovered with reasonable accuracy and objectivity. Yet with all the powers of observation that he possessed, he remained ignorant of the magnitude of his discoveries. He clung to the image of the world without realizing that his efforts had filled the void between the Atlantic and the Pacific Oceans. The world of Strabo and Ptolemy had been erased by one quick stroke of luck, determination, and faith. For Columbus, though, San Salvador was but the beginning of a long search for Cipango and its golden cities.

The following day, Sunday, October 14, Columbus proceeded to explore the leeward coast of San Salvador to the NNE with several of the caravels' boats. He saw two or three villages with many natives waving and shouting from shore. When they saw that he was not coming ashore, some of them swam toward the boats in great excitement and curiosity. Columbus was amazed at the generosity of the Indians who gave away their most valued possessions for mere trinkets. At one point, in fact, he entertained the thought of forbidding such unequal exchanges between the Indians and his men. He was also extremely impressed by the Indians' docility. So much so that he regarded building a fort—Columbus was a man of his times and being prepared for an eventuality was part of his "forma mentis"—almost unnecessary:

These people are very unskilled in arms. Your Highnesses will see this for yourselves when I bring you the seven that I have taken. After they learn our language, I shall return them; unless Your Highnesses order that the entire population be taken to Castile, or held captive here. With fifty men, you could subject everyone and make them do what you wished.[6]

These words should not be interpreted, as has been done, as a plan of conquest of the Indies by Spanish might. They are the observations of a man who lived through a bloody period in European history, where constant fighting among men was the order of the day, who marvels at how different the Indians are from Europeans. Columbus's remarks are meant to express his admiration for the Indians' innocence and childlike demeanors.

IN SEARCH OF CIPANGO

Columbus set sail from San Salvador on Sunday, October 14, and saw ahead of him so many islands that he could not decide where to go first. He then headed for the biggest island, about twenty-five nautical miles southwest of San Salvador. Darkness was creeping upon them as they were nearing the island, and the Admiral cautiously ordered the caravels to heave for the night. The island was Rum Cay, which Columbus named "Santa María de la Concepción." In the evening, some of the captured Indians told Columbus that the natives of this island wore very big bracelets of gold on their legs and arms. Columbus took this news with reservations, suspecting that they were lying in order to escape. At midnight one of the captives leaped overboard and swam to shore. At daybreak the following day, Tuesday, Columbus went ashore in the armed boats and was greeted by numerous Indians similar to those he had seen on San Salvador. Finding nothing new on this island, he returned to his ship. A large canoe pulled alongside the Niña and another captive Indian jumped into the sea and swam away. Some members of the crew chased the Indians to shore but they escaped into the woods. The Admiral then sailed eight leagues westward to a much larger island and anchored off its coast, which extended more than twenty-eight leagues from northwest to southeast. This island that the Admiral named "Fernandina" (now known as Long Island) was perfectly flat and surrounded by fine beaches.

On the way to Fernandina from Santa María, the fleet overtook a man in a canoe and picked him up. He had aboard a piece of native bread, about the size of a fist, a gourd filled with water, a clump of vermilion-colored earth, which the natives used to paint their bodies, and some dried leaves that the Indians greatly prized (probably tobacco). In a little basket, he carried a string of glass beads with two Castilian coins, by which they concluded that he had come from San Salvador, had passed over the Santa María, and was heading for Fernandina to spread the news of the coming of the Christians. He paddled up to one of the ships and together with his canoe was taken aboard. The Admiral ordered that he be given bread and honey and drink and sent ashore as soon as they reached Fernandina so that he might spread the good tidings about the Christians. The Indians' favorable account of the Christians assured them a good welcome. When the boats went ashore for water, the Indians showed the sailors not only where to find it, but carried the filled casks to the boats themselves, and took a great delight in pleasing the Christians.

While the natives resembled those of the other islands visited, in customs and language they seemed more intelligent and shrewder—driving harder bargains for what they traded. In their huts, they had cotton clothes that they used for bed coverings. Some women covered their genitals with clothes of woven cotton, others with wrapped skirts of woven cloths. Among the remarkable things the newcomers saw about the green and fertile island were trees that had on their trunks four or five different kinds of leaves and branches. For instance, one branch had leaves like a cane, others like mastic. The leaves seemed not to have been grafted but to have grown naturally. They saw a multitude of brightly colored fish, but did not find any land animals except lizards or snakes.

To learn more about the island, Columbus sailed to the northwest and anchored at the mouth of a beautiful harbor at whose entrance lay a small island, but after taking measurement of its depth, decided to anchor outside because the water was not deep enough. Noticing that the harbor was also the mouth of a river, Columbus sent men with casks to fetch water while he spent a few hours walking among some of the most beautiful trees he had ever seen. When the men returned they reported seeing a small village consisting of twelve to fifteen huts, shaped like Moorish tents, containing no ornament or furniture. The beds were nets that had the shape of slings, with the ends attached to two house posts; hammocks. The men also saw dogs that looked like mastiffs but could not bark.

After taking on water they returned to the ships and sailed northwest; the wind, however, proved unfavorable, and they turned back from the cape and sailed southeasterly off the windward shore of Fernandina. Finally, the wind stopped altogether, preventing the fleet from reaching the land to anchor. At midnight, it started to rain and it lasted until dawn. In his log of this date, Columbus referred to his discoveries as "the Indies."

On the following day, Thursday, October 18, the weather cleared. Columbus followed the wind around the island to what is now the village of Roses; and when the weather was no longer suitable for sailing, he lay offshore for the rest of the day. On Friday, October 19, the fleet weighed anchor at daybreak, and each ship was given orders to proceed to the next island by slightly different routes. The Pinta was instructed to head ESE and the Niña SSE and the Admiral's ship SE. Each captain was to keep to the course given until midday, at which time he was to change course to meet with the Admiral. However, before midday each ship steered eastward to meet at an island that the Indians called "Samoete" and the Admiral named "Isabela" (Crooked Island). They sailed along the west coast of this island and anchored off a cape for the night. Columbus had understood (or misunderstood) from the signs of the captured Indians that there was a gold mine on this island and that its chief, ruler of the surrounding islands, lived in a large city and possessed great treasures of jewels and gold. The dawn disclosed the most beautiful island the Admiral had ever seen, even more beautiful than the other islands; it had many very large trees and the landscape was dotted with hillocks.

According to the captives, there were also many lakes on the island. From this location, they proceeded NE to a bend in the coast that hid an open bay in which they anchored. Columbus named it "Cabo Hermoso" because of its beauty. He wrote the following in his log:

This island is one of the most beautiful I have ever seen, if the others are beautiful then this is more so. Of what I have seen so far, the coast is almost all sandy beach. It has many large, beautiful green trees.... There are many lakes and ponds in the middle of the island. I simply do not know where to go next. I never tire from looking at such luxurious vegetation, which is so different from ours. I believe that there are in it many plants and trees here that could be worth a lot in Spain for use as dyes, spices, and medicines; but to my great sorrow I do not recognize them. You can even smell the flowers as you approach the coast; it is the most fragrant thing on earth.[7]

In "The Great Sailor" the Italian Columbus scholar Paolo Emilio Taviani says that the Admiral had exceptionally good eyesight and an uncanny sense of smell, both of which contributed greatly to his mastery of the sea.[8] The last sentence of the quotation is eloquent enough. Sailing at some distance from the coast, Columbus was able to smell the flowers. Such a keen organ was to serve the Admiral well on many occasions, allowing him to forecast even weather conditions.

The following morning, Saturday, October 20, Columbus weighed anchor to try to locate the village and the wealthy ruler of the island. He sailed to the NE and E from the SE and S following the indications given by the captive Indians, but he ran into shallow waters and decided to turn back. There was a strong head wind and he was forced to lay to for the night, anchoring the fleet close to shore. The following morning, the fleet took off again and by ten o'clock they had arrived at the Cape of the Islet. The landing party went ashore hoping to find a village, but found only a single deserted house. The occupants had fled at the sight of the visitors. Once again, Columbus was impressed with the beauty of the place:

The woods and vegetation are as green as the April in Andalusia, and the singing of the little birds might make a man wish never to leave here; the flocks of parrots that darken the sun, and the large and small birds of so many species are so different from our own that it is a wonder. In addition, there are trees of a thousand kinds, all with fruit according to their kind, and they all give off a marvelous fragrance. I am the saddest man in the world for not knowing what kind of things these are because I am sure that they are valuable. I am bringing a sample of everything I can.[9]

No animals were seen in these islands except for the non-barking dogs and six-foot long reptiles—iguanas—that the Indians hunted for food. Columbus and his crew actually killed one of these "serpents" with their lances and reported that it tasted like chicken.

For several days, Columbus remained on the island to try to find its ruler. In reply to the repeated questions about the gold mine, the Indians made them understand that to the south lay a very large island that they called "Colba" (Cuba) abounding in gold and commerce. The Indians reported that many large ships came regularly to trade with its inhabitants. In addition to gold, pearls and spices were also found there. The Indians spoke of another large island beyond Colba that they called Bohio (Hispaniola). Columbus was now convinced that Colba was Japan. He decided to proceed to the mainland of China, without stopping at every small island in his path to present his credentials to the emperor in Quisay, the wealthy city described by Marco Polo. A lack of wind, however, and heavy rains delayed the departure.

On October 24, Columbus weighed anchor and headed for Cuba:

At midnight, I weighed anchors from the island of Isabela, from Cabo del Isleo, which is in the north part, in order to go to the island of Cuba, which the Indians tell me is very large and has much commerce, gold, spices, ships, and merchants. The Indians indicated that I should sail to the SW to get to Cuba, and I believe them because all my globes and world maps seem to indicate that the island of Japan is in this vicinity and I am sure that Cuba and Japan are one and the same.[10]

The trip to Cuba was difficult due to the vagaries of the winds, periods of heavy rainfall, and the danger posed by the reefs and shoals at night. The fleet set sail on a WSW course, but the wind died at daybreak; then it started to rain and it lasted all night. At midday, the wind began to blow ever so gently, and Columbus unfurled all sails to pick up speed to keep up with his other ships. In spite of this, by nightfall, the Santa María had managed to sail only twenty-one miles from Isabela's Bird Rock. Being a cautious sailor, when darkness fell, Columbus ordered all crews to strike sails except for the lowest ones; and as the wind grew strong, he issued the order to strip down to the base poles.

On Thursday, October 25, the fleet sailed from sunrise until 9:00 a.m. to the WSW and then changed course to the W traveling forty-four Roman miles by 3:00 p.m. Seven or eight islands all strung out N to S came into view. These were a string of cays that mark the eastern edge of the Great Bahama Bank. Columbus appropriately called them "Las Islas de Arenas" (the Sandy Isles). By Friday, October 26, the fleet had traveled five or six leagues when it anchored for the night in shoal waters. On Saturday, October 27, they weighed anchors at sunrise and traveled very cautiously in shoal waters in a SSW course until nightfall, when they sighted land. But rain began to fall so heavily at times that they jogged off and on at night. By sunset Saturday, they had made seventeen leagues to the SSW.

The heavy rain showers experienced by Columbus are normal for that season. The rainy season starts in late August, right after the scorching heat, and continues until November. Columbus marveled at the intense rain and on several occasions noted it in his journal. The island they had seen the night before was unlike any they had known. It was a huge land mass that filled out the entire landscape. Columbus was struck by its grandeur, its green valleys and long sweeping plains, but most of all by its high mountains that reminded him of Sicily. He was convinced that Colba was the Indian name for Cipango and his heart filled with anticipation. They sailed directly into the mouth of a large river, very beautiful and without danger of shoals and other impediments, and they dropped anchor.

Chapter Seventeen

THE CUBAN EXPERIENCE

Columbus's landfall in Cuba on October 28 took place on the northeast side of the island in a harbor in the Oriente Province, which he called "San Salvador" and which today is known as Bahía Bay. It was a beautiful harbor surrounded by green trees different from those in Spain "with flowers and fruits each according to its kind, many birds...which sing very sweetly."[1] Columbus went ashore with a small boat and saw two houses that belonged to fishermen, judging by the gear found inside. The occupants, however, had fled in fear on seeing the Europeans approach. In one of the houses there was a dog that did not bark. Columbus returned to his boat and proceeded up river for a good distance but saw no sign of Indians. The luxuriant vegetation, and the colorful plants and flowers that abound in the Caribbean, were a continuous source of marvel to the eyes of a European:

I have never seen anything so beautiful...the island is filled with very beautiful mountains, although they are not long, only high. All the other land is high like Sicily. According to what I can understand from the Indians from Guanahani who are with me, this land is full of rivers. They told me by signs that there are ten large rivers and that the island is so large that they cannot circumnavigate it with their canoes in twenty days.[2]

The island of Cuba runs 11° of longitude, extending from 74°5' to 84°55' longitude W. Circumnavigating the island required nearly 1,500 miles of navigation, a feat that no Indian could normally accomplish in a canoe. In his five-and-a-half-week stay in Cuba, Columbus himself was able to cover only about two hundred miles of the north shore from the eastern tip of the island. The Indians also said that in Cuba there were mines of gold and pearls, which was confirmed, in Columbus's mind, by the presence of shellfish. Large ships belonging to the Great Khan were reported by the Indians as covering the distance between the mainland and that island in ten days.

The following day, Monday, October 29, Columbus weighed anchors and sailed westward along the north coast to look for the ruler of the island. He sailed along the coast in a northwest direction and saw a river he named "Río de Luna," (River of the Moon), actually the narrow-mouthed Bahía Jururù, one mile from Bariay. Proceeding until the hour of vespers, Columbus saw the mouth of another river much greater than the others and he named it Río de Mares. (The word "Mares" was probably an error. Columbus may have meant "marte," or Mars, a logical choice considering he had just named the preceding river after the moon.) They also noticed a village on the bay and Columbus sent some sailors with an Indian guide to investigate. At the appearance of the visitors, everyone fled. Their houses resembled very large Moorish pavilions and looked like tents in an encampment. Columbus ordered the men not to take anything from the houses. They found many statutes of women and many heads shaped like masks. They also found nets, fishing hooks, and tackle, tamed wild birds, and the ever-present non-barking dogs. These dogs, according to Las Casas, belong to a breed that can grunt but cannot bark during infancy and young years. Dog experts have noted that Eskimo dogs today do not bark until they learn from mature dogs. The many references to these dogs by Columbus and Las Casas suggest that this particular breed domesticated by the Tainos was used largely for food.

On October 30, the fleet departed from Río de Mares and headed for the northwest. Before long, a cape covered with palms came into view and the Admiral named it "Cabo de Palmas" (possibly Punta Uvero, twenty-four miles west of Puerto Gibara). After having sailed another fifteen leagues:

The Indians who were on the Pinta said that behind the cape was a river, from which it was four days' journey to Cuba. The captain of the Pinta understood that Cuba was a city, and that it was on the mainland, a very large land that extends far to the north. He also understood that the king of Cuba was at war with the Great Khan, whom they called Cami and whose country or city they call Faba and many other names.[3]

Pinzón had studied Toscanelli's map, and had learned from Columbus specific facts concerning the coast of Asia. He therefore concluded that the Indians were talking about the Kublai Khan and the eastern provinces of China as described by Marco Polo. This information, accepted at face value by Columbus, changed his conviction that Cuba was Cipango. The Indians' information, Pinzón's acceptance of it, the huge size of the island, and perhaps Columbus's own eagerness were factors that convinced the great navigator that this island was the mainland of China after all. Under the circumstances, he decided to proceed beyond the cape to the river mentioned by the Indians to send a delegation to the ruler of the country and to bring gifts and the letter from the Castilian Sovereigns. That evening he set sail for the river, but his attempt proved futile as the wind veered wholly to the north and the coast trends NNW and SE. He saw a bay that he could not enter because of shoals. To make matters worse, a big storm threatened and he resolved to get back to Río de Mares.

At sunrise on the first of November, the Admiral sent some boats to inspect the houses but the natives had fled into the woods. After breakfast, he sent an Indian interpreter who, from a distance offshore, reassured the natives of the peaceful intentions of the Spaniards. The Indian told them that the Spaniards were good people and had not harmed anyone but instead had brought gifts to all the Indians with whom they had come in contact. To allay their fears, the Indian jumped into the water and swam ashore. The natives grabbed him by the arms and led him to a pavilion where he was interrogated. He must have been very convincing, for that afternoon there came out to the ships sixteen canoes bringing cotton yarn and other simple articles of no use to the white men. Columbus had forbidden all trading for anything but gold in order to tempt the natives to disclose its source. They had none to offer. None of the Indians wore gold ornaments; only one of them wore a piece of wrought silver in his nose. The natives confirmed that the ruler lived only four days' journey away and that merchants from his realm would arrive presently to trade with the Christians there and would give news to the king of that land.

Apparently, the news of the Christians' arrival had already reached the king's capital. Columbus consulted again Toscanelli's map, made some quick calculations, and became more convinced that he had found China:

I am certain now that this is the mainland and that I am before Zayto and Quinsay, three hundred miles distance, more or less. This is indicated by the sea, which comes in a different manner from how it has come up to now. Yesterday as I was going NW I found that it was becoming cold.[4]

THE LAND OF CIPANGO

Columbus now was convinced that the Grand Khan was within reach and he was most anxious to contact him. He decided not to wait for the arrival of the messengers and merchants but to press immediately for a meeting. For this important mission, he chose Rodrigo de Xerex and Louis de Torres, a converted Jew whom Columbus had taken along because of his knowledge of Hebrew, Aramaic, and also some Arabic; as near oriental languages they might be known by the Grand Khan's potentates. Columbus sent along two Indians: one from nearby, the other from Guanahani. The ambassadors carried strings of beads and other trinkets to buy food and meet expenses along the way, and had six days to go and return. Columbus instructed his representatives to inform the ruler of the Spaniards' arrival and their desire to discuss the establishment of friendly relations between Spain and China. Columbus asked them to learn all they could about the geographical features seen in their travels.

In the evening, the Admiral took the altitude with a quadrant and noted that the latitude north of the equator was 42°. This grossly erroneous reading has baffled historians because the reading at that location is actually 21°03'—almost half of Columbus's reading. How could be have been so far off?

S. E. Morison suggested that Columbus mistook another star for Polaris, possibly Beta Cephei (Alfirk) for which 42° latitude would be correct.[5] But, because Columbus had set his route from the Canaries at 28° north latitude and had proceeded SSW to Guanahani and then more SSW to reach Cuba, he surely must have realized that his reading should have been less than 28°N and not 42°N. As an angular dimension, 42°N is almost halfway to the North Pole. It is the boundary lines of the states of Oregon and California and the western part of the states of New York and Pennsylvania. It is possible, as suggested by some historians, that this was simply a copyist's error. In Roman numerals twenty-two is written XXII and forty-two XLII. Columbus must have meant 22°N. On November 21, off Puerto del Principe, Columbus obtained the same erroneous reading. This time, however, he noted that his reading was impossible and blamed it on his quadrant. I agree with Morison on this matter.

Sailors can spot the North Star in the northern latitude by locating the Big Dipper. The two stars, Dubhe and Merak (known as the two pointer stars, which form the front of the Big Dipper), are almost in a direct line with the North Star. This star appears to be five times as far from Dubhe as Dubhe is from Merak. Columbus was at a latitude where the pointer stars could not be seen to locate the North Star; hence, his error in using the wrong star to establish his bearing.

On the morning of November 3, the Admiral left the Santa María, got into a boat, and was rowed up the river on a field trip of exploration. Five or six miles up the river, he climbed up a mountain to explore the surroundings, but the nearby tall trees and groves obstructed the view. When he returned to his ship, he found that many Indians had come in their canoes to trade articles of spun cotton, notably the nets in which they slept and which they called "hammocks."

The following day, Martín Alonzo Pinzón showed Columbus two pieces of cinnamon obtained from a local Indian. He also stated that the same Indian carried some "red things," which he thought might be nutmeg. Presently, the Admiral showed some local Indians as small quantity of cinnamon and pepper he had brought from Spain, and they recognized them. They said that there was a great deal of both spices toward the southwest. Then he showed them gold and pearls, and certain old men assured him that in a place they call "Bohio" there was so much gold that people wore it around their necks, in their ears and noses, and on their arms and legs. Columbus decided that if his ambassadors returned from their mission without good news, he would explore the lands to the southeast. In his journal for Sunday, November 4, he wrote:

These people are very meek and shy: naked, as I have said, without weapons, and without government. These lands are very fertile. They are full of niames, which are like carrots and taste like chestnuts. They have beans very different from ours, and a great deal of cotton, which they do not sow and which grows in the mountains to the size of large trees. I believe that they can gather it anytime for I saw pods already open and others just opening, and flowers all on one tree and a thousand other kinds of fruit which I cannot describe, but which should all be very profitable.[6]

At dawn on Monday, November 5, the Admiral ordered the ships to be beached and repaired but specified that two of them should remain in service for security reasons, even though he did not feel in any danger from the Indians. The harbor was clear of rocks and it was an ideal place to careen the ships. The island had good beaches and plenty of wood to heat the tar. Careening consists of exposing the bottom of a ship on dry land, cleaning it of weeds and barnacles, and caulking it and pitching it to protect the hull from being destroyed by the teredo (shipworms), very common in warm waters. As the sailor burned the local wood to heat the tar, they noticed very aromatic fumes. They thought they were from mastic. Columbus reported in his journal that the local forest could easily supply a thousand quintals of this precious gum every year, more than was supplied normally by the island of Chios, including the entire Aegean archipelago. Columbus, who first became familiar with the mastic resin derived from the lentisk shrub at Chios, wrongly identified the Cuban mastic "almaciga" as one and the same.

On the sixth of November, the two ambassadors Columbus had sent into the interior returned and everyone gathered around them. They reported that after going inland for twelve leagues, they came to a town of fifty houses and one thousand inhabitants. The people received them with warmth and admiration and escorted them to a large house for an official reception. Believing the Spaniards were men form heaven, the Indians gazed at them in awe, touching them and kissing their hands and feet. The Indians made them sit down on two chairs of state with four legs, each made from a single piece of wood, gave them fruit, and then squatted on the ground around them. The guide who accompanied the ambassadors told the audience all about the Christians, their manner of living, their power, habits, and their friendly ways. The services of Louis de Torres, the Hebrew interpreter, were not needed because these Indians spoke the same language as the others. When the men left, the women came in and expressed the same curiosity and amazement. They examined the white men's skin, their bearded faces, and clothing, and begged them to stay longer. The women were entirely naked, except for a piece of cotton covering their genitals. The ambassadors showed them the cinnamon and pepper and other spices that the Admiral had given them and the natives told them by signs that many of the items could be found to the southeast and not around their area.

There were no signs of gold or other precious items. More importantly, there were no powerful rulers and no Grand Khan. Disappointed, the men decided to return to their ships. A leading man of the town and his son, attended by a servant, accompanied them. On the way back, the ambassadors met many natives who were going back to their towns and, for the first time, they witnessed the use of tobacco. They saw many of the natives with a firebrand in hand and certain dry weeds rolled up in a tube-like form. They lit one end and put the other in their mouths, inhaling the smoke and blowing it out. The Indians called the rolled weeds "tobacos" (cigars), and the name, erroneously, was applied to the plant. The Spaniards wasted no time in developing the habit of smoking the weeds. Las Casas reported that Spaniards were already smoking tobacco later on in Hispaniola. Columbus did not find gold in Cuba, but in introducing tobacco to the world, he found something of great consequence, albeit in a negative way. The ambassadors gave a favorable account of the beauty and fertility of the land. Columbus commented in his journal that his men had seen:

Many kinds of trees and grasses and fragrant flowers, as well as many different kinds of songbirds. Except for partridge and nightingales,[7] they were unlike those of Spain. And they saw geese,[8] of these there is a very great number here. They saw no four-footed beasts except dogs that do not bark. The land is very fertile and well cultivated with those niames, beans very different from ours, and panic grass.[9] *They saw a great quantity of cotton that had been gathered and spun and worked—in one house alone more than twelve thousand pounds of it. Two hundred tons could be had there each year.*

I have already mentioned that they apparently do not plant this cotton and that it bears fruit all year. It is very fine and has a large pod. All that these people have they will give for a very ridiculous price; they gave one great basket of cotton for the end of a leather strap.[10]

The report of the ambassadors must have been disappointing to Columbus, but he noted that even if gold and pearls were lacking, the land was not without value. He emphasized its fertility, its production of great quantities of cotton, and the gentle nature and generosity of the natives. While these factors are not immediately rewarding to those interested in exploitation, they are important for those who are interested in colonization. Columbus was interested in gold because he wanted to show a quick profit to the Spanish rulers and for that reason he always questioned the Indians about it. On this occasion, the Indians informed him by signs of a place to the southeast called "Bohio," and sometimes "Babeque," where the people gathered gold along the riverbanks by torchlight and afterwards hammered it into bars.

Once the Santa María was cleaned, Columbus made plans to sail on November 8; but strong adverse winds kept the fleet in the harbor of Río de Mares (Puerto Gibara) until November 12. Before leaving the harbor, Columbus detained five natives who had come aboard for a farewell visit and then sent the boat ashore to pick up seven women and three boys. The husbands and fathers of some of the captives came aboard and begged to be taken along to maintain the family unity and this was granted. Columbus desired to take both sexes, having learned from the Portuguese that men were always happier when accompanied by their women. The Indians were imprisoned; the project was to take them to Spain, teach them the Spanish language, and make good Christians out of them. Two of the young men, however, preferred to remain ignorant, jumped ship, and escaped at Tanamo Bay; the others were not so lucky. They did not survive the trip to Spain.

At dawn on Monday, November 12, the fleet finally left Río de Mares to visit the island of Babeque. Columbus set his course E ½ NE by S. After sailing eight leagues along the coast, he saw a bay, then another one after sailing four leagues. He decided not to stop because they did not look deep enough for his ships and also because the wind was favorable for Babeque. He reasoned that if any populous cities existed on the bays, they would be visible to him. By sunset the fleet had hardly traveled eighteen leagues, reaching a cape that Columbus named "Cabo de Cuba" because he thought it was the easternmost point of the island. All night he held his position off the cape; by daylight he headed toward the land, but a strong north wind came up, threatening to fling the ships onto the lee shore. Immediately the Admiral ordered a due east course for Babeque, but on the fourteenth a head wind and rough seas forced him back to Cuba after he had sailed almost halfway to Babeque. He found a secure haven in a deep harbor that was studded with many islands. He named the bay "La Mar de Nuestra Señora" (Bahía Tanamo), and the harbor near the mouth of the entrance "Puerto del Principe." Columbus noted that these islands may well have been the "…innumerable ones that are found on world maps at the end of the Far East, and I think there are immense riches and precious stones and spiceries in them."[11] This may be another indication that Columbus might have seen the terrestrial globe of Behaim, made at Nuremberg in 1492, in which the western segment of the globe is dotted with many islands at that location.

Columbus remained five days in Tanamo Bay, cruising around the islands in a boat, examining the flora and fauna and even erecting a huge cross on a nearby hill. The most interesting of the flora observed was a type of coconut that was not the coconut we know today but a smaller version of a different species, formerly very abundant in Cuba. Of the fauna, he found "great rats," large native rodents known as "hutia," still hunted and eaten in the Oriente Province.

The fleet departed Tanamo Bay on Monday, November 19, before sunrise with a light land breeze; and at midday the trade wind blew due E and the fleet sailed to the NNE in the direction of Isabela from which it had come to Cuba. It sailed all night and made only eighteen leagues by midday Tuesday. By nightfall on the twentieth it reached the vicinity of Puerto del Principe, but the ships could not reach it because it was night and the currents pushed them to the NW. The wind moderated and changed by 3:00 a.m. of the twenty-first.

At sunrise, the ships sailed to the E with the wind S and made little progress because of heavy seas until vespers (about 3:00 p.m.) they had progressed only eighteen miles to the eastward. The wind then backed to the E, forcing the fleets S by E. Thus, it had to beat about for three days between Isabela and Puerto del Principe, because of the vagaries of the wind.

At the third watch (between 3:00 and 7:00 a.m.), the wind began to blow NNW as the fleet headed to the S to reach land. Martín Alonzo Pinzón, however, did not follow Columbus.

Instead, he steered his Pinta due east to go to the island of Babeque, where the Indians had said that there was much gold. The Pinta, being a faster sailer than the Santa María, drew farther and farther away until it had vanished from the Admiral's sight by the end of the day. As night fell, Columbus slowed down his two ships and lit a lamp in the hope that Pinzón would return. Columbus wrote the following in his journal:

This day Martín Alonso Pinzón sailed away with the caraval Pinta, without my will or command. It was through perfidy. I think he believes that an Indian I had placed on the Pinta could lead him to much gold, so he departed without waiting and without the excuse of bad weather, but because he wished to do so. He has done and said many other things to me.[12]

Columbus had spoken well of Martín Alonzo Pinzón on the way to the Canaries when the Pinta's rudder was repaired, but their relationship had gradually deteriorated during the ocean-crossing to open dissension before the landfall on San Salvador. Columbus's fleet had in great measure been manned with competent personnel through Pinzón's influence and exertions. It was for these reasons that Pinzón did not relish the role of a subordinate, nor accepted the fact that he had to follow the slow-moving flagship at every turn. When he saw Columbus heading for Cuba again, looking for shelter, he was confident that the Pinta—a superior sailer to the Santa María—would overcome the heavy swells and safely reach Babeque. But greed and the quest for the much-touted gold was the primary reason for his deserting the fleet.

Columbus continued sailing all day Friday the twenty-third, without sight of the Pinta, and on Saturday the twenty-fourth at 9:00 a.m., the two ships were back in Cuba at the flat island of Cayo Moa Grande. The ships did not enter the harbor until three days later when the wind had finally calmed down. They sailed into a bay so large that it could safely hold all the ships of Spain without cables. The Admiral then went up to Río Mao in a boat and noticed on its bed and banks stones the color of iron, others associated with silver and iron pyrites, the fools' gold. He also saw many huge pine trees, very straight and very tall, suitable for ships' masts. The Admiral ordered sailors to cut a mizzenmast and a yard for the Niña.

On November 26, they weighed anchor from Puerto Cayo Moa and headed SE along the Cuban coast, encountering many capes and bays, the most prominent of which Columbus named "Cabo de Campana" (Cape Bell). Continuing SE along the coast twenty Roman miles away, he found a big village and saw many people come to the shore, shouting loudly, all naked with their darts in hand. When Columbus decided to speak to the hostile Indians, all the Indians aboard began to shake with fear and went to hide below the hatches. As three Spaniards headed for shore in a boat, the Indians adopted a defensive posture; but when they noticed that the Spaniards were unafraid, they took flight. The three Spaniards looked inside some houses; and when they saw that they were similar to houses they had already seen, they returned to their vessel.

At noon on November 27, the two vessels resumed their cruise and after sailing only two miles SE along the coast they came to another beautiful harbor that the Admiral named "Puerto Santo" (Puerto Baracoa), surrounded by open country and big villages. Columbus entered the harbor and described it as being round like a little porringer. He decided to fathom the harbor. As he went along in a boat, he was struck by the unspoiled beauty of the country—the tall, symmetrical trees, the abundant verdure, the crystal-clear water, and the fragrance of the air. He told the men in his company that a thousand tongues would not suffice to give an account to the Sovereigns of the things they saw. In his journal, he elaborated on his impression and on the value of his discoveries:

I do not need to write how great the benefits will be from here. It is certain, Lords and Princes, that where there are such lands there must be an infinite quantity of profitable things. But I do not linger in any harbor because I want to see as many lands as I can, in order to tell Your Highnesses about them. Also, I do not know the language and the people of these lands do not understand me, nor do I or any other person I have with me understand them. And these Indians I am taking with me misunderstand things many times; besides, I do not trust them very because they have attempted to escape several times. But now, Our Lord willing, I shall see all I can and little by little I will investigate and learn, and will have this language taught to persons of my house because I see that the language is all one up to this time. Then the benefits will be known, and one will labor to make all these people Christian, since it can easily be done. They have no sect nor are they idolaters; Your Highnesses will order a city and fortresses built in these regions, and these countries will be converted. And I certify to Your Highnesses that it does not seem to me that there can be more fertile countries under the sun, or any more temperature in heat and cold, with a greater abundance of good pure water—unlike those rivers of Guinea, which are all pestilent. Praise be to Our Lord, so far there has not been a single one of my people who has had a headache or who has been in bed because of sickness, except for one old man through pain from kidney stones, from which he has suffered all his life and even he became well at the end of two days. I say this in regard to all three ships. So may it please God and Your Highnesses may send learned men here, or that they shall come and they will see that everything I say is true.

I have already spoken of a village site or fortress on the Río de Mares, on account of the good harbor and the surrounding territory, and it is certain that all I have said is true, but there is no comparison between that place and this, neither with La Mar de Nuestra Señora. Here there must be large villages and a dense population inland and things of great profit for here, and in all the other lands I have discovered or hope to discover before I return to Castile, I say that Christendom will enter into negotiations, but most of all with Spain, to which all these lands should be subject. And I say that Your Highnesses must not allow any foreigner to set foot here or trade except Catholic Christians, since it was the beginning and the end of this enterprise that it should be for the increase and the glory of the Christian religion. No one should come to these regions who is not a good Christian.[13]

Bad weather kept the Santa María and the Niña in the Puerto Baracoa a whole week. This gave the crews an opportunity to explore the region and go ashore to wash clothes. The exploration of the interior revealed that the land was well cultivated with yams, maize, and pumpkins. The natives had huge dugout canoes moored under boathouses; one was over seventy feet long and big enough to accommodate 150 people.

On November 29, while exploring the countryside, members of the crew stopped at a village deserted except for an old man who had not been able to flee. They found in one house a cake of wax that when brought to Columbus's attention prompted him to say with assurance "...that where wax was found there should also be a thousand other good things."[14] Actually, Las Casas was of the opinion that no wax existed in Cuba—that what was found probably had come from the Yucatan. They also found a man's skull in a basket hanging from a post in another house, which Columbus interpreted as belonging to a family ancestor.

On Monday, December 3, the weather was still unfavorable, so Columbus with some of his armed men took some boats to explore to the southeast; at the foot of a cape he found a lovely bay, which he entered. He went ashore and climbed a mountain to look down on a valley where he saw extensive cultivations and a village. Columbus and his men came upon the natives suddenly, startling them and causing them to take flight. But the Indian guide coaxed them to stay, reassuring them that the visitors were decent people, not to be feared. Columbus ordered that they be given hawks' bells, brass rings, and green and yellow brass beads with which they were well pleased. Seeing that they had no gold nor other precious things, Columbus went back to where they had left their boats, then sent some crewmen to a place where he thought he had seen a great apiary. Before they were able to get back, many ill-intentioned Indians gathered and approached the boats where Columbus and his men were assembled. But the Admiral, who had previously noted with some amazement the Indians' meekness and fearfulness, and who claimed that ten armed Spaniards would rout ten thousand Indians, was not very impressed with their hostile posture. The situation was defused by the Indian guide who spoke of the Spaniards' mighty weapons and then by Columbus's amiable offering of the usual trinkets. The Admiral noted in his journal the great naiveté of the Indians, which allowed them to trade their spears for pieces of a shell. With a tinge of admiration for their innocence, Columbus wrote:

They believe that we come from heaven, and whatever they have they trade for whatever is offered them, without ever saying it is little. I believe they would do the same thing with spices and gold if they had them.[15]

On Tuesday, December 4, with the help of a light wind, Columbus left the harbor he called "Puerto Santo" and sailed along the coast past "Cabo Lindo" (presently, Punta del Fraile), east by south of "Cabo del Monte" (Punta Rama), after which there is a great bay, the Windward Passage. That night he spent at anchor off Cabo Lindo, the northern bulge of Cape Maisi. At sunrise on the fifth, the point of Cap Maisi was in view. From this cape, Cuba begins its trend southwest. On his second voyage, on April 29, 1494, Columbus named Cape Maisi "Cabo Alfa y Omega" (Cape Alpha and Omega) because he had decided that Cuba was not an island but a promontory of China and that this cape was the beginning of the East and the end of the West on the Eurasian continent. Thus, it was possible for someone who started walking westward from this point to eventually reach Cape St. Vincent in Portugal!

Chapter Eighteen

HISPANIOLA

On Wednesday, December 5, Columbus left Cuba with the intention of going to Babeque, but the wind that arose was NE. Accordingly, he changed his mind and headed SE by E in the direction of Bohio (Hispaniola), which could be seen in the distance. By sunset he had crossed the Windward Passage and reached the northern coast of the island within sight of a cape and harbor. His fleet lay at anchor all night off the coast and at dawn, on December 6, Columbus found himself four leagues from the harbor, which he first named "Puerto Maria" and later "Puerto de San Nicolao" because it was the feast of Sant Nicholas.

At the hour of vespers, he entered the harbor after some difficulty, as the wind was light. He was immediately struck by its beauty, which he said surpassed even the harbors he had seen in Cuba. It was spacious and very deep, surrounded by many trees loaded with fruit. Facing the harbor was a beautiful plain crossed by a river that spilled its clear waters into the bay. All the Indians of the villages in the plain ran away when they saw the ships.

When the dawn watch (7:00 a.m.) was relieved on Friday, December 7, the Santa María and the Niña left the harbor of

Saint Nicholas, rounded Cape Saint Nicholas Mole (present name) with a SW wind, and followed the north coast eastward, anchoring at 1:00 p.m. in a harbor Columbus named "Puerto de la Concepción," because it was the eve of the Conception of the Virgin Mother. Today it is called Moustique Bay. They went ashore and cast their nets and caught fish resembling the mullet and sole of Spain. They went a short distance into the country, which was all cultivated and "heard nightingales sing and other small birds like those of Castile."[1] The rain detained them for several days, thus allowing them an opportunity to explore the island.

On the twelfth of December, Columbus, with great solemnity, erected a cross at the entrance of the harbor and took formal possession of Hispaniola for Ferdinand and Isabella. On the same day, three sailors on a tour of exploration saw a large number of natives, who immediately took flight, but the sailors pursued them and captured a very young and beautiful girl whom they brought to the Admiral. She was completely naked except for a gold ring on her nose. Columbus assuaged her fears and ordered that she be appropriately dressed (with a sailor's shirt, no doubt) and gave her glass beads, hawks' bells, and brass rings and sent her back to land, as a potential lure to the natives, accompanied by some sailors and three of the captured Indians.

The men sent with her returned late that night to the ship without having ventured to her village, either because it was too far or because they were afraid. The following day Columbus, who was anxious to know more about the island from the natives, sent nine armed sailors with an Indian interpreter to the village, which was approximately four and a half leagues to the southeast. In a beautiful valley situated on the banks of a river (possibly the Trois Rivieres, which empties into the ocean half a mile west of Port de Paix), they found the village. It was a very large village of one thousand houses and more than three thousand men who, upon seeing the visitors, immediately took flight. The Indian guide ran after them, reassuring them that the Spaniards were not from Carriba but from heaven and that they gave many fine things to all those whom they met. Their fears allayed, at least two thousand of the natives came back and, as a sign of respect and reverence, placed their trembling hands on sailors' heads. Afterwards, the natives invited the Spaniards into their houses and offered them bread and "niamas" (sweet potatoes), fish, and fruits. And as the Admiral had expressed to the Indian guide a desire to have a parrot, they brought out as many parrots as were wanted. Soon, another large group approached, led by the husband of the young girl released the previous day. They brought her in triumph on their shoulders, and the husband gave things to the Christians for the kindness with which they had treated her and the magnificent gifts that they had given her.

His men also reported to the Admiral that the natives were more handsome and of better character than any of the others whom they had seen up to that time. As for their appearance, these were lighter in color. Two young women the men reported were as white as any in Spain. They also gave a glowing account of the beauty of the land, saying that all the fields were neatly cultivated, all the trees green and full of fruit, and that the air was like April in Castile.

According to these accounts of the first white visitors to the new continent, the people of Haiti in their primitive simplicity lived truly in an earthly paradise. The fertile earth provided them with plenty of food. Fish was abundant in their rivers and seacoast. Honesty and hospitality was a way of life with them, and hostility among them did not exist.

Ironically, it was their gentle nature and their simplicity that caused their undoing. The people of Hispaniola as well as the entire Caribbean were easily conquered and rapidly exterminated. The natives could not stand the hard work imposed on them by their Spanish conquerors who began the importation of African slaves to replace them. It is a sad commentary on western civilization that the entire native population of the Antilles was extinct by 1550.

VALLEY OF PARADISE—THE ROYAL VISITORS

On the fourteenth day of December, when the weather seemed favorable due to a land breeze, Columbus made another attempt to reach the island of Babeque but was again stalemated by lack of wind. Afterwards an east wind sprang up and he steered to the NNE, reaching an island he named Tortuga because of the many turtles he found there and because of its shape. This island, in the 1600s, was to become the base from which French pirates carried on their clandestine activities. Because the wind was still contrary for the course to Babeque, they returned that night to Moustique Bay.

The following day, they left the bay and tacked their way eastward in the Tortuga Channel to the mouth of a clear river today named Trois Rivieres, but which the Admiral named "Guadalquivir" because it reminded him of the river in Andalusia that flows through Córdoba and Seville. This river valley was one of the loveliest Columbus had ever seen and he named it appropriately, "Valle del Paraiso" (Valley of Paradise). He moored his ship and in a boat attempted to sail up the river, but was prevented from going too far by its current and shallow depth. In order to catch a land breeze, Columbus sailed away from the Valle del Paraiso at midnight, hoping to get through the Tortuga Channel before the onset of the trade wind. At the hour of tierce (9:00 a.m.), the wind began to blow from the east and, while tacking in the mid-channel, the fleet met a canoe with a solitary Indian in it, having a rough time in the turbulent sea. Columbus had him and his canoe taken aboard the ship and presented him with the usual gifts of glass beads, hawks' bells, and brass rings. He then set him ashore sixteen miles from where he had been picked up, at a village that appeared to have been recently established, as all the houses were new. The village probably stood on the present site of Port-de-Paix. As anticipated by Columbus, the Indian spread the news that the foreigners were not to be feared because they were good people. Apparently, word had already reached them that the Christians could be trusted. About five hundred people came down to the beach, soon to be followed by their leader, a subordinate to Cacique Guacanagari, ruler of that part of the island. He was a handsome youth of about twenty-one to whom all Indians showed great respect and reverence. Because many Indians of the village wore gold ornaments, they were asked where the gold came from; they answered by signs that there was much of it further south. The leader came aboard that evening and Columbus treated him with the respect due to a royal personage and offered him Castilian food to eat. He ate some of it but passed the remainder to some of his counselors who had come aboard with him.

The next day, on December 17, Columbus received visitors from two different quarters: the Cacique of that province with his retinue and forty Indians from Tortuga. While the Cacique was on the beach with his people trading away a large piece of gold leaf, bit by bit, Columbus saw the Indians from Tortuga approaching in their canoe, and began throwing pebbles in the water. Columbus ordered them back with threatening words.

The following day, Tuesday, December 18, was the Feast of the Annunciation, and Columbus decorated his two ships to celebrate the event. The sailors displayed banners and fired the lombards. Amid these celebrations there appeared at the hour of tierce a pagan procession. The Cacique with more than two hundred attendants, borne on a litter by four men, was heading toward the beach. The Admiral's account of this state visit and the Cacique's demeanor is vividly told by Las Casas:

The Cacique of the Isla Española had arisen early, for his house must be four or five miles from here, as best as I can judge, and he reached the village by nine o'clock in the morning. Some of my men were already in the village by then to see if any gold was brought. More than two hundred men came with the Cacique and four men carried him on a litter. The Cacique arrived while I was eating below the sterncastle. Without doubt his demeanor and the respect which they all showed for him would appeal to Your Highnesses, even though they are naked. As he entered the ship, he saw that I was eating and came quickly, to seat himself beside me, but he would not allow me to rise or interrupt my meal. I thought he might like to eat some of our food, so I ordered that something be brought for him.

When he entered under the sterncastle he signed with his hand that his entourage should stay outside, and they did so with all haste and respect, seating themselves on the deck, except for two mature men whom I took to be his counselors and governors, who seated themselves at his feet. Of the food I placed before him, he took a little of each thing as a salutation and then sent the rest to his people. They all ate some of it. He did the same thing with the drink, which he only touched to his mouth. He gave it to the others in the same manner; it was all done in a ceremonial style, with a very few words. Whatever he said, according to my understanding, was very formal and prudent, and the two with him spoke with him and for him with great respect.

After the meal, a servant brought a belt, shaped like those in Castile but made differently. He gave this to me, along with two very thin wrought pieces of gold. I believe that they get very little of this here, but I also believe that we are very near the place it comes from and that there is a great deal of it there. I saw that a cover on my bed pleased him, so I presented it to him, along with some very good amber beads that I wore around my neck. I also gave him some red shoes and a flask of orange flower water. This pleased him wonderfully. He and his governors and counselors were very sorry that they could not understand me, nor I them. Nevertheless, I understood he told me that if anything here would please me, the whole island was at my command. I sent for some beads of mine, on which, as a pendant, I have a gold coin with the images of Your Highnesses engraved on it, and showed it to him. I again told him that Your Highnesses command and rule over the best part of the world and that there are no other such great Princes. I also showed him the royal banners and the other banners that have a cross on them, which he admired greatly. He told his counselors that Your Highnesses must be great Lords, since you sent me here from so far without fear. And many other things were said that I did not understand, except that I very well saw that everything was wonderful.

Since it was getting late and he wished to leave, I sent him ashore in the boat with great honors and fired a salute with the cannons. When he reached land, he got into his litter and went away with his two hundred men and more, and his son was carried behind him on the shoulders of an Indian, a very honorable man. After that, whenever the Cacique encountered the sailors from the ships, he ordered that something to eat should be given to them and that they should be shown a great deal of honor. One sailor said that he had met the Cacique returning from the ship and had seen all the things I had given him. Each item was carried before the Cacique by one of his most important aides. His son was following behind the Cacique at some distance with the large number of people in the entourage and likewise a brother of the Cacique, except that the brother was on foot and two of the principal men were leading him by the arms. This brother had come to the ship after the Cacique and I had given him some things from the same articles of barter. It was then that I learned that the king, in their language, is called Cacique.

Today I traded for only a small quantity of gold, but I learned from an old man that there were many islands in the vicinity at a distance of three hundred miles or more, according to what I was able to make out, in which a lot of gold is found. I was told that on some of these islands there is so much gold that the whole island is gold. On others they gather it and sift it with sieves and melt it to make bars, and work it in a thousand ways. I was shown by signs how this is done. The old man indicated to me the course to take to get to those islands and the place where they may be found. I decided to go there, and if the old man had not been one of the principal persons belonging to the king, I would have taken him along. If I had known the language I would have begged him to accompany me, and I believe that we are on such good terms that he would have gone along of his own free will. But since I already consider that these people belong to the Sovereigns of Castile, it is not right to offend them. So, I decided to leave him alone. I placed a very large cross in the center of the plaza of that village and the Indians assisted me greatly in this work. They said prayers and worshipped it, and from their actions, I trust in the Lord that these islands are to be Christianized.[2]

ACUL BAY—THE WORLD'S LOVELIEST HARBOR

On the nineteenth day of December, Columbus made sail at night with the land breeze; but with the coming of dawn, the wind turned east and he could not get out of the Tortuga Channel—neither could he find a harbor for refuge. Therefore, from mid-channel eastward, he passed four capes that jutted out of the coast, some of the most prominent of which he called "Cabo Alto y Baxo" (Cape High-Low), possibly the Pointe Limbé of today. Further east, he saw Le Morne du Cap of the mountain range of Cape Haitien that he named "Monte Caribata." At sunset of the twentieth of December the fleet finally entered a harbor that was located immediately east of Cabo Alto y Baxo between the little island of St. Thomas and the Cape of Caribata. The following day, he went with the ships' boats to view the harbor and was convinced that this harbor surpassed all the other harbors he had ever seen. He stated:

I have been sailing the seas for twenty-three years, without laying off any time long enough to be counted, and I have seen all East and West (as it is called in going to the north, which is England), and I have traveled through Guinea, but in all regions, harbors as perfect as these will never be found. And it has been the case that each harbor I have come to has been better than the last one. I have considered what I have written very carefully, and I assert I have written correctly and now this harbor surpasses all the others.

All the ships of the world could be contained in it and it is so sheltered that the oldest line on the ship would hold it fast.³

Columbus gave this bay the name "Puerto de la Mar de Santo Tornás" because when they entered it was the eve of the Feast of St. Thomas the Apostle. It is now called Acul Bay, and is regarded as one of the world's loveliest harbors.

The next morning, December 21, Columbus began to explore the harbor with his boats. He ordered two men to land and climb a hill to see if there might be any towns, for he had noticed that most towns were not visible from the seashore but purposely built out of sight for protection from marauders. The men reported that a large village was situated not too far from the sea. Columbus ordered the men to row in the direction of the village until they came close to shore, where they saw a large crowd of men, women, and children on the shore. Columbus was amazed at the generosity of the natives who promptly brought the visitors bread made of cassava and water in gourds and clay pitchers. He also noticed that they were unarmed and naked:

These people have no spears, arrows, or any other arms, nor have the other inhabitants of this island, which I believe to be very large. They are as naked as their mothers gave them birth, men as well as women—unlike people of Juana and the other islands, where the women wore in front pieces of cotton, something like men's drawers, with which they covered their private parts, especially after the age of twelve. But here neither young nor old wore anything. In the other places we have been, the men made the women hide from us, through jealousy, but here they do not, and there are some very pretty women. They were the first who came to give thanks to Heaven and bring whatever they had, especially things to eat such as bread made from ajes, peanuts, and five or six kinds of fruit. I ordered some of the fruit preserved in order to take to the Sovereigns. The women in the other places did the same thing before the men concealed them.[4]

What a blissful paradise for love-starved sailors; pretty, naked Haitians and in no way inhibited! Columbus sent six men to look at the Indian village; during their absence, he received envoys from chiefs of other local villages on the bay inviting him to visit them, something he did with pleasure. The Indians received him with generosity everywhere he went.

At dawn on the following day, December 22, the two ships sailed out of the bay with the land breeze; they were just outside of Acul Bay when contrary winds (those easterlies again) forced them to return and anchor near the mouth of the bay. While tarrying there, Columbus received an invitation to call from Guacanagari, the most powerful Cacique of the northwest area of Haiti. As an enticement, the messengers brought a remarkable belt of white and colored fishbones, sewed in a pattern like embroidery, and to which was attached a mask with ears, tongue, and nose of solid gold. Columbus accepted the invitation as the Cacique's village was only on the other side of Cape Haitien. In the next two days and nights in which they could not get any sleep, Columbus stated that over a thousand Indians boarded the Santa María from canoes to bring gifts and that five hundred more swam to the ship even though she was anchored almost a league from shore. Columbus was now eager to leave for he had received reports about a place called Cibao in central Hispaniola where much gold could be found. Once again allowing for variations in pronunciation, "Cibao" was close enough to "Cipango" so that Columbus had visions of Japan with its roofs of gold.

Chapter Nineteen

SHIPWRECK—LA NAVIDAD

On December 24, before sunrise, Columbus set sail from Acul Bay. Aided by a land breeze, he steered eastward along the Haitian coast to reach the harbor of Cacique Guacanagari; it lay about three miles southeast of Cape Haitien, near the present Fort Libertè Bay. It was to have been a short trip, but the wind became so light soon after they left the bay that it could hardly fill the sails. They rounded Point Picolet, the promontory of Cape Haiten (Columbus named it "Cabo Santo" because it was Christmas Eve), and by tacking proceeded slowly, reaching Cape Haitien Bay at eleven o'clock at night. Despite the fact that they were only a few miles from the town of Guacanagari, Columbus, finding his ships almost motionless and the sea dead calm, decided to spend Christmas Eve off Cape Haitien Bay. Completely exhausted by the previous night's activities in Acul Bay, Columbus and his men retired for the night.

As a general rule, Columbus was always extremely watchful on his coasting voyages; and when the situation warranted it, he personally spent the night on deck to ensure the safety of his ship. On this particular night, he felt secure because the area had already been reconnoitered and found safe. Additionally, the sea was calm—a perfect situation for getting some sleep. Juan de la Cosa, the master of the ship, and the rest of the crew with the exception of the helmsman also retired for the night. As midnight approached the helmsman awakened the grommet, whose duty it was to turn the "ampolleta" (sandglass) as soon as the sand ran out. Then he made the fatal error of putting him in charge of the tiller, for he too found a suitable opportunity to catch some sleep. It was just seconds after the sand had run out of the top bulb, indicating the start of another day, that the Santa María gently floated into a coral reef of Caracol Bay. The boy felt the rudder scrape the reef and on hearing the sound shouted for help. Columbus, always a light sleeper, was the first on deck. Soon the master of the ship, whose duty it was to be on watch, appeared, as did all the men who began scurrying about in utter confusion. Columbus rose to the situation and, noticing that the ship had grounded bow on, with the stern drawing more water aft, immediately ordered Juan de la Cosa, who was part owner of the ship, to launch the ship's boat with an anchor and drop it out astern so as to lift the bow clear of the reef. However, instead of complying with the Admiral's orders, de la Cosa, with some of his friends aboard, thought more of saving themselves from a shipwreck and rowed toward the Niña, which lay about half a league windward. Vincente Yañez Pinzón, captain of the Niña, had already sent a boat full of his crew to aid Columbus and was surprised to see the cowardly sailors abandoning the foundering Santa María. He would not allow them aboard and ordered them to row back to their ship. In the meantime, the plight of the Santa María became more desperate as each swell of the sea lifted her up and then dashed her down on the reef, opening seams in her hull.

    Columbus ordered the heavy mainmast to be cut down in order to lighten her, but the ship had already suffered irreparable damage, and there was not much more they could do except to abandon her on the reef, transfer the crew to the Niña, and stand by for daylight to conduct salvage operations.

At daybreak on Christmas Day, Columbus sent ashore the Sovereigns' representative, Pedro Gutierrez, Butler of the Royal Household, and Diego de Harana, Marshal of the Fleet, to inform Cacique Guacanagari of his visit and of what had happened. When he heard the distressing news, he immediately sent all of his subjects with large canoes to help unload the stricken Santa María. So active and cooperative were they in their assistance that the whole task was completed before sunset on Christmas Day. Moreover, they saw to it that none of the salvaged goods was damaged or stolen. All the items were deposited near his palace, and armed guards kept watch until they could be safely stored in houses he provided. Concerned about the Admiral's wellbeing, the Cacique at various times in the course of the day sent one of his relatives, weeping, to console Columbus and to tell him not to worry about the loss of the ship. Deeply moved by the Cacique's affection and concern, Columbus wrote in his journal that these Indians:

Are an affectionate people, free from avarice and agreeable to everything. I certify to Your Highnesses that in all the world I do not believe there is a better people or a better country. They love their neighbors as themselves and they have the softest and gentlest voices in the world and are always smiling.... The King maintains a most marvelous state, where everything takes place in an appropriate and well-ordered manner.[1]

At sunrise the following day, Guacanagari came onboard the Niña to comfort the Admiral and to offer all assistance in his power. He told him that he had given the Christians who were ashore two very big houses and would give more if necessary. During their conversation, a canoe with Indians arrived from another place, bringing pieces of gold leaf to exchange for much-prized hawks' bells. Sailors also reported that other Indians in the village had bartered gold for hawks' bells, lace points, and other trifles. The king was delighted to see that Columbus was pleased by the sight of gold. Guacanagari told him that he knew where much of it could be found and if the yellow metal made him happy, he would give him as much as he desired. He said further that in Cipango, which they call "Cibao," they have it in such large quantities that they regard it with indifference. Moreover, that much more could be obtained on the island of Hispaniola, which they call Bohio, in Caribata province.

The Cacique dined onboard the Niña and the Admiral afterwards went ashore with him to visit his residence. Columbus reported:

He paid me great honor. Later we had a meal with two or three kinds of ajes, served with shrimp, game, and other foods they have, including their bread, which they call cazabe. Then the King took me to see some groves of trees near the houses, and fully one thousand people, all naked, went with us. The King was already wearing a shirt and a pair of gloves which I had given him and he was more excited about the gloves than anything else that had been given him.[2]

When the Indians had finished, Columbus ordered one of his men, who had served in the war against Granada, to give an exhibition of shooting with bow and arrows. The Cacique was amazed at the accuracy and skill of the Castilian. He also told Columbus that the Caribs, who made raids upon his territory and carried off his subjects, also used bows and arrows; the arrows, however, were not made of steel, unknown to the Indians, who were familiar only with gold and copper. The Admiral assured him that the Sovereigns of Castile would order the destruction of the Caribs. He then ordered a sailor to fire a Lombard and an arquebus. On hearing the loud report, the Indians fell to the ground as though they had been struck by a thunderbolt; when they saw the piercing effect of the balls, they were filled with wonder and dismay. Columbus assured them that the Spaniards would protect them against the fierce Caribs. This was the first demonstration of power of the Europeans, a power that was used to carve empires and to exploit defenseless peoples.

The kindness of the ruler was displayed again when he presented the Admiral with a large mask, which had large pieces of gold in the ears, eyes, and other places.

He placed this, along with other jewels of gold, on my head and around my neck. They also gave many things to the men with me. I derived a great deal of pleasure and consolation from these things, and when I realized that this mitigated the trouble and affliction I had experienced by losing the ship, I recognized that Our Lord had caused me to run aground at this place so that I might establish a settlement here. And so many things came to hand here that the disaster was a blessing in disguise. Certainly, if I had not run aground here, I would have kept out to sea without anchoring at this place because it is situated inside a large bay containing two or three banks of shoals. Neither would I have left any of my people here on this voyage; even if I had desired to leave them, I could not have outfitted them well enough nor given then enough ammunition provisions and material for a fort.[3]

The friendship of the natives and the provisions and supplies and the materials to build a fort were available to him now that the ship had been salvaged. Its lumber, armor, guns, and fittings would all be used to build the fort. Because it would have been impossible for all hands to return to Spain on the relatively small Niña, the crew of the Santa María, as well as other sailors who were eager to remain, would have the task of building and guarding the fort until Columbus returned.

LA NAVIDAD

Building a fort was a perfect solution to his problems. Columbus had most of the important materials: the Santa María's planks, timbers and fittings, guns and ammunition, and victuals to last a whole year. Such a fort, built in friendly territory, could actually become the nucleus of a future colony. The location was not the best because of reefs in the harbor, but it would do fine as a start. The neighbors were friendly and, in an emergency, could be depended upon as allies. The garrison could explore the area and determine locations of gold mines, as well as barter for gold with the natives. Most importantly, the sailors who remained could learn the natives' language and customs to facilitate future dealings. Columbus had no problem getting men to stay behind. Lured by the hope of finding gold, many of them actually volunteered. Columbus selected thirty-nine of the most able men, making certain that those who remained had different disciplines—among them two surgeons, a ship's carpenter, caulker, cooper, tailor, and men of arms. The command was given to Diego de Harana, Marshal of the Fleet. Second in command was Pedro Gutierrez; and third, Rodriguez de Escobedo. Louis de Torres, the interpreter, was also chosen to study the language of the Indians.

The fortress was completed in ten days, for the Spaniards received a great deal of assistance from the Indians. They built a large vault and over it they erected a sturdy wooden tower. They dug a wide ditch or moat around the fortress, mounted guns, and provided quarters for the men and storage space for supplies.

On the twenty-seventh, in the midst of these activities, some Indians reported that the Pinta was lying in a river two days' sail to the east. At the Admiral's request, Guacanagari immediately sent a canoe to make contact with the caravel and a seaman carrying a letter to Martín Alonso Pinzón, requesting that he return and join his old sea mates. Three days later the messengers returned without having contacted the Pinta.

As the time of departure drew near, Columbus assembled those men who were to stay in La Navidad for last-minute instructions. He stressed the importance of maintaining respect for Guacanagari and his chieftains for their assistance during the shipwreck and the building of the fort. Above all, he told them not to take advantage of the simple and unsuspecting natives, to treat them with kindness and to avoid disputes. He further pleaded with them not to use violence towards the women, causing scandals and destroying the image the Indians had of them as heavenly creatures. Lastly, he warned his men to respect the authority of the appointed leaders as they represented the vessel authority of the Sovereigns of Castile.

MEETING WITH PINZÓN

At sunrise on January the fourth, Columbus weighed anchor and with a light breeze from La Navidad set off for Spain. With only one ship at his disposal, he could not chance any further exploration. Furthermore, there was always the possibility that Martín Alonso Pinzón might get back to Castile before him. He had a boat tow the caravel out of the harbor and clear of the reefs:

I sailed to the east toward a very high mountain that looks like an island but is not. It is connected to the land by a low isthmus and is shaped like a very beautiful tent. I named this mountain Monte Cristi and it is exactly east of Cabo Santo at a distance of about twenty-four miles.[4]

A light wind prevented the Niña from reaching Monte Cristi that day, and the ship remained for two days in a large bay between Monte Cristi and Isla Cabra. On the sixth, they sailed with a land breeze and had advanced about ten leagues when at noontime the trade wind came up, forcing the Niña near some shoals. At this time, a sailor on the lookout shouted that he could see the Pinta in the distance moving towards them. Unable to anchor where he was, Columbus sailed back to Isla Cabra and waited for the Pinta. Pinzón came aboard the Niña and attempted to excuse his desertion, alleging that he had been separated from the fleet by adverse weather conditions and had tried ever since to rejoin the Admiral. Although Columbus was not fooled by Pinzón's explanations, he chose to ignore his desertion at least for the time being. The thought of sailing alone with the Niña was not very reassuring for Columbus. The Genoese, however, knew precisely why Pinzón had deserted him. One of the Indians aboard the Pinta had told Martín Alsonso about a region to the east where much gold could be found. Taking advantage of the superior sailing of this vessel, he had managed to push to windward, when the Santa María and the

Niña had been forced to turn back. He had sailed to Babeque and to Hispaniola east of La Navidad, where in three weeks' time he managed to collect a considerable amount of gold by trading with the natives. He kept half of the total and distributed the other half to his crew.

As a result of this incident, Columbus had lost complete confidence in the Pinzón brothers. Although he wanted to continue his explorations of the Isla Española, he felt insecure about his command. The two Pinzóns and their followers did not obey Columbus's commands and he decided to return to Spain, postponing a showdown. In the journal on January 8, the Admiral stated:

On account of this, in order to escape such bad company, which I have to ignore, I have decided to return with the greatest possible haste and not to stop longer. Although there are many disobedient people among the crew, there are also many good men. Now is not the time to think about their punishment.[5]

The following day, he began to get his ship ready by pumping out water that the caravel had taken in and caulking all seams. Some of the seamen went ashore to cut wood that would be used aboard for fuel.

At midday, the sailors went looking for water with the ship's boat in a river that is about one league SSW of Monte Cristi. They filled several barrels from the boat; upon returning to the caravel, they found bits of gold stuck to the barrel hoops, prompting the Admiral to name the river "Río de Oro." It is at present called the Santiago.

At midnight on January 9, Columbus set sail with the wind southeast and steered to the east-northeast, reaching a point he called "Punta Roja" (the present Punta Rucia), which he claimed was about sixty Roman miles due east of Monte Cristi. He dropped anchor in the shelter of the point three hours before nightfall because there were many reefs. Still smarting from the Martín Alonso incident, Columbus reported in this day's journal:

Tonight in the name of Our Lord, I will start on my journey without further delay for any reason, since I have found what I have sought. Also, I do not wish to have more trouble with Martín Alonso until Your Highnesses learn the news of this voyage and what he has done. Then I will not suffer from the evil actions of persons without virtue.[6]

On Thursday, January 10, they left the place off Punta Roja and at sunset had reached a river three leagues to the southeast that Columbus named "Río de Gracia." This was the place where Martín Pinzón had been trading and it long continued to be known as the "River of Martín Alonso." The natives of this locality complained that on his previous visit Martín Alonso had carried off four men and two girls. The Admiral discovered that they were being held aboard the Pinta and ordered their immediate release with presents and clothing. This gesture did not rest well with Martín Alonso and widened further their rift.

Eager to set sail, Columbus took advantage of the land breeze; he set out from the Río De Gracia at midnight on January 11 and sailed eastward within sight of a beautiful mountain that he called "Monte de Plata," known today as Loma Isabela de Torres. He discovered many capes, assigning such names to them as "Cabo del Angel," "Cabo de Hierro," "Punta Seca," "Cabo Frances," "Cabo del Buen Tiempo," and "Cabo Tajado." He did not tarry at these locations, but kept his distance for fear of shoals. For that reason, he spent the night hove-to outside Escocesa Bay.

Before dawn, he set out again to the east aided by favorable winds and before daylight he had already sailed twenty Roman miles. He continued on course and saw a cape that he called "Cabo de Padre y Hijo" (presently known as Punta Pescadores). Because both ships were making good time, they did not stop to explore some of the beautiful bays they were encountering. Following an easterly course, he saw a beautiful cape of jagged rock that he named "Cabo del Enamorado," possibly the present Cabo Cabron.

FIRST CONFRONTATION WITH THE INDIANS

The fleet sailed for about another twelve miles from Cabo del Enamorado and discovered another cape that reminded the Admiral of Cape St. Vincent in Portugal. Between these two capes there was a great bay, in the midst of which could be seen a tiny little island. They anchored there and sent the boat ashore for water and also to contact the local Indians, but the people fled on seeing the Spaniards. The fleet remained the night for lack of wind. The following day, Sunday, January 13, Columbus sent the boat ashore for a provision of yams. As the sailors landed, they found the natives quite different from the gentile pacific lot they had met on other islands.

According to Las Casas, Samana Bay at the time was inhabited by the well-armed Ciguayos tribe of the Arawaks, who in many ways were as ferocious and warlike as the Caribs. The landing party was met by men with bows and arrows with whom they started to talk. They bought two bows and many arrows and even talked one of the Indians into visiting with the Admiral onboard the Niña. Columbus reported that his face was uglier than that of the other Indians he had seen on the islands.

Columbus questioned the Indian through an interpreter who did not understand the language, and was convinced that he was among the fearful Caribs and that the gulf he had passed the day before was the strait dividing the land masses. The Indians also spoke of an island called Matinino (Martinique), which was populated by women only and in which gold and copper was mined. Columbus may have recalled the Amazonian Island populated by women and described by Marco Polo; they allowed men among them once a year from a nearby island. The male children resulting from such visits were delivered to the fathers; the females remained with their mothers. After the interview, the Indian was suitably entertained and presented with gifts as an incentive for others and sent ashore. As the Niña's boat approached the land, about fifty Indians armed with bows and arrows and war clubs were lurking in the trees ready to attack; but on a word from the visiting Indian who was in the boat, they laid aside their weapons and came forth to meet the Spaniards, who had been instructed by the Admiral to purchase some of their weapons to take back to Spain as samples of native armaments. The Indians parted with two of their bows but suddenly became suspicious and rushed back toward their weapons to attack or capture the Spaniards. Seeing the Indians running toward them with ropes, the Spaniards, who were greatly outnumbered, immediately took the offensive. One Indian was slashed on the buttocks and another one wounded in the breast with an arrow:

When the Indians saw that they could gain little, although there were only seven Spaniards and more than fifty of them, they took flight until not one remained. One left his arrows here; another his bow there. The men would have killed many of them if the pilot who went ashore as captain had not prevented it. The men then returned to the caravel.[7]

Thus ended the first skirmish between Indians and the white men in the New World.

Apparently, the clash with the Indians was all but forgotten when on the following day the local Cacique paid Columbus a visit. As an act of friendship, he had sent the admiral a string of beads, formed of small stones and sea shells, and then followed up by making a personal appearance with three aides. Columbus received the Cacique cordially and served a dinner of biscuits and honey. Columbus showed him the layout of the ship and gave them the usual gifts. The Cacique left, promising to reciprocate with a coronet of gold, a promise he fulfilled the following day.

Both caravels were leaking badly due, according to Columbus, to poor workmanship in the Palos shipyard. Finding a nearby beach to careen and caulk them was out of the question, for the Ciguayos could not be trusted. Thus, when a favorable wind appeared on Wednesday, January 16, Columbus decided to leave the bay he called "Bay of the Arrows" and be on his way. It was the last anchorage of the Niña and the Pinta in the New World.

Part V

HOMEWARD BOUND TO UNIVERSAL ACCLAMATION

Chapter Twenty

RETURN VOYAGE, 1493

On Wednesday, January 16, 1493, Columbus left Samana Bay, which he called "Golfo de las Flechas," three hours before daybreak, thus taking advantage of a favorable land breeze. His navigation plan was a simple one: to get the two ships out of the trade winds area by sailing N by E until reaching the region of the Westerlies, 32°15'N latitude, and then sail home. On leaving the bay, Columbus steered to the northeast, the direction that would lead him, according to the young Indian guides he had picked up in Samana Bay, to the island of Matinino, the land of the Amazons, and the island of the Caribs.

However, after sailing about fifteen leagues, the Indian guides changed their minds and began pointing towards the SE. Columbus, somewhat irritated at the change of direction, changed course, and had traveled only a few leagues when the most favorable breeze sprung up for the voyage to Spain. Considering that the two ships were taking water and the crews' desire to head for home, Columbus resumed his course for Spain. The longer he delayed his departure, the greater the possibility of encountering unforeseen dangers that would jeopardize his discovery.

BATTLING THE TRADE WINDS

The trade winds, which had been so helpful to Columbus on his outward voyage, became a hindrance on the homeward voyage, and this was overcome only by Columbus's superior navigational skills. With the wind nearly abeam as he headed N by E and with the proper sail setting, he was able to generate enough vectoral force to guide him in the desired direction. Of course, he could not count on great speeds by using this technique; nevertheless, he was able to move slowly to the latitude from which he could pick up the Westerlies.

Mild and pleasant weather and calm seas in the early part of the voyage elevated the crews' spirits and made everyone happy. On January 16, they saw land for the last time as they passed Cabo Engaño, the easternmost point of Hispaniola, and made twelve leagues to the E by N. The wind moderated somewhat on January 17 as they sailed to the NE by E and they made twenty-one leagues. They began to see a great deal of weed in the sea. The following day the weed had diminished, but they saw many tunas. A frigate bird flew around the caravel and made off to the SSE. They sailed with the light wind to the E by S for ten leagues and later to the SE by E for another seven and a half leagues. On January 19, they had good sailing, averaging seven knots at night and six knots during the day. They saw many tunas, boobies, and tropic and frigate birds.

On Sunday, January 20, the wind dropped at night and they had a few squalls. They sailed nineteen leagues and saw many tunas and birds. Columbus reported that the sea was very smooth and the air mild. However, he reported a change in the wind temperature on the following day, January 21, and predicted that it would become increasingly colder as the ships proceeded north.

Actually, Columbus had sailed approximately six degrees of latitude north of Samana Bay, as his present position was latitude 25°N. He had about another seven degrees to go before he would enter the zone of the Westerlies. He was concerned about the Pinta's performance, which slowed him down to some degree. In the entry of January 23, the poor performance of the Pinta was attributed to Martín Alonso Pinzón's greed:

If Martín Alonso Pinzón had taken as much trouble to provide himself with a good mast in the Indies, where there are so many good ones, as he did to separate himself from me with the intention of filling his ship with gold, he would have been better off.[1]

The following day, Thursday, January 24, they sailed eleven leagues to the NE during the night and another fourteen leagues to the ENE from sunrise to sunset. They continued sailing to the ENE the night of the following day, January 25, for another nine and a half leagues. After sunrise, because the wind had moderated, they sailed seven leagues to the ENE.

The sailors killed a porpoise and a very large shark. These were very necessary because we had nothing to eat except bread, wine, and ajes from the Indies.[2]

This is the first indication that sufficient provisions had not been taken for the trip back home. Apparently, Columbus had been more concerned in providing ample food for the garrison at La Navidad than filling the larders of the Niña, expecting after leaving La Navidad to pick up supplies as he sailed along the coast of Hispaniola. As it turned out, however, his departure was hasty and adequate preparation could not be made despite the fact that the ships were leaking. The Pinta needed a new mast and both caravels required additional ballasts for stability in rough seas.

On January 26, he proceeded at night fourteen leagues to the E by S; after sunrise he sailed at times to the ESE and to the SE, covering another ten leagues. Apparently, the wind direction had changed, hauling him eastward so he came about from the port to the starboard tack, steadily northing. This maneuver was used by Columbus when the wind headed him. As a general rule, he clung as close to N by L to NE by N on the starboard tack making northing pretty steadily. From January 27 to January 30, they sailed ENE and made only 112 miles in smooth waters, aided by a light southerly breeze. They did much better on the last two days of January as the wind picked up, almost reaching the latitude of Bermuda (32°15'N), which lay 450 miles to the west.

HOME WITH THE WESTERLIES

On February 1, Columbus realized that he had reached the region of the Westerlies, for he had an exceptional run, proceeding ENE for forty-five and three-quarters leagues over smooth seas aided by a western wind. On February 2, they were in the midst of the Sargasso Sea, and the effect of the moonlight on the sargassum-covered ocean gave the eerie effect of a sled swishing through soft snow. In the first three days of February, they sailed on the new course of ENE and made close to 360 miles. On February 3, Columbus noticed that the North Star appeared very high, as on Cape St. Vincent. He attempted, with both the astrolabe and his primitive quadrant, to take a reading of their altitude position but did not succeed because of the extreme rolling of the Niña. From all indications, he was now at a latitude of roughly 35°N, which is slightly south of the latitude of Cape St. Vincent.

The following day, the sky became overcast and then it started to rain. Columbus complained that it was rather cold. He changed his course for E by N to E and held this course from sunrise February 4 through February 7. On February 6, he made the best day's run of the entire voyage: two hundred nautical miles! A modern yacht of comparable size would have a difficult time making such a daily run. On February 7, they had reached a latitude of 36°45'N and longitude of 38°20'W and had sailed during the four days, February 4 to 7, a distance of nearly 600 miles averaging 150 miles per day and approaching speeds of eleven knots at times.

It was during this period of continued speed that Columbus began to wonder about the exact position of the Niña. Were they heading for the Azores[3] or would they miss the archipelago? Their position on February 7 indicated that if they sailed due east from that point they would run into the southernmost island of Santa María. Columbus called for a meeting of the pilots to fix the position of the Niña on February 6. Captain Vincente Yañez Pinzón estimated that Flores, in the Azores, bore due N and Madeira due E. Bartolomè Roldan, the amateur pilot, said that Fayal bore NE and Porto Santo E. Both were in error, estimating their position to be much farther south than they really were. To be more exact, Roldan estimated his position to be about 375 miles SE by E and Pinzón about 600 ESE from the true position. On February 7, Peralonso Niño declared that the Niña was already between the meridians of Terceira and of Santa María, and would pass thirty-eight miles north of Madeira. He was wrong on both counts, placing the position too far to the south and too far to the east than it actually was. The Admiral's estimate was the most accurate.

He placed the fleet seventy-five leagues south of the parallel of Flores, an overestimate of sixty-five miles.

In reality, Columbus did not relish the thought of making a landfall in the Azores. Because the Azores belonged to the Portuguese, he could be imprisoned as an interloper. However, he needed to reach the Azores as a point of reference from which he could get a bearing for Spanish port.

For the previous three weeks, Columbus had had good, clear sailing with favorable winds and fair weather allowing him the peace of mind to write an important document describing his recent discoveries. The letter is known by its Latin title, "Epistola de Insulis Nuper Inventis."[4] In this letter, addressed to Gabriel Sanchez and in another to Louis Santangel, Columbus describes eloquently the natural beauties of the New World. It was written to stimulate interest in his discoveries and to prepare the ground for subsequent voyages.

After sailing for another two days, again the pilots aboard the Niña began to have qualms as to their position. Vicente Yañez and the two pilots, Sancho Ruiz, who had been pilot on the Santa María, and Peralonso Niño, with Roldan, plotted the course and fixed their position and concluded that they were passing beyond the islands of the Azores to the eastward. The Admiral disagreed with them and insisted that they were actually west of their reckoning. On Monday, February 11, Columbus saw many birds overhead and concluded that land was not very far. Actually, he had reached the longitude of Fayal but was still 170 miles south of it. On this day, he proceeded on his course due E and averaged eleven Roman miles an hour during the night hours. The island of Santa María lay about 250 miles E by N.

CAUGHT IN VIOLENT STORMS

On Tuesday, February 12, Columbus sailed to the E at a speed of six Roman miles an hour during the night and by daylight he must have made sixty-six Roman miles. They were optimistic that perhaps soon they would be within sight of land. Instead they were confronted with violent winds and turbulent seas and were to experience the worst weather to fall upon them on either passage.

The storm increased in fury on the thirteenth and on the morning of the fourteenth, before dawn, the waves began to break over the Niña. The men set the main sail very low, as far as they could without having the fast of the sail torn by the rushing waves coming onboard. As the sea and wind increased, and seeing that the danger was great, he began to scud with the wind after he had made a run of twenty miles in three hours. The caravel Pinta with Martín Alonso aboard also began to scud and disappeared from view, contact being maintained during the night by flares. The lights gleamed more and more distant until they ceased entirely. Columbus continued to scud all night and was driven thirteen leagues to the NE by E. At sunrise, with no sign of the Pinta, Columbus began to fear for the safety of Pinzón and his crew. He also had forebodings about his own vessel. Still, he managed to set the main course low once again to enable the Niña to rise above the cross-swell so that it might not swamp her. In this fashion, he proceeded on the ENE course and afterward NE by E for six hours and made seven and a half leagues.

Columbus now sought divine intervention and solemnly vowed to make a pilgrimage to Santa María de Guadalupe and to offer a wax candle weighing five pounds. To select the man who would fulfill the promise, he ordered that:

A chick-pea be brought for every man on board; one was marked by a knife with the sign of the cross, and they were shaken up in a cap. I was the first person to draw, and it was I who took out the pea marked with the sign of the cross. Thus, I was elected by chance, and from that time I considered myself obligated to fulfill the vow and make the pilgrimage.[5]

Another lot was cast in the same way for a pilgrimage to Santa María de Loreto and the lot fell on a seaman of Puerto Santa María named Pedro de Villa. The Admiral promised to pay the expenses for the journey. A third lot was cast for a pilgrimage to Santa Clara de Moguer, a church near Palos, to perform a solemn Mass and make an all-night vigil, and this likewise fell to Columbus. To propitiate heaven further, the Admiral and all the mariners made a vow that upon reaching the first land they would all go clad only in their shirts, in procession to make a prayer in a church that was dedicated to Our Lady. Finally, convinced that they would perish at sea, each one made his own private vow.

The Niña was being tossed about like a walnut shell down a mountain stream because of the lack of ballast in her hold. The consumption of the drinking water and other provisions had lightened the vessel so much that she rolled crazily among the waves. The Admiral ordered that all the pipes of the ship be filled with seawater, and this remedied the situation.

This was a most difficult moment for the Admiral. He feared that the Pinta had foundered in the storm; and if the same thing happened to the Niña, the whole record of his discoveries would be lost forever. He began to reflect first on his relationship with God and then on his life's experiences, and on the future of his two sons. The entry as told by Las Casas in his journal for Thursday, February 14, is a testament to his great faith:

It seems to me that the great desire I have to bring this wonderful news to Your Highnesses, and to show that I have been proven truthful in what I have said and volunteered to discover, causes me to fear greatly that I will not succeed in doing so. It seems to me that even a gnat can disturb and impede it. I attribute this to my little faith and lack of confidence in the Divine Providence. On the other hand, I am comforted by the favors that God has bestowed upon me by giving me such a victory, in discovering what I have discovered. And after so many adversities and contradictions in Castile, God had fulfilled all my desires. And as before, I have committed myself to God and have conducted my enterprise for Him, and He has heard me and given me all that I have asked, and I believe that God will fulfill what was begun and that He will deliver me safely. This is especially so since He delivered me from the difficulties I had at the outset of the voyage, when I had greater reason to fear than now, on account of the trouble with the sailors and people who were with me, who all with one voice determined to return and rebel against me, making protestations; and the eternal God gave me strength and courage against them all. And there are many other wonderful things that God has manifested in me and by me on this journey, besides those which Your Highnesses know from persons of your household. Therefore, I ought not to fear this storm. But my weakness and anxiety will not allow my mind to be reassured.[6]

Columbus then stated his concern for his two sons: Diego, who was a teenager, and Ferdinand, who was only four years old, both in Córdoba at school.

I also feel great anxiety because of the two sons I have in Córdoba at school, if I leave them orphaned of father and mother in a foreign land. And I am concerned because the Sovereigns do not know the service I have rendered on this voyage and the very important news I am carrying to them, which would move them to help my sons.[7]

He entertained the thought that if the Pinta survived the storm and the Niña went down, the world would know only Pinzón's version of the discoveries. He was convinced that Pinzón would not tell the truth. Therefore, he wrote on a parchment an account of his discoveries with the hope that whoever found it might bring it to the attention of the Sovereigns. He wrapped the parchment securely in a waxed cloth, put it in a barrel, and threw it overboard in the raging sea.

After sunset on that day, the blue sky began to appear in the western quarter, and the storm abated somewhat even though the sea was still very high. He proceeded to the ENE at four Roman miles per hour all night, and in thirteen hours made thirteen leagues. After sunrise on Friday, February 15, they sighted land appearing to the ENE; but no one was certain as to what land it was. Some said it was the island of Madeira; others that it was the Rock of Sintra in Portugal, near Lisbon; and some of the pilots were optimistic enough to say it was Castile. By his own reckoning, Columbus figured it was one of the islands of the Azores. Land at last! Their prayers had been answered, but there were still rough and angry seas to overcome before landing.

All night they went beating to windward, and as they drew closer, they recognized the land to be an island. They sailed to the NE and then to the NNE until sunrise on February 16, when they took the southward tack to reach the island, which was hardly discernible because of a great cloud mass. From the stern, Columbus saw another island (São Miguel) eight miles away. Unfortunately, a heavy head wind and a choppy sea sprang up, and he went tacking from sunrise to nightfall, when they sang "Salve Regina" upon seeing a light to the leeward on the island, which they had first seen the previous day.

Columbus was now completely exhausted, as he had not slept since the storm began and was suffering from arthritis from the constant exposure to the elements. He decided to take a nap while the vessel beat to windward, hoping to reach land by sunrise; however, the Niña had already overtaken the island of Santa María during the night. At sunrise of February 17, they sailed to the SSW and finally reached land by dusk, but they still did not know what island it was.

CONFRONTATION IN THE AZORES

After sunset on February 17, they sailed around the island to find a safe anchor; the lingering storm still prevented Columbus from learning where he was. They dropped an anchor, but the cable parted and they put out to sea again, where they stood, at intervals, all night. After sunrise on February 18, they found shelter on the northern side of the island, and sent a boat ashore. They had landed on the island of Santa María, the most southern of the Azores. The people of the island were surprised to see the caravel riding at anchor and astonished that it had been able to withstand the violent storm that had been raging for the past fifteen days. They rejoiced on learning that the Admiral had reached the Indies.

On advice of local sailors, Columbus shifted his anchorage from the northwestern point of the island off the village of Nossa Senhora dos Anjos (Our Lady of the Angels), to a more secure location about one and a half miles eastward near Cape Punta Frades, completely out of sight of the village. He had left three men ashore to get fresh provisions and water. After sunset, three men of the island hailed the caravel and Columbus sent a boat to take them aboard. They were the official greeters sent by the captain of the island, called João de Castanheira, who claimed he knew Columbus. As a gesture of welcome and friendship, they brought aboard bread, chickens, and various refreshments—courtesy of de Castanheira—apologizing that he personally did not come calling, due to the lateness of the hour; he promised to come the following morning with more refreshments and the three Spanish sailors whom he still kept with him to learn more about the voyage. The Admiral was very courteous and hospitable to the messengers, ordering that they be given bunks for the night to sleep aboard the Niña, because it was a long way to row home in the dark.

The following morning, as the three messengers were getting ready to leave, Columbus reminded his crew of the vows they had made the previous Thursday at the height of the tempest to march in a penitential procession, clad only in their shirts, in the first land where there might be a shrine to the Blessed Lady. He decided that half of the crew should go in fulfillment of the vows to a small chapel or hermitage that was near the sea, and he would go later with the other half, after the first group came back to take over as shipkeepers.

The people of the island, judging by the messengers' behavior, seemed trustworthy; moreover, Castile and Portugal were now at peace and Columbus did not suspect any treachery on the part of the islanders. Indeed, Columbus prevailed upon the three messengers to seek the local priest to celebrate Mass at the shrine of Our Blessed Lady, which they agreed to do. The ten penitent crew members of the Niña undressed themselves, took their shoes off and, clad only in their shirts, took the boat to shore with the three messengers and marched in procession to the tiny chapel. Their penitential rites, however, were rudely interrupted by a multitude of people on horseback and on foot, led by the Captain, who fell upon them and took them prisoner. The Niña's men were caught with their pants down, literally.

At about 11:00 a.m., seeing that his men and boat were not returning, the Admiral began to fear that the pilgrims might have been detained by the Portuguese—or worse, that the boat might have hit the rocks surrounding the harbor and sunk. He decided to investigate, but because he could not see the chapel from where he was anchored, he weighed anchor and sailed a short distance toward the chapel. He saw that his boat, occupied by armed men under the command of de Castanheira, was heading toward the Niña presumably to arrest the Admiral. Columbus ordered his men to arm themselves and be ready to fight if called upon to do so. In the meantime, he told them to stay out of sight.

Approaching the Niña, de Castanheira stood up in the boat and asked for safe conduct to board the vessel. Columbus replied that he would give him permission to do so if de Castanheira would tell him what he had done to the men of the Niña. Afraid that Columbus might take him as a hostage if he went aboard, the captain became wary and kept his distance. Columbus accused him of breaking his word. The Admiral also reminded him that his act of perfidy would certainly offend the King of Portugal and the Sovereigns of Castile, who were at peace. Moreover, he told the captain that he was dealing with a duly authorized Castilian Admiral and Viceroy of the Indies, warning him that he would face dire consequences from Castile if he persisted in his acts of enmity. De Castanheira replied that all he was doing was in conformance with orders received from the King of Portugal.

Columbus became very angry, and when the captain ordered him to sail into the harbor with the Niña, he threatened to sail away with half of his crew, but not before he had depopulated the whole island and carried to Castile a hundred Portuguese prisoners. The dispute was not resolved—the Captain of Santa María headed for shore in the barge and Columbus returned to the harbor where he had first anchored because weather conditions did not permit doing anything else. On the following day, February 20, Columbus ordered his vessel repaired and the pipes filled with seawater for ballast. The weather became so bad that he lost his anchorage when the cables parted once again and he was forced to sail towards the island of San Miguel to find a harbor to ride out the stormy sea and high winds. He sailed until nightfall without sighting land. The Admiral was also concerned because he had only three seamen aboard competent enough to deal with the high seas. Fortunately, although the waves ran high, they came from one direction only. If there had been a turbulent sea as before, he would have been too undermanned to cope with it.

After the sun rose on the morning of February 21, he decided to return to Santa María to try to recover his people, the boat, the anchors, and the cables he had left there. The weather seemed to be moderating. Columbus reflected on the contrast between the weather in these Azorean islands and what he had enjoyed in the Indies, where he had sailed all winter without encountering a single storm. The Admiral was led to conclude that:

Theologians and learned philosophers were quite correct when they said that the early paradise is at the end of the Orient, because it is a most temperate place, and so those lands which I have discovered are at the end of the Orient.[8]

This notion became an obsession with for him. He believed, as did many of his contemporaries, that the Garden of Eden, as described by Cardinal d'Ailly's *Imago Mundo,* was in the East.

Soon after his arrival at the island of Santa María at the Baia da Cres, east of Punta Frades, where he had first anchored, he saw a boat approaching; on it were five seamen, two priests, and a notary public who, upon receiving assurance of safe conduct, boarded the caravel. Because it was late, they passed the night there. In the morning, the party said that they had been sent by the captain of the island to learn for certain where the Admiral had been and if he had a commission from the Sovereigns of Castile. The Admiral immediately answered that he had been to the Indies, then showed them the general letter of credence from the Sovereigns to all princes and lords, and other documents. This apparently satisfied the Portuguese party, who went ashore and released the captured sailors. While in captivity, the sailors had learned that the captain had been ordered by the Portuguese King to take the Admiral prisoner at all costs. That being the case, why were the Admiral and the sailors set free? Because the Portuguese had bungled the whole incident. They had failed to detain Columbus and his crew, and that failure would certainly have brought repercussions both from King João of Portugal and the Sovereigns of Castile.

The weather improved the following day. Columbus weighed anchor and proceeded to sail around the island to find some good anchorage to take on wood and stone for ballast, but could not come to anchor before 9:00 p.m. The following day, he tried to take on wood and ballast but was prevented from doing so by heavy surf that broke upon the shore. But while the wind, which was veering south, was dangerous for vessels at anchor off the island, it was fair and favorable for the voyage to Spain. Columbus, always eager to exploit opportune moments, decided to leave the Azores and head for Spain.

Chapter Twenty-One

INTERLUDE IN PORTUGAL—JOURNEY'S END

On Sunday, February 24, Columbus left the island of Santa María for Castile and ordered a course to the east. He covered a total of twenty-eight leagues. Other than the possibility of foul weather, Columbus did not expect any problems on this route as it was normally used by Portuguese sailors, Lisbon-bound from the Mina and other ports of the west coast of Africa, who found it more convenient to head in the direction of the Azores and then rely on the Westerlies to get to Lisbon or Cape St. Vincent. They had no problem sailing due east from Santa María, but by Wednesday, February 27, they experienced some adverse winds that drove them off course. However, they had already covered almost half of the 770 miles that separate Cape St. Vincent from Santa María. Columbus remarked that it was very painful to have such a tempest when he was so close to home, but he had yet to meet the full weight of the storm. He fought the variable winds for the next two days, making moderate headway.

On Saturday, March 2, he proceeded to the N by N and covered a distance of forty-eight leagues. On Sunday, March 3, after sunset he got back on his course to the east, but a sudden squall blew up, splitting all the sails and imperiling the ship. In this hour of need, the men again sought divine help. Once more they drew lots to send a pilgrim to Santa María de la Cinta in Huelva, barefoot and in his shirt, and again the lot fell—as one might have guessed—on the Admiral. Ferdinand, who is not known for his modesty, ventured to say that perhaps "God found his offerings more acceptable than those of others."[1] Las Casas, on the other hand, stated that this recurrence was God's way of humbling Columbus's pride, as he had not yet realized that the glory of a discovery was the work of God—that he himself was merely the chosen instrument. It is possible that there may have been some sleight of hand on the part of some clever crewman to help Columbus's good fortune.

The situation was serious enough that they also vowed to fast the first Saturday after they arrived. They had already sailed sixty Roman miles before the sails split and they had already seen signs of land. Now, they were scudding under bare poles because of the great tempest of wind, and the sea that came upon them from two directions. The following night the tempest increased to such a degree that they thought they were lost. The waves were pounding the vessel from two sides and powerful winds seemed to lift the caravel into the air. Thunder and lightning filled the sky with a vengeance against the daring mariners who had violated the secrets of the sea.

By the first watch (7:00 p.m.) the sailors had sighted land in the moonlight but they did not know where they were. Columbus managed to set a storm squaresail that had not been blown off and with the aid of the northwest wind made some headway. With great peril, keeping off the rocky and dangerous lee shore until daybreak, they recognized the land to be the Rock of Sintra, a mountainous peninsula that juts out from Portugal just north of the Tagus River, which the Admiral decided to enter because he could not do anything else.[2] This laconic statement was Columbus's excuse for placing himself at the mercy of the Portuguese. They sailed up the Tagus and at 9:00 a.m., March 4, anchored at Restello, the outer port of Lisbon. The natives from various parts of the shore came to see the vessel that had escaped the most vicious storm in years. They had been watching the struggling ship the whole morning with great anxiety. They told Columbus that the storm had sunk twenty-five ships trading in Flanders, and that other vessels had been detained in port for months without being able to get out.

Mindful of the unpleasant reception he had received from the Portuguese at Santa María, Columbus decided to use his diplomatic skills to contact directly King João II to apprise him of his arrival and to reassure him that he had come from the Indies and not from Guinea.

He asked for permission to proceed upstream to Lisbon as he feared some ruffians, thinking that he carried a large quantity of gold, might be planning some acts of mischief against him. At the same time, he sent his "Letter to the Sovereigns" written early in February off the Azores to Ferdinand and Isabella, adding a postscript to apprise the Sovereigns of his safe return.

RECEPTION IN LISBON
THE ADMIRAL AND KING JOÃO II

On Tuesday, March 5, once again the Admiral's presence in Portuguese waters was challenged by the local authorities. Anchored not too far from the Niña was a Portuguese warship. Her master, the famous Bartolomé Dias, the discoverer of the Cape of Good Hope, approached the Niña in his armed boat and came aboard, ordering the Admiral to come with him and give an account of himself to the king's ministers as was required of all ships that arrived there. Adopting a defensive posture, Columbus replied that he was Admiral of the Sovereigns of Castile and that he would give no such account to anyone, nor would he leave his ship unless by force of arms. Dias then requested that he should send the master of the caravel. The Admiral replied that neither his master (captain) Vincente Yañez Pinzón, nor even a grommet, would be sent unless compelled by force.

In defense of his position, one must realize that it was the custom of the Admirals of the Sovereigns of Castile to die rather than surrender themselves or their people. Dias then asked to see the letters of authority of the Sovereigns of Castile, which Columbus was pleased to show him. Convinced of Columbus's credentials, Dias returned to the warship and told his story to the captain of the vessel, Alvaro Daman; duly impressed, the latter came aboard the Niña with a great fanfare of drums, trumpets, and pipes. He spoke with the Admiral and offered to do all he required.

The next day, Wednesday, when it became known that Columbus had come from the Indies, it aroused the curiosity of nearly everybody in Lisbon even though the city had become accustomed to many maritime discoveries. This one, though, was different as the navigator had come from the west and had brought back not only human specimens but specimens of unknown plants, animals, and artifacts. They were enthralled by the stories of a beautiful new world where spices and exotic plants grew wild, gold was cheap, and the natives friendly and generous. According to Ferdinand's description:

So many people swarmed aboard to see the Indians, and hear the story of the discovery, that there was not room for them all;

and the surrounding water could not be seen, so full was it of the Portuguese boats and skiffs. Some of the Portuguese praised God for so great a victory; others were angry that the enterprise had slipped through their fingers because of the King's skepticism and indifference.[3]

There were also countless people visiting the caravel on Thursday, expressing their enthusiasm for a voyage so beneficial to mankind and for the propagation of the Christian faith.

On Friday, March 8, the Admiral received a letter from the King of Portugal, brought by Martín de Noronha, one of the king's attendants, inviting him to the royal residence in the country. He congratulated Columbus on his safe arrival and assured him that he had issued orders that everything the Admiral required for himself or his vessel should be supplied promptly and without cost. The Admiral had misgivings about going, but at the same time he did not want to offend the king as he was now totally at his mercy. Moreover, he wanted to dispel any suspicion that he might have been in Portuguese territories.

Columbus left the same day for the Valle del Parayso, nine leagues from Lisbon, accompanied by Don Martín, who had provided mules for the trip. He brought along with him several of his healthiest specimens from among the ten captive Indians who had endured the stormy ocean voyage. He also brought some Indian artifacts that he planned to present to the King. The route north led through Lisbon then to Sacavem, where they spent the night. They continued the following morning along the west side of the bay through Alhandra and followed the right bank of the Tagus River through Villa Franca and Castanheira. Because of the rain, they did not arrive in the Valle del Parayso until nightfall of Saturday, March 9. At that time, the king, in order to escape the pestilence, was staying at the monastery of Santa María das Virtudes, situated at the foot of the Valley del Parayso, a beautiful farming region thirty miles north of Lisbon. The reception by the king was very formal. On approaching the royal residence, Columbus was greeted by the principal officers and cavaliers of the household, who conducted him with great ceremony to the palace.

Then the king ordered him to seat himself in his presence, an honor accorded only to persons of royalty. He congratulated the Admiral on the results of his voyage and assured him that everything in his kingdom that could benefit or be of service to his Sovereigns or himself was at his command. Columbus gave an account of his voyage and the various territories he had discovered and the king listened attentively, interjecting at one point whether some of the territories discovered did not belong to Portugal according to the Treaty of Alcacovas (1479). In this treaty, confirmed by the papal bull "Aeterni Regis" in 1481, Spain recognized exclusive Portuguese rights on the west coast of Africa and the Cape Verde Islands, and Portugal recognized Spanish sovereignty in the Canary Islands:

The Admiral rejoined that he knew nothing of that treaty but that he scrupulously observed his orders not to go to the Portuguese Mina nor any port of Guinea, and that so he had ordered it proclaimed in all harbors of Andalusia, before they departed on the voyage. The king graciously replied that he was sure that there would be no need for arbitrators in this matter; and handed him over as guest to the Prior of Crato, who was the most eminent person there and from whom the Admiral received many courtesies and favors.[4]

INTERLUDE IN PORTUGAL—JOURNEY'S END

After Mass on the following day, Sunday, March 10, the king continued to question Columbus on the new territories discovered and made direct inquiries as to soil, countries, people, gold and pearls, stones, and other precious things, of the courses they had followed, and what happened on the return trip. Columbus replied in full, stressing that these were regions heretofore undiscovered by any Christian power. The king listened attentively and even challenged the two Indians to show the positions of the islands by rearranging beans on a flat table; both of them rearranged them in the same fashion. Trying to contain his anger, the king was now convinced that this upstart Admiral, whom he had dismissed as a braggart in 1483 for proposing a western voyage under Portuguese auspices, had indeed discovered new territories for Spain—even surpassing his own territories of Guinea.

His only consolation lay in the possibility that perhaps some of these new lands could very well be under the domain as defined by the Treaty of Alcacovas. Possibly by direct negotiations with Ferdinand and Isabella, he would attempt to extend the line of demarcation as defined by the Treaty of Alcacovas farther westward. To deal with the existing Spanish pope for an abrogation would be hopeless. In any event, there was not much for the king to do at this time but to bite the bullet and press on to greater achievements of the future. Some of the king's advisers, however, did not share his nonchalant attitude. They reasoned that the easy way out was to have Columbus killed. They would provoke the Admiral and, believing him to be arrogant and overbearing person, they could fix it so that his demise would appear to have been caused by his shortcomings.[5]

But King João forbade any assassination attempts. On the contrary, he showed the Admiral great courtesy and affection and considered him to be a distinguished benefactor of mankind.

On Monday, March 11, the king bade farewell to Columbus and gave him messages for Ferdinand and Isabella. On the way back to Lisbon, Columbus and his entourage, including Martín de Noronha, stopped at a monastery to see the queen, who had sent word that he must not leave without calling on her. Doña Leonor was staying at the Convent of São Antonio de Castanheira fifteen or twenty miles south of Vertude and west of Villa Franca. Columbus, with his Indians, knelt before Doña Leonor, kissed her hand, and paid homage. With her were the father of his guide, D. Pedro de Noronha, Marquis de Villa Real, and the queen's brother, the Duque de Bejar, who was to ascend to the Portuguese throne a few years later as Manuel I. She was very pleased to see Columbus and showed him such favor and courtesy as might befit a lord.

The Admiral and his retinue left the Queen in the evening and proceeded to Alhandra, a town on the Tagus, about twenty-two miles above Lisbon, where they lodged for the night. He complained that after spending the better part of three days on the saddle he was sore and preferred to take a boat down to Restello the following day. In the morning, while they were making arrangements to hire a boat, a squire of Don João came calling to say on the king's behalf that if he wished to go to Castile by land, he would accompany him, obtain lodgings for him on the journey, and provide all he needed as far as the Portuguese border.

Columbus, who was tired of traveling on land, declined. Also, he was a bit suspicious of the offer. Why was it not mentioned at Virtude? The Portuguese court chronicler, Rui de Pina, confirms that Columbus's suspicions were justified.[6] Columbus did not fall into the trap and boarded the Niña that night. The following morning, March 13, at 8:00 a.m., with a strong ebb tide and a NNW wind, he weighed anchor and sailed for Spain, where he arrived safely at the bar of Saltes at sunrise on the fifteenth. At midday, he entered the harbor of Palos, from which he had sailed for his great enterprise on August 3 of the preceding year. Columbus's final remarks in his journal summarized in a few bold strokes an accomplishment that succeeded only by the grace of God, which helped him overcome all manner of man-made obstacles, especially among the Sovereigns' courtiers. Surprisingly, the difficult part of the journey was experienced before his departure. Columbus's personality is expressed in this short paragraph—his ambition, his desire to establish himself as a supreme mariner, his bravado, his faith in himself and in God, and his obsessive identification with a cause:

This voyage has miraculously proven this to be so as can be learned from my writings, by the remarkable miracles which have occurred during the voyage and for me, who has been in the Court of Your Highnesses for such a long time, with the opposition and against the advice of so many of the principal persons of your household who were all against me and treated this undertaking as a folly. I hope to Our Lord that it will be the great honor of Christianity although it has been accomplished with such ease.[7]

Chapter Twenty-Two

COLUMBUS'S LETTER—AN ACCOUNT OF HIS DISCOVERY

The letter of Christopher Columbus (*Epistola Cristoferi Colom*), written on the Niña before the Admiral reached the Azores, was sent from Lisbon on March 6. The rapidity with which it traveled by courier to its destination is astounding. As early as March 19 the Duke of Medina Celi, from his castle about fifty miles northeast of Madrid, announced to the world that Columbus had arrived in Lisbon after finding the lands he had sought. In our times of instant communication and slow mail delivery, it takes four days for first class mail to cross the American continent from California to New Jersey—and this is by air mail!

SPREADING THE AMAZING NEWS

Within a few weeks after the end of the voyage on March 15, 1493, the news of the discovery spread rapidly throughout Spain, Portugal, and Italy. Many Italians, established in Spain as merchants, diplomats, or churchmen, wrote letters to their friends in Italy about Columbus's great accomplishment. Thus, Tribaldo de Rossi reports that the Signoria of Florence received a letter from Spain in the last week of March 1493, announcing that a very great island inhabited by naked people had been discovered by "certain youths with three caravels." Columbus was not identified in this message, but a Barcelona merchant named Annibale Gennaio wrote a letter to his brother in Milan on April 9, 1493, identifying a "certain Columbo" in a lengthy letter in which more details were given. The envoy of Milan for the city of Ferrara immediately sent a copy of this letter to Ercole D'Este, Duke of Ferrara, on April 21, followed later by a copy of Columbus's letter.

On April 18, the pope in Rome received a copy of the letter of Columbus, as did Ludovico Sforza (Il Moro) in Milan. Columbus's letter of his first voyage, addressed to Louis de Santangel, must have been printed in Barcelona even before he came to court there in mid-April to have circulated so quickly. This same version was translated into Latin by the Catalan Leanardo de Cosco and printed in Rome in May 1493 under the title *De Insulis inventis Epistola Cristoferi Colom*. Copies were printed not only in Rome, but in Antwerp, Basel, and in Paris at a later date.

Guiliano Dato translated it into Italian as *Storia Della Inventione delle Nuove Insule de Chanaria Indiane*, and printed in Rome on June 15, 1493. The text by De Lollis in the *Raccolta di documenti e studi pubblicati dalla R. commissione columbiana* (1892–96) is a hybrid made up of the Latin and Spanish versions.

News of the letter and the discovery reached Columbus's native city of Genoa by the return of her ambassadors Francesco Marchesi and Antonio Grimaldi, and was recorded among the great events of 1493. While the news of the discovery of the Indies spread quickly from Spain to Italy through the private letters of Italians living in Spain, Northern Europe did not receive any news until early autumn. At first it did not arouse much enthusiasm, but the northern Europeans took notice after the second voyage had established a permanent settlement in the Indies. King Henry VII of England finally took the initiative to engage another Genoese-Venetian navigator living in Bristol, John Cabot (Giovanni Caboto), to seek a western route to the Indies by sailing a northern route at a latitude of 51°N in a tiny ship called the *Matthew*.

While there were some skeptics who doubted Columbus's claim that he had reached the Indies or even the outlying islands of Cipangu, his letter filled the civilized world with wonder and delight. Naked native women! Rivers filled with gold dust! Beautiful unspoiled lands with trees that seem to reach the sky, always luxuriant in all seasons! Exotic flowers and birds! Nightingales and other birds of a thousand varieties singing in November! Spices, cotton, and mastic, as much as anybody would want, readily available! Columbus stressed the docility of the natives and the possibility of their conversion to the Christian religion. The wonders reported in the letter stirred the world more than any other event had done before.

This letter was not directly written to Ferdinand and Isabella, but to Louis de Santangel, the queen's Keeper of the Privy Purse, together with other documents for the monarchs. Another copy of the letter was addressed to Gabriel Sánchez, General Treasurer of Aragon. A letter of transmittal, addressed to Their Highnesses, making reference to the letter, announcing his arrival and asking for a court audience to explain his trip in person, was also included. This letter of transmittal has never been found. Columbus's letter, printed in Barcelona in the spring of 1493 by Pedro Posa, was lost until 1889, when a copy was found in Spain. This copy, acquired by a London art dealer, was eventually sold to the New York Public Library and is today in its Lenox Collection. The original letter to Santangel has never been found.

The translation that follows was made from the original Spanish (not from the Latin translation) by the eminent historian Samuel Eliot Morison, who refers to it as "...the first and rarest of all printed Americana." It is reprinted with the permission of the Heritage Press, New York City.

Columbus's Letter to the Sovereigns on His First Voyage 15 February–4 March, 1493

Sir, forasmuch as I know that you will take pleasure in the great triumph with which Our Lord has crowned my voyage. I write this to you, from which you will learn how, in twenty[1] days I reached the Indies with the fleet which the most illustrious King and Queen, our Lords, gave to me. And there I found very many islands filled with people without number, and of them all have I taken possession for Their Highnesses, by proclamation and with the royal standard displayed, and nobody objected. To the first island which I found I gave the name "San Salvador," in recognition of His Heavenly Majesty, who marvelously hath given all this; the Indians call it "Guanahani." To the second I gave the name "Isla de Santa María de Concepción"; to the third, "Ferrandina"; to the fourth, "La Isla Bella;"[2] to the fifth, "La Isla Juana"; and so to each one I gave a new name.

When I reached Juana, I followed its coast to the westward, and I found it to be so long that I thought it must be the mainland, the province of Catayo.[3] And since I found neither towns nor cities along the coast, but only small villages, with people of which I could not have speech because they all fled forthwith, I went forward on the same course, thinking that I should not fail to find great cities and towns. And, at the end of many leagues, seeing that there was no change and that the coast was bearing me northwards, which was contrary to my desire since winter was already beginning, I proposed to go then to the south, and as moreover the wind was favorable, I determined not to wait for a change of weather and backtracked to a certain harbor already noted,[4] and thence I sent two men upcountry to learn if there was a king or great cities. They traveled for three days and found an infinite number of small villages and people without number, but nothing of importance, hence they returned.

I understood sufficiently from other Indians whom I had already taken, that continually this land was an island, and so I followed its coast eastward 107 leagues up to where it ended. And from that cape I saw toward the east another island, distant eighteen leagues from the former, to which I once gave the name "La Española." And I went there and followed its northern part, as I had in the case of Juana, to the eastward for 178[5] great leagues in a straight line. As Juana, so all the others are very fertile to an excessive degree, and this one especially. In it there are many harbors on the sea coast, beyond comparison with others which I know in Christendom, and numerous rivers, good and large, which is marvelous. Its lands are lofty and in it there are many sierras and very high mountains, to which the island Centrefrei[6] is not comparable. All are most beautiful, of a thousand shapes, and all accessible, and filled with trees of a thousand kinds and so tall they seem to touch the sky; and I am told that they never lose their foliage, which I can believe, for I saw them as green and beautiful as they are in Spain in May, and some of them were flowering, some with fruit, and some in another condition, according to their quality. And there were nightingales and other little birds of a thousand kinds singing in the month of November, there where I went. There are palm trees of six or eight kinds, which are a wonder to behold because of their beautiful variety and so are the other trees and fruits and plants; therein are marvelous pine groves, and extensive meadow country; and there is honey, and there are many kinds of birds and a great variety of fruits. Upcountry there are many mines of metals, and the population is innumerable. La Española is marvelous, the sierras and the mountains and the plains and the meadows and the lands are so beautiful and rich for planting and sowing, and for livestock of every sort, and for building towns and villages.

The harbors of the sea here are such as you could not believe without seeing them; and so the rivers, many and great, and good streams, the most of which bear gold. And the trees and fruits and plants have great differences from those of La Juana; in this [island] there are many spices and great mines of gold and of other metals.

The people of this island and of all the other islands which I have found and seen, or have not seen, all go naked, men and women, as their mothers bore them, except that some women cover one place only with the leaf of a plant or with a net of cotton which they make for that purpose. They have no iron or steel or weapons, nor are they capable of using them, although they are well-built people of handsome stature, because they are wondrously timid. They have no other arms than arms of canes, [cut] when they are in seed time, to the ends of which they fix a sharp little stick; and they dare not make use of these, for oftentimes it has happened that I have sent ashore two or three men to some town to have speech, and the people without number have come out to them, and as soon as they saw them coming, they fled; even a father would not stay for his son; and this not because wrong has been done to anyone; on the contrary, at every point where I have been and have been able to have speech, I have given them of all that I had, such as cloth and many other things, without receiving anything for it; but they are like that, timid beyond cure. It is true that after they have been reassured and have lost this fear, they are so artless and so free with all they possess, that no one would believe it without having seen it. Of anything they have, if you ask them for it, they never say no; rather they invite the person to share it, and show as much love as if they were giving their hearts; and whether the thing be of value or of small price, at once they are content with whatever little thing of whatever kind may be given to them. I forbade that they should be given things so worthless as pieces of broken crockery and broken glass, and lace points, although when they were able to get them, they thought they had the best jewel in the world; thus it was learned that a sailor for a lace point received gold to the weight of two and a half castellanos, and others much more for other things which were worth much less; yea, for new blancas[7]—for them they would give all that they had, although it might be two or three castellanos' weight of gold or an arroba or two of spun cotton; they even took pieces of the broken hoops of the wine casks and, like animals, gave what they had, so that it seemed to me to be wrong and I forbade it, and I gave them a thousand good, pleasing things which I had brought, in order that they might be fond of us, and furthermore might become Christians and be inclined to the love and service of Their Highnesses and of the whole Castilian nation, and try to help us and to give us of the things which they have in abundance and which are necessary to us. And they know neither sect nor idolatry, with the exception that all believe that the source of all power and people came from the sky, and in this belief that they everywhere received me, after they had overcome their fear. And this does not result from their being ignorant (for they are of a very keen intelligence and men who navigate all those seas, so that it is wondrous the good account they gave of everything), but because they have never seen people clothed or ships like ours.

And as soon as I arrived in the Indies, on the first island which I found, I took some of them by force in order that they might learn [Castilian] and give me information of what they had in those parts; it so worked out that they soon understood us, and we them, either by speech or signs, and they have been very serviceable. I still have them with me, and they are still of the opinion that I come from the sky, in spite of all the intercourse which they have had with me, and they were the first to announce this wherever I went, and the others would run from house to house and to the neighboring towns with loud cries of, "Come! Come! See the people from the sky!" They all came, men and women alike, as soon as they had confidence in us, so that not one, big or little, remained behind and all brought something to eat and drink, which they gave with marvelous love. In all the islands, they have very many canoes like rowing fustas, some bigger and some smaller, and some are bigger than a fusta of eighteen benches. They are not so beamy, because they are made of a single log, but a fusta could not keep up with them by rowing, since they make incredible speed, and in these they navigate all those islands, which are innumerable, and carry their merchandise. Some of these canoes I have seen with seventy and eighty men on board, each with his oar.

In all these islands, I saw no great diversity in the appearance of the people or in their manners and language, but they all understand one another, which is a very singular thing, on account of which I hope that Their Highnesses will determine upon their conversion to our holy faith, towards which they are much inclined.

I have already said how I went 107 leagues in a straight line from west to east along the coast of the island Juana, and as a result of that voyage I can say that this island is larger than England and Scotland together; for beyond these 107 leagues, there remain to the westward two provinces where I have not been, one of which they call "Avan,"[8] *and there the people are born with tails. Those provinces cannot have a length of less than fifty or sixty leagues, as I could understand from those Indians whom I retain and who know all the islands. The other, Española, in circuit is greater than all Spain, from Colonya by the coast to Fuenteravia in the Vizcaya, since I went along one side 188 great leagues in a straight line from west to east. It is desirable land and, once seen, is never to be relinquished; and in it, although all I have taken possession of for their Highnesses and all are more richly supplied than I know or could tell, I hold them all for their Highnesses, which they may dispose of as absolutely as of the realms of Castile. In this Española, in the most convenient place and in the best district for the gold mines and for all trade both with this continent and with that over there, belonging to Grand Khan, where there will be great trade and profit, I have taken possession of a large town to which I gave the name "La Villa de Navidad," and in it I have built a fort and defenses, which already, at this moment, will be all complete, and I have left in it enough people for such purpose, with arms and artillery and provisions for more than a year and a fusta, and a master of the sea in all [maritime] arts to build others; and great friendship with the king of that land, to such an extent that he took pride in calling me and treating me as a brother; and even if he were to change his mind and insult these people, neither he nor his people know the use of arms and they go naked, as I have already said, and are the most timid people in the world, so that merely the people whom I have left there could destroy all that land; and the island is without danger for their persons, if they know how to behave themselves.*

In all these islands, it appears, all the men are content with one woman, but to their Maioral, or king, they give up to twenty. It appears to me that the women work more than the men. I have been unable to learn whether they hold private property, but it appeared true to me that all took a share in anything that one had, especially in victuals. In these islands I have so far found no human monstrosities, as many expected, on the contrary, among all these people good looks are esteemed; nor are they Negroes, as in Guinea, but with flowing hair, and they are not born where there is excessive force in the solar rays; it is true that the sun there has great strength, although it is distant from the equator 26°.[9]

In these islands, where there are high mountains, the cold this winter was severe, but they endure it through habit and with the help of food which they eat with many excessively hot spices. Thus I have neither found monsters nor had report of any, except in an island which is the second at the entrance to the Indies, which is inhabited by people who are regarded in all the islands as ferocious and who eat human flesh; they have canoes with which they range all the islands of India and pillage and take as much as they can; they are no more malformed than the others, except that they have the custom of wearing their hair long like women, and they use bows and arrows of the same stems of cane with a little piece of wood at the tip for want of iron, which they have not.

They are ferocious toward these other people, who are exceedingly great cowards, but I make no more account of them than the rest. There are those who have intercourse with the woman of "Matremomio,"[10] which is the first island met on the way from Spain to the Indies, in which there is not one man. These women use no feminine exercises, but bows and arrows of cane, like the above-said; and they arm and cover themselves with plates of copper, of which they have plenty. In another island, which they assure me is larger than Española, the people have no hair. In this there is countless gold, and from it and from the other islands I bring with me Indios[11] as evidence.

In conclusion, to speak only of that which has been accomplished on this voyage, which was so hasty, Their Highnesses can see that I shall give them as much gold as they want if Their Highnesses will render me a little help; besides spice and cotton, as much as Their Highnesses shall command; and gum mastic, as much as they shall order snipped and which up to now has been found only in Greece, in the island of Chios, and the Seigniory[12] sell it for what it pleases; and aloe wood, as much as they shall order shipped, and slaves, as many as they shall order, who will be idolaters. And I believe that I have found rhubarb and cinnamon, and I shall find a thousand other things of value, which the people whom I have left there will have discovered, for I tarried nowhere, provided the wind allowed me to sail, except in the town of Navidad, where I stayed [to have it] secured and well seated. And the truth is I should have done much more if the vessels had served me as the occasion required.[13] This is enough. And the Eternal God, Our Lord, Who gives to all those who walk in His way victory over things which appear impossible; and this was notably one. For, although men have talked or have written of these lands, all was conjecture, without getting a lot at it, but amounted only to this; that those who heard for the most part listened and judged it more a fable than that there was anything in it, however small.

So, since our Redeemer has given this triumph to our most illustrious King and Queen, and to their renowned realms, in so great a manner, for this all Christendom ought to feel joyful and make great celebrations and give solemn thanks to the Holy Trinity with many solemn prayers for the great exaltation which it will have, in the turning of so many peoples to our holy faith, and afterwards for material benefits, since not only Spain but all Christians will hence have refreshment and profit. This is exactly what has been done, though in brief.

Done on board the caravel off the Canary Islands,[14] on the fifteenth of February, year 1493. At your service.

— *THE ADMIRAL*

Additional Note, Which Came with the Letter

After having written this, and being in the Sea of Castile, there rose up on me so great a wind south and southwest,[15] that I was obliged to ease the ships.[16] But I ran hither today into this port of Lisbon, which was the greatest wonder in the world, and whence I decided to write to Their Highnesses. In all the Indies I have always found weather as in May; I went thither in thirty-three days and would have returned in twenty-eight but for these tempests which detained me twenty-three days, being about in this sea. Here all the seafarers say that never has there been so bad a winter or so many losses of ships.

Done the fourteenth[17] day of March.

Chapter Twenty-Three

THE CONQUERING HERO RETURNS HOME

The Niña, sailing with an ebb tide up the Saltes, arrived in Palos, after a thirty-two-week voyage, on March 15, looking pretty and in grand shape despite the ordeal with the Atlantic storms. Taking advantage of the carte blanche that King João of Portugal had offered, Columbus had had the vessel completely overhauled in the royal shipyards. The dirty hold of the ship was cleaned and disinfected, probably with vinegar; leaks caulked; new stone ballast installed to replace the saltwater; and most importantly, new sails and rigging had replaced the shredded sails torn by the last storm. Finally, she had received a fresh coat of paint.

Close behind and on the same tide came Martín Alonzo Pinzón with the Pinta! No doubt, Columbus was very happy to see the Pinta and grateful that she had not been lost. Apparently, during the storm of February 13, when the two vessels had been separated, the Pinta sailed past the Azores without sighting any of them and eventually reached Bayona, a Spanish harbor just north of the Portuguese border. Because Pinzón did not tarry in the Azores, he missed the storm that nearly sank the Niña within sight of the Portuguese coast.

Having reached Spain ahead of Columbus, Martín Alonso immediately dispatched a courier with a letter to the Sovereigns, at that time holding court in Barcelona. He requested an audience so that he could make a report on the discovery. They sent a quick reply requesting that he come to court with the Admiral—which he interpreted as a snub and over which he grieved all the way home to Palos. Without reporting to the Admiral, or even hailing his brother, Vicente Yañez, Martín Alonso left his ship, went to his country home, and died soon after on March 20. Historians claim he died of grief, but chances are that he must have been a sick man as a result of the hardships suffered on the voyage. Grief and depression were the catalysts of his demise. He was buried in the monastery of La Rábida on the banks of the Río Tinto, an appropriate resting place for a great navigator.

ANDALUSIAN RECEPTION

Columbus received a tumultuous reception in Palos when the inhabitants learned that his voyage of discovery had been successful. As the news spread throughout the town, bells rang and businesses suspended as the entire community rushed to the ship to greet the Admiral. Soon a procession was formed and headed for the local church to give thanks to God for the success of the expedition and the safe return of the Admiral and his crew.

Columbus was now anxious to meet with the Sovereigns, who were still in Barcelona. He had already dispatched his letter describing his first voyage from Lisbon. Now he sent another copy of it, requesting that a reply be sent to Seville, where he would await their orders. Seville, approximately fifty-five miles west of Palos on the Guadalquivir and a large prominent city even at that time, had an efficient courier service to Barcelona, nearly 750 miles diagonally to the northeast of Spain.

Considering the painful sores Columbus had experienced on the overland journey from Lisbon to Valle del Parayso on his visit to King João, one wonders why he did not proceed by sea instead of by land to Barcelona. A sea voyage around the Strait of Gibraltar northeast in the Mediterranean to Barcelona was longer by 150 to 200 miles but definitely more comfortable, as he would be sailing along the Spanish coast in familiar territory. Morison states that haste was a consideration because of the possibility that Martín Alonso might reach the Sovereigns ahead of the Admiral. My own conclusion is that Columbus chose the overland route primarily for spreading the good news of his discovery and, to some extent, to bask in the glory of his discovery. After all, he had been accused of being a braggart, a dreamer, and a nobody. He had endured six long years of rejection in Spain, and now was his moment; he wanted a public vindication.

During this period, Columbus fulfilled his vows at Santa Clara de Moguer and Santa María de la Cinta at nearby Huelva and spent nearly two weeks at La Rábida with Fray Juan Pérez and some of his friends. By the end of March, he left for Seville with six of his healthy Indians, as one had died and three sick ones were left behind at Palos. His short trip to Seville was a triumphant parade as Columbus took along, besides the Indians, the various exotic items—rare birds and other curiosities brought from the New World. He arrived in Seville on March 31, Palm Sunday, and was greeted with much honor and acclamation, as the people poured forth to marvel at the feathered Indians who seemed to be inhabitants from another planet. The Admiral was presented to the city's nobility and bishops, and had the honor of dining with the alcalde, the archbishop, and the Duke of Medina Sidonia, his early sponsor.

Columbus spent the Holy Week in Seville and must have been deeply moved by the spectacular pageantry, which even today is considered the world's most extraordinary religious spectacle. The confraternities or brotherhoods of the religious faithful garbed in their colorful hooded vestments trod as penitents all week long down the narrow streets in solemn processions. Floats with tableaus depicting the Virgin Mary in tears and the agony of Christ on the cross were pushed forward by penitents, making their way through the wailing crowds. The Holy Week celebrations at the Cathedral culminated in the Easter Triduum commemorating the crucifixion, burial, and resurrection of Christ. Whether by design or not, Columbus arrived in Seville as Christ had arrived in Jerusalem, in triumph, and on the same day! The time was propitious, and he must have been deeply moved by the experience of the Holy Week.

With the culmination of the Easter Festivities that April 7, Columbus was pleased to receive the very important letter from the Sovereigns addressed to "Don Cristóbal, Our Admiral of the Ocean Sea, Viceroy and Governor of the Islands that he hath discovered in the Indies." There was no question from this formal salutation that Columbus had finally arrived! The letter commended Columbus for his great discovery, but the tone of the letter was one of haste:

We wish you to come soon…that you should hasten your coming as much as possible so that everything may be seen to, and as you see that summer is with us and we must not let miss the best time to return, see whether something could not already be prepared in Seville or in other places for your return to the lands you have discovered. And write soon…so that we may be in a position to see things while you are on your way here and back, so that when you return from here [Barcelona] all may be ready.[1]

It was sent from Barcelona on March 30, 1493. The need for the great haste was obvious: a fear that the King of Portugal might consider Columbus's discoveries as encroaching on Portuguese possession and act accordingly. Columbus complied with the Sovereigns' request, immediately divulging for their scrutiny and acceptance a plan for the colonization and administration of Hispaniola. The salient points of the plan were:

a. Two thousand volunteer settlers should be allowed to go.
b. These settlers to be distributed among three or four towns to be built in convenient places.
c. Each town is to have an alcalde and a clerk for public administration and priests for worship.
d. Nobody should be allowed to collect gold without a license from the governor or alcalde.
e. All licensed gold-gatherers must hand over their takings to the town clerk, who will take half of the gold for the Crown and one percent for the support of religion.
f. All trade between Spain and Hispaniola should be conducted between Cadiz and selected ports on the island to protect the Crown's interest.
g. Anyone who wishes to make further discoveries should be allowed to do so.[2]

The letter was signed with an enigmatic signature whose meaning has baffled historians throughout the centuries and which may never be deciphered. Columbus attached great importance to it and even described how it should be written. It was:

S

SAS

XPO FERENS

The last signature, "XPO Ferens," is simply the Greek-Latin form of the name. The other letters are conjectural and may be interpreted in many ways. As a matter of fact, this signature has been a favorite puzzle for mystery hunters, and the interpretation of it ranges from the ingenious to the absurd. The triangular form itself raises many interpretations. For example, de Madariaga suggests that it is a cabalistic interpretation translated into the shield of David, suggesting Columbus's Jewish origin.[3] Here are three interpretations of the three top lines as suggested by Landström:[4]

SERVUS

SUM ALTISSIMI SALVATORIS

XRISTE MARIA YESU

I am the servant of the Most Exalted Savior Christ, Mary, Jesus;

SALVO

SANCTUM ALTISSIMUM SEPULCRUM

XRISTE MARIA YESU

I shall save the Holy, Most High Sepulcher of Christ, Mary, Joseph;

SERVIDOR
SUS ALTEZAS SACRAS
XRISTE MARIA ISABEL

The Servant of the Most Exalted Majesties Christ, Mary, Ysabella.

Having sent this letter ahead by a swift courier, Columbus left Seville for Córdoba with his entourage, which now consisted of not only the six Indians and some of his officers, but also two servants, befitting his status of Admiral. Here he visited his mistress, Beatriz Enriquez de Harana, and his sons, Diego and Ferdinand. The city gave her "adopted son" a great ovation and he was entertained by the alcalde and his entire municipality.

ROYAL WELCOME IN BARCELONA

The cavalcade then continued to Murcia, reaching the Mediterranean coast at Valencia. It proceeded along the coastal route to Tarragona and arrived in Barcelona between April 17 and 20. His son Ferdinand describes Columbus's arrival in Barcelona as follows:

This news [Discovery of the Indies] caused them [Their Highnesses] great joy and happiness, and they ordered that a solemn reception be held for him, as befitted one who had rendered them so great a service. All the court and the city came out to meet him, and the Catholic Sovereigns received him in public, seated with all majesty and grandeur on rich thrones under a canopy of cloth of gold. When he came forward to kiss their hands, they rose from their thrones as if he were a great lord, and would not let him kiss their hands, but made him sit down beside them. After he had given them a brief account of the voyage and its success they permitted him to retire to his lodgings, to which he went accompanied by the whole Court. So much did their Highnesses favor and honor him that when the king rode about Barcelona the Admiral rode on one side of him and the Infante Fortuna [the king's cousin] on the other. Never before had anyone been permitted to ride with the king, save his very close kinsman, the Infante.[5]

The round of receptions continued the following day when Columbus was publicly received in the Alcazar by the king and queen. The most aristocratic families of Spain were assembled for this state reception. Columbus entered the hall surrounded by a crowd of cavaliers. The Admiral was conspicuous for his stately and regal bearing, which with his gray hair gave him the appearance of a Roman senator. As he approached, the Sovereigns rose as if receiving a person of high rank, and when he knelt to kiss their hands, they told him to rise and be seated beside them and the Infante Don Juan.

At their request, he now gave an account of his voyage and a description of the islands discovered and later he paraded the Indians and all the exotic birds and other trappings, which were admired with intense interest. Finally, all adjourned to the royal chapel where the "Te Deum Laudamus" was chanted by the choir and accompanied by instruments. Everyone was deeply moved. At the end of the service, Columbus, attended by the whole court, retired to a special guest residence provided for him.

During his stay in Barcelona he spent some leisure time with the royal family. The queen took much delight in discussing his enterprise with him. As for the king, he appeared on horseback with Prince Juan on one side and Columbus on the other. Also, Pedro Gonzalez de Mendoza, the Archbishop of Toledo and Grand Cardinal of Spain, a man of high virtue, invited Columbus to a banquet where he was assigned the most honorable place at the table. Columbus's shining star had reached its zenith. Honored by the Sovereigns, lionized by the nobility, idolized by the people—his cup was truly running over. He bore all these attentions and adulations with restrained modesty, knowing only too well that many of these same people had derided him as an adventurer and a braggart in that very court. Columbus was now enjoying his finest hour, but it was a prelude of bitter years to come. Jealousy would raise its ugly head and attempt to discredit and destroy him.

A COAT OF ARMS FOR THE ADMIRAL

To perpetuate the glory of his achievement in his family, a coat of arms was bestowed on Columbus. He was accorded the honor and privilege of including in it the castle and lion, the official emblems of Castile and Leon, in the two top quarters. In the lower-right quarter, his proper bearings, which were a group of islands surrounded by waves, are indicated; while in the lower-left quarter, his family coat of arms, used before ennoblement, is retained. To this, the following legend was later added:

A Castilla y a León
Nuevo mundo diò Colón

To Castile and to León
Columbus gave a new world.

Later still, after he had discovered the mainland of America at Paria in 1498, Columbus included terra firma with the islands on the lower-right quarter. As befitting his status of Admiral of the Ocean Sea, a new lower-left quarter was introduced consisting of five gold anchors horizontal on a blue field. The family arms were retained by squeezing them between the two lower quarters.

REPARTITIONING THE NEW WORLD

In 1492, the Spaniard Rodrigo Borgia became pope with the title of Alexander VI. His election to the throne of Saint Peter was due in part to the influence of Ferdinand and Isabella. As a courtier and cardinal, he had fathered a large family including Cesare Borgia, the famous and ruthless *condottiere*; Lucrezia Borgia, a lady of much controversy; and another son, Pedro Luis, on whom Ferdinand had conferred the dukedom of Gandia. Previously, Ferdinand had favored the future pope with three Aragonese bishoprics and nominated the teenager, Cesar, to the bishoprics of Pampeluna and Valencia. Pope Alexander's administration was a remarkable one, lasting until his death in 1503. It became his lot to keep peace between the kings of Spain and Portugal by repartitioning between them their discoveries in the New World.

When the news of Columbus's discovery reached King João II, the Spanish Sovereigns were alerted by their ambassador in Lisbon that King João was equipping a fleet to reach the newly discovered Indies. Alarmed at that news, the Sovereigns requested that a Bull be issued by the pope to protect their interests. The first Bull, "Inter Caetera," dated May 3, 1493, was motivated by Columbus's famous letter and granted to Spain the lands discovered by Columbus and laid down a demarcation line between Spain and Portugal for future discoveries. This Bull, however, did not abrogate the previous one, "Aeterni Regis," of 1481, which King João interpreted as a horizontal line of demarcation running through the Canaries westward.

Any land discovered south of this line would be disputed by the Portuguese. This line, which would have been at approximately 28°N latitude across the Atlantic, would have jeopardized Columbus's discoveries of Cuba and Hispaniola, which fall below that line. Because of the confusion, Spain immediately sent a delegation to Rome. Pope Alexander consequently issued a second "Inter Caetera" describing a line of demarcation drawn from the North Pole to South Pole one hundred leagues towards the west and south from the Azores and Cape Verde Islands. West of this meridian, which falls on 38°W longitude, all future discoveries of land to the west shall belong to Castile. This line was suggested by Columbus, as in passing that meridian on his first voyage, the compass needle northwested a full point. Additionally, the stars and temperature of the air and water abruptly changed. This Bull, however, did not sit well with the Portuguese, who demanded a line of demarcation further west. Rather than risk a naval encounter, the two nations decided, without the interference of the pope, whom the Portuguese felt was partial to Spain, to settle the problem between themselves. The result was the Treaty of Tordesillas, satisfactorily concluded on June 7, 1494, in which the line of demarcation was moved 370 leagues west of the Cape Verde Islands or on the longitude meridian of 46°W. On the basis of this treaty, Portugal later was able to claim Brazil. But it allowed both Spain and Portugal to pursue their projects of discoveries in relative harmony.

Part VI

THE SECOND VOYAGE TO THE INDIES

Chapter Twenty-Four

THE SECOND VOYAGE OF DISCOVERY

The great solemnity with which the king and queen had received Columbus, and the fact that they had issued orders that he should be honored by all the grandees in the land, raised quite a few eyebrows. The king and queen astounded their courtiers by giving Columbus a reception worthy of the best traditions of the Crown. The Sovereigns were prepared to reward him with still more honors for his accomplishments. Yet, strangely enough, the festivities would not have taken place if Columbus had arrived two months earlier—or at least not at the same level of magnitude and opulence.

Queen Isabella, despite her deep religious convictions and austere life, was a pleasure-loving monarch and loved stately ceremonies for worthy causes. Since December 7 of the previous year, she had been distraught and despondent because of a near-fatal attempt on the king's life. On that day, the king had been sitting in court in Barcelona adjudicating legal cases. As he rose to go after completing his hearings, a man attacked him and struck him with a cutlass, giving him a deep gash from the top of his head by the ear and neck down to the shoulders. Fortunately, though it was a deep and horrible wound, no arteries were severed as the king wore a gold necklace. For nearly three months, when the king's survival seemed in doubt, the queen was in mourning. When the king, though pale and sickly, was out of danger, it was time to celebrate. And she made the most of it as Columbus had brought good news, good enough to lift her spirits.

MORE HONORS FOR THE ADMIRAL

In addition to the festive events they had planned for the Admiral, Ferdinand and Isabella rewarded Columbus for his accomplishments with tangible assets. In chronological order, they were:

1. Columbus was granted the honor of a coat of arms with a castle and a lion—the royal symbols of Castile and León reserved for royalty. (May 20)
2. To raise his station in life, he was given a present of 1,000 gold dobles (335,000 maravedis). (May 23)
3. He was granted the right to lodge with five of his servants wherever he went at government expense, paying only for his own food. (May 26)
4. All the rights, honors, and privileges agreed upon in the Capitulation of Santa Fé were solemnly confirmed. (May 28)
5. His appointment as Captain-General of the second fleet going to the Indies was approved. (May 28)
6. The right to submit three persons for the government of the Indies as defined in the Capitulations was confirmed. The Sovereigns, however, retained the power to choose one of the three persons proposed by the Admiral.

7. The Sovereigns granted Columbus the ten thousand maravedis promised by them to the first man who sighted land on the first voyage.

This last item has caused much controversy among the chroniclers. Why did Columbus claim the reward? Because he claimed that on October 11, at 10:00 p.m., before moonrise, he was standing on the sterncastle of the Santa María and thought he saw a light; he called Pedro Gutierrez and later Rodrigo Sánchez, who claimed they saw it too. Rodrigo later claimed he saw nothing because he was in no position to see it, but had merely yessed Columbus. Later, at 2:00 a.m., October 12, Rodrigo de Triana, the lookout on the Pinta's forecastle, saw what seemed to be a white sand cliff gleaming in the moonlight and shouted, "*Tierra! Tierra!*" This time, indeed, it was land. Martín Alonso Pinzón had a Lombard fired to alert the fleet, and Columbus approached the Pinta and confirmed the sighting. He reckoned that the land was but six miles away.

Ferdinand dismissed the whole thing by admitting that:

A sailor named Rodrigo de Triana first sighted it [the land] while they were still two leagues away. It was not he who received the grant of ten thousand maravedis from the Catholic Sovereigns, however, but the Admiral, who had first seen the light amid darkness, signifying the spiritual light with which he was to illuminate those parts.[1]

I don't believe that it was greed that made him accept the reward. I think somehow the glory of discovery would have lost some of its luster if his eyes had not seen the land first.

THE GREAT ARMADA

The preparation of the fleet for the second voyage proved to be a more arduous task than anticipated. It took longer than the monarchs had hoped for, despite the competent administration of the Archdeacon of Seville, Don Juan de Fonseca, nephew of the Archbishop whom the Sovereigns had appointed to prepare a large fleet for the second voyage, in collaboration with Columbus. They could not have appointed a more competent person for the job. According to Las Casas, Don Juan de Fonseca, who occupied a high position in the Church—he was the Bishop of Burgos, until he died—was a very capable and resourceful man, especially gifted in the manning of fleets. The king and queen always depended on his services for the preparation of their fleets.

To assist Fonseca in his duties, the Crown appointed Francisco Pivelo as treasurer and Juan de Soria as comptroller. An office of administration and procurement was established at Seville, and a custom-house, as suggested by Columbus, established in Cádiz. Financing of the great enterprise was partially provided by a loan and by the expropriated properties of the exiled Jews. Ponder the mysterious ways in which contemptible historical decisions become providential. In this case, Spanish rulers illegally took away the possessions of persecuted people to help establish a new country that many years later would provide a haven for the persecuted people of the world.

Columbus and Fonseca were given the responsibility to purchase or charter whatever ships were required, as well as provisions and stores to supply a complement of 1,200 men, which by departure time had swelled to 1,500. The fleet consisted of seventeen vessels of various types; three of them including Columbus's flagship, the Capitana, later renamed the Santa María, were large naos in the two-hundred-ton class. They were roomy and carried those items they needed to introduce Spanish civilization into the Indies: furniture, building materials, provisions, seeds, seedlings, sugarcane and grapevine shoots, and horses for transportation. Twelve of the vessels were caravels, of the middle tonnage, perhaps as much as one hundred tons. Finally, there were three small caravels of the Portuguese type, including the dauntless Niña, recommissioned and renamed Santa Clara after the monastery in Moguer.

All the vessels were well manned as many volunteers had flocked to enlist, affording Fonseca and Columbus the opportunity to be selective. Nearly five hundred of them were young soldiers, veterans of the Granada War, eager for new adventures in the New World. Of this group, many were hidalgos—men of nobility—and others aspired to be hidalgos by acts of valor. Among this group was Alonso de Hojeda, a chivalric adventurer, already noted for his skill in the martial arts and for feats of remarkable ability. Trained for a military career in the ducal court of Don Louis de Cerda, Duke of Medina Celi, erstwhile patron of Columbus, Hojeda would become in due time a famous explorer and conquistador.

The commander of the armed forces was Francisco de Pensalosa, uncle of historian-bishop Bartolomé de Las Casas, whose father, Pedro, also sailed on this voyage. There were a number of Genoese mariners including Michele de Cuneo, childhood friend of Columbus, whose accounts of the second voyage, notably a letter to Hieronymo Annari in 1495, is of interest in relation to the discovery of the Virgin Islands, Jamaica, and Puerto Rico and a lively source of information on fauna, flora, and native manners and customs.

Other well-known historical figures who sailed with the fleet were Ponce de León, conquistador of Puerto Rico and discoverer of Florida; Columbus's younger brother Diego (Giacomo); Juan de la Cosa; another of that name, a famous chart-maker of Puerto Santa María; and Dr. Diego Alvarez Chanca, a physician of Seville whose interest in birds, trees, herbs, and maladies left us a detailed account of the flora and fauna.

Missionary work was an important aim of the voyage; a dozen ecclesiastics were aboard headed by Fray Buil, a Benedictine entrusted by the Sovereigns with the task of converting the Indians to Christianity. The queen had charged three Franciscans to build the first church in the New World, donating fixtures and equipment for building it. Other priests, missioners, and chaplains were on board as well.

Despite the marvelous job done by Fonseca and Columbus, the Sovereigns grew impatient with the progress being made and issued several royal orders to make haste. The first royal letter was sent to Columbus on June 12, soon after he had left Barcelona for Seville. But instead of going directly to Seville, Columbus, with five of his baptized Indians, took a longer route to fulfill his vow of pilgrimage to Guadalupe in Estremadura, made aboard the Niña on the homeward voyage. This was another triumphal journey for the Admiral for he headed westward to Zaragoza then southwest to Madrid through Medina Celi. From Madrid he followed a tortuous route through Talavera de La Reina, then Trujillo and finally Guadalupe. There, in the monastery's gothic church in front of the image of Nuestra Señora de Guadalupe, Columbus fulfilled his vows. Still riding the crest of success, the Admiral, of course, was received with great admiration wherever he went. The monks of the monastery asked him to name an island after their city on his next voyage.

The Lady of Guadalupe, thanks to Columbus and to the conquistadores from Estremadura, such as Cortes and Pizarro, is now venerated in many countries of the New World. She is especially venerated in Mexico, where the Virgin appeared to a poor native boy in 1531 in New Guadalupe. The shrine created there is perhaps even more popular than the original one in Estremadura.

From Guadalupe, Columbus continued southward to Córdoba, where he said farewell to his mistress, Beatriz, and his two sons, then eventually reached Seville, possibly in late June but most likely in early July.

On July 25, the king and queen sent letters to both Fonseca and Columbus, urging them to move quickly with preparations for the second voyage. On the fourth of August, the royal couple wrote to Francisco Pivelo, the treasurer of the fleet, with a similar request. On August 18, another request to Fonseca and Columbus—and on September 5, still another urging both men not to delay. Why the concern and urgency of the Sovereigns? They feared that King João of Portugal, not pleased with the second Papal Bull, might send his own fleet to the Indies. An intelligence report had been received that a Portuguese caravel had set sail from Madeira westward, giving indication that she might be heading for the newly discovered lands. Columbus contacted the Sovereigns about the possibility of intercepting this caravel with part of his fleet, which was being assembled. But apparently cooler heads prevailed, and remonstrances made to King João, who indicated that the caravel had sailed without his permission, caused it to be ordered back.

THE GRAND FLEET DEPARTS

Early in the morning of September 25, 1493, the fleet departed from Cádiz. Unlike Columbus's first departure, the second was a festive occasion, a procession of happy people and gaily decorated ships with colorful banners flying from the rigging and royal standards waving in the breeze, high on the mainmasts. The shores echoed with the roar of cannons, the sounds of trumpets, the braying of clarions, and the cheers of the jubilant population. Cheering and waiving "Goodspeed!" from shore were the youthful sons of the Admiral, Diego and Ferdinand. "...while my brother and I looked on, the Admiral weighed anchor in the harbor of Cádiz...for the Canary Islands,"[2] wrote Ferdinand. A fleet of Venetian galleys, which was in the harbor at the time, escorted the armada to sea.

Columbus had been warned by the Sovereigns to stay clear of any Portuguese possession and to be on the lookout for their caravels. He headed towards the Canaries, and after seven days, the fleet arrived at the Grand Canary. They set sail again at midnight, after making some repairs on one of the ships, and on October 5 reached San Sebastian, Gomera, where Doña Beatriz de Peraza greeted Columbus with cannon salvos and showers of fireworks. Michele de Cuneo, in his letter to Annari, mailed from Savona on October 15, 1495, reported that the fleet had taken onboard fresh supplies and live animals to start herds in Hispaniola. During this time, Columbus had an opportunity to spend some time with Doña Beatriz.

"On the tenth of October," reported Cuneo, "we sailed on our direct course, but because of contrary weather, we remained for three days near the Canary Islands. On the morning of October 13, a Sunday, we left the island of Ferro, the last of the Canary Islands, and our course was W by S."[3]

Every captain had been given sealed instructions as to what to do if the ships were separated from the fleet. On leaving the Canaries on his first voyage, Columbus had set his course due west. Now, with his west by south course, he wanted to go farther south than Hispaniola to find the islands that according to the Indians contained a great quantity of gold. The island of Matinino was still on his mind. Another reason, as recorded by Dr. Chanca, was that "these islands were nearer to Spain."[4] They were indeed! Furthermore, by sailing farther south, the fleet went deeper into the trade wind zone so that this new course shortened the ocean crossing by a week.

The fleet had clear, speedy sailing for most of the trip except for a short period about two-thirds of the way across. It was a thunderstorm of considerable violence, which frightened marines terribly. Once again from de Cuneo's letter:

On 26 October, the vigil of SS Simon and Jude, at about 4:00 p.m., the fortune of the sea began to strike us in such a way that you would not believe it. We thought our days had come to an end. It lasted all that night and until day in such a manner that one ship could not see the other; in the end it pleased God that we should find each other.[5]

Columbus also kept a journal for his second voyage, but it has never been found and is presumed lost. When writing his father's *Life of the Admiral,* Ferdinand had access to it, as did other early chroniclers. However, information on the second voyage was recorded by contemporaries who were with Columbus such as de Cuneo and the hidalgo Guillermo Coma of Aragon, who corresponded regularly with Niccolò Scillacio, a Sicilian professor of philosophy at the University of Pavia, who was staying with Giovanni Antonio Birreta.

Scillacio translated all the letters he received from his friend Coma into Latin and printed them at Pavia late in 1494 or early

1495, in a twenty-page pamphlet dedicated to the reigning Duke of Milan, Ludovico Mari Sforza.

Scillacio's account of the storm, which makes reference to an electrical discharge well known to sailors, is even more dramatic than de Cuneo's:

Finally, in response to their unceasing prayers and their pious and tearful entreaties...fiery humors were released which dissolved the thick cloud of the furious storm. It was a certain St. Elmo, who harkens to the cries of sailors and is gracious toward victims of shipwreck, two lighted candles flashed out in the dark of the night from the flagship's masthead. Straightway, the storm began to abate, the sea to temper its wrath, and the waves their violence.[6]

After the storm abated, flocks of birds flying westward and land-type cloud formations were seen in the distance. Columbus, with his uncanny sense of perception, had already sensed that land was not too far. On November 2, he was so confident that he ordered all ships to shorten sail. In the early morning hours of Sunday, November 3, 1493, the watchman at the Admiral's masthead saw the high peak of an island against the misty gray morning sky. "*Tierra! Tierra!*" he shouted. The sound of his voice was echoed by other shouts of *Tierra! Tierra!* over the silent ocean. They had reached an island farther south and fifteen degrees nearer the Old World than San Salvador. The Admiral summoned all hands to pray and give thanks to the Lord, after which they sang the "Salve Regina."

Chapter Twenty-Five

A LITANY OF SAINTS

Columbus's first sight of land on Sunday, November 3, was an island in the Lesser Antilles he named "Dominica" because it was discovered on Sunday. It is a beautiful, lush island cut by sparkling streams, in those days inhabited by the fierce cannibalistic Carib Indians.[1] After an unsuccessful attempt to land on the northeastern shore of Dominica, Columbus sailed northward and spotted another island, round and flat and much smaller than Dominica. That he named "María Galante." On this island, he found good anchorage on the lee side, possibly in the vicinity of the present-day Grand Bourg. On landing on María Galante, the Admiral—with many men watching—displayed the royal standard and with appropriate ceremonies took possession of the archipelago in the names of the King and Queen of Spain. They found no people on this island, but some sailors regretted their eagerness to taste the local fruit, as Dr. Chanca explains:

On this island the trees were amazingly dense, and they were of great variety of species known to none of us. Some were in fruit, some in flower, and all therefore were green. We found one tree, like a laurel but not so large, the leaves of which had the finest scent of clove that I have never smelt. I think it must have been a species of laurel. There were wild fruit [possibly the manzanillo]...which some rashly tried. But no sooner did they taste them than their faces swelled, growing inflamed and painful that they almost went out of their minds. They cured themselves with cold compresses.[2]

Before daybreak on the following day, November 4, they headed west by north, sighting on the port side four small islands (present Terre-de-Bas, Terre de-Haut, Grand Ilet, and Ilet à Cabrit) that Columbus named "Todos los Santos" after All Saints Day, recently past, a name the French have maintained with "Les Saintes." A few miles ahead rose a great mountain mass. Columbus named it "Santa María de Guadalupe," fulfilling a promise made to the monks of the famous shrine in Estremadura. Actually, two islands, Grande Terra and Basse-Terre (Guadeloupe today), form one of the two French departments in the Caribbean. Like Martinique, it enjoys the status of a province of France.

On approaching Guadeloupe from the east side in the direction of the present city of Capesterre-Belle-Eau, a waterfall in the Soufriere Mountains, rising 4,870 feet above sea level, makes an imposing sight, as described by Dr. Chanca:

Three leagues away could be seen a waterfall of considerable breadth, which fell from so high that it seemed to come from the sky. It could be seen from so far off that many wagers were laid on board. Some said that it was white rock and others that it was water. When we got nearer, the truth was apparent. It was the most beautiful thing in the world to see the height from which it fell and from how small a place such a force of water sprang.[3]

ADVENTURES IN GUADELOUPE

The fleet began to circle the island looking for a suitable anchorage; this they found at the southernmost point of the island between the present Vieux Fort and Trois Rivières. Early the following day, in order to ascertain who inhabited the island, Columbus, who had already guessed that they might be Caribs, sent out several of the caravels' captains to reconnoiter. Some of the men brought back boys who reported that they had been held captive by the Caribs, others captured women who opposed resistance. Another group of women came back of their own accord, claiming they too had been made prisoners.

Six men under the command of Captain Diego Marquez penetrated the dense forest and did not report back that evening, causing much consternation in the ranks of the fleet. They were forced to remain in Guadeloupe for eight days, until the men returned. In the meantime, the Admiral had an opportunity to learn the customs and habits of the natives. In visiting the dwellings and villages near the coast, the Spaniards found a great number of human skulls and bones hanging inside the houses. They encountered mostly women, and very few men, who told them that ten canoes full of Caribs had gone to raid other islands. When the Spaniards made it clear they disliked the Caribs because of the cannibalism, the women rejoiced. They were, in fact, all prisoners. The Caribs periodically raided other islands, traveling as far as 150 leagues in their canoes hewn out of a single tree. Dr. Chanca reported that:

They carry off all the women they can take, especially the young and beautiful, whom they keep as servants and concubines. They had carried off so many that in fifty we found no males and more than twenty of the captives were girls. These women say that they are treated with a cruelty that seems incredible. The Caribs eat the male children they have by them and only bring up the children for their own women; and as far as men they are able to capture, they bring those who are alive home to be slaughtered and eat those who are dead on the spot. They say that human flesh is so good that there is nothing like it in the world; and this must be true for the human bones we found in their houses were so gnawed that no flesh was left on them except what was too tough to be eaten. They castrate the boys they capture and use them as servants until they are men. Then when they want to make a feast, they kill and eat them, for they say that the flesh of boys and women is not good to eat. Three of these boys fled to us and all three had been castrated.[4]

Apparently, the Caribs also disliked the flesh of the brown-robed monks, for the first time they ate one they all came down with indigestion. Thereafter no Carib would eat a man dressed in the habit of a monk. Spanish sailors would deliberately dress in this ecclesiastical garb to be spared, in case of capture by the aborigines, the honor of becoming an entrée.

Aside from the horrible practices of its inhabitants, the island of Guadeloupe left a memorable impression on the Spaniards because of its lofty mountains, silvery streams, and exotic flora. In many ways, the Caribs were better artisans, judging from their belongings, than the docile Taino Indians. For example, their towns, which consisted of a group of houses built around a public square, were better planned. The houses were more sturdily constructed with trunks of trees interwoven with reeds and thatched with palm leaves. The houses were square, not round like those the Spaniards had seen in Cuba and Hispaniola, and they were laid out so that each had its portico for shelter against the tropical sun. For furniture, they had hammocks of cotton netting and seats hewn out of tree trunks. Their utensils, formed of earthenware, were equal or superior to those seen in Hispaniola. Their cloth was woven so tight and of such texture as to equal the clothes made in Spain. They had domesticated geese like those seen in Europe, but what caught the eye of the Spaniards were the beautiful huge parrots with blue, green, white, and scarlet plumage. Being an aggressive war-like people, they made their bows and arrows powerful enough to pierce the shields of the Spaniards, as the arrows were tipped with sharp fish bones. In Guadeloupe, the Spaniards also discovered the pineapple, which Ferdinand described as:

Fruit that looked like green pine cones but were much larger, these were filled with solid pulp, like a melon, but were much sweeter in taste and smell.[5]

Columbus was in a hurry to reach the men he had left behind in La Navidad. For this reason he sent out four search parties of fifty men each to look for the Diego Marquez party, according to de Cuneo, but they returned without finding any trace of the men.

Just as Columbus was thinking seriously of leaving the lost party behind, some sailors saw smoke rising from a mountaintop. A boat was sent immediately to the nearest place on the shore, and a rescue party, led by an old native woman, reached the lost group and helped them back to safety. When asked how they had gotten lost, they replied that the trees were so thick that they could not see the sky to look at the stars for a bearing. Columbus was not impressed by their story. Indeed, for their long delay (de Cuneo said they had been looking for gold), he ordered that the captain be put in chains and the rest of the party on short rations.

At daybreak on Sunday, November 10, the Admiral and his fleet weighed anchor and headed north along the west coast of Guadeloupe for Hispaniola, but lay becalmed on the lee side of the island and lay-to for the night until the following morning. By midday of November 11, they reached a medium-sized island, which the Admiral named "Santa María de Monserrate" after the famous monastery of Monserrat near Barcelona. Columbus did not stop at the island, as he wanted to make time for Hispaniola. Some of the Indians aboard had told him that the Caribs had depopulated that island by eating all of its inhabitants. It was just as well, for this island—now owned by the United Kingdom—is barely ten miles long and lacks good harbors. Today it remains one of the least-developed islands in the Antilles. The only attraction of this lush island is a live volcano.

On passing Monserrat, Columbus saw a larger island he named "Santa María la Antigua," boasting an ideal anchorage and superb beaches, which lie within its sheltering reef. Continuing in a northwesterly direction, they passed a tiny island—actually a huge rock—a mile long. Columbus named it "Santa María la Redonda" because, as Ferdinand explained, "…it is so round and so smooth that it is impossible to climb its sides without a ladder."[6]

They sailed past this island and in a northwesterly direction. Not too far along, they managed to find shelter and anchorage in the lee of a much larger island that Columbus named "San Martin" after Saint Martín of Tours. The name did not last long on this island, for in the next century it was changed to "Nuestra Señora de Las Nieves" (Our Lady of the Snows), in honor of the virgin who caused snow to fall in August on the Esquiline (one of the seven hills in Rome) to pinpoint the site of a church that a pious couple wanted to build in her honor. The result was the construction of the Basilica of Santa María Maggiore, where, on the feast day of August 5, synthetic snow is made to fall at the celebration of the commemorative Mass. Once again, the Virgin Mary was being honored, this time by someone other than Columbus. But the name was too cumbersome for the English to handle after they occupied the island, and the name was abbreviated to "Nevis," short enough for a small island. The island was the birthplace of Alexander Hamilton.

Columbus left his Nevis anchorage on November 12 and held the lee side of nearby St. Kitts, another possession of the United Kingdom barely four miles to the northwest, on his way to Hispaniola.[7] Again sailing leeward to the northwest and not too far away, Columbus passed another small island, which he named after the virgin martyr Saint Anastia; the Dutch who took possession of it in the seventeenth century named it "Saint Eustatius."[8]

Continuing his northwest trek, Columbus passed another tiny island that rises vertically from the sea—with no beaches at all—which he named "San Cristóbal" and which is known today as Saba.[9] Columbus hove-to for the night near San Cristóbal. On the morning of November 13, they headed due west to an island about seventy-five miles away that the Indians aboard called Aya, but by nightfall they had not made the island, so once again they hove-to. Columbus had become extremely cautious after the loss of the Santa María, and he refrained from approaching unknown islands in the darkness of the night.

On the morning of the fourteenth, Columbus weighed anchor and proceeded on his westerly course closer to the island that he named "Santa Cruz," after the Holy Cross. The island is shaped like an isosceles triangle with its apex pointing eastward, parting the trade wind like an airfoil.[10] It was there at almost noon that Columbus anchored his fleet.

A well-manned boat, consisting of about twenty-five men, was ordered ashore to fetch water and procure information from the natives. As usual, as they landed, the natives fled, but the part of the party that ventured inland found a small village that was seemingly deserted; however, they were able to free a few Arawak slaves, girls, and boys. As the boat was getting ready to return to the flagship they spotted a canoe, on which there were three or four Carib women and two Indian slaves whose genital organs had been severed.

The natives were dumbfounded at the sight of the strange men in the boat and the colorful masted fleet in the harbor. As they stopped to gawk in amazement, the boat maneuvered so as to cut off the canoe's ability to head toward shore. Feeling themselves trapped, the Caribs decided to fight despite the great odds, rather than be taken prisoners. For the first time, the Spaniards were to see the courage of the Carib Indians and feel their ferocity in battle. They picked up their bows and arrows and began to shoot arrows at the invaders with uncanny accuracy. The Spaniards tried to protect themselves with shields, which, though made of wood and leather, did not protect at least two men—one of whom was wounded on his side and the other was hit with an arrow which pierced the shield and penetrated three inches into his chest. Seriously wounded, he died a few days later. There might have been more casualties had the boat not rammed the canoe, spilling its human cargo into the water. Dr. Chanca reported:

When the boat was upset, the Indians remained in the water, sometimes swimming and sometimes standing, since there were shallows there and our men had some difficulty in catching the enemy, for they continued to shoot when they could. There was indeed one that they could not take until he was mortally wounded with a spear thrust and they brought him thus wounded to the ships.[11]

Peter Martyr gives a more vivid account of the ferocity of the Caribs and the hostile behavior of "the mortally wounded" Carib. Even when they were aboard the ship, presumably subdued, Martyr said, they did not put off their fierceness and cruel countenances any more than do the lions of Lybia. The captive's wound was so wide his intestines hung out of his body. They threw him overboard to drown, only to see him swim aboard the shore, holding his intestines in place with one hand. The fearful Arawaks demanded that he be brought aboard for a coup de grace. He was brought aboard, bound hand and foot, and thrown into the sea, but he managed to free himself and swim for shore again. He was finally dispatched with a shower of arrows.

Michele de Cuneo was involved in this skirmish with the Caribs and managed to capture a Carib girl, whom Columbus allowed him to keep as a slave. Apparently, she was imbued with the Carib ferocious spirit but was soon domesticated in a decidedly natural fashion by the not-so-gallant but persistent Italian, as he reports:

While I was in the boat I captured a very beautiful Carib woman, whom the said Lord Admiral gave to me, and with whom, having taken her into my cabin, she being naked according to their custom, I conceived desire to take pleasure. I wanted to put my desire into execution but she did not want it and treated me with her bare fingernails in such a manner that I wished I had never begun. But seeing that (to tell you the end of it all), I took a rope and thrashed her well, for which she raised such unheard of screams that you would not have believed your ears. Finally, we came to an agreement in such a manner that I can tell you that she seemed to have been brought up in a school of harlots.[12]

The Admiral became convinced that unlike the docile Arawak Indians he had met in Cuba and Hispaniola, the Caribs would be fierce impediments in the exploration of the West Indies. It would require more than the donation of hawks' bells to subdue these defiant and menacing warriors. He weighed anchor as soon as some order had been established and named the eastern cape of the harbor "Cabo de la Flecha" (Cape of the Arrow) because of the incident.

The Admiral sailed directly northward, interrupting his eastward course, which would have brought him to Hispaniola and Navidad. In view of the fact that he was extremely anxious to reach the Navidad settlement—the local skirmish with the Caribs had changed his attitude of concern to one of foreboding—the delay can only be blamed on the instabilities of the wind, particularly because it took him two days to cover the thirty-five-mile stretch to the Virgin Islands. He had reached an archipelago of so many islands that he could not possibly assign individual names to them; hence, the group was named after Saint Ursula and her companions, the eleven thousand virgins. According to legend, Ursula was a maiden from Britain who was martyred together with eleven thousand maiden companions.[13]

The small caravels of the fleet sailed as far north as Virgin Gorda, 18°30'N latitude on November 17, and then headed southwest again possibly joining the rest of the larger caravels south of St. John, from which point they sailed along the south coast of Vieques, which he named "Gratiosa," on November 18; then due west along the south coast of a large island "as big as Sicily" that Columbus named "San Juan Bautista" (Puerto Rico), making a landfall on the lee side of the island in the Bahia de Boqueron on November 20.

Columbus had a sentimental reason for naming the island of Vieques "Gratiosa," for Graziosa Geraldine was the mother of his friend Alessandro Geraldine.[14] On many occasions the Admiral had heard his friend Alessandro extol his mother for her holiness, gentle manners, and total devotion to her family. Columbus promised his friend that someday he would name an island after his mother and he was pleased to do so on November 18. The fleet remained in Boqueron Bay for two days; the seamen fished and rested and the caravels took water.

Chapter Twenty-Six

RETURN TO NAVIDAD

During the fleet's brief stay in Puerto Rico, a shore party wandered inland and found a deserted town of neatly-built huts placed around a common square. Conspicuous among the huts was a large, well-built house, possibly the Cacique's residence, which dominated the grouping. A road from this large house to the sea had fences on both sides made of interwoven reeds separating well-maintained gardens. At the end of the road was a wattled terrace, also constructed of reeds and overhanging the sea. All was silent. Not a human being was in sight. It was obvious that the natives, fearful of the strange visitors and their ships, had sought concealment in accordance with a well-established plan of survival, based no doubt on their experience with the Caribs.

The warlike Caribs of the Lesser Antilles were a factor that influenced the exploration of the New World. They posed a threat to Columbus and his men and their belligerence undoubtedly had some effect on the Spaniards. One of the reasons that induced Columbus to sail south on his second voyage was to visit these Indians and observe firsthand the cannibalism that the Arawak Indians of Cuba and Haiti had told him about.

THE CARIB INDIANS

The Carib Indians belong to a Native American race that originated in the valley of the Orinoco River in South America, spread throughout the Amazon basin, the Guianas, and the Caribbean and which, at the time of Columbus's second voyage, had seized the Lesser Antilles. If Columbus had not come when he did, they probably would have continued northward and conquered the Greater Antilles as well. Spreading fear and terror wherever they went, they were the "Vikings" of their day. They were expert sailors with the ability of roaming all over the Antilles. They were skilled in building and handling canoes used in their raids; some of these dugouts had planks built upon the sides and were large enough to hold fifty people. They were also fierce fighters, trained for war from infancy. Their mothers put in their small hands the bow and arrow to prepare them to take part in their fathers' military excursions at an early age. The island Carib practiced both fishing and agriculture like the Arawaks of the north, but unlike the Arawaks, they practiced cannibalism and were nomadic, their constant wanderings keeping alive the savage customs and ferocious spirit of the predator. They went naked, except for a small cotton apron worn by the women. They painted their bodies and faces to protect them from the heat of the sun and from the insects. For purposes of decoration and to distinguish members of one family or community from those of another, they would paint designs of animals and plants on their bodies.

Additionally, they painted the brows and the area around the eyes to enhance their fierce looks. They wore their hair long to distinguish themselves from the Arawaks and they were beardless. Dr. Chanca described a common practice of the Caribs—that of wearing around each leg two rings of woven cotton—one below the knee and one at the ankle. In this way, they made their calves appear large by constricting the knee and ankle.

Their social organization closely resembled that of the North American Indians, the unit of organization being the clan ruled by a Cacique.

Columbus at first received the impression that the Caribs lacked religious beliefs. But later, he became convinced that they worshiped many supernatural beings, whom they represented by idols called "zenis." They had temples for this purpose in which the idols were set up to be consulted as oracles by the priests.

Michele de Cuneo's observations of the Caribs, their customs, manners, and lifestyle are reported in his famous letter, which is reproduced herewith:

As I have told about the nature and variety of the brute beasts, it now remains to tell something about the people. I must then say that people of both sexes are of an olive complexion like those of the Canaries. They have flat heads and the face tattooed; of short stature; as a rule, they have very little beard and very well-shaped legs and are thick of skin. The women have their breasts quite round and firm and well-shaped. These, as a result, when they have given birth, immediately carry their infants to the water to wash them and to wash themselves, nor does child-bearing give them folds on the belly, but it always stays well stretched, and so the breasts. They all go naked, but it is true that the women, when they have had knowledge of man, cover themselves in front either with the leaf of a tree, with a cotton clout, or panties of the same cotton. They eat all sorts of wild and poisonous beasts such as reptiles of fifteen to twenty pounds each; and when they meet the biggest ones they are devoured by them; and whenever they wish to eat those reptiles, they roast them between two pieces of wood. When we were left without food we ate some and there are some which are very good and their flesh very white.

The Caribs and those Indians, although they are innumerable and inhabit an extensive territory, are scattered in distant groups one from another. Nevertheless, all have one language and all live alike, in appearance like one nation of their own, save that the Caribs are more ferocious and more astute men than those Indians. Whenever they catch these Indians, the Caribs eat them as we would eat young goats and they say that a boy's flesh tastes better than that of a woman.

Of this human flesh they are very greedy, so that to eat of that flesh they stay out of their country for six, eight, and even ten years before they repatriate; and they stay so long, whenever they go, that they depopulate the islands. And should they not do that, those Indians would multiply in such a way that they would cover the earth. That happens because as soon as they are of procreating age, they procreate, respecting only their sisters; all the rest are common. We wished to hear from those Caribs who catch the Indians, and they told us that during the night they hide themselves and when day comes they surround their houses and catch them.

Those Caribs and Indians shave their hair and their beard and so do the women, and they shave with canes and the hair from the nose they uproot with their fingers. Their knives are stones which cut like real knives, and they make handles, and with these they cut and work their boats called canoes, which are trees hollowed out with those knives, and in which they navigate from island to island; but they do not use sails, only oars, which look like those paddles we use to beat hemp. When those Caribs hunt the said

Indians, their weapons are very big clubs with a knob on top carved like the head of a man or of some other animal. They also carry very big bows like the English bows. The bowstrings are made of that above-mentioned grass, the arrows of canes, the shaft of very strong wood, made in the shape of a column, inside which they force that cane and bind closely; and the feathers are taken from parrots' wings. With these arrows, they do great destruction. Also, instead of iron they use fish bones.

We went to the temple of those Caribs, in which we found two wooden statutes, arranged so that they look like a Pietà. We were told that whenever someone's father is sick, the son goes to the temple and tells the idol that his father is ill and that the idol says whether he should live or not; and he stays there until the idol answers yes or no. If he says no, the son goes home, cuts his father's head, and then cooks it; I don't believe they eat it but truly when it is white they place it in the above-mentioned temple; and this they do only to the lords. That idol is called "Seyti." They take a man whom they have proclaimed holy and who is dressed in a cloak of white cotton. This holy man never speaks, and in their fashion, they treat him very tenderly; and they say that in the morning he places himself in the middle of the temple and the first woman who enters has intercourse with him, and then all of the other women go to kiss her as if she was a most worthy object because that holy man has condescended to do business with her.

The said Caribs and Indians, apart from that idol, do not worship anything else nor do they sacrifice in any way to that idol, nor do they know God or devil; they live like proper beasts. They eat when they are hungry, use coition openly whenever they feel like it, and apart from brothers and sisters, all others are common. They are not jealous, and in my opinion, they are cold-blooded people, not too lustful, which may come from the fact that they eat poorly. According to what we have seen in all the islands where we have been, both the Indians and the Caribs are largely sodomites, not knowing (I believe) whether they are acting right or wrong. We have judged that this accursed vice may have come to the Indians from those Caribs; because these, as I said before, are wilder men and when conquering and eating those Indians, for spite, they may also have committed that extreme offense, which proceeding thence may have been transmitted from one to the other.

The Caribs and Indians, in our opinion, live a short time; we have not seen a man who in our judgment could have been past fifty years of age. They sleep mostly on the ground like beasts. Their lords, whom they call Cacique, all sleep over cotton sheets. These lords they honor extremely and respect. When they are together to eat, no one would dare eat if that Cacique had not eaten first. The women do all the work. There are plenty of mosquitos in those countries which are extremely annoying and that is why the Indians anoint their bodies with those fruits which are red or black in color, and which are an antidote to their annoyance; but we could not find a better remedy than to stay in the water.[1]

The sensational stories written about the Caribs may not be totally justified. There is no doubt that the writers exaggerated concerning their customs and manners. In many instances, they wrote what people wanted to hear. Columbus and other discoverers, finding human skulls and other human bones in the Caribs' residences, concluded that they might have been leftovers from their dinners. We should recognize, however, that the Caribs, being ancestor worshippers, might have preserved these human relics in honor of the deceased members of their families. This is not to say that cannibalism may not have been practiced among them, although a number of scholars have begun to question the reports of cannibalism as a myth.[2] Writers of the period probably sensationalized to shock the sensibilities of their readers.

RETURN TO NAVIDAD

At daybreak on November 22, the fleet left Puerto Rico, steering a northwesterly course for Hispaniola and familiar territory. Between the two islands they passed a small island that the Admiral later named Mona; by the end of the day, they made landfall on the easternmost promontory of Hispaniola named "Cabo San Rafael," later renamed by the Spaniards "Cabo Engaño" (Cape Deceit). The Admiral cautiously lay-to for the night. The following morning, November 23, they sailed along the north coast and soon reached Balandra Head of Samana Bay, from which Columbus had sailed on his return trip to Spain on January 16. By noon, they had sailed into the bay and put ashore at Las Flechas, home of one of the two Indians who Columbus had taken to Spain. The other Indian who had been captured on the island of San Salvador had been baptized in Barcelona with the name Diego Colón and remained faithful and devoted to the Spaniards. The sailors had the unpleasant task of burying the seaman who had been wounded in the skirmish with the Caribs at St. Croix. The first funeral in the New World went off with restrained dignity on the beach, under the gaze of natives who were received later aboard the María Galante. Columbus did not tarry long at Samana Bay—he even excused himself from calling on the local Cacique because he was anxious to reach his comrades at Navidad.

On November 25, Columbus anchored in the Harbor of Monte Cristi after covering 170 miles in two days. A shore party sent out to survey the area discovered two dead bodies bound with ropes on the banks of the river. One of them had arms extended and tied by the wrists to a stake in the form of a cross. Both were so badly decomposed that it was impossible to tell whether they were Indian or Spanish. On the following day, two more bodies were discovered, also decomposed. One of them had a beard and was obviously the corpse of a white man. The sense of expectation that Columbus had felt at the thought of seeing the men he had left behind in the fort at Navidad turned to foreboding. The macabre discovery cast a gloomy pall over everyone. The recent experience with the fierce Caribs at St. Croix had made Columbus fearful for the safety of his outpost in the New World.

The fleet weighed anchor on the morning of November 27 from Monte Cristi and headed with all possible speed toward Cape Haitien. By the evening, they had arrived opposite the harbor of Navidad and cast anchor about a league from land, not daring to enter the harbor in the dark. Columbus remembered only too well the Santa María disaster of the previous year. Flares were ignited aboard the fleet but no similar signal was shown from land. He ordered two cannons fired, and the report echoed all around the bay—but again there was no reply from the fort. Every ear was strained for some welcome sound; every eye was focused in the darkness for a response light beam; but there was no sound, no light, no sign of life. The suspense was broken at 10:00 p.m. when Indians in a canoe approached the ships, asking to see the Admiral. When directed to his ship, they would not come aboard until they could see the Admiral's face. Columbus recognized the leader of the group as a cousin of Guacanagari, who sent his greetings to the Admiral and brought two golden masks, one presumably for Martín Alonso Pinzón.

Through his interpreter, Diego Colón, Columbus asked about the Spaniards who had remained on the island. The reply was somewhat confused or perhaps deliberately obfuscated either by the visitor or by the interpreter. Several of the Spaniards had died of sickness, others had perished fighting among themselves, and others had gone to live on a different part of the island where they had taken Indian wives. He further added that Guacanagari had been wounded in a battle with the fierce Cacique of Cibao named Caonabo, who had attacked and burned his village, and that now he remained ill of his wound in a neighboring hamlet.

That is why he had not come personally to greet the Admiral. Of course, Columbus was greatly saddened to learn of the destruction of the fort but reassured that the local Indians had not been the attackers and that his good opinion of these people had not been misplaced. It was also heartening to learn that some of the men were still alive. They would surely hear of his arrival and rejoin him to give a qualified account of the destruction of the fort. The Indians who came aboard were well treated and departed late in the night, promising to return in the morning with the Cacique Guacanagari. When Guacanagari did not appear, the crew began to suspect treachery, but Columbus, satisfied with the friendly attitudes of the natives, would not entertain such thoughts. He sent a boat ashore to reconnoiter the site of the fortress. It was in total ruin. It had been sacked and burned to the ground. The following morning, Columbus and Dr. Chanca set out to do their own investigation. They took the boat to shore and walked about a league to a hamlet, whose inhabitants had fled. Inside the houses they found many articles of European origin, such as stockings, pieces of cloth, an anchor of the wrecked Santa María, and a beautiful Moorish robe folded in its original wrap. When they walked back towards the fort, they met some Indians who took them to a site not far from the fort and showed them the graves of eleven Spaniards buried in different places. Apparently, they had been dead for some time, for grass had already grown on the graves.

The Indians confirmed that Caonabo, from another part of the island, had invaded their territory and killed the Spaniards, possibly out of vengeance, because the white men had seduced the wives and daughters of the Indians. A meeting with Guacanagari might shed more light. The opportunity presented itself when Melchior Maldonado, commander of the caravel scouting for a new settlement site, found the Cacique lying on a hammock nursing an injured leg. The Cacique expressed a desire to see his old friend, the Admiral. The next morning, Columbus went to see Guacanagari. Scillacio in his "letter to the Duke of Milan" describes the event vividly:

The Admiral made ready to visit the king, who had his seat some ten miles from the shore. He took along one hundred of the more distinguished Spaniards and started out for the region from which smoke was rising and in which the largest number of reefs were seen. They proceeded to the royal palace in martial array to the accompaniment of flutes and drums. They were given the customary royal welcome, and a delegation selected for this purpose was sent to the king. They saluted Guacanagari as he lay in his swinging couch, skillfully worked to resemble silk, and exchanged pledges of loyalty. The king rejoiced in the presence of the Spaniards. When friendly relations had been re-established and good will restored, the king reported the death of the Christians in unhappy tones.

He gave details mournfully, told of the battle, described the king's furious behavior and remarked on the superior forces of the enemy, discussed the perilous situation, and exhibited his wound.[3]

Not mentioned by Scillacio, but reported by Dr. Chanca, was the examination of the wound by the fleet's surgeon, who removed the bandages and noticed that "…he was no more wounded in this thigh than in the other, although he made a cunning pretense of being in great pain."[4] There was then an exchange of gifts between the Spaniards and the Indians and some bartering in which the Spaniards got the better deal. Again, from Scillacio:

So it was that in exchange for the most worthless little trinkets, the Spaniards that day carried off more than thirty bosses of gold, the Indians grinning gleefully over the cheap brass [that they got] and our men in turn at this trade of gold for brass, since the Indians paid huge sums of gold for a single brass boss.[5]

The cordial relationship between Columbus and Guacanagari seemed to suffer a setback when Columbus made known the purpose of his expedition:

The Admiral then summoned his Indian interpreter and bade him inform the king of the reasons for their expedition. The Spaniards had set out for foreign parts for the purpose of civilizing the inhabitants thereof by precept and admonition, and for the purpose of taking possession of the islands for the mighty monarchs of Spain, but Guacanagari above all others was to be treated as a friend and an ally. As soon as the king heard this from the Indian, he sprang to his feet and pounded the ground with his foot, raised his eyes toward Heaven, and called out for his people. Thereupon, the rest of the Indians assembled there, some six hundred in number joined the outcry. This startled and alarmed our men so much (we had one hundred light-armed men on the spot) that some grasped their sword-hilts, thinking that the business was to be settled by force of arms.[6]

That evening Guacanagari accompanied the Admiral to the ships and was astonished to see horses—animals unknown in the Indies. He was amazed at their great size, strength, fearful appearance, and docile behavior. Little did he suspect that these animals would play an important military role in the subjugation of his people and the conquest of the Indies. He also marveled at the power and grandeur of the Spaniards as he beheld the huge fleet at anchor. Columbus guided the Cacique on a tour of his ship, where the plants and fruits of the Old World, domestic fowls of various kinds, sheep, swine, cattle, and other animals brought to stock the island, were all wonders to him. The Cacique had supper on the ship and later in the evening returned ashore.

The friendly relationship between Columbus and Guacanagari did not rest well with many members of the fleet. After the Cacique had gone ashore, a brief meeting was held in which Fray Buil questioned the innocence of the Cacique and suggested that he be seized and executed for his complicity in the massacre. He reiterated that the Cacique's leg wound was a sham, despite his assertion that it had been violently bruised by a stone. The Admiral was not thoroughly convinced, as some of the Cacique's men had been wounded by fish-bone spearheads, mainly by Caonabo's soldiers, and the destruction of his own village were strong evidence of his innocence. Besides, there was nothing to be gained by killing Guacanagari, as any settlement established by the Spaniards on that same island demanded a harmonious relationship with the neighbors—at least until the Cacique's guilt could be proven beyond any doubt. As more evidence was obtained through a better understanding of the Taino language, a clearer story of the massacre emerged, exonerating Guacanagari.

According to Las Casas and Oviedo, Don Diego de Arana, put in command of the fort by Columbus, could not cope with most of the seamen, who did not know how to conduct themselves with restraint or sobriety on shore. No sooner had the Admiral departed than the men began to quarrel over gold and women. Avarice and lust prevailed as the seamen began to accumulate, by any and all devious means, all the gold ornaments they could get from the natives. Others indulged in sexual orgies. Not content with the two or three wives allowed by Guacanagari, they began to seduce the natives' wives and daughters. Many left the fort and lived outside the compound. Diego de Arana tried to assert his authority, but even his trusted lieutenants took advantage of the disorder. In fact, Rodrigo de Escobedo, the secretary, and Pedro Gutierrez, the royal butler, killed Giacomo, the Genoese grommet, and left the fort with nine companions to search for gold in other territories.

Having learned of gold mines in Cibao, they headed for that district in the interior of the island within the province of Mayguana ruled by Caonabo, a Cacique of Carib stock. This fierce king had known of Columbus's landing on the island and had been relieved at the Spaniards' departure. However, the building of a fort at La Navidad had aroused his anger so that he promised himself to destroy it. Hence, when the group led by Escobedo and Gutierrez appeared in his territories, Caonabo, aware of the discord at the fort, concluded that it was vulnerable. He put the group of Spaniards to death and made plans to attack the fortress. First, he made an alliance with the Cacique of Marien, whose territories adjoined those of Guacanagari, and then moved against Navidad without being discovered. Ten men were at the fort at that time, living in huts with five women each. The compound was not guarded. The rest of the men were quartered in houses in the vicinity. Caonabo attacked in the middle of the night. His men burst in on the Spaniards with frightful yells. They killed three of them and others, awakened by the screams, were chased into the sea, where they were drowned. The rest who were quartered in the town were eventually massacred. The fort was set on fire and razed to the ground.

Guacanagari and his men fought faithfully but too late. They were no match for Caonabo, who invaded his village and burned it. There was no doubt that if the men had been vigilant, the fort would not have been sacked. Columbus's warnings had gone unheeded. Law and order had become relaxed; the public good sacrificed to lust, passion, avarice, and private interest.

Now a site for new settlement had to be found at some distance from the present one. The land in the vicinity was considered damp and unhealthy. Columbus decided to beat back eastward, perhaps into the area of Monte Cristi.

Chapter Twenty-Seven

ISABELA AND CIBAO

During his short stay at Navidad, Columbus had sent crews east and west along the coast looking for a favorable site for a settlement, without success. Accordingly, on Saturday, December 7, the fleet left Navidad and sailed eastward seeking the harbor of Puerto Plata, which the Admiral had seen and admired on January 11, 1493, during his first voyage. The advantage for this site was its proximity to the gold mines of Cibao.

He reached Monte Cristi the following day and cruised leisurely among the several islands in the bay to admire the flora. From there he attempted to proceed eastward but was stalemated by the easterly trade winds, which kept the fleet from making any headway. Indeed, it took nearly twenty-five days, struggling against the undiminishing winds, to put into a harbor only thirty-two miles from Monte Cristi. Columbus was now confronted with a very serious problem aboard his fleet. The seamen were sick and weary of manning the sails, and the animals were dying. It was senseless to proceed further to Puerto Plata. He decided to select a bay, which he called "Isabela" in honor of his queen, for a permanent settlement.

It had a very large harbor open to the northwest and was protected on one side by a natural rampart of rocks and by a deep forest on the other. Fresh water was available as two rivers, one large and the other small, flowed into the beautiful plain. There was an Indian village on the banks of one of the rivers. The gold mines of Cibao, according to the Indians, were inland—not too far away.

Without further delay, as soon as the site had been chosen, the troops, artisans, laborers, and other personnel charged to lay out and build the settlement. Cattle, livestock, (including horses, which had suffered greatly from the confinement), provisions, guns, and ammunition were brought to shore. There was a great deal of excitement at starting the first settlement in the New World. The thrill of feeling the good earth, strolling among the luxuriant vegetation, and breathing and smelling the perfumed air imbued everyone with a sense of renewed vitality. The layout of the town was quickly drawn; streets, squares, and public buildings located in the traditional Spanish layout in which the church, government buildings, and governor's palace dominated a square plaza. This pattern would serve as model for every new settlement in the New World.

About two hundred wattled and thatched huts were planned—all to be made mainly from native growth. The public buildings, however, were built of stone. The town was built primarily as a trading post much like the towns built by the Portuguese on the coast of Africa. Everyone pitched in with pride and zeal in the work.

The colonists fell ill. Exposure to the elements, distasteful native food to which they were unaccustomed, and hard work took their toll on the men. Columbus himself fell sick and, according to Ferdinand, "…was unable to keep a journal at all from December 11, 1493, to March 12, 1494."[1] It should be mentioned that there were also many malcontents among the colonists, especially the hidalgos, who considered themselves above labor of any kind. These well-to-do gentlemen had joined the expedition primarily for adventure and the prospects of finding gold. There were also many volunteers, not on the royal payroll, who had enlisted for self-enrichment but found instead poor food, labor-induced body aches, and illness. Much has been said about the widespread illness of the colonists—several hundred of them being sick—as being due to syphilis, unknown to the western world at that time, but Dr. Chanca's accounts seem to discount its being of venereal origin.

THE CIBAO EXPEDITIONS OF HOJEDA AND GOBALÁN

Once the activities of the settlement had been performed and all the ships had discharged their cargoes, it would be very costly to keep the ships at anchor. But how could the Admiral send the ships back to Spain without fulfilling the promises he had made to the Sovereigns? He had promised them an appreciable amount of gold, accumulated by the men left behind at Navidad, or at least an assurance that gold mines had been discovered and that the precious metal would be forthcoming. Something had to be done to justify his commitments. It was necessary to send an expedition inland to Cibao, indicated by the Indians as the source of much gold. The very name of its Cacique "Caonabo," meaning "the Lord of the Golden House," indicated the wealth of his dominion. Cibao was situated in a range of mountains directly inland, south of Isabela, approximately three or four days' journey away.

Columbus lost no time in ordering two expeditions to explore the interior of the island for gold. One expedition, under

Alonso de Hojeda, was to go to Cibao and look for the gold source; the other, under Gines de Gorbalán, was to go to Niti, the residence of Caonabo. On January 6, 1494, at the Feast of the Epiphany, Fray Buil celebrated the first Mass in the New World, attended by all, in the unfinished structure that was to be the colony's chapel. Soon afterward, Hojeda and Gorbalán headed south with about forty well-armed men and some Indian guides, crossing the Cordillera Setentrional and descending into the Vega Real. They then forded the Río Yaque del Norte and continued southward toward the Cordillera Central, reaching the vicinity of the confluence of the Río Janico and the Río Bao, where they paused, afraid to ford the rivers swollen by heavy rains. Michele de Cuneo, who was along with the Hojeda expedition, reported:

Being more or less near that place of Cibao, and the weather being terrible, and having to cross another very wild river, being afraid of the outcome, we turned back to the nearest settlement (of Indians) to talk to them and they told us that, positively, in the place of Cibao there really was gold in large quantities; and they presented our captains with a certain amount of gold which included three big pieces, viz. one worth nine castellanos, another fifteen castellanos and the last of twelve, which included a piece of rock. This gold they brought to the Admiral telling him all that we have related above, as seen or heard.[2]

Apparently, Hojeda did not want to press his luck. He had found out what he wanted to know: the natives were friendly and the high range that the natives called "Cibao" was indeed the source of much gold. As soon as the weather abated, he headed north again and arrived at Isabela on January 20 to report to the Admiral.

Gorbalán and his party, more stubborn and resourceful than Hojeda, requisitioned a dugout canoe from the natives and crossed the raging river with the help of friendly Indians swimming along the canoe to stabilize the craft. Once on the other side, they were treated with respect by the natives and the local Caciques. They even showed him how the native goldsmiths hammered the malleable gold into thin sheets. Later, Gorbalán, as he continued his march towards the district of Niti, found more evidence that gold was indeed abundant in the kingdom of Caonabo. He did not seek out Caonabo—just as well, for it might have been a fatal mistake—but decided to go back to Isabela, arriving there on January 21, a day after Hojeda. The return of Hojeda and Gorbalán to Isabela with the discovery of gold was happy news for the Admiral and the colonists. De Cuneo expressed it in jubilant but brief terms:

With this [gold] he and all of us made merry, not caring any longer about any sort of spicery but only for this blessed gold. Because of this the Lord Admiral wrote to the king that he was able shortly to give him as much gold as the iron mines of Bicsay.[3]

This sudden elation was short-lived; Columbus, who had been sick himself and was still ailing, was deeply concerned about an epidemic of illness that had struck the Spaniards on this trip. This was a complete reversal of the first trip, when he had boasted that no one had fallen ill because of the salubrious environment of the Indies.

Dr. Chanca reported that at least three hundred men had fallen sick within a week after landing. He claimed that the change of climate, diet, and hard work were responsible for most of the illness. The heavenly climate that Columbus had boasted of on his first trip had changed to torrential rains. A lot of food had been spoiled and most of the wine was lost due to leaky barrels. Columbus had complained that the coopers had done a shoddy job, as leakage had been discovered soon after they had left port. The colonists tried to get accustomed to the Indian diet of fish, maize, yams, and cassava instead of their customary pork, beef, bread, and wine. The situation had become critical. His soldiers were getting restless—they had come to fight and seek gold, not to dig ditches and build huts. There were many malcontents who wanted to return to Spain. Indeed, Bernal de Pisa, the "Contador" appointed by the Crown to keep count of the gold, had already been caught in an abortive attempt to seize several caravels and return to Spain.

The Admiral realized that the fleet had to be sent back immediately to replenish the colony's food and supplies. Relief could arrive, at best, in four months. He simply could not wait to fill the fleet with gold and spices, as he had desired.

THE FLEET RETURNS HOME

Preparations for the return of the fleet began soon after the Cibao expedition. On February 2, 1494, the Admiral ordered twelve ships back to Spain under the command of Antonio de Torres. He kept five ships for himself—three small ones, the Niña, the San Juan, and the Cardera, for coastal explorations—and two larger ships, the flagship María Galante and the Gallega, for military action, if required and for storage.

Columbus did not send home the large quantity of gold originally promised but was able to accumulate approximately thirty thousand ducas worth of gold recently found in Cibao.

More gold would be forthcoming, Columbus believed. Gorbalán, returning on this trip, would give the Sovereigns a good account of his expedition to Cibao and of the inexhaustible supply available once mines had been established there. More exotic plants, spices, and herbs for medicines were shipped, as well as sixty parrots of different colors. The Admiral reported that the plants and seeds brought from Spain and planted in the New World were already showing a more vigorous growth than in Spain and cited in particular the luxuriant growth of the sugarcane. Harvest time, however, was still a long way off, and the colony was in dire need of provisions. One thousand people, most of whom were ill due to a diet of poor unfamiliar native food, depended on the supplies from Spain. Columbus requested three or four caravels with salt meat, wine, oil and vinegar, sugar, molasses, and wheat flour, as well as medicines for the sick and ailing. Shoes and clothing were also requested. Anticipating construction of towns and forts, Columbus asked for more laborers and beasts of burden to do the heavy work, and for the exploration of the Cibao region, expert miners, soldiers, and military equipment. To improve the morale of the colonists he sent a report to praise Hojeda, Dr. Chanca, Margarit, and several other officers and asked that they be given a raise in salary. He also requested that the two hundred hidalgos be put on the royal payroll so as to control them.

Lacking any great quantities of gold, and having to show that there was value in the Indies, Columbus resorted to a practice initiated by the Portuguese in their raids against the African coasts. That is, capturing slaves and sending them back to the mother country. Men, women, and children were abducted and sent to Spain to be sold as slaves. The Indians were taken to Spain ostensibly so they could be taught the Spanish language and converted to Christianity. Of the hundreds put on board, many died on the crossing.

Antonio de Torres followed Columbus's orders to sail northward until he picked up the westerlies, arriving at Cádiz on March 7—twenty-five days, the fastest crossing of the Atlantic to that date. The requests that Columbus sent to the Sovereigns were accepted without reservation. The Sovereigns ordered that the Admiral be given everything he had requested in the most expeditious way. The Admiral had sent the report with trepidation because of the Navidad massacre and feared some repercussions but received instead commendation for a report well planned, objectively thought out, and feasible. They vouched their complete faith in his endeavors.

Columbus's actions were highly praised by the Sovereigns in a subsequent letter, which stated: "…we consider ourselves well served and obliged by you, so that we shall confer upon you favors, honors, and advancement as your great services require and deserve."[4] History, as we shall see, would prove otherwise as Columbus was to receive no favors, no honors, and no advancements.

SPANISH SETTLEMENT IN CIBAO

With the departure of most of his fleet and his health once again restored, Columbus was now in a position to follow up on the Hojeda and Gorbalán expeditions. An expedition in force was organized and left for the Cibao on March 12, 1494, to establish an inland fortress in the vicinity of the source of gold. All able-bodied men, except those required to garrison Isabela, were enlisted. It was a heterogenous group consisting of foot soldiers well-armed with swords and arquebuses, cavalry troops, crossbowmen, and artisans of all sorts required to build a fort.

Columbus asked for a well-disciplined army to impress the natives. With banners flying and trumpets sounding and in full military formation, the Castillians left Isabela and headed south—the precursor for many armies of Spanish conquistadors in the New World. Within a few miles they crossed the Río Bajabonico, marched another twelve miles across a dry plain, and camped for the night at the foot of the Cordillera Setentrional. The following day, they climbed the mountain, which rises, in some places, to a height of several thousand feet at its summit and reached a pass that Columbus named "El Puerto de los Hidalgos" (the Pass of the Gentlemen).

From this pass, they could see below the most beautiful valley mortal eyes had ever seen; Columbus named it "Vega Real" (Royal Plain) because he was profoundly moved by its beauty. They crossed this fertile valley and reached the Río Yaque del Norte, where they camped for the night. The following day they crossed this river in rafts and canoes as it was too deep for fording, except for the horsemen. Friendly Indians carried across, on top of their heads, the Spaniards' belongings. They continued southward to the foot of the Cordillera Central, where, according to Hojeda, gold could be found.

They marched until they reached the Río Janica, where they stopped at the recommendation of Hojeda. It was in this general locality, possibly in the vicinity of the present small village of Fortaleza, up in the adjoining hills that on Sunday, March 16, 1494, Columbus ordered that a fort be built. He named it "Santo Tomás" after the doubting Thomas in the Scriptures, because one of the hidalgos had refused to believe the existence of gold on Hispaniola until he could touch it. The Admiral made a layout of the fort and appointed Mosen Pedro Margarit commander with about fifty men and a number of horses to build and garrison the fort.

The sight of the animals struck fear in the hearts of the Indians. Columbus then sent Juan de Luxán with a party of men into the mountains to look for gold and was assured upon their return that the Cordillera Central was a veritable source of gold deposits and that the location of the fort as a center to mining operations was well chosen. The local Indians were very friendly and hospitable and brought to the fort site gold nuggets worth at least three thousand castellanos.

On March 21, Columbus headed north again for Isabela but had a difficult time traveling because of foul weather and swollen streams. On March 29, Columbus was welcomed back to Isabela to the sounds of trumpets and musket shots. But the red carpet of welcome was not justified, as he found the morale of the men he had left behind very low. Some of the sick men had died and food and provisions were nearly gone. Luckily, some of the crops planted, especially wheat, were nearly ready for harvesting. On April 1, he received news from Margarit at St. Thomas that, according to the Indians, Caonabo was on his way to attack. The Admiral immediately sent reinforcements consisting of seventy men with provisions and ammunitions.

During Columbus's absence the building of Isabela had proceeded very slowly. It was now necessary to accelerate construction before the next fleet arrived from Spain; however, illness and hard work had taken their toll of the construction and labor force. Columbus drafted the young hidalgos to do the work but met with a great deal of resistance because the sons of Spanish noblemen regarded work as an offense to their honor as gentlemen. While they had no choice but to obey, they vowed to take their revenge on Columbus, a foreigner who did not understand Spanish traditions. Columbus was forced into a role that he did not relish—that of martinet—to cope with dissension and insubordination. It was obvious that the Admiral could not keep eight hundred men in check for any great length of time, especially when he did not know when the relief fleet would arrive.

It was at this point that Columbus felt the necessity of setting up a local governing body to explore, colonize, and govern the new territories of the Indies in an orderly, equitable fashion.

SHARING THE RESPONSIBILITIES

As Admiral of the Grand Fleet, Columbus assumed an awesome responsibility for the safety of his ships and the well-being of 1,200 men. With unerring accuracy, he crossed the Atlantic to the Lesser Antilles and sailed over uncharted seas to the Greater Antilles and to Navidad without the loss of a single ship and with only one fatality. No other person in the history of navigation has accomplished such a feat. Now he had been thrust into a very demanding role of governor, army general, city planner, and builder, explorer, and navigator. He had to cope with such diverse problems, such difficult personalities, and such conflict that he looked forward to pursuing the work he liked best—that of maritime discovery. It had become apparent to him that Cibao was not Cipango. His original mission had been to reach Asia. He began to make preparations to pursue that mission. First, he had to appoint a governing council for the island during his absence. He named a council, consisting of his brother, Don Diego, as president, and Fray Buil, Juan de Luxán, Alonso Sánchez de Carvajal, and Captain Coronel as members. He appointed Alonso de Hojeda captain of a task force consisting of four hundred men to relieve the impatient Margarit at the Fort of

St. Thomas; with the bulk of the force Hojeda would be free to reconnoiter the island and intercept Caonabo if possible. By delegating these responsibilities to other people, Columbus hoped to acquire the freedom to continue his own work of discovery.

On April 9, Hojeda left Isabela with the expeditionary force heading for St. Thomas. On the way, when he came to the Indian village of Pontón on the bank of the Yaque, he met three Spaniards returning to Isabela from St. Thomas. They reported that the Indians had robbed them of some clothes and had taken them to the local Cacique. Hojeda immediately ordered that the ears of one of the Indians be cut off and that the Cacique be taken to Isabela for execution. Fortunately, another Cacique, friendly to Columbus, interceded and saved the life of the Cacique of Pontón. Hojeda's was the first act of violence against the friendly Indians. The first shedding of blood—just a trickle at this time, but a profusion in times to come.

Having freed himself of most responsibilities, Columbus ordered his three caravels reconditioned and re-equipped, and on April 24, left the island on his quest of the mainland.

Chapter Twenty-Eight

IN SEARCH OF TERRA FIRMA—
THE EXPLORATIONS OF CUBA, 1494

When Columbus left Cuba, during his first voyage on December 5, 1492, he had suspected it might be a peninsula of Asia. It was his intention to ascertain whether this land mass was truly an appendage of the Asian continent by sailing around it. His fleet consisted of the highly dependable Niña and two smaller caravels, the San Juan and the Cardera, each displacing about forty tons, compared with the Niña's sixty tons. Columbus chose to travel lightly as the total complement of men in the entire fleet was about sixty men and grommets. The Niña was piloted by Francisco Niño, the original owner; Alonso Medel of Palos sailed as her master; Juan de la Cosa, who was to gain fame for drawing the first map of the New World, shipped as seaman. Also aboard were Pedro de Terreros, boatswain, and Diego Tristan as passenger volunteer. There were aboard altogether twenty-five men and grommets, including two Genoese and one Venetian. The San Juan had Alonso Perez Roldan as master and a total complement of fifteen, while the Cardera, whose master was Cristóbal Perez, had only fourteen, of which the boatswain was a Genoese named Fernerin(o) and the crew a very young lot of five grommets and seven able seamen.

The tiny fleet left on April 24, 1494, and did not return to Isabela until September 29, 1494.

VOYAGE TO THE SOUTH COAST OF CUBA

They sailed eastward along the north cost of Hispaniola to Navidad, then through the Tortuga Channel, where they were becalmed, anchoring finally at Trois Rivières. On the fourth night out, they reached port St. Nicholás at the northwest point of the island. The following day, April 29, they crossed the Windward Passage to Cuba's Cape Maisi, which Columbus had named "Cape Alpha and Omega" on his first voyage. At Cape Maisi, Columbus went ashore and with proper ceremonies set up a cross and took formal possession of the island once again, as he had done on his previous voyage at other Cuban ports. This was to reaffirm the belief that between this cape and Cape Vincent in Portugal lies the land mass of Eurasia. Thus, if Columbus were to keep going westward from Cape Alpha and Omega he would reach Cape Vincent in Portugal, without crossing any ocean! On April 30, they decided to sail along the southern coast of Cuba, heading westward almost along a 20°N parallel.

Unlike the north shore of the Oriente province, which the Admiral had found lush with vegetation on his first voyage, the southern shore is comparatively arid and mountainous at the eastern end of the island, where the Sierra Maestra range rises to 8,400 feet in Turqurino Peak. They sailed on an emerald sea along the rugged coastline, pounded by the waves. A scent of cactus flower and sea grape permeated the air. Near the end of the day, they sailed into a large harbor, which because of its size Columbus named "Puerto Grande," which at present is Guantanamo Bay, site of a large United States naval station.

The entrance of this bay was narrow, but as the fleet sailed into the bay, it expanded into a wide expanse resembling a great lake. Several fires blazing on shore confirmed the presence of inhabitants, but when the Spaniards landed, although the fires were still burning, the Indians had scattered into the woods. The visitors had interrupted the preparation of a very large barbecue. There were great quantities of fish, iguanas, and hutias (West Indian rodents)—some roasting and others suspended from branches of trees. The Spaniards, who had a voracious appetite, partook of this bounteous banquet with great delight but abstained from eating the iguana, which they regarded as a kind of serpent. After eating, the Spaniards roving about the seashore noticed a great number of Indians peering down upon them from a nearby hillside. Diego Colón, the interpreter, approached the Indians, speaking to them in their native language with words of friendship and telling them of the good intentions of the Spaniards and thus dispelling their fears. The Indians descended from their hideouts and approached the Spaniards, first with apprehension, then with awe. Columbus learned that they had been ordered by their Cacique to procure victuals for a great banquet to be given to a neighboring Cacique. They roasted the animals to prevent spoilage in transportation. The Spaniards presented the Indians with trinkets and hawks' bells as payment for the fish they had eaten.

They spent the last night of April in the bay, and early on the morning of May 1 they continued sailing westward, hugging the coastline until, forty miles away, they came across the Bay of Santiago de Cuba, another deep bay, narrow at the entrance and very wide within. They found friendly natives there who brought to the visitors cassava bread, fish, and water. This bay is the present site of the city of Santiago de Cuba.

They departed before dawn on May 2 and continued eastward; the Sierra Maestra mountains now touching the coast, out to the westernmost point of the southern coast to a prominent cape that Columbus named "Cabo de Cruz," a name that has survived to this day. At this point, the coast turns northeastward into the Golfo de Manzanillo. Rather than turn backward to follow the coast of Cuba to determine whether it was a peninsula of the mainland, Columbus interrupted his quest when he was told that the island of Jameque lay directly to the south. Columbus misunderstood this to be the island of Babeque, which he was told on his first voyage contained gold mines. On May 3, he sailed directly southward from Cabo de Cruz for Jamaica.

DISCOVERY OF JAMAICA

The trip to Jamaica, a distance of ninety-five miles from Cape Cruz, proved to be a rough one. According to de Cuneo, they crossed in very bad weather under bare poles to that island. The northeast trade wind blew with hurricane velocity, forcing the fleet to bare poles and heave-to for the time. On Monday afternoon, May 5, they saw Jamaica, etched against the setting sun, and the Admiral sailed directly ahead into St. Ann's Bay, which he named "Santa Gloria" because of the majestic beauty of the island. Jamaica seemed more densely populated than any other island.

The Jamaican Indians were more warlike than the other Taino Indians. As Columbus sailed into the bay, about seventy canoes full of warriors, bent on hostile actions, moved toward the fleet. To avoid a fight, the fleet fired several blank salvos from its lombards, their thunderous sound and repercussion scaring and scattering the native fleet. Columbus then sent his Indian interpreter, Diego Colón, in a boat to assure the Jamaicans that they had come in peace and did not wish to harm anyone. The Indians responded in kind, even sending a canoe to the flagship to greet the Admiral and pick up some gifts. They spent only one night at Santa Gloria, the Admiral already having convinced himself that there was no gold on this island.

On the following morning, May 6, they sailed fifteen miles westward along the Jamaican coast to the harbor Columbus named "Puerto Buena," called the same to this day. Here, too, the Indians were hostile, casting wooden spears and stones at the caravels as the seamen tried to land. Because the Admiral wanted to stay a few days at the most convenient harbor for caulking his ships and taking on wood and water, and because the Indians posed an unwanted danger, the Admiral resorted to a show of force to impress them with Spanish might. He dispatched several boatloads of crossbowmen against the canoes; these killed a few Indians and disbanded the rest to shore, where the Spaniards let loose a large dog on them.

This show of force had the desired effect, for the following day, six Indians showed up at the shore with conciliatory gifts of fish, fruit, and cassava, which the Admiral accepted with pleasure. There followed, during their brief stay, a show of amity in which the Spaniards accepted more provisions in exchange for the usual trinkets. None of the natives wore gold ornaments, and no gold objects of any kind were evident anywhere, much to the disappointment of the Spaniards. On May 9, having completed the repairs on his fleet and taken on provisions, the Admiral sailed again westward thirty-four miles along the north coast to El Golfo de Buen Tiempo (the Gulf of Fair Weather), now called Montego Bay. Disappointed at not finding gold in Jamaica,

Columbus decided not to waste precious time here. On May 14, he was back at Cape Cruz, in Cuba, to resume his exploration of the island.

THE CUBAN SOUTH SHORE ODYSSEY

Columbus did not tarry long on Cape Cruz, remaining only long enough to be greeted by the local Cacique before taking off again, following the Cuban coast in a northeasterly direction. They sailed through the Balandras Channel and entered into the Gulf of Guacanayabo, following its coastline until it swung west again. At sunrise the following morning, May 15, they were amazed to see directly ahead that the sea was full of islands covered with lush vegetation "the fairest that eyes beheld." Columbus, remembering that Sir John Mandeville, in his famous travels in the Indies and Cathay nearly 150 years before, had reported seeing an archipelago with thousands of islands, became convinced that perhaps he too was approaching the land of Grand Khan. He named the archipelago "El Jardín de la Reina," the Queen's Garden (today called Jardínes de la Reina). The archipelago, located from twenty to fifty miles from shore, extends from the Gulf of Guacanayabo through the Gulf of Ana María to the coast city of Casilda, a distance of about 150 miles. They continued westward along the shore until they reached the present city of Santa Cruz del Sur and then swung northwestward into the Jardínes de la Reina channel and into the Gulf of Ana María at the Cayo Santa María, where they made a ninety-degree turn to the southwest into the cays now known as Laberinto de Doce Leguas. There they made a landfall, on May 22, at a large island on which there was a deserted village. The natives had fled, leaving behind a large number of non-barking dogs, which were promptly roasted and eaten by the Spaniards.

They put out to sea again and followed the various islands from Cayo Grande to Cayo Breton, from which they could see to the northwest the Sierra de Trinidad rising from the coast between the town of Casilda and Cienfuegos. The fleet sailed fourteen leagues directly toward this mountainous landmark, and as they approached the shore, they found it to be full of shoals. With night approaching, they decided to waft for the night on the land breeze, which kept them safe from the shoals and lay-to until the morning of May 26, when they sailed cautiously along the coast and entered the mouth of the Río las Misas (River of the Masses).

They were greeted by many Indians who approached them and brought out bread, birds, and cotton skins. As they continued their trek along the coast, they saw many villages from which the natives came out cheerfully, and bearing the usual gifts to the "people from heaven." Perhaps it might have been for this distraction that Columbus missed the bay in which the present large city of Cienfuegos is located. Cienfuegos Bay is twenty miles long and has a fine harbor. But they did not miss the next large bay that they encountered, the Gulf of Cochinos, which is fifteen miles deep and which some of the sailors regarded as a channel between Cuba and Asia. The northeastern shore of this bay is noted for its water springs, which caught the attention of the Admiral, who described them as Bernáldez.

From the Gulf of Cochinos, the fleet skirted the southern part of the Peninsula de Zapata and found themselves in the Banco Jardines, where they encountered such trouble in the shallow waters as truly tested the mettle of the Admiral's crews. The cays off the Zapata Peninsula are difficult to navigate because of the variable colors of the water, which at times are crystal clear, and other times milk-white or as black as the night. This is due to the variable colors of the ocean bottom and the oceanic residues accumulated thereon. Thus, in some places the gulf has a bottom of white chalk, which, when churned by the waves, is mixed throughout the surface, giving the appearance of milk. In the same manner, when the bottom is covered with fine black sand, the action of the waves colors the surface ink-black; when the sediment is green, the ocean appears green. The variation of colors occurs primarily in the shallow waters, but what alarmed the mariners most was the recollection from old Arabic tales that the outermost edge of the earth was covered with green shoals and the fear that they might have reached the point of no return.

They did not sail off the edge; instead they found themselves in only two fathoms of water, and they could not stop the forward movement of the vessels as the anchors were being dragged along the bottom, the fine sediment providing no holding reaction. They went along for thirty miles dragging their anchors until they approached an island where they found two and a half fathoms of water. There they anchored, in a state of extreme distress. Early the next day, on May 27, the Admiral sent one of the caravels in search of freshwater on the Cuban shore but found none as the shore was covered with mangroves. In the afternoon, they arrived at a western point of the Zapata Peninsula, at a low headland; the Admiral gave it the angelic name of "Punta del Serafin" because it was the Feast of All Angels. In looking directly north from this point they had a clear ocean view of mountains on the opposite shore; after taking soundings, the Admiral headed for the mountains in at least three fathoms of water. With the help of fair wind they reached the opposite shore the following day. They found springs of fresh water there and a beautiful large palm grove. This anchorage must have been the present site of the city of Batabano.

Columbus now reversed his usual direction and headed eastward along the coast into the Ensenada de la Broa for a distance of several miles, but noticing that he was landlocked, he headed westward again. Despite assurance from the local Cacique that deep water lay ahead, they became stymied on shoals in waters less than a fathom deep, in Canal del Cayamas. Columbus extricated his fleet by kedging, which had been unsuccessful with the Santa María at Navidad on Christmas Eve of 1492, but which proved successful with the lighter caravels in this dangerous situation. This is a laborious process in which a boat carrying an anchor is rowed ahead of a stricken ship. The anchor, dropped in the sea, is the point of attachment of the hauling cable, which pulls the ship ahead when the windlass is actuated by the crew. If the bottom is soft and devoid of sharp rocks, the keel will plow a channel without damage to the ship. They eventually extricated the ships without damage and were fortunate to sail thereafter on depths of three fathoms.

The fleet sailed along the coast within many islands for several days seeking freshwater, but could not go ashore because of swamps and mangroves. Eventually, they found a palm grove where they landed, took water, and refreshed themselves. From May 29 to June 12, they sailed along the coast and anchored nightly. They passed the Cayos San Felipe, located to the south and, on June 12, reached the Bahía Cortes, where the coast begins to swing southwest. Columbus had reached a point that was less than fifty miles from Cape Corrientes, the southwestern extremity of Cuba. Had he persevered for another day or two of sailing, he might have discovered that Cuba was an island—but that was not to be, for the Admiral had already convinced himself that Cuba was the Chinese province of Mangi and that the southwest-trending shore was the beginning of the Malay Peninsula. The caravels were at this time in bad shape—they needed caulking and, in many instances, re-rigging. The morale of the officers and men was low. It was a good time to head back to Isabela. But there were some legal matters to be settled first.

This remarkable voyage placed Columbus in the unique and exalted rank of being the greatest navigator. Michele de Cuneo, who accompanied him on this voyage, stated in his letter to Annari:

There is one thing that I wish you to know, that in my humble opinion, since Genoa was Genoa, no other man has been born so magnanimous and so keen in practical navigation as the above-mentioned Lord Admiral; for, when navigating only by looking at a cloud or by night a star, he knew what was going to happen and whether there would be foul weather; he himself both conned and steered at the helm; and when the storm had passed over, he hoisted sail while the others were sleeping.[1]

Chapter Twenty-Nine

RETURN TO ISABELA—JUNE 13–SEPTEMBER 19

Columbus began his return voyage from the Bahía Cortes to Isabela on June 13. He chose a southeasterly course, seeking clear, open-sea sailing to avoid the cays and shoals he had encountered on his westward voyage. He soon sighted a large island he named "San Juan Evangelista," later universally known as the Isle of Pines, but more recently, under the Castro regime, it was renamed Isla de la Juventud (Isle of Youth). Columbus approached the island from the west, at the present Punta Frances, then followed a channel and found himself enclosed in a deep bay from which there was no way out. Finding themselves completely landlocked, the men became frightened; Columbus cheered them with encouraging words, reassuring them that he would lead them out of the bay—which he did. They then attempted to circle the island around the north shore but made very little headway. They fought the head wind all the way to the eastern part of the island, where they anchored to take in a supply of water and wood. They took off again, but failing to beat the head winds, returned to Bahía Cortes, anchoring there on June 22. They took off again, navigating this time through the groups of islands between San Juan Evangelista and Cuba, struggling against the trades by tacking and beating to windward. On the thirtieth of June, the Niña ran aground on one of the shoals, suffering considerable damage. Kedging with cables would not release her, so it was necessary to drag her over the shoal by the prow.

They continued beating to windward and were beset with more problems—this time with evening rain squalls, which drenched them to the bone. They crossed the Gulf of Batabano and the milk-white sea, encountering huge sea turtles, so huge and so numerous that the ships had to push them out of their way. Hunting the turtles and searching for pearls in the large quantities of oysters caught provided an interlude of relaxation for the seamen. It took them twenty-five days to cover two hundred miles to windward. The wind and currents finally eased up and the ships managed to extricate themselves from the dangerous shoals and mangroves. They crossed the Gulf of Cochinos (Bay of Pigs) where they had made a landfall on their westward voyage and reached Ornafay, located between Cienfuegos and Trinidad. Here Columbus began to seek some convenient harbor where he might make a landfall to allow his crews some rest. They were exhausted; the toils, the privations, the struggle with the elements, and the scarcity of food and water had taxed the men. It was with great joy that they anchored on Sunday the seventh of July in Río San Juan, which they had seen on the westward voyage. The friendly natives received them with joy and affection and shared the bounties of their district: cassava bread, fruits, hutias (rats), and birds of various kinds. Columbus ordered the men to raise a large wooden cross on the banks of the river. He also asked the priest to celebrate a Mass of thanksgiving. The Indians and the local

Cacique looked with awe and reverence as the rituals of the Mass were performed by the priest. His gestures and words and devotion of the Spaniards must have appeared as mysterious but awesome proceedings. A venerable, dignified old Indian was moved by the religious ritual and told the Admiral, according to Ferdinand, "It was well to thank God because the souls of the good would go to heaven, their bodies remaining on earth; but the souls of the wicked would go to hell.[1]

Columbus was greatly moved by the Christian-like philosophy of the elderly Indian. He named the Río San Juan "El Río de Las Misas," as Mass had been celebrated there.

Columbus now had a very important decision to make: to sail through the Jardín de la Reina and struggle through the hundreds of islands and cays, or head for the open sea directly to Cabo de Cruz and confront the head wind and current outside. He departed on July 8 from the River of the Masses and chose to sail towards the open sea outside Cayo Breton, leaving the Laberinto de Doce Leguas on the port side. It turned out to be a most unfortunate decision as they met the trade winds head-on and foul weather all the way. Furious gusts of wind and rain struck the fleet without respite for several days, harassing the already tired and disheartened crews. As they approached Cape Cruz, a violent squall struck the ships and threw them on their beam ends. They stuck sails and let go of their largest anchors to ride out the gale. The Niña, which had already been damaged on the shoal the thirtieth of June, began to take on water at every seam and was miraculously saved by the tireless pumping of the crew, who had a most difficult time. They were all very weak from lack of food. According to Ferdinand, Columbus wrote in his journal:

I am on the same ration as the others. May it please God that this be for His service and that of Your Highnesses. Were it only for myself I would no longer bear such pains and dangers, for not a day passes that we do not look death in the face.[2]

After ten days of continuous hardships, in which they made a good 180 miles to windward, they arrived on July 18 at Cabo de Cruz to be greeted once more by hospitable Indians, who brought the seamen cassava bread, fish, fruits, and other refreshments—as they had done on their westward voyage.

The docile and faithful Indians came to the rescue of the Spanish invaders on many critical occasions. Without their help, the exploration of the Greater Antilles would have been a dismal failure. Their repeated acts of generosity accelerated their own enslavement and eventual decimation at the hands of the "civilized" white men.

JAMAICA REVISITED

On Tuesday, July 22, lacking a fair wind for Hispaniola, Columbus sailed directly southward to El Golfo de Buen Tiempo in Jamaica (Montego Bay), from where he had departed three months before. From Montego Bay, the fleet circled the island in a counterclockwise direction around Negril Point, the westernmost point of the island to Bahía de la Vaca (Portland Bight), where they dropped anchors. Columbus found the south coast of Jamaica very fertile and full of harbors. The whole coast was crowded with towns and friendly natives who would follow the fleet in their canoes, bringing the Spaniards food and refreshments. Every afternoon there was a rain squall. The Admiral reasoned that this was to be expected because of the great forests on the island—the same thing used to happen in the Canary,

Madeira, and Azores Islands before those islands were stripped of their forests. These squalls forced him to take shelter every afternoon and slowed down his progress so that it took him nearly three weeks to sail around the southern coast from Montego Bay to Portland Bight, which he named "Bahía de la Vaca" (Cow Bay).

Columbus was particularly impressed with this bay as it contained seven islets and was surrounded by many villages. He had a strong desire to stay longer in this beautiful bay and explore its countryside, as the natives were much friendlier than those of the northern shore with whom he had had some confrontations on his westward voyage, but the leaks in his vessels and the low morale of his crews made it impossible. The Cacique of the large village came down from the hills, attended by a great number of servants bearing refreshments. A very curious person, he inquired about the Spaniards, their ships, and where they came from. Through his interpreter, Diego Colón, Columbus replied in his customary manner, stressing the power of the Spanish Sovereigns and their peaceful intentions. Diego Colón, however, added his own glowing impressions of his Spanish visit and the power of the Admiral in routing the Caribs.

The next day this same Cacique, with his own fleet of three canoes, overtook Columbus's fleet as the Admiral was slowly sailing away, aided by a light wind. The largest canoe, beautifully carved and painted, was occupied by the Cacique and his family, consisting of his wife, two daughters, two sons, and five brothers. One of the daughters was eighteen years of age and very beautiful; her sister was somewhat younger and not as alluring. Both of them were naked as was customary in these islands. In the prow of the canoe stood the standard bearer of the Cacique proudly wearing a mantle of red feathers with a coronet on his head, also embellished with feathers, and in his hand he carried a white banner. Two Indians with helmets of feathers of varied colors and painted faces beat a rhythmic sound upon tabors, while two others, similarly painted, held trumpets ingeniously carved of black wood. Six other Indians, possibly guards, in large white feather hats completed the retinue.

The Cacique went aboard the Admiral's ship with all of his people appearing in full regalia. Around his head was a cornet of small precious stones of various colors. Gold pendants were suspended from his ears and various ornaments of guanin strung in the form of a necklace hung around his neck. His body was mostly exposed, with the exception of a girdle, which was made of the same material as the coronet on his head. His wife was naked like the daughters but she had a small apron of cotton to cover her. Bands of cotton also were worn around her arms and legs, and around her middle was a string of small black stones from which hung a pendant like an ivy leaf, made of green and red stones.

As soon as the Cacique saw the Admiral he said:

I have determined to leave my country and to come with you. Your interpreter and other Indians have told me of the great power of your Sovereigns and the many nations you have subdued in their name. All our islands are in fear of you; for who can resist you now that you have discovered the secrets of our land and the weakness of the people. Rather than see you take way my dominions I will embark with all my household in your ships and will go do homage to your Sovereigns.[3]

Columbus was greatly moved by the Cacique's speech and was touched by his sincerity and fervent declaration of subservience. He knew the dangers that this proud king and his family would face: the cold weather, the licentiousness of the crew with respect to the women, and most importantly, the adjustment to a new culture and a different mode of living. For these reasons, he chose not to take them away from their realm but sent them back after receiving their homage and loyalty.

With westerlies filling the sails, the fleet had an easy run from Portland Bight directly eastward to Morant Point, the eastern point of Jamaica, on the south coast, which Columbus called "El Cabo del Farol" (Cape of the Lighthouse). In his haste, he failed to see Port Royal Bay, site of the present capital city of Kingston.

RETURN TO HISPANIOLA

The fleet negotiated the Windward Passage in less than twenty-four hours, and on August 20, Michele de Cuneo was the first to sight land, a southwestern cape of Hispaniola. Columbus named it appropriately "Cabo de San Miguelde Saona" in honor of Michel de Cuneo from the city of Savona (later called Cape Tiburon and recently Cape Carcasse). Columbus was now in a position to explore the southern coast of Hispaniola and had favorable winds until he made a landfall in Jacmel Bay, 130 miles east of Cape Tiburon.

At the end of August, he anchored at a small island named "Alta Vela" (Isla Alto Velo), located offshore at the present boundary of Haiti and the Dominican Republic; this also marks the southernmost point of Hispaniola. It was at this point that Columbus waited for the other two ships, which had become separated during a storm the previous Friday. He sent men ashore to climb to a high point on the island, but they did not spot any sails. The sailors seized the opportunity to add fresh meat to their diet by killing a few seals.

The ships finally showed up six days later, and all three then sailed together for the island of Beata, off Cabo Beata, about thrity miles northeast of Alta Vela. When the natives learned of the arrival of the Spaniards, they came in their canoes to report that some Spaniards had arrived there from Isabela and that all were in good health. Wanting to inform the garrison in Isabela of his arrival, the Admiral sailed further east to the Río Jaino in Santo Domingo, where Hispaniola narrows down, and sent nine men ashore to cross the Vega Real, call at Santo Tomás, and proceed to Isabela.

The fleet continued eastward along the coast; the Admiral sent three boats ashore near a large village to look for water, but they were confronted by Indians armed with bows and poisoned arrows. They carried ropes in their hands and seemed intent on capturing the intruders. But when the boats came ashore, the Indians had a change of heart, put aside their arms, and offered to bring the Spaniards bread, water, and all else they had.

Sailing always along the coast, they found mountainous shores and good harbors; several times they landed to replenish their water supply and pick up provisions, finding the natives always generous. One day they saw a large sea monster:

As big as a whale, with a carapace like a turtle's, a head the size of a barrel protruding from the water, a long tail like that of a tunny fish, and two large wings. From this and from other signs the Admiral knew they were in for foul weather and sought a port where they might take refuge.[4]

As expected, on September 15 they sighted an island off the eastern end of Hispaniola and took refuge there in time to avoid the gale that struck soon afterwards. This island, which the Indians called "Adamaney," was named by Columbus "La Bella Saonese" in honor of Michele de Cuneo, who hailed from Savona, twenty-five miles from Genoa. In doing so, Columbus was honoring his own origins in Liguria.

While taking refuge from the storm behind Saona, Columbus observed a total eclipse of the moon on September 14. Having in his possession an almanac that gave the time of the eclipse at Nuremberg, the Admiral, noting that the eclipse occurred at Saona five and a half hours after, tried to calculate Saona's longitude. There are fifteen degrees to each hour. But he miscalculated. He came up with a longitude of 91°30'W, which corresponds with the Pacific Coast of Guatemala. Because the western half of the island of Cuba was situated farther to the west than Saona, Columbus figured that he had traveled to China. In reality, Isla Soana lies just short of 69°W longitude.

The storm abated by September 24; the fleet then left Saona and sailed to Cape Engaño, the easternmost point of Hispaniola. Instead of picking up the trade winds and rounding the cape to the north shore of the island to Isabela, Columbus turned southwest toward Puerto Rico, where he intended to raid the Caribs and destroy their canoes so that they could no longer pose a danger to the natives of Hispaniola. In the channel between Hispaniola and Puerto Rico, the Admiral was suddenly stricken with a high fever and collapsed from exhaustion. Ferdinand recorded the occurrence thus:

From that point on, the Admiral ceased to record in his journal the day's sailing, nor does he tell how he returned to Isabela. He relates only that because of his great exertions, weakness, and scanty diet, he fell gravely ill in crossing from Saona to San Juan; he had a high fever and a drowsiness, so that he lost his sight, memory, and all his other senses. Because of his illness, the ship's people decided to abandon the project for exploring the Carib islands and instead make for Isabela, here they arrived five days later, September 29. There by God's favor, the Admiral's health was at last restored, though he lay ill for more than five months. This illness was caused by his great exertions on that voyage and the resulting exhaustion, for he sometimes went eight days with less than three hours' sleep. This would seem impossible did he not himself tell it in his writings.[5]

Morison theorized that Columbus had had a nervous breakdown. The Admiral had endured great physical and mental hardship as he sailed among the innumerable uncharted islands. Continuously exposed to the elements, drenching downpours, and limited food and drink, Columbus developed arthritis during this voyage, a condition that was to plague him for the rest of his life. The adventure lasted over five months, every day of which brought additional proof, if any were needed, of Columbus's supreme skills as a navigator. They must have covered at least four thousand miles and battled through a number of storms, and suffered hunger, thirst, loss of sleep, and other deprivations. They finally returned to Hispaniola without loss of life or ships, but the stress was too much for the forty-three-year-old Admiral. He had, however, proved to himself, at least, that Cuba was part of the Asian mainland, in spite of his failure to find the cities of the Grand Khan and the "Indies" described by Marco Polo and Sir John Mandeville.

Chapter Thirty

DISCORD IN ISABELA—TROUBLE WITH THE INDIANS

There was joy on Isabela when Columbus's fleet appeared in the harbor on September 29, 1494. Many of the colonists had begun to suspect that the fleet had met with disaster in some unknown sea. Perhaps the most overjoyed of all was his brother, Bartholomew, whom Columbus had not seen for nearly six years. Only a year or two younger than the Admiral, Bartholomew had been very close to his brother and had shared his spirit of adventure and dreamed of discoveries while they were working together as chart-makers in Lisbon until 1485.

It will be recalled that Columbus had sent Bartholomew to England to propose his project of discovery to King Henry VII, and had been refused. He then had gone to France to petition Charles VIII, but he too had not been ready for the great enterprise. He had remained in France in the service of Ann de Beaujeu, the king's sister. It was from the lips of the King of France that Bartholomew heard the news, in 1493, of Columbus's discovery. A letter Columbus had written to him from Spain, soon after his first voyage, had never reached him. The French court gave Bartholomew a purse of one hundred crowns for his traveling expenses; unfortunately, he arrived in Seville after Columbus sailed with his fleet from Cádiz in September. In Seville, following written instructions from his brother, he went to Valladolid where the Sovereigns were holding court, taking with him his two nephews, Diego and Ferdinand, who were to serve as pages to the Infante Don Juan. He made a favorable impression on the monarchs, for they treated him as a distinguished visitor and knighted him so that he could be addressed as "Don Bartolomé." They also discovered that he was an able and accomplished navigator, gave him three ships loaded with supplies, and sent him to aid his brother in Hispaniola.

The fleet must have sailed from Spain late in April or possibly in early May, for it arrived in Isabela on June 21, 1494. It was then a pleasant surprise for Columbus to learn that his brother had been waiting for him. In the few months that Bartholomew had been in Isabela, he had been able to see firsthand the deplorable state of the colony. The council headed by his brother and appointed by Columbus before he left for his exploration of Cuba, Don Diego, could not cope with the discord and violence caused by Margarit, Father Buil, Hojeda, and other malcontents. Don Diego was totally incompetent as an administrator because of his mild and peaceable disposition.

What was needed in the colony was a man of strong will and intellect who knew how to command. Bartholomew Columbus was such a man, according to Las Casas:

Bartholomew was of a different and more efficient character. He was prompt, active, decisive, and of a fearless spirit; whatever he determined, he carried into instant execution, without regard to difficulty or danger. His person corresponded to his mind; he was tall, muscular, vigorous, and commanding. He had an air of great authority but was somewhat stern, wanting that sweetness and benignity which tempered the authoritative demeanor of the admiral. Indeed, there was a certain asperity in his temper, and a dryness and abruptness in his manners, which made him many enemies; yet notwithstanding these external defects, he was of a generous disposition, free from all arrogance or malevolence, and as placable as he was brave.

He was a thorough seaman, understanding both the theory and practice of his profession; having been formed in a great measure under the eye of the Admiral, and being only slightly inferior to him in science. He was superior to him in the exercise of the pen, according to Las Casas, who had letters and manuscripts of both in his possession. He was acquainted with Latin, but does not appear to have been highly educated; his knowledge, like that of his brother, being chiefly derived from a long course of varied experience and attentive observation. Equally vigorous and penetrating in intellect as the Admiral, but less enthusiastic in spirit and soaring imagination, and with less simplicity of heart, he surpassed him in the subtle and adroit management of business, was more attentive to his interests, and had more of that worldly wisdom which is so important in the ordinary concerns of life. His genius might never have enkindled him to the sublime speculation which ended in the discovery of the world, but his practical sagacity was calculated to turn that discovery to advantage.[1]

Las Casas thinks that Bartholomew gained some of his expertise in navigation from sailing with Bartholomew Dias on the latter's historic expedition down the coast of Africa to the Cape of Good Hope. He bases his opinion on notes written in the margin of Pierre d'Ailly's *Imago Mundi*, ostensibly by Bartholomew, in which he describes that he had reached a promontory called Cabo de Boa Esperança, to which he added that he was present in all of it. Washington Irving is of the opinion that Bartholomew accompanied Dias in 1486 before proceeding to England to see King Henry VII. This may account for his two-year delay in reaching England. Ferdinand claimed that his uncle had been held by pirates encountered on his way to England. But if Bartholomew had been with Dias, then surely his brother Christopher, who was in Lisbon when Dias returned late in 1488, must have had knowledge of it. Morison solves the puzzle by insisting that the marginal note was written by Columbus himself and not by his brother Bartholomew and that the claim that he had witnessed all of it merely indicated Columbus's presence at the arrival of Dias in Lisbon.

Columbus, weakened by his illness, found in Bartholomew the leader he could trust to bring peace and tranquility to the colony. Accordingly, he immediately appointed him Adelantado, an office equivalent to that of Governor. Columbus had a perfect right to do so from the articles of administration agreed upon with the Sovereigns, but King Ferdinand looked upon the appointment as an undue assumption of power.

The Sovereigns asserted their right to make such a high appointment, but to avoid further difficulties they confirmed Bartholomew to that office.

TURMOIL IN HISPANIOLA

Before leaving on his voyage of exploration of Cuba, Columbus had charged Alonso de Hojeda to relieve Mosen Pedro Margarit at the fort of St. Thomas. Margarit had been put in charge of an army consisting of some 250 hidalgos and crossbowmen, 110 musketeers, and 16 troopers. His orders were to reconnoiter the island and intercept Caonabo if possible. Margarit was instructed that his military objectives were to impress the natives with a display of military might while maintaining their good will. He was also ordered to live off the country by bartering for food and provisions as he went along, and to do the Indians no harm unless they committed acts of theft, in which case the culprits' ears and noses should be slit. More importantly, he was to explore the island and report on useful products for exportation.

Leaving Hojeda in command of the fortress of St. Thomas, Margarit and his army did not explore the rough mountains of Cibao but descended into the fertile Vega Real, demanding gold from the natives and raping their women. For a time, the Indians supplied them with food, but their scanty stores were soon exhausted by the Spaniards, one of whom, Las Casas declared, consumed more in a day than would support an Indian for a month. If provisions were withheld, the Spaniards took them with violence, subjecting the Indians to whippings and torture. Instead of being welcome guests, the Spaniards assumed the role of masters, taking boys to use as slaves. News of the excesses soon reached Don Diego Columbus, who, with the consent of the council, reprimanded Margarit and ordered him to proceed on his military tour according to the Admiral's instructions. Margarit took offense. He felt that he did not have to answer to the council. Moreover, he considered Don Diego's reproach a reflection on his honor as a nobleman and friend of the king. He regarded Don Diego and Columbus himself as foreign upstarts, lacking his own noble lineage.

He went back to Isabela to complain to the council, but with the exception of Fray Buil, his fellow Catalan, the council would not condone his actions. Fray Buil had been a consistent critic of Columbus and found it very convenient to ally himself with Margarit and support his arrogant defiance of authority.

He had been a constant thorn in the Admiral's side, possibly because of Columbus's less than deferential treatment of the hidalgos, including himself. Obviously, humility was not his forte, and unlike later missionaries who braved all hardships and privations of the New World in the hope of converting pagans to Christianity, Fray Buil longed for the comforts of the Old World despite the fact that he had not converted a single soul.

Encouraged by Margarit's insubordination, the monk became his ally in a plot to seize the ships that had brought Bartholomew to Isabela and to leave the colony for Spain. The plot was carried out in great haste, for, as soon as they were able to interest a group of malcontents, they took possession of the ships in the harbor and sailed for Spain before the Admiral's return. They reached Spain early in November 1494. Why such great haste on the part of Margarit? Ferdinand states that Margarit was unwilling to await the arrival of the Admiral because he would have had to account for his actions in office; Washington Irving, though, mentions another possible explanation for the haste. Margarit, according to Irving, "…in the course of his licentious amours, contracted a malady at that time new and unknown, and which he attributed to the climate, and hoped to cure by medical assistance in Spain." We may speculate that the disease was syphilis.[2]

POLITICAL DIVISION OF HISPANIOLA

In 1494, the island of Hispaniola was divided into five domains, each governed by a Cacique of absolute and hereditary power to whom hundreds of inferior local Caciques yielded tributary allegiance.

The reader has already become familiar with Guacanagari, who befriended Columbus on his first voyage and helped him to build Navidad after the Santa María foundered off Cape Haitien. His domain, called Marien, extended along the northern coast from Cape St. Nicolás at the western extremity to the great river Yaque del Norte and included the northern part of the Vega Real. He was generous, hospitable, peaceful, affectionate, kindhearted, and always loyal to Columbus.

The fierce chieftain of the domain called Maguana was the dreaded Carib Cacique Caonabo, who had massacred the sailors at Navidad and was still an inveterate enemy of the Spaniards. Columbus hoped to bring him to justice for his wanton acts. His mountainous domain comprised the main part of the center of the island situated along the southern face of the mountains of Cibao. The fort of St. Thomas was built on his borders.

The most important domain comprised the central part of the Vega Real. It was lovely country partly covered with forests, with many towns, and with many rivers rolling down the mountains of Cibao, and on its southern frontier had gold dust mingled with their sands. It was named Magua, and the Cacique of this domain was Guarionex.

The Higuey domain ruled by the Cacique Cotubanama occupied the whole eastern part of the island, which included Samana Bay and part of the River Yuna on the north side and on the west side the river Ozema. The inhabitants, who had learned how to use the bow and arrow from the Caribs, were the most active and warlike people on the island. Columbus had had his first skirmish in the New World with the Indians of this area on his first voyage, when he had been attacked by them with bows and arrows in the Golfo de las Flechas (Bay of the Arrows).

The fifth domain, named Xaragua, was the most populous and largest. It comprised the whole southwest coast, including the long promontory of Cape Tiburon, which Columbus called

"Cabo San Miguel," extending along the southern side of the island for a long distance, including the large Lake Enriquillo of today. The head Cacique was named Behechio; his sister Anacaona, celebrated throughout the island for her beauty, was Caonabo's favorite wife.

OPEN HOSTILITIES WITH THE INDIANS

With Pedro Margarit's sudden departure, the army in the field was left without a leader. They separated into small groups and began to scatter among the Indian villages, demanding food, terrorizing the natives, and raping the women. Aroused by these activities, the Indians began to deny them food and eventually exacted bloody vengeance on the invaders whenever they met them in small groups or as individuals. Encouraged by these petty triumphs, the Indians became more militant. Guatiguana, Cacique of a small town in the dominion of Guarionex, was bold enough to kill ten Spaniards who had quartered themselves in his town, outraging the natives by their licentious conduct. Then he secretly ordered that fire be set to the hut occupied by forty sick Spaniards. Other marauding soldiers were ambushed and killed. Confronted with an open rebellion, Columbus decided to crush it immediately before it got out of hand. He sent a force into the interior, consisting of a number of horsemen, some foot soldiers, and many hounds, to punish the wretched Indians indiscriminately and return to Isabela with about 1,500 prisoners including women and children. Columbus knew that these poor creatures were really the innocent victims of a situation that could not be immediately resolved. But he knew that he had to deal with it harshly and without mercy to avoid a larger conflict. The problem of what to do with the prisoners was held in abeyance. The solution was not long in coming.

Early in the fall of 1494, four caravels under the command of Antonio Torres, bringing an ample supply of provisions, arrived in Isabela. Torres also brought letters from the Sovereigns, dated August 16, 1494, expressing a great deal of satisfaction for the report sent in February by the Admiral. They approved of everything the Admiral had recommended and done, but requested that all of the islands discovered on the outward voyage be identified. They showed a great deal of interest in the affairs of the colony and expressed a desire to receive more frequent information, even proposing that a caravel should sail each month from Isabela and Spain. They also informed him that in adjusting the line of demarcation with Portugal (the Treaty of Tordesillas), separating their newly discovered possessions, it was important to have the best and latest information at hand, and suggested that the Admiral return to Spain and be present at the convention. They reiterated, however, that if he found it difficult to get away, he should send his brother or some other competent person fully briefed and prepared to take his place.

Here was a good opportunity for Columbus to go home immediately and avoid the turmoil brewing in Hispaniola. His brother Bartholomew, the new Adelantado, could take over and give Columbus not only a much-needed rest in a civilized country and an opportunity to defend himself against the charges that surely would be made by Fray Buil and Margarit. But Columbus was a man of dedication and not one to shirk his responsibilities, despite his lingering illness. No, he would not leave his post to vindicate himself and his enterprises against the aspersions of his enemies, neither would he send his brother Bartholomew, now that he needed him in the crisis. Instead, he would send his younger brother, Don Diego, as his advocate at court. As for the agreement about drawing the line of demarcation with Portugal, it would have to be postponed for the time being.

A decision now had to be made as to what to send back to Spain with the Torres fleet to help defray the expenses of colonization. The Cibao "mines" had not yielded much gold, and it was apparent that there were no actual mines but alluvial deposits, which yielded very little gold. Nevertheless, he sent all the gold that he could gather, which was not much. He also sent specimens of other metals and minerals, fruits, and exotic plants and specimens that he had collected either locally or in the course of his voyage of exploration. These items would hardly fill the holds of three caravels. Columbus knew that he had to justify the expenses of the expedition with immediate and tangible benefits to the Crown. That meant gold or pearls and, lacking these short-term commodities, he had to come up with a substitute. He opted for slaves, a practice that had been used by the Portuguese. He ordered that about five hundred of the healthiest Indian prisoners be sent to Spain to be sold as slaves in Seville. In a previous letter, Columbus had approached the Sovereigns about the possibility of slave traffic but they had not looked kindly on the American slave trade. However, the Sovereigns had favored the practice of slave-selling in their recent Moorish war. Indeed, the practice had been sanctioned by the Church itself as a method of converting the infidels, the barbarians, and the pagans to Christianity.

Michele de Cuneo, who returned to Spain with Don Diego Columbus, gives a vivid but pitiful account of this slave incident:

When our caravels in which I wished to go home had to leave for Spain, we gathered together in our settlement 1,600 people male and female of those Indians; of these, 550 souls among the best males and females, we embarked on our caravels on February 17,

1495. Concerning the rest who were left an announcement was made that whoever wanted them could take as many as he pleased; and this was done. And when everybody had been supplied there were some four hundred of them left; these were granted permission to go wherever they wanted. Among them there were many women who had infants at the breast. In order to better escape us, since they were afraid we would turn to catch them again, these mothers left their infants anywhere on the ground and started to flee like desperate people; some fled so far that they were removed from our settlement of Isabela seven or eight days beyond the mountains and across huge rivers; as a result from now on scarcely any will be had. Among these people who were taken was one of their kings with two chiefs who it was decided should be killed with arrows on the following day, so they were tied up, but in the night they knew so well how to gnaw one another's ropes with their teeth that they freed each other from their bonds and escaped.[3]

De Cuneo then went on to explain that many Indians never made it to Spain:

When we reached the waters around Spain about two hundred of those Indians died. I believe because of the unaccustomed air—colder than theirs. We cast them into the sea…when we reached Cádiz, in which place we disembarked all the slaves, half of them were sick. For your information, they are not working people and they very much fear cold, nor have they long life.[4]

To which we may add that naked people crossing the Atlantic in February and March might very well catch pneumonia, even if they were Caucasians!

Chapter Thirty-One

A PERIOD OF DISCONTENT

Following the enslavement of the Indians and their dispatch to Spain and the continued profligate conduct of the Spaniards, Guatiguana, the Cacique who had escaped by gnawing through his bonds, assembled a large army in the Vega Real to march on Isabela and drive the intruders into the sea. Through his friend Guacanagari, Cacique of Marien, Columbus received the news that some allied chiefs were assembling a great force in the Vega, within two days' march of Isabela. Guacanagari, an ever-faithful ally, offered to take the field with him to repel the attackers. Columbus, however, had by this time recovered from his illness and resolved not to wait for the assault but to carry the fight to the enemy. This was not only good military strategy, but it also afforded better protection for the women and children of Isabela recently arrived with the Torres fleet.

On March 27, 1495, assisted by his brother Bartholomew as the new Adelantado and Alonso de Hojeda, who was always ready for a good fight, the Admiral left Isabela to encounter the enemy with two hundred infantrymen, twenty horsemen, and twenty hounds. They were armed with crossbows, swords, lances, and heavy arquebuses. With these formidable weapons, the small army in steel armor and shielded with bucklers took on thousands of naked savages. They were aided by a force of Indian allies under Guacanagari, but the Spaniards were not expecting much from them. They marched up to the Puerta de los Hidalgos and descended into the Vega Real to meet the forces of Guatiguana, which, according to Las Casas, consisted of one hundred thousand men—obviously a gross exaggeration. But their numbers must have been great as they included the combined forces of several Caciques. It was commanded by Manicaotex, the brother of Caonabo, who upon learning from his scouts that only a scant number of soldiers would challenge this large army, sneered contemptuously. With his little but powerful army, Columbus advanced to a place where the present large city of Santiago is located. The Indian army, under Manicaotex, was stationed on a plain dotted with clusters of trees.

Bartholomew, who had scouted the large force of the enemy, advised that the little army be divided into platoons to attack the Indians at the same time from different directions. His plan was adopted. At a given signal, the platoons of the infantry began to advance with great sounds of drums and blasts of trumpets. The thunder and lightning of the arquebuses, from behind the trees, added to the din and threw the Indians into utter confusion. Immediately Hojeda with his cavalry charged into the main body, slashing and carving their way through the human masses with sword and spear. As the horses bore down on the terrified Indians, the bloodhounds were let loose, tearing at their naked bodies. The Indians fled in every direction, but could not escape the shower of arrows that fell on them. The skirmish was of short duration. Many Indians were killed or taken prisoner. The remainder of their army was broken up and dispersed. Guacanagari and his forces were not even needed, as the rout of the enemy was complete.

THE CAPTURE OF CAONABO

Now that Guatiguana had been dealt with, it was necessary in order to ensure tranquility in the Vega Real that Caonabo, the most feared of all Caciques, be captured. Open warfare with this wily Carib was out of the question, for it involved invading his mountains and exposing the meager Spanish army to the danger of ambush at every turn. Hojeda proposed to trick Caonabo into their hands, by inviting him to be a special guest of the Admiral in Isabela and capturing him alive without striking a blow. The plan was bold and dangerous, characteristic of Hojeda, who seemed to enjoy extravagant exploits and feats of bravery.

Choosing ten hearty soldiers, well armed and well mounted, he made his way to Caonabo's retreat on the southern slopes of the Cibao mountains, located past the Cordillera Central near the city of San Juan. Approaching the Cacique with the deference due a great king, he told him that he had come to extend him an invitation to visit Isabela to make a treaty with the Christians, at its satisfactory culmination, and that he would be presented with the bronze bell of the church. The Indians had always looked upon the chapel's bell as a supernatural object whose sound, like a voice from heaven, urged the Spaniards to enter the chapel. Caonabo had heard the sound of the bell from a distance and was curious to see it. Now that it was being offered to him as a gift of peace he could hardly wait to lay his hands on it and agreed to set out for Isabela with the Hojeda party. When the time came to leave, Hojeda was surprised to see a powerful force of warriors acting as the Cacique's bodyguards, ready to march with him. When asked why such a large force was needed on a friendly visit, Caonabo replied that on such an important occasion it was necessary to have a large retinue.

Hojeda was somewhat disturbed by the excessive show of force but had to give in so as not to arouse suspicion. It was necessary, however, to get rid of the Cacique's army along the way. The opportunity came in the course of their march when they set camp near the Little Yaqui River. Hojeda took out of his saddlebags a pair of burnished steel handcuffs and another of foot irons that he claimed the King of Spain wore on special occasions when he rode horseback.

The Indians always had a fascination for metal objects and greatly admired gold and brass, which they called "turey." Hojeda assured the Cacique that these were made of "negro turey de Vizcaia"—black brass from Biscay—Biscay being famous for steel even in those days. Hojeda then invited Caonabo to climb on his horse with him and try them on. The Cacique was flattered by the idea of riding on the huge animal, so dreaded by the Indians. He was assisted to mount behind Hojeda, the shackles and bracelets adjusted to feet and hands, and his body bound to Hojeda's so that he could not fall off. The Spaniards then gave them a riding exhibition and all of them with their prancing horses rode around the Indians to confuse them. At a given signal, they veered off at great speed, leaving the confused warriors behind. They crossed the river with the Cacique and headed in the direction of Isabela. Utmost vigilance was required to prevent his escape during the journey. They also had to be careful not to arouse suspicion, for they traveled in enemy territory. They had rough going but made it in safety and entered Isabela in triumph and to great acclaim after a most daring enterprise.

Columbus ordered that the Cacique be treated with kindness and respect and that a room be provided in his house for his imprisonment, as he did not trust the local prison. The captive, however, was to be kept in chains at all times. Despite his precaution, Columbus considered Caonabo too dangerous to be kept in Hispaniola as attempts might be made to liberate him. It was agreed that he be sent to Spain at the first opportunity. During his captivity, Caonabo confessed that he had killed twenty of the Spaniards who remained under Harana in Navidad after Columbus returned to Spain. He also indicated that he planned to destroy Isabela at the opportune time. Caonabo's capture was deeply felt by his loyal subjects. It was reported that Caonabo's brother-in-law, Behechio, Cacique of Xaragua, was assembling an army of more than seven thousand warriors in a plan to capture the fort of Santo Tomás and use the Spanish prisoners as hostages in exchange for Caonabo. Once again, Hojeda was sent to garrison Santo Tomás. After reinforcing the troops there, he headed over the mountains to fight Behechio.

Hojeda's cavalry charge threw the Indians into a panic. Many were slain, and many more taken prisoner, among them Behechio, who later escaped and retired to his remote domain away from the influence of the white man.

IMPOSITION OF TRIBUTES

With the defeat of Guatiguana and the capture of Caonabo, "The island was so peaceful that a Christian could safely go wherever he pleased, and the Indians themselves offered to carry him piggyback as they do nowadays at the post stages," wrote Ferdinand.[1] With the island under some measure of control, Columbus began to give some thought to going back to Spain and taking care of his affairs. Unfortunately, in June 1495, a violent "hurricane"—a word adopted from the Indian language—struck the island and sank all the ships except the

Niña, which weathered the storm. The San Juan, Cardera, and Gallaega were all broken up and lost. The Admiral ordered that a new ship be built from the salvaged parts of the sunken vessels. The shipwrights that Columbus brought along were equal to the task, and the first vessel constructed in the New World and built like the Niña was launched. They named it officially Santa Cruz, but the seamen nicknamed her "India."

The need to extract whatever riches were on the island to justify the expenses of the voyages and to assure future support made it imperative for Columbus to turn his victories into cash. A system of taxation was imposed on the vanquished Indians. The natives had to pay a heavy tribute of gold to the Spanish. It applied specifically to those of the Vega Real, Cibao, and all the regions of the mines. Each person above the age of fourteen was required to pay every three months the measure of a Flemish hawks' bell of gold dust. The Caciques had to pay a larger amount, and Manicaotex, the brother of Caonabo, had to give a calabash of gold valued at 150 castellanos every two months. In the districts that produced no gold, each individual was required to furnish an arroba (twenty-five pounds) of cotton every three months. Each person who complied received a copper medal as certificate of payment to hang around his neck. Failure to comply meant certain torture and execution. The natives had been enjoying the pleasant life of the islands too long. Their lives, so they reasoned, were meant to be enjoyed, not to produce wealth. The beautiful life—to dream under the shade of a tree, to slumber during the sultry noontide heat, to sing, to dance, and to love—came naturally to them. Putting them to work would make them productive and keep them from waging war against the invaders. But it did not work out that way at all because they were not used to forced labor.

Anticipating the possibility of a local rebellion, it was decided that in addition to the fortresses of Isabela and Santo Tomás in the mountains of Cibao, other fortresses should be built throughout the island. These would prove to the natives that the Spaniards were there to stay permanently. The forts would become the nuclei around which future cities would grow. The Spaniards built a fort at Magdalena in the Vega Real near the site of Santiago, at Santa Catalina near the Estencia Yaqui, and at Esperanza on the banks of the River Yaqui. The most important one was Fort Concepcion in the Vega Real, fifteen leagues to the east of Esperanza, built to control the extensive and populous domains of Guarionex.

The system of taxation was a total disaster for the Indians, who could not and did not know how to find the required gold. To make it more palatable, the Admiral decided to lower the tribute by fifty percent, but even that was exorbitant. Some complied and for others it was impossible. The option for the latter was either to be killed or seek refuge in the mountains, where they would be hunted by hounds. In desperation, many committed suicide. Of the original native population estimated by some at three hundred thousand people—Las Casas claimed there were three million natives—one-third were killed off between 1494 and 1496. Life on the island was never the same for the Indians. By 1508 only sixty thousand remained; by 1548, Oviedo estimated a native Indian population of only five hundred African Negroes were brought early in the sixteenth century to do the work the Indians had been expected to do and more African slaves were brought later on, thus changing radically the ethnic aspects of the Caribbean Islands.[2]

ARRIVAL OF AGUADO

Juan Aguado had been with Columbus on his second voyage to the Indies and had returned to Spain with the Antonio de Torres fleet, which left Isabela on February 2, 1494. Columbus had commended him in a letter to the Sovereigns and had recommended that his pay be increased. Perhaps it might have been this commendation that motivated the Sovereigns to nominate Juan Aguado as a special agent to report on Columbus's conduct as Viceroy and Governor and collect information on the existing situation in Hispaniola for the benefit of the Crown. He was put in commanded of a fleet that consisted of four vessels that sailed from Seville on August 5 and arrived in Isabela in the month of October 1495. He brought along much-needed supplies and a competent metallurgist requested by the Admiral, one named Pablo Belvis, who came prepared with the tools of the trade for mining, assaying, and purifying gold. Also aboard were several priests to replace Fray Buil and his colleagues and Don Diego Columbus. Aguado carried a letter from the Sovereigns to be delivered to Columbus, ordering him to reduce the number of colonists on the royal payroll to five hundred people, but he could not deliver it to him as he was absent from Isabela, waging war against the Indians. Aguado also carried a letter of introduction from the Sovereigns addressed to the colonists. It stated:

The King and Queen: Gentlemen and Squires and other persons who are in the Indies at our behest, we send you thither Juan Aguado, our butler, who will speak to you on our behalf. We order you to have faith and trust in him. From Madrid, April 9, 1495.

I the King—I the Queen
By order of the King and Queen, our Lords, Hernan Alvarez[3]

This curt statement of authority was not addressed to the viceroy—Columbus was ignored, indicating that Aguado was on an impartial fact-finding mission, outside the influence of the Admiral.

Despite the fact that he was simply a delegated agent of the Crown employed to collect information, Aguado overplayed his role by assuming a tone of supreme authority. He interfered in public affairs and even ordered several persons to be arrested. He ordered his letters of credence from the Sovereigns to be pompously proclaimed by sound of trumpets and began at once to countermand the orders of the Adelantado by assuming the functions of Viceroy. Bartholomew sent word to his brother about the insolent conduct of Aguado, thus forcing the Admiral to return to Isabela. Aguado had expected a violent confrontation with his former boss, but Columbus would not be embroiled in an undignified altercation. Instead, he first listened to Aguado with solemn deference because he represented the Sovereigns, then assured him of his complete cooperation in helping him gather all of the information he sought. As expected, Aguado had no difficulty in obtaining plenty of testimony against the oppression and suspected transgressions of Columbus, because every person in the colony was discontented and eager to go home. All the ills in the colony, even those produced by the misdeeds of the colonists, were blamed on the administration of Columbus. Yet, it was doubtful whether any other administrator could have done much better than he with a group of malcontents who had come to Hispaniola just to get rich and not to do menial work. Hunger was the worst grievance, for the colonists could not adjust to the native diet. There was little or no food, and according to Las Casas, the Spaniards wanted nothing more than to return to Spain. The most commonly heard expression was "Así Dios me lleve a Castilla" (So may God take me to Castile).

There is no doubt that Columbus was deeply humiliated seeing himself treated as an equal by the king's emissary. His authority and, worse yet, his prestige jeopardized by a civil servant, and his pride wounded—he had no recourse but to go to Castile and present his case to the king and queen.

Chapter Thirty-Two

COLUMBUS RETURNS TO SPAIN
MARCH 10–JUNE 11, 1496

Following his discussions with Juan Aguado, Columbus resolved that it was in his best interest to return to Spain. According to Ferdinand:

> *To report to the Catholic Sovereigns about many things relating to their service. He decided on this especially because many spiteful envious men were giving the Sovereigns false accounts of what was happening in the Indies, to the great prejudice of the Admiral and his brothers.*[1]

Columbus did not sail away until March 10, 1496, because the new ship India (Santa Cruz), built in Isabela, lacked proper equipment for her maiden voyage across the Atlantic. The Niña (Santa Clara) had been damaged in the June 1495 hurricane, when the other caravels had foundered and required repair on her hull and rigging. Following that devastating hurricane, the Admiral was also convinced that he needed better and safer anchorage for the fleet—one that provided protection from the north and northeast winds. Isabela was unsatisfactory not only as a haven for the ships but also because its location was too far from the Cibao mines. To reach them, his men had to cross the Cordillera Setentrional, the Vega Real, several rivers, and the mountains of the Cibao. It was important that a new site, preferably on the south coast of the island, be chosen before he embarked for Spain. The selection of the new site may very well have been influenced by a love story.

THE DISCOVERY OF GOLD MINES AND A NEW SETTLEMENT

Oviedo tells the story of young Miguel Diaz, in the service of the Adelantado, who found a new settlement site as a result of his romantic involvement with Catalina, a female Cacique. This young Aragonese had become a fugitive following an altercation with another Spaniard in which he had critically stabbed his adversary. Wandering about the island with some of his friends, he came to an Indian village on the southern coast in the Higuey domain, where the present city of Santo Domingo is located. The hospitable Indians were friendly and the Spaniards decided to live with them for some time. The lady Cacique of the village was a beautiful woman with whom Diaz fell in love, and they lived happily together for some time until the Aragonese began to get homesick. Catalina, fearful of losing her lover, devised a sure way of keeping him from leaving. Knowing that gold was the primary attraction for the Spaniards, she told him that rich mines of the precious metal existed in the vicinity and urged him to persuade his countrymen to abandon Isabela and settle on the banks of the nearby Ozema River. Her people would receive them with utmost kindness and hospitality.

Diaz was receptive to the idea and immediately made an exploratory survey of the mines, and was convinced that they were superior to the mines of Cibao. He was also impressed with the beauty of the land, the excellence of the river, and the security of the harbor at the river's mouth. It dawned upon him that the communication of this valuable intelligence to the Adelantado might earn him a pardon. Without wasting time, he crossed the island and arrived at Isabela. To his relief, the man he had wounded had recovered. Appearing before the Adelantado, he told him about the gold mines. He could not have come at a more opportune time, for the Admiral had been anxious to move the settlement to a safer and healthier place. He was very eager to bring home conclusive proof that there was gold in Hispaniola, to silence his enemies. An expedition was immediately ordered to confirm Diaz's claim. The Adelantado, accompanied by armed men, and by the metallurgist Francisco de Caray and Diaz, set out for the River Ozema about fifty leagues away.

They crossed the Cordillera Setentrional through the Puerto de los Hidalgos, the Vega Real, to the fortress of Concepción, another range of mountains, and descended into the beautiful plain of Bonao (called by the same name today). They continued for some distance to a large river called "Hayna." On the western bank of this river, about eight leagues from its mouth, they found gold. It was not a sedimentary gold dust but gold ores in large particles. In several places, they saw deep tunnels, which indicated that the mines had been excavated years earlier. The Adelantado was convinced that Miguel Diaz's information was correct. Accordingly, he was not only pardoned but given important assignments in various capacities in the affairs of the colony. The Admiral was overjoyed at the favorable report presented by the Adelantado and ordered that a new city be built during his absence. The building of Santo Domingo was started after Columbus won the approval of the King and Queen, which he had received in Cádiz, following his second voyage. The message reached Isabela at the beginning of July 1496, and it is certain that construction started soon afterwards. Ferdinand Columbus stated that the name was chosen because Domingo (Domenico) was the name of the Admiral's father; Las Casas says that it was chosen because the Adelantado arrived there on Sunday ("Domingo," in Spanish).

PERILOUS CROSSING

With the first caravel India (Santa Cruz) built in the New World, equipped for the long voyage, and the Niña (Santa Clara) repaired, Columbus prepared to leave Isabela for Spain. He left the command of the colony and island to his brother Bartholomew, to be succeeded by his brother Diego in case of his death.

There were 225 passengers aboard the two caravels, at least double the ships' capacities. Obeying the orders of the Sovereigns, all those who were sick, all those who could be spared from the island, and all those with wives and relatives in Spain whom they wished to see returned in these caravels. There were thirty Indians aboard, including the captive Caonabo, who was to die at sea; his brother and nephew and a selected group were chosen to be trained as interpreters.

The two ships set sail at daybreak, March 10, 1496, at a time of the year when the westerlies are strongest. The right choice for the crossing would have been to scud downwind through the Bahama Channel to the latitude of Bermuda and then take advantage of the west wind. This was the route Columbus had used on his first voyage and the route he had advised Torres to take in 1494. In view of the crowded condition of his vessels and the hundreds of mouths to feed, what could have prompted Columbus to fight the westerlies by retracing the path of the outward voyage of his second trip? The only valid explanation that can be advanced is that the Admiral feared for the safety of his large human cargo and chose a route with the shortest oceanic passage. The India, built in Hispaniola, was an untested ship and sailing for several hundred miles within sight of land would provide a shakedown cruise and a haven in case of trouble. The trade-off was then the chance of encountering head winds to slow down the vessels for a longer journey or the safety of his passengers. He chose the latter, and that proved to be almost a fatal mistake.

The Adelantado sailed aboard the Niña as far as Puerto Plata, where the brothers landed to look at the site for the new capital. Columbus had admired the place on his first voyage and had been heading towards it during his second voyage, after quitting Navidad for a new site, but adverse winds had forced him to settle on Isabela, short of his destination at the present site. The new site pleased them. The Adelantado returned to Isabela by land, after wishing his brother farewell.

Columbus took off from Puerto Plata with the trade winds blowing against his fleet and did not negotiate Cape Engaño, the easternmost point of Hispaniola, 175 miles east of Puerto Plata, until March 22. With the trades bowing unabated, he crossed the Mona Passage, tacked along the coast of Puerto Rico, and swung south along the Lesser Antilles. By the sixth of April, with his crews very tired and sick of fighting the trades and periodic calms, and his provisions running dangerously low, the Admiral decided to stop at the Island of Guadeloupe for food and water.

On Saturday, the ninth of April, he anchored at the little satellite island of Mariagalante just south of Guadeloupe, the island where the Admiral had taken formal possession of the Caribbean Islands on his outward voyage. The following morning the Admiral proceeded northeast to the Grande Anse Island, another satellite of Guadeloupe, and sent an armed boat ashore, expecting trouble from the Caribs. He was correct with his instinct, for even before the boat touched the shore it became the target of a shower of arrows, launched by a large group of women who were rushing out of the woods where they had been hiding. Fortunately, all the arrows fell short of their mark.

Undaunted by this inhospitable reception, Columbus had two Indian women swim ashore to reassure the Amazons of the Spaniards' good intentions—that they were seeking food for which they would exchange articles of great value. The Amazons replied that they had no food to give, but their husbands who were at the northern end of the island might satisfy their needs. The Admiral sailed there with the Niña and India and noticed a number of natives on the beach shouting and yelling at the white men. Once again, an armed boat was sent ashore only to be greeted with a shower of arrows, which fell far short in the water. As the boat came closer to shore, the Indians prepared to resist them until a discharge from the lombards sent them running into the woods. The Spaniards landed unharmed and proceeded to loot and destroy the huts, finding nothing of value, only a human arm roasting on a spit. Columbus sent forth armed men to explore the interior of the island and they returned with three boys and ten women, one of whom was the wife of a Cacique—a woman of great strength and regal manner. Columbus let it be known that these women and boys would be held as hostages unless a quantity of provisions were made available to the Spaniards. The women obliged by teaching the invaders the art of making cassava bread.[2]

AGONY ON THE HIGH SEAS

The fleet remained in Guadeloupe for nine days, baking mounds of cassava bread, filling their casks with water, and storing a supply of firewood. Finally, on the twentieth of April, they released their hostages, with the exception of the Cacique and her daughter, who chose to remain aboard. They headed for Spain, keeping their route well south on approximately 22°N latitude to avoid the north Atlantic storms that nearly sank the Niña in 1493. But at this latitude Columbus was sailing against the whole current of the trade winds, and his progress was so slow that after a month's sailing he was still on the high seas. By May 20, the provisions were already so reduced that everyone was put on a daily allowance of six ounces of bread and a pint of water. As they kept going, the scarcity of food grew more severe, and the situation became more alarming as the pilots aboard were not certain of their location. They all had different opinions, but according to Ferdinand, the Admiral was confident that their position lay somewhat to the westward of the Azores. By the beginning of June and six weeks from Guadeloupe, famine was rampant aboard the ships.

With death staring them in the face, it was suggested by some Spaniards that they should kill and eat their Indian prisoners. Others with more humane feelings suggested that they should throw them into the sea to preserve the food. According to Ferdinand, "They would have done it too if the Admiral had not forbidden it, saying that as Christians and human beings, they should not be treated worse than others."[3] Columbus appealed to them to have a little more patience because, according to his dead reckoning, they were not too far from Cape St. Vincent. Some of the pilots disagreed with him, affirming that they were approaching the English Channel, while others believed they were heading for Galicia (sic) (northwest Spain). Columbus was so confident that he was right that he ordered the sails to be taken in that night to avoid crashing on the shore in the dark; this only brought cynical laughter from the pilots.

The next morning, however, they became convinced that the Admiral's confidence was justified when they signed land ahead—the Portuguese coast about thirty-five miles north of Cape St. Vincent, his destination. This brilliant execution of dead-reckoning navigation prompted Ferdinand to write in his biography of his father, "From that time on the seamen regarded the Admiral as most expert and admirable in matters of navigation." The fleet sailed southward along the coast rounding Cape St. Vincent, their spirits high and thankful to God for their narrow escape. Now, in a festive mood, they decorated their ships. Every available banner and pennant was displayed for the homecoming. On June 11, the vessels anchored in the Bay of Cádiz, after a weary voyage of three months. At best, it was a pathetic homecoming in contrast to the gallant and colorful fleet of seventeen ships that had left Cádiz on September 25, 1493. He had left as a hero; and now, two years, eight months, and seventeen days later, he came home to defend himself against the calumnies of his subordinates who had become his enemies, bent on undermining his popularity with the Sovereigns.

In the harbor of Cádiz, Columbus found three ships commanded by Peralonso Niño, ready to sail with supplies for the colony. Columbus read the royal letters and dispatches addressed to him that Niño had delivered. Then he took the opportunity of writing to the Adelantado, urging him to bring the island into a peaceful and productive state and send to Spain all Caciques who had taken the lives of the Christians. He also added that the new gold mines recently discovered on the River Hayna should be worked with diligence and that a new seaport should be built in the vicinity. Peralonso Niño set sail with his three ships on the seventeenth of June with more provisions for the colonists, along with the Admiral's hopes for a peaceful and productive colony.

Part VII

THE THIRD VOYAGE TO THE INDIES
JUNE 11, 1496–MAY 25, 1498

Chapter Thirty-Three

APPROVAL AND PREPARATIONS FOR THE THIRD VOYAGE

Columbus's popularity, which had reached its zenith when he had left for his second voyage, was completely undermined by the malcontents who had returned to Spain prior to him. It had waned as a result of the negative rumors spread by the likes of Fray Buil, Margarit, and Aguado. Even the crew and passengers who had returned with the Admiral, visibly run-down and emaciated by the unhealthy conditions of Hispaniola, lent credence to the stories told by his enemies. Columbus attempted to dismiss the charges by citing his recent accomplishments: his discoveries along the southern coast of Cuba and his arrival at the outskirts of what he presumed to be the Golden Chersonese (Malay Peninsula). His detractors, however, remained unconvinced. Columbus began to believe that his misfortunes were indeed due to his own pride, that God was displeased with his lack of humility; therefore, he began to wear the habit of a Franciscan friar with the cord of humility around his waist. In fact, it was in this penitential vestment that he appeared before the bewildered Curate of Palacios, Andrés Bernáldez, Chaplain to Diego Deza, Archbishop of Seville, with whom he was to lodge while in Spain.

In the Curate, the Admiral found a devoted friend with an inquisitive disposition and an inclination for writing everything down in his diary. Columbus delighted in telling him about his explorations and recounted vividly his recent voyage along the southern coast of Cuba. Bernáldez recorded it in minute detail in his *Historia de los Reyes Católicos*.

News of Columbus's arrival finally reached the Sovereigns, who had feared him dead. They wrote a gracious letter from Almazan, dated July 12, 1496, congratulating him on his safe return and inviting him to come to court as soon as he was strong enough to undertake the long trip. Almazan, 150 miles northeast of Madrid, required an overland trip of over 500 miles. The pleasant tone of the letter gave Columbus new encouragement as he had considered himself out of favor with the Sovereigns following the uncomplimentary reports of Fray Buil, Margarit, and Aguado.

The long journey to the north of Spain gave Columbus an opportunity to rekindle the interest of the population in his discoveries. His train was less ostentatious and more puzzling than the triumphant procession of his first homecoming. Instead of a magnificently clad Admiral, a humble man in Franciscan garb looking much older than the proud and haughty leader of four years past now led the train. His ascetic mien complemented not only his brown vestment but his role of "poverello" from Assisi. He took along with him several Indians in full regalia decorated with gold ornaments; one of them was the brother of Caonabo. Whenever they passed through a populous center, Columbus put a massive collar of gold around his neck that according to Bernáldez weighed 600 castellanos (261,000 maravedis). Hideous masks of animals or idols and many cages of brightly colored parrots were also displayed along the way to Burgos, where the Sovereigns were expected to meet Columbus.

Ferdinand and Isabella received Columbus warmly and with dignity despite his puzzling habit. Encouraged by their friendly reception, Columbus presented them with a considerable quantity of gold dust and some gold nuggets as big as pigeon eggs in addition to Indian crafts and booty. He then gave a detailed account of his recent voyages along the southern coast of Cuba, his discovery of Jamaica, and the discovery of the gold mines off Hayna. Most important, he let them know that he had learned from some Indians of the existence of *terra firma* south of all the islands he had discovered and proposed a new enterprise to add more extensive territories to their dominions. For this new venture, he asked for eight ships: two to be sent with supplies directly to Hispaniola as soon as possible and six to explore the mainland, which even the King of Portugal believed existed to the south of the Caribbean islands. The Sovereigns readily agreed that a third voyage was necessary and promised to grant his request.

The reader may wonder at this point why the Sovereigns quickly approved Columbus's plan despite all the negative reports they had received from his enemies. After all, Columbus had not made good on his promise to fill the royal treasury chests with gold. The Sovereigns, while fascinated with the power of gold, actually considered it as just another valuable metal no doubt welcome to their exchequer, but definitely not the most important commodity in their future plans to make Spain a great and powerful Christian nation. Their aim was to colonize the Indies with Spanish subjects. They thought in terms of farms, husbandry, and people working and producing for the common good. And it is for this purpose that they constantly urged Columbus to provide the best possible information on the new territories: geographical location, climate, flora and fauna, minerals, fisheries, and land produce.

Of great concern to the queen was the spiritual salvation of the Indians, which could only be done by spreading the Gospels. The natives had to be treated humanely so that evangelization could proceed more smoothly.

Columbus was still a valuable asset to the Sovereigns' plans for colonization and exploration, in spite of charges made by the Catalan clan, but he had made many enemies among the members of the court, and these would eventually humiliate him. Despite the Sovereigns' good intentions, Columbus had to wait nearly two years before embarking on his third voyage. This delay was caused by the Sovereigns' preoccupation with dynastic marriages for their children and by Ferdinand's involvement in Italy. Through these marriages, which required lengthy and delicate negotiations, the Sovereigns established a complex network of relationships with Portugal, Austria, Flanders, and England.

A more worrisome event that preoccupied the Sovereigns at this time was Ferdinand's military campaign in Italy against Charles VIII of France, which succeeded in restoring the Kingdom of Naples to the Aragonese Federigo III. The pursuit of alliances through marriage and the projection of Spanish might in Europe were obviously more important for the moment than the financing of a third voyage to the Indies. No doubt the royal treasury was overburdened when you consider the enormous expenditures incurred in the pursuit of war and in the celebration of princely weddings; two such weddings between Margaret of Austria and Juan of Spain, and Juana of Spain and Philip of Hapsburg, were attended by twenty thousand guests brought to Flanders and back to Burgos by 130 vessels. The marriage that took place in Burgos on March 19, 1497, was attended by Christopher Columbus.

An event relating to the arrival of the fleet that brought Princess Margaret to Spain boosted Columbus's stock with the king and queen. The queen had been deeply concerned about the fate of the fleet, which was late in arriving. The court had already left Burgos on a Saturday, but the Sovereigns had lingered until Monday hoping to greet their future daughter-in-law. The weather had been bad and the possibility of a French foray against the Spaniards was real. Columbus sent a reassuring note to the queen in which he placed himself in the captain's shoes and predicted, in view of the weather conditions, that the fleet would arrive at Laredo on Monday. Indeed, on Monday one of the ships that had not called on the Isle of Wight sailed into the harbor of Laredo in northern Spain. After the queen was notified of the happy event, she sent Columbus a letter expressing her gratitude.

Shortly after Columbus attended the marriage of Don Juan and Princess Margaret, the Sovereigns finally issued the first orders about the ships that were to go to the Indies. Nine months later, the dependable Niña with its companion, the India, returned to Hispaniola with food, supplies, and women, all of these cargoes sorely needed; however, it was not until four months afterward, on May 25, 1498, that the Admiral was able to leave for his third voyage.

The two-year respite had not been wasted by Columbus, for it enabled him to regain favor with the Sovereigns, following the reports of Fray Buil, Margarit, and other malcontents. The Privileges of April 1495 were reconfirmed and the monarchs allowed Columbus to prepare a "mayorazgo" for the perpetual care of his estate. During this period, the Admiral received the news that four Portuguese ships under the command of Vasco da Gama had left on July 8, 1497, to sail around the Cape of Good Hope to India. There were also rumors that John Cabot (Giovanni Caboto) had left Bristol for the west at the order of King Henry VII. Sailing in the North Atlantic, Cabot had reached Newfoundland and had returned to Bristol early in August of 1497. This single event eventually was the basis for the English claim to North America and the establishment of the first, but short-lived, settlement on Roanoke Island in North Carolina in 1585, and subsequently of a more permanent colony in Jamestown, Virginia, in 1606. A new age of exploration had started in earnest—an age which with the beginning of the sixteenth century would involve the entire globe. Columbus was the man who had started it.

CONFIRMATION OF COLUMBUS'S PRIVILEGES AND OTHER ORDERS

The rights and privileges of April 1492, granted to Columbus in Santa Fé, were again confirmed. An additional concession was made by the Sovereigns. The cost of the two expeditions to the Indies had exceeded the income; Columbus not only had not gained any profits from his trips but had actually incurred debt. Therefore, the Sovereigns relieved Columbus of bearing one-eighth of the cost of the supply ships for the voyages already undertaken and would allow him instead one-eighth of the gross proceeds and one-tenth of the net profit for the ensuing three years; at the expiration of that period, the original terms of the agreement were to be enforced.

Columbus was offered a tract of land in Hispaniola of considerable size, fifty leagues from east to west by twenty-five leagues from north to south, and along with it the title of Duke or Marques; he gratefully declined the land gift to avoid arousing envy from his many enemies at court. Columbus brought to the attention of the Sovereigns a Royal Order issued on April 10, 1495, which ran counter to his privileges, which should never have been issued and indeed should be declared null and void. Specifically, as a result of the malicious reports received in April 1495 from Fray Buil and Pedro Margarit, the Sovereigns had issued a decree entitling any Castilian searching for gold in Hispaniola to keep one-third of what he had found and turn the remaining two-thirds to the Crown. After due investigation, the Sovereigns agreed with Columbus that the order did interfere with his prerogatives; they issued a Royal Edict on June 2, 1497, retracting the prejudicial statement, explaining:

It never was our intention in any way to affect the rights of the said Don Christopher Columbus, nor to allow the conventions, privileges, and favors which we have granted him to be encroached upon or violated; but on the contrary, in consequence of the services which he has rendered us, we intend to confer still further favors on him.[1]

This apology by the monarchs, seldom encountered in those days, was a clear indication of his renewed favor at the royal court. Thus, it was under these beneficial circumstances that Columbus was able to arrange, after the death of Don Juan, that his two sons be appointed as pages to the queen. By Royal Edict signed by the queen on the eighteenth and nineteenth of February 1498, his two sons were to be paid a pension of 9,700 maravedis each for being brought up at court.

As a friendly retribution, the Sovereigns also granted Don Bartholomew the title of "Adelantado of the Indies," which the

Admiral had dared to give him previously of his own accord, but which they had ignored as an abuse of the Viceroy's powers. This light slap on the wrist was the only royal rebuke to the Admiral, who by now was much elated with his success.

COLUMBUS "MAYORAZGO" OR PERPETUAL RIGHT OF SUCCESSION OF HIS ESTATE

To perpetuate in his family the gains made by his deeds of exploration, Columbus was allowed the right of establishing a "mayorazgo" so that the titles of nobility might be passed on to succeeding generations. In a solemn testament executed in the early part of 1498, Columbus specified that upon his death his estate should pass on to his own male descendants, starting with his sons Diego and Ferdinand. The heir was always to bear the arms of the Admiral, to seal with them, and to sign with his signature. In all signatures, the title of "the Admiral" should always be used, regardless of whatever other titles might have been given by royal order.

In his testament, he made provisions also for his brothers Bartholomew and Don Diego. He ordered that one-tenth of the revenues earned by the "mayorazgo" should be devoted to pious and charitable purposes and to provide welfare assistance to the poor persons of his lineage. Of particular interest to those who doubted Columbus's Genoese origin is the following:

Item: I also enjoin Diego, or anyone that may inherit the estate, to have and maintain in the city of Genoa, one person of our lineage to reside there with his wife, and appoint to him a sufficient revenue to enable him to live decently, as a person closely connected with the family, of which he is to be the root and basis in that city;

from which great good may accrue to him, inasmuch as I was born there, and came from thence.

Deeply concerned as he was about the future welfare of his native city, he ordered that his entail contain the following:

Item: I command the said Diego, or whoever may possess the said estate, to labor and strive for the honor, welfare, and aggrandizement of the city of Genoa, and to make use of all his power and means in defending and enhancing the good and credit of that republic, in all things not contrary to the service of the church of God, or high dignity of our king and queen, our lords and their successors.

Columbus also provided for financial help to needy relatives and specified dowries for the young women of his lineage. Other items included the specification that:

A church be built on the island of Hispaniola…to be called "Santa María de la Concepción" to which is to be annexed a hospital upon the best possible plan, like those in Italy and Castile.

Another item provided for the establishment of a school of theology, "to spare no pains in having and maintaining in the island of Hispaniola, four good professors of theology to the end and aim of their studying and laboring to convert to our holy faith the inhabitants of the Indies."

In still another item he provided for the recovery of the Holy Sepulchre by investing in the Stocks of the Bank of St. George in Genoa:

Item: As it becomes every man of property to serve God, either personally or by means of his wealth, and as all monies deposited with St. George are quite safe, and Genoa is a noble and powerful city...the said Diego or such persons as may succeed him in this trust is to collect together all money he can and accompany the King our Lord should he go to the conquest of Jerusalem.[2]

PREPARATIONS FOR THE THIRD VOYAGE

Very much pleased with his success with King Ferdinand and Queen Isabella, Columbus began in earnest to prepare for his third voyage. At the request of the queen, he sought colonizers for Hispaniola, not adventurers. To this effect three royal charters were issued on June 22, 1497, concerning colonization and land grants.

Permission was granted to send out three hundred colonists on royal pay including forty escuderos or servants, thirty sailors, thirty grommets, twenty miners, fifty farmers, ten gardeners, twenty mechanics of various kinds, and thirty women. They were to be paid prevailing wages and twelve maravedis a day for keep, except for the women, who were expected to work for their passage. Columbus was also allowed to take along fifty more persons if they were willing to pay for their own passage. However, there were not too many takers in this category. Indeed, gone were the good days of the second voyage when he had many more volunteers than he needed. This time to fill his complement it was decided to take along convicts. For inducement, the orders stated that the time served in the colony was to count twice as much as in Spain. Ten years in Hispaniola would be equivalent to a life sentence, and with some exceptions, permanent settlement in Hispaniola would justify a reprieve of the sentence—the exceptions being heresy, treason, sodomy, counterfeiting of coins, and lèse majesté. In another order, the Viceroy was given authority to grant and distribute land to persons who would stay and work the land for at least four continuous years.

Some delay was encountered in fitting out the expedition. This responsibility had been assigned to Antonio de Torres; in fact, the official documents had been made out in his name as well as in Columbus's. But because of his unreasonable demands, Torres was removed from his responsibility and Don Juan de Fonseca, Bishop of Badajoz, was reinstated. The competent bishop had done a good job in fitting out Columbus for his second voyage, but their relationship had gradually soured to the extent that he had become extremely envious of the Admiral, not only uncooperative but obstructive as well. All the papers had to be drawn anew and new contracts made out with the bishop's name. A stickler for details, royal orders, and requisitions for supplies meant nothing to him unless he was certain that money was available to pay for the requisitioned items. The fact of the matter is that the money was not available in many instances as the royal treasury had been hard-pressed with the unusual expenditures related to the dynastic marriages and the Italian wars.

While the bishop was extremely dedicated to the Sovereigns, he looked upon Columbus as a pretender bent on deceiving the Sovereigns. Accordingly, through the efforts of his minions they threw all kinds of impediments in Columbus's path in order to delay his voyage. One of the most insolent of the bishop's followers was his treasurer, Ximeno Breviesca, who became a veritable thorn in Columbus's side. The very day that the squadron was about to sail, Columbus was so irritated by the vitriolic remarks of this man that he lost his self-control and knocked him to the ground, an unusual and regrettable act on the part of the

Admiral, who was known to control his emotions. He deplored his loss of self-control and openly apologized to the Sovereigns in a letter written some time afterward.

Columbus's fleet for his third voyage consisted of six vessels. Three vessels were ordered to proceed directly to Hispaniola with men and supplies sorely needed in the colony. These ships, whose names are not known, were commanded respectively by Alonso Sánchez de Carvajal, mayor of Baeza, who had accompanied Columbus as a captain on his second voyage; by Pedro de Harana, brother of Columbus's mistress; and by Giovanni (Giannetto) Colombo, son of Columbus's uncle, who had written to the Admiral in previous years asking for a seagoing job. The other three vessels Columbus equipped and reserved especially for his voyages of exploration consisted of his flagship, a nao, the Santa María de Guia, of approximately one hundred tons and similar to the Santa María of his first voyage, and two caravels, the smaller one named El Correo and the other of seventy tons called La Vaqueños. Pedro de Terreros, a veteran steward on Columbus's first voyage, was one of the captains and Hernan Perez the other. A total sum of 2,324,326 maravedis was appropriated by the Sovereigns for the third voyage. By the last week of May 1498, everybody except the Admiral was aboard at Seville, ready for another eventful voyage.

Chapter Thirty-Four

THIRD VOYAGE OF DISCOVERY—LANDFALL IN TRINIDAD

Columbus joined his fleet at Sanlúcar de Barrameda, the seaport of Seville at the mouth of the Guadalquivir River. On the thirtieth of May 1498, he set sail for his third voyage, with a squadron of six vessels. The route he proposed to take was considerably farther south than on his previous voyages. He intended to sail first to the Cape Verde Islands at approximately 15°N latitude and then, with the help of the trade winds, attempt to reach the equatorial territories at the longitude of Hispaniola. Various factors prompted the Admiral to plan this course. During his previous voyages, he had been told by the Caribbean Indians that a large mainland existed southward of their islands. According to rumors, King João II of Portugal entertained the same idea; therefore, it was important to find any lands that would belong to Portugal by virtue of the Treaty of Tordesillas. There were other reasons for exploring the equatorial area; Columbus had received a letter by a renowned lapidary named Jayme Ferrer, who had informed him through Queen Isabella that according to his experience, gold, precious stones, spices, and drugs could be found in more abundance and of better quality in the regions about the equinoctial line.

Columbus wanted to test these conjectures. There is no doubt, however, that the Admiral, ever a consummate mariner, had another interest in mind: studying the effects of ocean currents, the weather, the constellations (especially the North Star), and the effects of the torrid zones on marine and human life.

Upon leaving Sanlúcar, Columbus had been warned that because of the recent war with France, a French squadron was lurking off Cape St. Vincent. Accordingly, he sailed to the southwest toward the Madeira Islands, arriving on June 7, at the island of Port Santo, where he planned to hear Mass and take on water, wood, and other necessities. This was the island where his father-in-law and brother-in-law had been captains, where he had lived after his marriage to Doña Felipa, and where his son Diego was born. No doubt it must have brought back many memories. Unfortunately, most of the inhabitants had fled to the hills, having mistaken his fleet for French corsairs, so that no homecoming reception took place. He left the same day for the nearby city of Funchal on the island of Madeira, located about forty miles southwest of Porto Santo. It took the fleet nearly three days to get there because there was not enough wind to fill the sails. Once there, however, the Admiral received a warm reception because, as a former resident, he was very well known.

Columbus spent six days in Funchal socializing with old friends and, more importantly, replenishing his vessels with water, provisions, and wood. He also employed as a pilot for one of his ships a man from Seville named Pedro de Ledesma, who was to become a mutineer on the fourth voyage. On Saturday afternoon, June 16, the fleet departed from Funchal with favorable winds and sailed southward to Gomera in the Canary Islands, 290 miles away. It arrived there on the third day out. The

Spaniards were surprised to find at anchor a French warship that had captured two Spanish vessels. At the Admiral's approach, the French warship put to sea in great haste followed by the captives. The Admiral made no effort to pursue them, thinking that they were merchant ships fleeing because they had mistaken his fleet for French corsairs. But when he learned the truth he sent three ships after them. The French warship abandoned one of the captured ships and attempted to flee with the other that had onboard four Frenchmen and six captive Spaniards. Seeing that help was on the way, the Spaniards overpowered the French crew and returned to Gomera. The Admiral returned the vessels to the rightful owners and gave up the French prisoners to the governor of the island in exchange for the six Spaniards carried off by the French warship.

On Thursday, June 21, the Admiral left Gomera. He divided his squadron off the island of Ferro with specific instructions. Three of the vessels were ordered to proceed directly to Hispaniola to carry supplies to the colony. Exact instructions were issued to their captains Harana, Carvaja, and Colombo. These captains were to alternate the command and bear the signal light a week at a time.

Columbus set their course W by S before the trade winds for a distance of 850 leagues to reach Dominica Island. From there they were to sail WNW to Puerto Rico, then cross the Mona Passage leaving Mona Island on the starboard side and follow the south coast of Hispaniola for approximately twenty-five leagues to Santo Domingo. On Thursday, June 21, while the three ships set a course for Hispaniola, the Admiral with his flagship, the Santa María de Guia, and the Vaqueños and Correo, headed for the Cape Verde Islands.

During this stretch of the voyage the Admiral suddenly fell ill. As Ferdinand reported it:

The Admiral was suddenly seized by grievous pains of gout in the leg, and four days after by a terrible fever, but despite his illnesses he remained sound of mind and diligently noted the runs made by the ship and the changes in the weather, as he had done since the beginning of the third voyage.[1]

Holding on course, the fleet made good time covering 750 miles. On Wednesday, June 27, the Admiral sighted the island of Sal, one of the islands of the Cape Verde archipelago. He bypassed it and sailed on to the island of Boa Vista, which means "good view." This name is misnomer for the island is barren and poor. Columbus anchored his fleet in a bay on the western shore, near a tiny island facing some houses that belonged to a leper colony. Having noticed that the visitors were Castilians, the captain of the island, one Don Rodrigo Alfonso, paid the Admiral a courtesy visit and offered to satisfy all his wants. The Admiral reciprocated by offering the captain a drink and some refreshments—a luxury for the captain because Boa Vista's inhabitants led a dreary life, for the island is very dry and barren without trees or good water. The inhabitants ate nothing but fish and goat meat, as bread and vegetables were not available. The island was full of goats, which may explain its barrenness. The inhabitants slaughtered a great number of them and the pelts were salted and exported to Portugal.

The Admiral was curious to learn how the lepers cured their disease and was told that the hot climate was a primary factor. A second factor was their diet of turtle meat and their smearing themselves with the turtle's blood. By prolonged treatment with the blood, they were eventually cured. On Saturday afternoon, June 30, the Admiral set sail from Boa Vista for the island of São Tiago to the southwest, the principal island of the archipelago, which they reached at vesper time the following day. He sent a boat ashore to buy some black bulls and cows, in the belief they would thrive in Hispaniola, but he had no success in obtaining any.

The Cape Verde Islands left a bad impression on Columbus. He claimed, "From the time of his arrival in those islands he never saw the sky nor any star save through a haze so thick and warm that three-fourths of the natives of the country were sick, and the rest had a sickly color."[2]

HOT WEATHER TO TRINIDAD

On Thursday, July 5, the Admiral left the island of São Tiago, bound for the southwest, intending to sail to the equatorial zone and then proceed due west until he struck land. But on account of the very strong north and northwest currents between these islands, he could not make such headway. Additionally, the wind was so light that for three days he was within sight of the volcanic island of Fogo, barely three miles west of São Tiago. The Admiral remarked that the island seen from afar "resembles a great church with a campanile on its east side in the shape of a very high steep peak, which emits fire and smoke when the winds blow from the east as also happens on Tenerife, Mount Vesuvius, and Mount Etna."[3] Finally, a moderate wind sprang up on July 7, and the fleet was on its way southward and heading towards trouble with the doldrums and hot weather. He held his course to the southwest and soon began to navigate through weeds of the type he had met on his direct voyage to the Indies. At nightfall, after he had gone 480 miles, he took his wood quadrant, made a sight on the North Star and found that he was within 5° of the equator. This position has been challenged by several observers; Las Casas commented that Columbus must have sailed nearly eight hundred miles to the southwest to get on a 5° latitude position.

On Friday, July 13, the wind abruptly stopped according to Las Casas:

And he came into such great, vehement burning heat that he feared lest the ships catch fire and the people perish. So suddenly and unexpectedly did the wind cease and the excessive and unusual heat come on that there was no one who would dare to go below to look after the casks of wine and water, which burst, snapping the hoops of the pipes; the wheat burned like fire; the bacon and salt meat roasted and putrefied. This heat and fire lasted eight days. The first day was clear with a sun that scorched them; God granted him a respite, for on the six following days, it rained and was cloudy. But despite all this, they got no relief to give them hope that they would not burn to death; and if the seven days had been bright and sunny like the first, the Admiral says that it would have been impossible for even one of them to escape with his life.[4]

During this scorching period, on July 14, Columbus took another sight of the North Star and found that he was 7° above the equator. During this period Columbus again suffered an attack of gout and insomnia—ailments that would plague him to the end of his days. Finally, the wind returned just as abruptly as it had left him; the Admiral sailed westward seventeen days with the intention of eventually turning southward, according to his original plan. But he had problems: the repair of his vessels damaged by the heat and the necessity of obtaining suitable provisions to make up for the provisions lost to the heat.

On Sunday evening, July 22, they saw many birds flying from the WSW toward the NE; then they were certain that land could not be very far. On Monday and Tuesday, they saw more birds; one of them, an albatross, alighted on the Admiral's ship. They were running short of water and the Admiral changed his course due west and turned to the starboard hand in the hope of making a landfall on Dominica or any of the Caribbean islands. So he gave orders to steer to the N by E; he continued on his course until midday, when land was sighted:

But as His Divine Majesty ever showeth mercy towards me, fortuitously and by chance a seaman from Huelva, my servant named Alonso Pérez, climbed to the crow's nest and saw land to the west, distance fifteen leagues and it appeared to be in the shape of three rocks or mountains.[5]

Columbus wrote this in his journal. He named this land "the Island of Trinidad" in honor of the Blessed Trinity. Because Columbus had already committed himself to name the next island to be discovered "Trinidad," he was convinced that this was truly a miracle, the three peaks of the mountain representing the Trinity. They gave thanks to God and with great joy sang the "Salve Regina." Columbus wrote:

It pleased our Lord by his Divine Majesty that on the first sight there were three rocks, I mean mountains, all in a group, all at once and in a single view. May His Almighty power guide me by his charity in such wise He be well served and Your Highnesses have much pleasure, for it is certain that the finding of this land in this region was a great miracle, as great as the discovery on the first voyage.[6]

There was an additional miracle involved in the discovery of Trinidad. His calculations that he lay due south of the Windward Islands was amazingly accurate. The North Star sights from as low a latitude as 10°N are nearly impossible to be seen or read correctly, especially with a crude wooden quadrant. Yet it is interesting to speculate that if Columbus had followed his southwest course to the equatorial region, he would have landed on the coast of Brazil, thus discovering the shortest ocean route to the Indies. Moreover, assuming he would have made landfall either at the present location of Natal or at São Luis, both sites laying east of the 45°W meridian or longitude, he would have landed on territory allocated to Portugal by the Treaty of Tordesillas. And this was exactly one of the problems that Columbus had set out to investigate on his voyage. Instead, he made landfall at approximately 62°W longitude, not expecting that Portugal would eventually lay claim to Brazil.

TRINIDAD AND TERRA FIRMA

Having sighted the three-peaked island, the Admiral abandoned his course for the Caribbean islands, and headed instead towards the new island. He turned westward and that evening reached a cape that reminded him of a galley under sail; accordingly, they called it "Cabo de la Galera" (Galley Cape). There was a good harbor that was not deep enough so the fleet slowly continued westward in the moonlight along the south coast of the island. When dawn came on Wednesday, August 1, he saw that the land was carefully cultivated and beautiful. He sailed five more leagues and discovered a bay deep enough to anchor the fleet.

The men took on water from springs and streams and bathed. Columbus named the place "Punta de la Playa" (Beach Point). There were signs of people of many farms and well-cultivated areas. There were aloes, large royal palm groves, and expanses of great beauty. To the south there appeared to be another island more than twenty leagues long, but in fact, it must have been Punta Bombeador, Venezuela—Columbus's first sight of the continent!

When Columbus noticed the rising current of the water in the channel, he decided, after a day's stay, to continue sailing westward along the southern coast to the end point of the island, which he called "Punta del Arenal," or Sandy Point. Around the point, there were calmer waters on the lee side and the fleet anchored there in the gulf named "Golfo de la Ballena" (Gulf of the Whale). Soon on Thursday, August 2, a large canoe came from the east with twenty-five men aboard; when they got within range they began to shout and talk incomprehensibly. Columbus displayed some brass chamber pots and other bright objects to coax them to come closer, then ordered the grommets to beat the tabors and strike up a dance on the poop deck. The Indians mistook these actions to be a war dance and began to shoot arrows at the Spaniards. The Admiral immediately ordered the grommets to stop and to bring crossbows on deck and fire at the Indians to frighten them. Nothing more was seen of them. Columbus, who expected all people living in the equatorial region to be black, was surprised to find these natives actually lighter than the Indians he had seen in the Caribbean. He described them as well-formed, young, with very fine manners and handsome bodies; their hair was long and smooth, cut in the manner of Castile. They were naked but wore cotton bandannas woven with designs and colors around their heads.

The Admiral was pleasantly surprised with the very mild climate of the region. He believed that out beyond a point one hundred leagues west of the Azores there is a change in the sky, sea, and climate. This was the reason why in Trinidad, so close to the equator, it was cold every morning, "although the sun was in Leo." With respect to the local tides, he found that the waters ran westward stronger than the river of Seville and that the rise and fall of the tide differential was large enough so that they could careen carracks. In fact, the current flows so strong as to pour between Trinidad and the opposite island of Isla de Gracia at great speed. Obviously, Columbus noticed the hydrodynamic effect, which the Swiss mathematician Daniel Bernoulli was to prove nearly 250 years later. The Spaniards found the fruits, trees, lands, and climate to be similar to those on Hispaniola. From the ocean, they marveled at the large size of the oysters and the countless fish.

From Punta del Arenal, westernmost point of Trinidad, Columbus looked towards N by E at a distance of approximately fifteen leagues and saw a cape jutting out from the mainland; he mistook it for an island and called it "Isla de Gracia." On Saturday, August 4, he decided to go see the Isla de Gracia and sailed through the narrow channel separating Trinidad from the mainland to enter the Gulf of La Ballena:

There came a current from the south as strong as a mighty flood, with such great noise and din that it terrified all hands, so that they despaired of escaping, and the ocean water which confronted it coming from the opposite direction, caused the sea to rise, making a great lofty tidal wave which tossed the ship on top of the bore, a thing which none had ever heard of or seen; and it tripped the anchors of the other vessel (which ought already to have weighed) and forced her farther out to sea; and he made sail to get out of the said bore. It pleased God that they were not damaged.[7]

Because of this perilous experience, Columbus called the strait "Boca del Sierpe," the Serpent's Mouth.

Following this frightening experience, which today is generally accepted as being caused by a volcanic disturbance, the Admiral made great haste to leave Boca del Sierpe and had a smooth sail across the Gulf of Paria to the mountainous Isla de Gracia; he anchored at a harbor at the extreme eastern tip on the evening of August 4. This tip, which Columbus called "Cabo de Lapa" (Barnacle Cape), was the tip of the Paria Peninsula, an appendage of the mainland. This anchorage is believed to be the modern Bahía Celeste. On the following morning, Sunday, August 5, the Admiral began to sail south and west along the southern coast of the Paria Peninsula and anchored in a good harbor five leagues away, possibly Ensenada Yacua. It was here that Columbus sent boats ashore—thus marking the first European landing on this continent since the Norsemen back in the eleventh century.

Chapter Thirty-Five

DISCOVERY OF THE GULF OF PARIA AND THE NEW CONTINENT

From Ensenada Yacua, Columbus continued westward along the south shore of the supposed island of Gracia, intending to keep on until its end and then to proceed northward into the open ocean on his way to Hispaniola. He marveled at the beautiful coast, indented with many fine harbors. The land appeared on very high ground and had many valleys. It was neatly cultivated in many places, in others covered with fruit trees and majestic forests watered by numerous rivers. They found innumerable monkeys but had yet to see any local Indians. "This island," he says, "is full of harbors; this sea is fresh, although not wholly so, but brackish like that of Cartagena."[1] It is important to mention at this time that the whole area south and southwest of Trinidad consists of the huge Orinoco delta and the enclosed body of water that Columbus called "Golfo de la Ballena," presently known as the Gulf of Paria, which is a natural basin filled by many rivers—notably by the five channels of the Orinoco and, further west, by the many channels of the Río Grande and Río San Juan. This explains, of course, the "seawater" being fresh.

On Monday, August 6, Columbus sailed five leagues to a bay, possibly Guiria, at the mouth of the Río Guiria in Venezuela. He landed and laid claim to the territory. The ceremony was conducted by Pedro de Terreros, as Columbus was "indisposed." It was not performed on their landfall the previous day because no natives were present. Four Indians in a canoe came to the caravel closest to the shore. The pilot called out to the Indians to take him ashore with them, and as he approached and entered the canoe, the pilot deliberately overturned it, forcing them to swim about. Then, with the help of his comrades, he captured and brought them to the Admiral. La Casas quotes from the Admiral's journal:

As soon as these Indians came here, I gave them hawks' bells and beads and sugar and sent them ashore, where there was a large throng of them, and after they heard of the good treatment accorded their fellows, they all wanted to board the vessels. Those who had canoes came, and they were many, and all were warmly received and kindly bespoken, and given things which pleased them.[2]

The hospitable Indians brought bread and water and some beverages that looked like green wine. The Admiral noticed that all of them were heavily armed with bows and poisoned arrows and shields. He asked them many questions but they did not understand him.

On Tuesday, August 7, many of the Indians came to visit the Admiral and all brought offerings of bread and maize and other food, together with pitchers of beverages, some of it white like milk, some green, and some a dark color, all made of fruit. Once again, they were all armed with bows and arrows and once again the Admiral reciprocated with gifts of beads and hawks' bells.

The Indians smelled everything that was given them. They did not care for the beads but found the hawks' bells highly desirable. Using the sense of smell as their criteria, they valued brass more than gold because of the presence of copper, as this was the alloying element in "guanin," the alloy of mainly copper and gold, which they valued more than gold.

From these Indians Columbus learned that the name of their country was Ilaria and that further westward he would find the country more populous. On Wednesday, August 8, in the company of six Indians who had been seized by force, the Admiral set sail further west; after he had sailed eight leagues, he reached a point he called "Punta del Aguja" (Needle Point) located in a country that was the loveliest and most populated land he had ever seen. Proceeding further on he arrived at another place so beautiful that he called it "Los Jardínes" (the Gardens). He found there many houses and people; many of the Indians wore clothing. Thinking that he had come across a new Indian culture area, Columbus decided to anchor there, and many canoes approached the vessels:

Every one wore his kerchief so worked in colors that it looked like an almayzar; one tied around the head and one covering the rest, as has already been said. Of these people who this day came to the vessels...some wore some gold leaf around the neck and one of the Indians he had taken told him that there was much gold thereabouts and that they made large mirrors [actually shiny gold disks] out of it, and he showed how they gathered it.[3]

That evening more natives from that whole region came aboard, many of them wearing pieces of gold in the shape of horseshoes around the neck. Though they valued their gilded ornaments highly, they would gladly have exchanged them for hawks' bells, but Columbus had forbidden such bartering.

On the following day, more canoes filled with people came aboard, and while all wore gold collars, some women came who wore on their arms strings of small beads interspersed with pearls of high quality. The Admiral was very much interested in the pearls and asked where they found or fished for them. They replied by unmistakable signs that they were produced and gathered toward the west behind that island which was Cape Lapa, the Point of Paria, and the mainland, which he believed to be an island (Gracia). Columbus was very much thrilled to learn that pearls were found in the vicinity and he sent two boats ashore to investigate, but not without some concern for the length of time it would take to locate the oyster beds. As he put it:

I rejoiced greatly when I saw these things [pearls] and spared no effort to find out where they obtained them, and they told me that they got them there, and in a land further north. I had wished to remain there, but the supplies I had with me, corn and wine and meat for the people here [on Hispaniola], were beginning to go bad; and I carried them so far and with such great labor. Accordingly, I sought only to bring them to safety without delaying on any account.[4]

As future events would prove, this was a consequential error. The reader will recall that during the exploration of the south coast of Cuba in his second voyage, Columbus had decided to quit and return to Isabela just as he was approaching the western extremity of Cuba; this would have proven it to be an island. Instead, by stopping just short of his goal, he went on believing to his dying days that Cuba was part of the Asiatic continent.

Similarly, in his haste to bring aid to his comrades in Hispaniola, Columbus missed the opportunity of finding the oyster beds off the north coast of Gracia and the southern cost of Margarita Island. It remained for Hojeda and Vespucci, in 1499, to find the oyster beds and gain great favor with the Sovereigns.

The boats Columbus had sent to obtain pearls were greeted by the villagers with great enthusiasm and the sailors were invited ashore for a warm reception. During the festivities, many ornaments of gold were seen, but all of an inferior quality. One Indian had an ornament of gold the size of an apple. But what really interested the sailors were the pearls, of which they saw many necklaces and bracelets among the women. These kind and hospitable ladies gladly gave them to the sailors in exchange for hawks' bells and other brass trinkets. Several specimens of fine pearls were procured for the Admiral for eventual delivery to the Sovereigns. The sailors, while enjoying the hospitality of their hosts, regretted much not understanding their language, and resorted to conversation by means of signs. At the hour of vespers, they returned to their ships to report to the Admiral. Upon seeing the quantity of fine pearls brought for his inspection, Columbus was elated and expected that the territory of Paria he had claimed for Spain would be a source of wealth richer than gold for the Sovereigns. His active imagination began to take for granted that which was merely supposition. The jeweler Ferrer was correct after all—that approaching the equator one would find the rarest and most precious production of nature. In reading Pliny, Columbus had learned that pearls are formed from drops of dew that fall into the mouths of oysters. That being the case, the coast of Paria was a natural habitat for pearl-producing oysters. Because of the cool nights and hot days, the dew formation occurred very frequently. As a result, the oysters were so plentiful that they clustered on the roots of the mangrove trees, which grew on the edge of the sea.

Hoping to find the site where the pearls were to be found and then aim for a northward channel to the sea on his way to Hispaniola, Columbus sailed westward from Los Jardínes on August 10 for about five leagues, sighting many islands to the west and south and giving them his usual characteristic names.

As he sailed along, he began to notice that the water became shallower and fresher, until he could not venture any further with his large nao of one hundred tons. He came to anchor and called on the small El Correo to ascertain whether there was an outlet channel to the open sea. The caravel returned that same evening with the report that it had reached the western end of the gulf and found four river channels from which flowed a great quantity of water—the mouths of the Río Grande. Columbus would gladly have continued in his search for a channel to the open sea, but his eyes were giving him trouble and the supplies for the colony were in danger of spoiling. On the eleventh of August, he set sail eastward for the Boca del Drago, and on Sunday, August 12, he anchored in a beautiful harbor on El Caracol Island in the middle of the channel; he gave it the name of "Puerto de Gatos" from the species of monkey called "gato paulo."

Early the following morning, Monday, August 13, the fleet weighed anchor and proceeded to sail through the Boca del Drago, steering northwestward between the Paria's Cabo de Lapa and the El Caracol Island. At about 9:00 a.m., Columbus reached the middle of the channel where:

He found a great contest between the freshwater seeking an exit to the sea and the saltwater of the sea seeking an entrance into the gulf; and it was so furious and violent that it raised a great tidal bore with a very high crest, and with this the two waters raised from east to west a noise and a thundering, very great and terrifying, with a wave, succeeded by four other waves, one after the other, with conflicting currents. They thought they would perish no less than in the Boca del Sierpe off Cabo del Arsenal, when they were entering the gulf.[5]

Columbus was totally unprepared for this dangerous situation. Fortunately, the wind was constant so that the vessels could be directed away from the rocks, but then even the wind abandoned him. The recourse was to drop anchors to save the ships, but the water was 120 fathoms deep and they could not hit bottom:

It pleased the goodness of God that from that very danger sprang safety and liberation, for the same freshwater overcoming the salt, swept the vessels out without a scratch and thus they were saved for when God wishes that one or many should live, water becomes their medicine (instead o their poison).[6]

Having escaped from the treacherous waters, the Admiral reflected that he had literally escaped from the dragon's mouth and named the channel "Boca de Drago" (Mouth of the Dragon).

Once past the channel, Columbus headed for the open sea with the intention of sailing westward along the north shore of Paria and to visit the Gulf of Pearls at its western end. On the way, he discovered many islands, the first directly to the north from the Boca, which he named "Isla de la Asunción," then another he called "La Concepción," both names given in honor of the Feast of the Assumption of Mary falling on August 15, the following day. The Isla de la Asunción has been identified as the island of Grenada situated twenty-six leagues north of the Boca and discernible from that distance only on a clear day.

Because the Admiral also spotted a group of three small islands that he called "Los Testigos" (the Witnesses) ten leagues above the coast of Paria, he obviously was not sailing close to shore but some distance north of it. Near these small islands he saw other small islands: "El Romero" (the Pilgrim), now called La Sola, and "Las Guardias" (the Sentinels), now called Los Frailes, near the much larger island of Margarita. We now know through the writings of Las Casas why the fleet kept itself at a considerable distance offshore. It had been Columbus's intention, as usual, to keep close to shore, but he had lost so much sleep during the previous month, and his eyes were so bloodshot because of his constant vigilance, that he went to bed that night earlier than usual, and the pilots played it safe by cautiously maintaining a great distance offshore. The fleet then must have been well offshore by the time it reached longitude 63°W, which is exactly the position of the small Los Testigos Islands. Apparently, Columbus had learned his lesson off Navidad on Christmas Eve 1492 with the loss of the Santa María, and the crew was not about to risk the safety of the vessels again.

While sailing along Paria, Columbus began to notice that the land stretched out wider and appeared flatter and more beautiful toward the west, and that the Gulf of Pearls had no outlet with the ocean as he had expected; he gradually came to the realization that such a great expanse could not have been an island. Columbus, according to Las Casas, came to believe that what he had before him was:

A mighty continent which was hitherto unknown. I am greatly supported in this view by reason of this great river, and by this sea which is fresh, and I am also supported by the statement of Esdras in Book 4, Chapter 6, which says that six parts of the world consist of dry land, and one part of water....Moreover, I am supported by the statements of several cannibal Indians whom I captured on other occasions, who declared that there was mainland to the south of them. At that time, I was in the island of Guadeloupe. Furthermore, as Your Highnesses know, a short time ago it was not known that there was more land than that described by Ptolemy and there was no one in my own time who believed that a man could sail from Spain to the Indies. For this reason, I spent several years in Your Court, and not a few took part in the discussions. But finally, only the extraordinary daring of Your Highnesses decreed that the venture be made, against the judgment of all those who said it could not be done. And now the truth appears and will before long appear in great measure. And if this is a continent, it is a wonderful thing and will be so regarded by all men of learning, since from it flows as a large a river as to form a sea of freshwater forty-eight leagues (in extent).[7]

In a letter to the Sovereigns, Columbus mentioned that no Princes of Spain had ever gained territory outside their borders, save now. He wrote, "Your Highnesses have another world (Otro Mundo) here by which our holy faith can be so greatly advanced and from which great wealth can be drawn..."[8] Yet, there were many reasons why he could not pursue further this voyage of discovery. It was very urgent that he get back to Hispaniola with the much-needed supplies and to check on the situation there; if the situation warranted it, he would send his brother, the Adelantado, to continue the exploration of the mainland.

There were other reasons that promoted the Admiral to hasten to Hispaniola. His health and his eyesight were beginning to fail him, owing to lack of sleep. The mariners in his fleet had not been told that he was setting out with the intention of discovery for it would have meant more pay than he could give—besides, they were tired of sailing. He was not too pleased with the size of his ships, which were totally too big for voyages of discovery. The Santa María de Guia was over one hundred tons and the La Vaqueños over seventy tons, with only the El Correo capable to reconnoiter the coast and waters because of its shallow draft. And so, on Wednesday, August 15, on the Feast of the Assumption, after sunrise, he gave orders to weigh from his anchorage, which was within the gulf south of Margarita and north of the Paria Peninsula, and set sail northward for Hispaniola.

THE TERRESTRIAL PARADISE

Upon leaving the Paria Peninsula, Columbus let his mind soar beyond rational reasoning. After nearly suffocating in the torid doldrums after leaving the Cape Verde Islands, he had feared that the climate might become even more unbearable as he got closer to the equator. On reaching Trinidad he found, however, the temperature relatively mild and the vegetation more lush; delicious fresh fruits of all varieties were in abundance and the currents in the Gulf of Paria were freshwater. The natives had lighter skins and were more hospitable and more civilized. Moreover, now that he had discovered an Other World, could this be the land where the Terrestrial Paradise was located?

He recalled that Cardinal d'Ailly's *Imago Mundo*, which he had read so avidly, had placed the Terrestrial Paradise at the first point of the Far East. He also remembered the Old Testament:

Then the Lord God planted a garden in Eden in the East, and there he put man he had formed. He made all kinds of beautiful trees grow there and produce good fruit. In the middle of the garden stood the tree that gives life and the tree that gives knowledge of what is good and what is bad.

A stream flowed in Eden and watered the garden; beyond Eden it divided into four rivers. The first river is the Pishon; it flowed around the country of Havilah. (Pure gold is found there and also rare perfume and precious stones). The second river is the Gishon; it flows around the country of Cush; the third river is the Tigris, which flows east of Assyria, and the fourth river is the Euphrates. (Gen. 11)

Recalling this biblical passage, Columbus identified the four mouths of the Río Grande, discovered by El Correo, as the four rivers of Eden—and were not the natives wearing gold as around the country of Havilah in the Bible? In writing to the Sovereigns two months later, Columbus located the Terrestrial Paradise in "the Land of Gracia." In the same message Columbus made another astonishing observation: that the portion of the earth near the Terrestrial Paradise is not spherical but pear-shaped—or "like a woman's teat on a round ball." Columbus arrived at the "pear-shaped" concept by noticing on the ocean-crossing that the elevation of the North Star with his quadrant varied 10° on the same latitude. He concluded, therefore, that the polar distance of the North Star (that is, the radius of the circle that it describes around the celestial pole) was 5°. He recalled, however, that on earlier voyages he had found it to be but 2½°.

Rather than suspect errors on his sightings, he concluded that the earth was not round at the latitude but in the shape already mentioned. The Terrestrial Paradise was then located on "the teat" as the elevated position was near to heaven. The gradual increase in the North Star's orbit indicated that Columbus was sailing closer to heaven. The Admiral's exhaustion may be responsible for this mental lapse.

Chapter Thirty-Six

REBELLION IN HISPANIOLA

On August 16, 1498, Columbus left Margarita Island at daybreak and set his course NW by N for Santo Domingo. He made good sailing, averaging about one hundred miles daily, but he lowered his sails at night for fear of encountering islands or reefs in the unknown sea. While sailing slowly off and on at night he noticed a westward draft that carried his fleet off course so that on August 19 he recognized the landfall on an island that he had named Saint Catherine on his second voyage. He renamed it Madama Beata. This island is located about seventy-five miles west of Santo Domingo. On the following morning, the fleet approached the southern coast of Hispaniola and Columbus noticed another smaller island immediately south of Beata; this one he called "Alto Velo" (Tall Sail) because it has a mountain peak profile that looks like the ship's sail from afar. The Admiral was annoyed that he had fallen off so much from his course, but he correctly concluded that his error had been due to the strong currents toward the west. Despite this error, Columbus performed an amazing feat of seamanship in sailing from an uncharted island to another uncharted point in an unknown world, using his crude quadrant and the dead-reckoning technique. He anchored in the strait between Beata Island and the coast of Hispaniola and sent a boat ashore to seek Indian messengers to relay an overland message to the Adelantado at Santo Domingo. Six Indians were brought to the ship, one of them carrying a Spanish crossbow complete with cord, bolt, and rack. Immediately the Admiral suspected trouble on Hispaniola, either mutiny or another situation similar to that in Navidad.

The next day, the Admiral had a joyful and unexpected reunion with his brother Bartholomew. The Adelantado had sighted the three caravels that Columbus had dispatched from Ferro with supplies and provisions for the colony, sailing westward past Santo Domingo. Apparently, they had overshot their objective. The Adelantado had set out in pursuit, with the hope of showing the fleet the way to the settlement, but he had lost them. Instead he had encountered the Admiral's fleet. It was a happy reunion because the two brothers had not seen each other in nearly two and a half years; it was especially so for Bartholomew, who had heard rumors that the colony was in a state of rebellion.

Sailing the one hundred miles from Beata to Santo Domingo is an arduous task, due to the strong ocean currents and trade winds. On some occasions, early navigators had struggled for months to negotiate the distance. Columbus and the Adelantado were fortunate because they left Beata on August 22 and anchored in Santo Domingo's Ozama River on August 31. The brothers were confident that the lost fleet carrying the provisions that had overshot Santo Domingo would eventually find its way back to the colony. When Columbus finally arrived at the new settlement, which was originally called "New Isabela" but which the Adelantado finally named "Santo Domingo," he was almost blind, tired, and suffering from arthritis. He was looking forward to a well-deserved rest. Instead he found the colony in a state of rebellion. Many settlers had died, and over 160 of the survivors were suffering from an illness later identified as syphilis. The reasons for the rebellion were manifold: insufficient food supply from Spain, too much work and meager remuneration for it, the Spaniards' greed for more gold, and most importantly, dislike of the stern rule of the "foreign" Adelantado.

FRANCISCO ROLDAN'S REBELLION

Peace reigned in the colony for about a year after Columbus sailed for Spain in March 1496. Juan Aguado's investigation and his report to the Sovereigns had created an impression among the colonists that Columbus would not be coming back and that perhaps a new administration might be delegated to take over the island government.

In the summer of 1496, Peralonso Niño arrived with two supply ships and reported that he had seen the Admiral at Cadiz. Another year went by without any news or supplies reaching the colony. With provisions nearly exhausted and hunger and sickness rampant, the situation was ripe for rebellion. Such an individual was Francisco Roldan, whom Columbus had appointed Alcalde Major (Chief Justice), a position of prestige and authority in the colony; during Columbus's absence he was accountable only to the Adelantado, whom he detested for not being an appointee of the Sovereigns and to Don Diego also, who was in charge of the city. An opportunity to seize control from the Adelantado presented itself to Roldan when the former was away in the province of Xaragua, about eighty leagues away from Isabela, at the southern tip of the island, collecting tributes from the Caciques of that region. Bartholomew had left the military control of the colony to Roldan but under the authority of Don Diego, for whom Roldan had such little respect that he ignored him in all dealings.

While the Adelantado was away, Roldan and his conspirators made an attempt to seize a caravel that the former had built as a standby to send to Castile in case of provision shortage. His aim was to send the ship to Castile to make a formal complaint to the Sovereigns about the miserable situation in Isabela. Don Diego objected that the vessel could not be launched for lack of tackle and other equipment. Roldan was not convinced and claimed that it was simply an excuse to prevent him from informing the Sovereigns of the distressing situation in Hispaniola caused by the Columbus brothers. Don Diego refused to provide Roldan with additional ammunition to incite his followers. According to Roldan, this incident was simply one more act of subjugation by the tyrannical brothers who had forced the colonists to work in the fields and build forts without remuneration, whereas the "foreigners" themselves were getting rich. All the wealth of the island should be equally divided among the colonists, Roldan proclaimed; they should be allowed to use the heathen Indians, men, and women for labor or for whatever they pleased instead of being punished for their licentiousness. Focusing the frustrations and anger of the colonists on the Columbus brothers, Roldan roused them to such intensity that they began a plot to murder the Adelantado. Apparently, the Adelantado had condemned to death a Spaniard by the name of Berahona, who had raped the favorite wife of Guarionex, the Cacique of the Vega. The plot counted on the Adelantado to make an appearance at the execution and to be stabbed during the attendant tumult. Fortunately, Berahona was pardoned and the assassination was thus unwittingly foiled.

In the Adelantado's absence, Don Diego got wind of the brewing rebellion but was reluctant to take steps to impede or crush it. Instead, to gain time until the Adelantado returned to Isabela from Xaragua, he ordered Roldan with forty men to Vega to pacify the Indians of that area who had openly refused to pay their tribute.

Roldan marched to the Vega, not to punish the Indians but to strengthen his own position. He made friends among the recalcitrant Caciques and Indians, promising to dispense them from taxation and forced labor in return for their help in overthrowing the Columbus brothers. Having gained their support, Roldan and his followers planned to assault the fortress of Concepción, a road station between Isabela and Santo Domingo still under construction. At that time, the fortress was under the command of Miguel Ballister, a loyal and dedicated soldier who promptly sent a message to the Adelantado, who had returned to Isabela but quickly hastened back to Concepción to help. Roldan requested and obtained a safe-conduct to enter the fort and discuss a settlement with the Adelantado. Roldan again demanded that the caravel be launched as soon as possible, otherwise he enjoined that he and his rebel friends be permitted to launch the vessel and sail away to Xaragua with it. The Adelantado was angered by Roldan's effrontery and retorted that neither he nor his friends were capable of launching or sailing the ship.

Roldan marched away in anger and set out for Isabela, where with sixty-five of his men he attempted to launch the caravel, but to no avail. Failing that, the rebels plundered the arsenal and storehouse, taking whatever food, clothing, and arms they needed. Powerless to prevent the plundering and fearing for his life, Don Diego took refuge in the fortress with his servants. Roldan hoped to settle in Xaragua, which, as he had learned from many Spaniards, had a beautiful climate, hospitable Indians, and beautiful women. But before heading for Xaragua, he wanted to surprise the Adelantado in the fortress of Concepción and vanquish him in battle. The Adelantado, however, had heard rumors of the impending attack and was prepared. Foiled once more, Roldan decided to head for Xaragua to spread along the way vicious slanders about the Adelantado to all the Caciques he met. He told them that the Adelantado was the tyrant of the Spaniards and the oppressor of the Indians. The Indians, in turn, confused by the dissension among the white men and encouraged by Roldan's promise of protection, stopped sending their tributes and even withheld allegiance to the government. Roldan now posed as the champion of the Indians, and even cultivated a close association with the Carib Cacique Manicaotex, brother of the late Caonabo.

It was during this critical period of the colony's existence that news was received that Pedro Fernandez Coronel, with two advance vessels of Columbus's fleet, had arrived at the port of Santo Domingo, bringing supplies and reinforcement of troops. This was a crushing blow to Roldan, as the additional supplies and men strengthened the government's position. Additionally, the royal confirmation of Adelantado's title legitimized it and inversely characterized his own as traitorous. Rather than exercise his renewed authority with haughtiness, Bartholomew sought instead to heal the wounds of the past and promised amnesty to all. He even prevailed upon Coronel to visit Roldan and attempt to reach an amicable settlement before the arrival of the Admiral. Roldan was at this time within five leagues of Santo Domingo. Upon approaching the encampment, Coronel was met by a body of archers with their crossbows leveled. Coronel tried to reason with Roldan, who said that he would never submit to the rule of the Adelantado but would be ready, instead, to submit to the Admiral on his arrival. When Coronel returned with accounts of Roldan's obstinacy, the Adelantado proclaimed him and his followers traitors to the Crown.

Roldan now left his encampment in the Vega and headed for the promised land of Xaragua. In the meantime, the natives, who had been instigated by Roldan under the leadership of the Cacique Guarionex, made plans to attack the fortress of Concepción. Upon hearing of this new conspiracy, the Adelantado immediately advanced with his army to aid the garrison. Lacking in the element of surprise, Guarionex abandoned his plans and chose to leave his realm, and followed by a small band of faithful natives, he headed for the mountains of Ciguay, seeking asylum in the domain of the Cacique Mayobanex, who received him with open arms. Mayobanex, as the reader may recall, was the Cacique who had visited Columbus after the incident in the Bay of Arrows at the end of his first voyage.

The Adelantado wasted no time in mounting a campaign to subdue the recalcitrant Caciques. Upon discovering the Guarionex had retreated into the mountains of the Samana Peninsula, he set out to battle against him in the spring of 1498 with ninety men, a few horsemen, and a body of Indians. This proved to be his most daring and most difficult military campaign. It was brought to a conclusion when Guarionex was captured through the cooperation of the Indians themselves. Another outcome of the campaign was that it extended the Spanish rule to a part of the island considered inaccessible until then.

THE ARRIVAL OF COLUMBUS'S SUPPLY FLEET

The three ships that left Columbus's fleet at Gomera on June 19 under the commanded of Carvajal, Harana, and Giovanni

Colombo had fair sailing to the Caribbean Islands; however, they had not steered a proper course to Santo Domingo and had been carried by the currents westward to the coast of Xaragua. When Roldan and his men initially spotted the ships, they believed they had been dispatched to quell the rebellion. But they soon realized the truth. Roldan went aboard pretending to be stationed in that area and introduced himself as "Alcalde" (mayor). He and his men were thus able to procure swords, lances, crossbows, and other military equipment from the unsuspecting captains. It was not until the third day that Alonso Sánchez de Carvajal became suspicious. By then it was too late. Roldan's men had convinced the crew that the life they were leading in Xaragua was much better than could be expected in Santo Domingo. The captains tried to convince Roldan to end his rebellion, pointing out that with Columbus's imminent arrival their differences could be resolved. Roldan indicated that this might very well come about, and that he had acted against the injustice and oppression of the Adelantado but was ready to submit to the Admiral on his arrival. Because of the contrary winds and the opposing currents, it was arranged among the captains that a large number of people aboard, especially craftsmen and others who were most needed in the colony, should proceed to Santo Domingo by land.

They would be traveling under the leadership of Giovanni Colombo. Harana was to proceed with the ships, wind permitting, and Carvajal was to remain, in an effort to induce the rebels to be loyal. On the following morning, as Colombo prepared for his trek, he was astonished to find himself deserted by all but eight of the forty men in his company. The deserters very casually had gone over to the rebels' side, much to his dismay and despite his remonstrances. They were mostly convicted criminals who had volunteered to serve in the colonies to obtain suspended sentences but who now sought a more adventurous method of gaining their liberty. An appeal to Roldan brought only an excuse that he had no means of enforcing obedience on his new volunteers.

It was with great difficulty, as expected, that the fleet under Harana reached Santo Domingo. By the time of their arrival, most of the provisions had been either used up or were spoiled. Alonso Sánchez de Carvajal arrived a little later by land, having been escorted most of the way by a group of rebels. He brought a letter from Roldan to the Admiral.

On their arrival at Santo Domingo from Xaragua, the captains found that Columbus had been well briefed about the rebellion on Hispaniola. In return, they informed Columbus of the defection of the new arrivals to Roldan's ranks and of the latter's movement of his forces closer to the Vega, an act belying his confidence in the superiority of his forces. He was aware of a strong desire among many men to return home. Moreover, it became clear that reinforcements from Castile would be necessary to reach a balance of power. Obviously, his position was precarious and he had to strike a bargain with Roldan. The rebels had to be brought back by peaceful means. Despite his failing health, he decided that he would do all in his power to settle the insurgency amicably. On September 12, he issued a proclamation offering free passage and provisions for the voyage to all who desired to go back to Spain in the five vessels being prepared for departure. This offer would get rid of those who had no inclination for living on primitive islands, of the dissatisfied, as well as of the homesick. It would also weaken Roldan's insurgent army. Thus, he decided to open full communications with Roldan despite the Adelantado's warning that the best way to deal with the rebels would be with a tough and determined military force.

THE GENTLE ARBITRATOR; PEACE AT ANY COST

Having been once again apprised by the Adelantado of the rebels' intransigence and of the charges of sedition leveled against them, the Admiral nonetheless adopted a moderate attitude to bring about a peaceful settlement. On September 22, 1498, he issued a decree promising food and free passage to any settler who desired to go back home. He also ordered Miguel Ballister, commander of the fortress of Concepción, to direct Roldan and his followers to meet with Columbus to consider how the interests of the Catholic Sovereigns could best be served. Roldan defiantly declared that there could be no meeting until they had released all the Indians captured in the siege of Concepción. He also stipulated that the Admiral send Carvajal, a man he trusted and found reasonable, to negotiate with him. At first Columbus had some reservations about sending Carvajal. But once again, for the sake of the peace, he sent Carvajal and Ballister to negotiate a pact. However, on October 15, Roldan made further demands by sending the Admiral his own terms for peace in writing. These demands were immoderate and insolent, putting all the blame for the revolt on the Adelantado. On October 17, Roldan and his leaders wrote another letter claiming that they had left the Adelantado because he plotted to kill them, and that they had been waiting for the Admiral's return to seek justice. But because the Admiral, on his arrival, showed displeasure at their actions and even had plans to harm them, they would hereafter show no allegiance to him.

Before receiving this letter, Columbus had already sent Ballister, with whom Roldan could speak in confidence as if he were the Admiral himself. Roldan would find the Admiral amenable to discuss every reasonable proposal that he chose to discuss. Historians have been puzzled by Columbus's unusually conciliatory attitude. With all the prestige of a viceroy, he dealt with Roldan from a position of weakness. He should have asserted himself and dealt with the rebellion firmly and decisively. Was it because the mutineers outnumbered him, or because of his recurring illness? He had proved himself a man of great courage, yet in this particular instance he was being inveigled by a rebel who was evidently guilty of treason and who deserved to be hanged.

On October 18, the Admiral sent five ships back to Spain; Roldan and his men were not on board, as Columbus had hoped and as they had promised. He also wrote Roldan an apologetic letter that he could not hold the ships in port any longer. Why the apology? The report to the Sovereigns stressed the need of new blood in the colony of dependable persons who could gradually replace the rebels and malcontents who had been unproductive and destructive. Then, with the colony in capable and loyal hands, a new colony could be started in the Paria and in the "Terrestrial Paradise" on which the Admiral had already sent complete reports. To defray the cost of colonization, he once again proposed the trade of slaves and of brazil wood. The conversion of the Indians to Christianity was proceeding very slowly and he requested that more priests—preferably monks—be sent to the colony. Moreover, he asked that a very competent and experienced person be sent to preserve peace and administer justice. On a more positive note, he was pleased to inform the Sovereigns that the island now could provide its own cassava bread and meats of pork, cattle, and hutia.

With the ships gone, the Admiral tried once again to settle amicably the Roldan incident. There was more correspondence between Columbus and the rebels, but it seemed that the more concessions the Admiral made, the more Roldan demanded.

Finally, a formal agreement was signed November 16, 1498, which defined explicitly the conditions for settling the dispute and for the departure of Roldan and his rebels to Castile. It stipulated in part:

1. That the Lord Admiral shall give him (Roldan) two ships…properly equipped to be delivered at the port of Xaragua…where the said Alcalde Mayor and his company will embark for Castile.

2. That his Lordship shall order paid the wages due them up to the day of sailing.

3. That he shall grant them slaves from the distribution made to the people, as compensation for the sufferings they have endured on this island and for the services they have rendered, confirming this grant.

4. That his Lordship shall order the said ships loaded with all the provisions they may need for the voyage.

5. That inasmuch as the said Alcalde Mayor and his company fear that his lordship or some other person acting for him may seek to do them some mischief with the ships remaining on the island, he will give them a safe-conduct promising in the names of the Catholic Sovereigns and on his faith and word as a hidalgo…that neither his lordship nor any other person shall harm them or prevent their sailing.[1]

For his part, Roldan pledged to abide by the agreements made with de Carvajal and Diego Salamanca, adding a few more provisions:

First, that from this day till he gives his reply, which will be in a space of ten days, I shall not admit into my company any of the Lord Admiral's people.

That within fifty days after the said reply is brought and delivered to me in Concepción with his Lordship's approval of what has been agreed upon and signed (which shall be within ten days) we shall embark and sail for Castile....It is understood that all the said articles are to be signed and executed by his Lordship just as they are carried in writing by the said Alonso Sánchez de Carvajal and the said Diego de Salamanca. It shall await his reply here in Concepción for eight days from this time. And if he should not reply, I shall not be bound by anything said herein.

In witness whereof, and that I and all men of my company shall observe and carry out all that I said, I have signed this instrument with my hand. Done in Concepción this day, Saturday, November 16, 1498.[2]

The agreements were approved and signed by Columbus on November 21; on November 24, Ballister delivered the Admiral's letter to Roldan at Concepción, whereupon they set out for Xaragua to await the ships for their departure within the next fifty-day period promised. In the meantime, Columbus was having a difficult time gathering provisions for the Niña and Santa Cruz so that departure was delayed until late January 1499; however, a great storm arose during the trip to Xaragua, forcing the ships to seek another port until the eve of March. Because of the delay, Roldan and his men refused to abide by the agreement, which specified a fifty-day interval. The ships finally arrived in Xaragua and remained there until April 25, when they were recalled by Columbus because the shipworms were destroying them and the crews were suffering severely from lack of provisions.

Roldan now was in a position to tighten his terms even more. He demanded that fifteen of his men should be allowed to return to Castile in the first ships coming from Spain; second, that those who chose to remain should be given houses and grants of land in lieu of their pay; third, that he should publicly proclaim all that had happened was caused by false testimony of a few evil men; and fourth, that he should restore Roldan to his office of perpetual Alcalde (mayor). These terms were humiliating to the Admiral, but he accepted them in September 1499, as the rebellion had been going on for two years and he feared the possibility of a state of anarchy in the making. On November 5, Roldan began to exercise the duties of his office and peace once again came to the island, albeit for a short respite.

Chapter Thirty-Seven

COLUMBUS IN DISGRACE

Once the dispute with Roldan had been settled, the Admiral was convinced that a rapprochement between his adversary and the Adelantado could never be achieved—there was too much bad blood between them. Columbus felt that he could best serve the Sovereigns by returning to Castile with his brothers and have the monarchs appoint another governor for Hispaniola. He was also convinced, in retrospect, that he had paid too high a price for peace on the island. The final condition demanded by Roldan, namely "that those who choose to remain in the colony should be given houses and grants of land in lieu of their pay," made landlords of many criminals. And if everybody became a landlord, who would do the work in the fields? The Indians, of course! Thus, a system of exploitation known as "repartimiento" (distribution) and later "encomienda," or trust, was created at the proposal of the Roldanites: the distribution of Indians among the settlers was a compromise between the royal opposition to slavery and the settlers' determination to be served. It was a New World feudalistic system. Each settler was given a large acreage of farm land, which included ownership of the Indians living on it. The system took hold throughout the

American Spanish Empire and lasted for centuries. Apparently, the Caciques consented to this new social order in the hope of ridding themselves of the abominable system of the gold tribute and other demands made by the Spaniards.

Roldan lost no time in presenting to Columbus a list of more than one hundred of his followers who demanded grants of land in Xaragua. Columbus, however, feared a partisan takeover in so remote a province, and thus insisted on a more even distribution throughout the island. This involved allocating, instead, some settlements in Bonao, on the bank of the Río Verde and other places in Vega. Additionally, arrangements were made with the local Caciques to supply Indians to assist the colonists in the cultivation of their lands, free of pay. Roldan himself demanded and obtained large grants of land in Xaragua with a variety of livestock of cattle and other animals belonging to the Crown.

Having made peace with Roldan by acceding to his demands, Columbus prepared to return to Spain with his brother Bartholomew and account for his actions to the Sovereigns. But his plans had to be changed when he received news that four ships, possibly unauthorized, had arrived at the western part of the island on September 5.

ARRIVAL OF HOJEDA

Additional reports disclosed that the landfall had been made in a harbor below Jacquemel (modern Jacmel). The newcomers apparently intended to carry off Indians as slaves and cut down brazil wood. The ships were commanded by Alonso de Hojeda, the bold and adventurous hidalgo who had performed valiant deeds against the Indians on Columbus's second voyage.

To test Roldan's fidelity, Columbus wisely called upon him to intercept Hojeda. Accepting willingly and with pride, perhaps to prove to the Admiral that he could be trusted in matters concerning public safety, Roldan departed from Santo Domingo with two caravels and landed with twenty-five well-armed men within two leagues of the harbor where Hojeda's ships were anchored in an attempt to surprise him from land. Hojeda, however, had learned of Roldan's approach and immediately presented himself with only a small escort; he claimed that he had landed on the island to repair his damaged ships and pick up provisions.

Roldan demanded to see the orders under which he was sailing, and Hojeda showed him a license signed by Bishop Fonseca authorizing him to sail on a voyage of discovery. When the flagship Santa María de Guia and the caravel El Correo had returned to Spain in the fall of 1498, the discovery of pearls at Paria became known. Hojeda, who was a favorite of Bishop Fonseca, managed to secure the chart of the area and maps of the route made by Columbus. The idea of exploring this new wealthy region became an obsession with him. He communicated his desire to Bishop Fonseca, who was only too glad to give him a personal license in order to vitiate the Admiral's successes. Under this license, Hojeda was able, with the help of wealthy speculators, to outfit four ships at Seville. Included among the crew were Amerigo Vespucci, a Florentine merchant and pilot living in Seville; Bartholomé Roldan, who had been with Columbus on his first voyage; and Juan de la Cosa, the mapmaker of the second voyage. Hojeda's voyage and a strange sequence of events resulted, later, in the naming of the new continent after Amerigo Vespucci.

Hojeda's expedition had sailed in May 1499 and, following the charts made by Columbus, reached the Gulf of Paria, sailing past Margarita, where they discovered the rich pearl fisheries of Cubagua. The fleet had continued westward, reaching the islands of Bonaire, Curaçao, Aruba, and the Gulf of Maracaibo, which Vespucci named the "Gulf of Venezuela" because of a village in the bay built on piles that resembled Venice, hence "Venezuela" (Little Venice). They sailed a few leagues further west and then turned northward. They reached Puerto Brazil (Jacmel) on Hispaniola on September 4, 1499, and soon began to cut down brazil trees and hunt Indians.

Roldan reported to the Admiral what he had learned. Columbus was shocked to hear that a voyage to the Indies had been approved without his knowledge and consent. Furthermore, he was deeply grieved that information that he had sent to the Sovereigns, in confidence, should have fallen into the hands of adventurers like Hojeda.

Columbus patiently waited for Hojeda's visit to get a full explanation, but having duped Roldan, Hojeda sailed instead to Xaragua. Arriving there in February of 1500, he attempted to start a counter-revolution with the aid of former Roldanite dissenters who had settled there. Roldan proceeded to Xaragua to force him into submission, but Hojeda retired to his ships, refusing to come ashore. Roldan offered to come aboard to speak to him, provided he send a boat ashore; this was done. After Roldan and some of his men came on board, they overpowered Hojeda's men, killing several of them and rowing the boat ashore with the rest. Hojeda was not as concerned about his men as about the boat, which was sorely needed by his fleet. The boat was eventually returned in exchange for the hostages and the release of some of Roldan's men. Hojeda also agreed to leave Hispaniola within an established time. He did indeed leave, but on his way to Spain he raided the Bahamas, capturing 232 timid and gentle Indians on an island that Vespucci called "Iti." They were easy prey because they had learned to trust the "men from heaven." Unfortunately, thirty-two of them died on the way to Cadiz, where the rest were sold as slaves.

It is difficult to understand how Vespucci, an intelligent Florentine gentleman, condoned young Hojeda's acts of piracy.

Hojeda's voyage was not the only one licensed for exploration, in violation of Columbus's agreement with the Sovereigns. In the same year, 1499–1500, two of Columbus's former shipmates on his first voyage obtained licenses for exploring the Indies. Peralonso Niño, former pilot of the Santa María and the Niña, sailed to Paria and returned with a valuable cargo of pearls gathered around Margarita. Vicente Yañez Pinzón, former captain of the Niña on Columbus's first voyage, had also seen Columbus's letter of 1498 about this Pearl Coast and prevailed upon Bishop Fonseca to issue him a license to go there. He sailed from Palos with four caravels on November 18, 1499, for the Cape Verde Islands, and from there sailed westward intending to make a landfall further south than the Paria Peninsula. He was the first European to cross the equator on the American side of the Atlantic and, late in January of 1500, he reached Brazil's easternmost bulge in the vicinity of the present-day Recife, approximately 8°S or further north in the vicinity of Fortaleza, approximately 4°S, both on the Portuguese side of the Line of Demarcation. In following northwestward along the coast, he discovered the mouth of the Amazon River before reaching the Paria Peninsula. From there he sailed northward to Santo Dominigo. Unlike Hojeda, Pinzón's arrival caused no trouble with Hispaniola, as he had always been loyal to Columbus and his actions were not suspicious. He picked up provisions, repaired his ships, and headed back to Castile, possibly taking along with him the fifteen Roldanites whom Columbus had promised to send back to Castile at the first opportunity. Unfortunately, in July, on the way home, the fleet was struck by a terrible hurricane that sank two of his caravels with their entire crew.

DOWNFALL OF THE VICEROY: ARRIVAL OF BOBADILLA

The admiration of the Sovereigns felt for Columbus after the discovery of the Indies was clearly shown by the honors and wealth they showered on him. This admiration waivered somewhat with the negative reports that Margarit and Fray Buil brought home during the second voyage, but their confidence in their Viceroy remained unabated as he left for his third journey. Columbus was on the high seas to Trinidad when the Sovereigns received the report of the vulgar scene that had scandalized Seville—when he floored and kicked Bishop Fonseca's agent, Ximeno. According to Las Casas, this was the main cause of Columbus's fall from grace. His status suffered another setback when in the fall of 1498 the five ships returning from Hispaniola brought reports of latent mutiny in the colonies and the Adelantado's harsh treatment of the colonists and natives. They were particularly annoyed by the message sent by Columbus advocating continuation of the slave trade.

Columbus looked upon the slave trade as legitimate. The Portuguese had engaged in this activity with the Africans and the Spaniards had done the same with the Moors. However, especially when it concerned the Indians, the king and queen were opposed to the idea and irritated by the Admiral's proposal.

Along with the pearls and map of Paria came also a report of Roldan's rebellion, as told by the Admiral and later as explained by Roldan. The Sovereigns concluded that Columbus was a great Admiral but an incompetent Viceroy.

Further reports were received from Hispaniola and from other colonists who had returned to Castile "against the Admiral and his brothers, claiming they were cruel and unfit to govern because they were foreigners and had no experience in governing men of quality."[1] Another complaint on the part of the colonists who had returned home was lack of pay for their services in the colonies—in some cases for several years. Ferdinand tells the following story:

I remember when I was at Granada, at the time of the death of Prince Miguel, more than fifty of these shameless wretches bought a quality of grapes and sat down to eat them in the court of Alhambra, loudly proclaiming that their Highnesses and the Admiral had reduced them to that pitiful state by withholding their pay, adding many other insolent remarks. They were so shameless that if the Catholic King rode out, they would crowd about him, shouting "Pay! Pay!" And if my brother and I, who were pages to the Queen, happened by, they followed us crying: "There go the sons of the Admiral of the Mosquitoes, of him who discovered lands of vanity and illusion, the grave and ruin of Castilian gentlemen," adding so many other insults that we took care not to pass before them.[2]

It was with great reluctance that the king and queen finally accepted Columbus's suggestion in the letter he sent in October 1498, and sent a learned man to administer justice in Hispaniola. They selected a man of high integrity and an old member of the Royal household as their agent, Francisco de Bobadilla, Knight Commander of the Order of Calatrava. He was chosen because the Sovereigns wanted this delicate task to be carried out with the utmost tact and deference towards Columbus. At first, the powers given him on March 21, 1499, were limited merely to judicial inquiry into the rebellion against the Admiral and the punishment of the rebels. However, more disquieting news was received from Hispaniola, and on May 21, 1499, Bobadilla was appointed Governor and Chief Magistrate, a post that impinged on the powers of the Viceroy and Adelantado.

Bobadilla's voyage was delayed for over a year and he did not arrive in Santo Domingo until August 23, 1500, by which time Roldan had made peace with the Admiral and the situation in Hispaniola, with minor pockets of resistance, was well under control. Unfortunately, it did not seem that way to Bobadilla who, upon landing, beheld with shock the corpses of seven rebels hanging from the gallows. This spectacle goaded him to immediate action. At that time Columbus was in Concepción restoring order following a rebel attack, led by Adrian de Maxica, one of Roldan's former lieutenants, against Don Bartholomew.

Bobadilla told Don Diego, who was in charge of the city, to stop all executions and to hand over the five prisoners scheduled for hanging the following day. Don Diego refused, insisting that he took orders only from the Admiral who held powers superior to any possessed by Bobadilla. The following day, after the morning Mass in front of the church, Bobadilla had his orders read and exhorted Don Diego and the population to obey him. Then he proceeded to take over the city's fortress and the Admiral's house, including all documents. To gain support, he issued an order exempting everyone from paying tributes and even permitted the gathering of gold without interference from the authorities and at a reduced tax to the Crown. He placed Don Diego under arrest and summoned the Admiral to appear before him by sending him the following royal order:

Don Christopher Columbus, our Admiral of the Ocean Sea. We have sent the Knight Commander Francisco de Bobadilla, the bearer of this letter, to say certain things to you on our behalf. We desire you to give him full faith and credit and to act accordingly.

From Madrid, May 26, 1499
I the King, I the Queen
By Their Order, Miguel Pérez de Almazan[3]

As soon as Columbus received the summons, he immediately left for Santo Domingo. Nonetheless, on his arrival, Bobadilla, without holding a hearing or inquest, had him cast in jail. The Adelantado was still at large at that time with an armed force; he could have come to his brother's rescue but was convinced by Columbus to submit to Bobadilla and trust in the justice of the Sovereigns. Having imprisoned all three brothers, Bobadilla went through the ritual of an inquest, which, of course, was predisposed against the brothers by perjured malcontents.

Early in October 1500, he put the Admiral and Don Diego in irons aboard the caravel La Gorda and sent them off. The Adelantado was to be sent on another ship later. The captain offered to remove his chains, but the Admiral stubbornly refused, saying that he had been ordered chained in the Sovereigns' name and would wear them until they ordered them removed. The caravel entered the Bay of Cádiz late in October after a fast passage.

Columbus had been condemned by Bobadilla and was in disgrace, but he had not been judged properly. There is no doubt that Bobadilla overreacted in jailing Columbus and his brothers. In obtaining testimony from the settlers to indict Columbus, he should have realized that most of the settlers were former convicts who could not be trusted. Hojeda's visit did not help

Columbus's cause as he had announced that the queen was dying and Columbus would soon lose all authority and be recalled to Castile. The situation in Hispaniola was an unsavory one, but it is doubtful whether any other "foreigner" could have done any better, considering both the human and physical elements the Admiral had to deal with. History has shown that many civilized nations bound on colonizing distant lands inhabited by primitive and, at times, savage aborigines have failed miserably not because of the resistance of the natives but because of the internal dissension, lack of provisions, greed, and fear of never being able to return to the homeland. England, over a century later, was to experience similar pains in establishing a permanent colony in Virginia.

They judge me there as a governor who had gone to Sicily or to a city or town under a regular government, where the laws can be observed in toto without fear of losing all; and I am suffering grave injury. I should be judged as a captain who went from Spain to the Indies to conquer a people numerous and warlike, whose manners and religion are very different from ours, who live in sierras and mountains, without fixed settlements, and where by divine will I have placed under this sovereignty of the King and Queen our Lords, an Other World, whereby Spain, which was reckoned poor, is become the richest of countries.

I ought to be judged as a captain, who for a long time, up to the present day, hath borne arms without laying them down for an hour and by knights of the sword and not by [men of] letters, unless they were Greeks and Romans or others of modern times, of whom there are so noble in Spain; for otherwise, I am greatly aggrieved since in the Indies, there is neither a town nor a settlement.[4]

This statement is from the famous letter Columbus wrote to Doña Juana de Torres, former governess to Infante Don Juan in the Infanta, his sister, with whom Columbus had formed a friendship during this last days at court. Doña Juana was now a confidante of the queen, and Columbus, in unburdening his innermost feelings to her, was certain that they would reach the queen. Columbus probably wrote it on shipboard, or more likely after he landed in Cádiz. It is of great historical importance because it tells us not only of his deep mortification over Bobadilla's treatment but is also Columbus's own account of the situation in Hispaniola before his incarceration. He also lashes out at Bobadilla:

Observe the discernment of Bobadilla, to give all for nothing and four millions' worth of permits without reason or necessity, without first notifying Their Highnesses! And that is not the entire damage.[5]

Then the Admiral becomes apologetic:

I know that my errors have not been committed with malicious intent, and I think Their Highnesses believe me when I say so. I know and see they use mercy to one who seeks maliciously to do them ill! I believe and am certain that they will be kinder and more charitable toward me, for I have fallen into error through ignorance and by force, as they will learn fully hereafter.[6]

Part VIII

THE FOURTH VOYAGE TO THE INDIES
MAY 1502–NOVEMBER 1504

Chapter Thirty-Eight

PREPARATIONS FOR A FOURTH VOYAGE

The voyage of La Gorda, which carried Columbus in chains back to Spain, was blessed with favorable weather. The ship crossed the Atlantic swiftly as if to minimize Columbus's affliction, which was also made less disagreeable by the solicitous conduct of the master of the caravel, Andrés Martín, who felt sympathetic towards Columbus. Exactly eight years earlier, in October of 1492, Columbus had discovered a new world. Now, he was returning to Spain in disgrace and in chains. The La Gorda made Cádiz before the end of October, and at the invitation of the Carthusian fathers, Columbus went to stay at the monastery of Las Cuevas in Seville—still in chains.

The sight of Columbus in chains produced a general burst of indignation among the people of Seville and it was echoed throughout the nation. It aroused widespread sympathy even among those who had been critical of his conduct. After all, whatever his indiscretions, he had done so much for Spain. On November 20, 1500, the Admiral wrote to the Sovereigns that he had arrived in Cádiz; it is reasonable to assume that the outcry of the people and possibly his own long letter to Doña Juana de la Torres had preceded his letter to the court, held at the time in Granada. Columbus did not receive an answer until December 12, as there were more pressing problems preoccupying the Sovereigns. There was the problem of the insurrection and conversion of the Moors—that faction that had been allowed to remain in Spain after the Granada Wars had become restive. The Italian Wars were entering a second phase of action with Louis XII of France. On November 11, 1500, in the secret Treaty of Granada, the two monarchs had decided to divide between them the Kingdom of Naples. But despite these important commitments, the Sovereigns ordered that the Admiral be set free and wrote him a letter expressing their good will toward him, assuring him also that he would be treated with honor and understanding when he came to court. Moreover, to assuage his hurt feelings and to help him meet current expenses, they sent him the sum of two thousand ducats.

COLUMBUS DAY IN THE ROYAL COURT

Columbus, with his brothers Bartholomew and Diego, appeared at the royal court in the Alhambra at Granada on December 17, 1500. The meeting with the Sovereigns was a highly emotional occasion. Columbus wept as he kissed their hands and continued crying when he declared that any errors he may have made had been due to lack of experience rather than any deliberate intent all the while asserting his everlasting loyalty and love. The monarchs, and especially the queen, were deeply moved and assured him that his imprisonment had not been by their wishes or command, that they were much displeased by it, and would see to it that the guilty parties were punished and he was given satisfaction for his wrongs.

But while this promise of "satisfaction" involved the restoration of all income, possessions, and rights that had been sequestered and detained when he was arrested, it did not include the punishment of Bobadilla nor the restoration of his own title of Viceroy, which the Sovereigns had promised to reconsider. But the months went by, and it became apparent to the Admiral that a restitution of his viceroyalty would never take place.

King Ferdinand had already come to the conclusion that while Columbus was a great admiral, he could not be trusted to govern any island. He began to feel more and more that he had made a bad bargain with Columbus. He had never anticipated that so much territory, and consequently so much wealth, would come under the command of this foreigner. Columbus's rewards would be huge if the agreement were respected by the monarchs. This was totally unnecessary now as Bishop Fonseca was granting licenses to many individuals, some of them former mariners who had sailed with Columbus; these were willing to finance their own voyages from which the Crown benefited not only by the share of the proceeds but also gained from the extension of their territories. Thus, while Columbus had been away on his third voyage, Alonso Hojeda, Pedro Alonso Niño, and Vicente Yañez Pinzón used the Admiral's charts and journal and made voyages from which the Crown derived income and new territories without investing a single ducat. It should also be mentioned that in the last few years of the fifteenth century, voyages of discovery had been undertaken by other nations as well. In 1497, John Cabot (Giovani Caboto) sailed on the north Atlantic to Newfoundland. In the same year, Vasco da Gama had opened the long-sought route to India for Portugal, and early in the new century, on the ninth of March 1500, a Portuguese fleet under the command of Pedro Alvarez de Cabral, sailing for Calicut, kept far west of the Cape Verde Islands to avoid the calms and sighted the coast of Brazil, taking possession of that country for Portugal.

This exploration fever made Ferdinand very uneasy. He decided on a colonial administrative plan in which local governments would be established in all-important places, all to be subject to a central government to be located at Santo Domingo, which in turn would become the capital of the overseas empire.

APPOINTMENT OF DON NICOLÁS DE OVANDO

The person whom the Sovereigns selected to replace Bobadilla was Don Nicolás de Ovando, Commander of Lares, of the Order of Alcantara. A favorite of King Ferdinand, he was a man of great prudence, according to Las Casas, and capable of governing many people. He was a humble person, sober in his mode of living, yet projected a figure of authority.

Replacing Bobadilla, Ovando would rule as governor and supreme justice over all the islands and mainland, but out of deference to Columbus, he was not given the title of Viceroy; however, he was given a send-off in a manner befitting a king. He was permitted seventy-two squires as his bodyguards, ten of whom were horsemen. The fleet conveying Ovando to his domain consisted of thirty ships, five of them from 90 to 150 tons; twenty-four caravels from 30 to 90 tons; and one bark of 25 tons. Twenty-five hundred persons embarked in this fleet, including seventy-three married men with their families. This was to be a new wave of respectable people—no jailbirds—to be distributed among four towns, forming in each the nucleus of a stable and productive population. It was the Sovereigns' intention that the newcomers should displace the malcontent and dissolute who would be sent home with the returning fleet. Don

Alonso Maldonado, appointed chief justice and mayor, sailed with his expedition to replace Roldan, who was to be sent home. Obviously, the Sovereigns had made it possible for Ovando to start his new administration with a clean slate and with the right people, a situation unavailable to Columbus on his third voyage.

Columbus's interests were not overlooked, as Ovando was instructed to examine his accounts and to ascertain the damages he had sustained during his imprisonment. All the property confiscated by Bobadilla was to be restored or, if it had already been sold, it was to be made good. All the arrears of his revenues were to be paid to Columbus, and all his future revenues were to be punctually paid. The Adelantado and Don Diego were also to be indemnified for all their confiscated belongings and properties. Columbus was allowed to have a factor, or personal agent, to look after his interests. For this responsibility Columbus appointed his good friend Alonso Sánchez de Carvajal, who performed his duties with diligence and honesty, so well in fact that at the time of his death Columbus was a rich man. The Sovereigns approved the choice of Alonso Sánchez, the seafaring mayor of Baeza. He was devoted to the Admiral and had been, as we have seen, the captain of a ship on the second voyage and of one of the provision ships on the third.

Ovando's fleet did not leave Spain until February 13, 1502. In the meantime, word was received from recent arrivals that Bobadilla's administration in the island had been so bad that he had lost complete command over the community. He had attempted to pacify the colonists by liberal concessions rather than by strict discipline, only to find that the more he gave the more they wanted. Thus, his imprudence weakened his power base and lawlessness prevailed once again.

THE PROPHECIES: THE BOOK OF PRIVILEGES

Columbus had returned to Spain in late October 1500. Ovando left for the Indies in mid-February of 1502. In the intervening sixteen months Columbus had time to lick his wounds, to seek consolation from some correspondents, to try to obtain pardon and reinstatement from the Sovereigns, to gather all the documents pertaining to his discovery into a *Book of Privileges*, to pen a *Book of Prophecies*, to design a new type of vessel, and to plan for a fourth voyage.

What Columbus wanted most of all from the Sovereigns was the complete restoration of all his rights and privileges exactly the way they had been before 1500. But this was not to be, as evidenced by Ovando's appointment as governor and supreme justice. He remained in Granada for nearly nine months, hoping always to get a favorable decision from the Crown. With each passing month it became apparent to him that things would never be the same, for despite the Sovereigns' generous offers of restoration of rights at the time of his arrest, they had never indicated that he would be reinstated in the government as Viceroy of all the lands discovered overseas. Apparently, he would remain in disgrace, to some degree. His imagination began to soar. No, he would not be passive. He would interest the Sovereigns in greater enterprises. And what greater enterprise was there than the capture of the Holy Sepulcher? He had entertained this idea earlier in his mayorazgo; now he was proposing that a force consisting of fifty thousand foot soldiers and five thousand horses be assembled for driving out the infidels from Jerusalem and recovering the Holy Sepulcher. The Sovereigns had already driven the infidels out of Granada; why not drive them out of Jerusalem? The profits accrued from his discoveries would be dedicated to that end. It was important, therefore, that he put forth convincing arguments. He would seek them in the Holy Scriptures, the writings of the saints, and in all sacred and philosophical writings. From these sources, he also hoped to cull revelations that might be constructed to bear upon the discovery of the New World.

This was to be the *Book of Prophecies*: a prediction of the discovery of America wherein he is the central figure chosen by destiny to conquer another world. He returned to Seville and received help for his mystic and portentous research from Fray Gaspar Gorricio, a Carthusian monk from the Monastery of Our Lady of the Caves (Nuestra Señora María de las Cuevas) across the Guadalquivir River from the city of Seville. He cited to Columbus various sayings in the Apocalypse of St. John and in the prophecies of Isaiah and other prophets and religious figures. About Columbus's activities as discoverer of new lands, the monk quoted from Isaiah:

The Lord hath called me from the womb; from the bowels of my mother hath he made mention of my name....Surely the isles shall wait for me, and the ships of Tarshish first, to bring thy sons from far, their silver and their gold with them....For behold, I create new heavens and a new earth; and the former shall not be remembered, nor come into mind.

At about the same time Columbus met a Genoese diplomat, Niccoló Oderigo, who gave his fellow Genoese some worldly advice on how to protect himself and his heirs from being robbed of the fruits of his enterprise. He advised him to make a collection of the documents that had a bearing on his titles and privileges and then store them in a bank or other secure places. Accordingly, Columbus put together copies of forty-four documents dealing with these matters, which he titled *The Book of Privileges*. Four copies were made: one was kept at the Monastery of Las Cuevas in Seville; one was given to the Admiral's son Diego; the two others went to the Bank of St. George in Genoa. The copy that was left at the Monastery of Las Cuevas is now in the archives of the U.S. Library of Congress.

He hoped eventually to write the *Book of Prophecies* as a poem, possibly in the style of Dante's allegorical *Divine Comedy* and with its religious overtones, but Columbus was either too busy with his dreams of further discoveries or, more likely, unequal to the task. While the *Book of Prophecies* was written for the edification of the Sovereigns, it is not certain that they ever even saw it, as there is no record of any royal commentary on the subject.

THE FOURTH VOYAGE APPROVED

On February 26, 1502, Columbus sent a message to the Sovereigns setting forth his plans for another voyage to the New World and indicating some very important reasons for the undertaking. Unfortunately, the message and its contents have never been found, but it must have been convincing enough to exact such a prompt approval from the Sovereigns. There is reason to believe that Columbus proposed the discovery of a western passage to India, motivated possibly by Vasco da Gama's recent departure for India on February 10, 1502. During his second voyage, when Columbus had traveled along the southern coast of Cuba to the Golden Chersonese, he had been convinced that Cuba was not an island but an appendage of terra firma. In like manner, during his third voyage he had discovered that Paria was also an appendage of terra firma. This was later corroborated by Hojeda, who sailed even further westward to the Gulf of Venezuela. Columbus then concluded that between the land mass stretching from Cuba southward to Venezuela should be explored for a western passage to India. In other words, he suspected that a Central America existed and that a western passage could be found in what is now Panama! If we discount the existence of the Yucatan Channel, this was an amazing intuition. Columbus then concluded that he could sail through the passage to India and from there return to Spain and thus become the first person to sail around the world. Another but less important goal, he would upstage Vasco da Gama's voyage to India. With these accomplishments, Columbus hoped to retain the respect of the Sovereigns and recover all his rights and privileges. On March 14, 1502, the Admiral received the following letter from the king and queen:

Be assured that your imprisonment was very displeasing to us, as we made clear to you and to all others, for as soon as we learned of it we caused you to be set free. You know the favor, with which we have always treated you, and now we are even more resolved to honor and treat you very well. All that we have granted you shall be preserved intact according to the privileges that you have received from us, and you and your heirs shall enjoy them, as is just, without any contravention. And if it should be necessary to confirm them anew, we shall do so, and we shall order your son placed in possession of everything, for it is our wish to honor you and reward you in more than this. And be assured we shall look after your sons and brothers as is just and your office shall be vested in your son. But all this can be attended to after you have sailed; we therefore pray you do not delay your departure.

From Valencia de la Torres, March 14, 1502
I the King, I the Queen[1]

The cordial tone of this letter has been a bone of contention among many historians who have interpreted the letter as being used merely as a pretext to get rid of the restless Admiral for a few years and divert him from his constant and repetitious claims. This is an unfair conclusion, as the Sovereigns always had a very high opinion of Columbus as their greatest mariner and discoverer. They might have lost confidence in his administrative ability, but they had no doubt whatsoever of his ability as a mariner. In fact, there were valid reasons for allowing Columbus to undertake the voyage. First, it would keep the Admiral busy elsewhere, away from Hispaniola; second, Ferdinand's cupidity was aroused at the idea of a more direct route to those countries from which Portugal was planning to derive a lucrative trade. If such a strait really existed, what person was more qualified than Columbus to discover it?

Final instructions for the fourth voyage specified that Columbus was not to go to Hispaniola and thus embarrass Ovando. He was allowed ten thousand pesos for ships, provisions, and armaments. He was to discover islands within the Spanish side of the Line of Demarcation. An official comptroller, Francisco de Porras, would be in charge of all gold, pearls, silver, and other valuable items that should be officially recorded. Most importantly, no Indian slaves should be exported. Because Vasco da Gama had left for his second voyage to India, the Sovereigns found it opportune to furnish Columbus with a letter of introduction as they supposed that sailing westward he might conceivably meet Da Gama on his eastward voyage. Columbus still believed that he had been sailing in the Asiatic waters and the passage he was seeking would lead him into the Indian Ocean and a possible meeting with Da Gama.

Columbus altered his will to provide for Beatriz Enriquez de Harana, Ferdinand's mother, and then made final preparations for his fourth voyage.

Chapter Thirty-Nine

START OF FOURTH VOYAGE—FRIGHTFUL HURRICANE

Columbus was fully aware that the fourth voyage would be his last. For several years, since the end of his second voyage, his health had been steadily failing and now, at fifty-one, in the early years of his old age, he dared to undertake *El Alto Viaje*—the High Voyage—to exceed in historical importance of all his previous ones. The voyage lasted approximately two and a half years, and it was the most exacting of all. The dreadful violence of the raging seas and the overwhelming horrors of the tropical hurricanes almost drowned the intrepid mariners in their open vessels. In desperation, they turned to God continuously and in many situations even prayed for death as a welcome relief from such storms. And as if the forces of nature were not enough to plague the crews, the human passions of vile men and the hostility of ferocious Indians, who felt threated by the invaders, added infinitely to their misery.

Columbus's High Voyage may be compared to the epic poems of Homer's *Odyssey* and Virgil's *Aeneid* in terms of drama and adventure.

THE FLEET FOR THE FOURTH VOYAGE

Columbus was provided with a fleet of four vessels: the flagship La Capitana of seventy tons; the caravel Santiago de Palos, also called the Bermuda of sixty tons; the caravel La Gallega of sixty tons; and the caravel Vizcaína of fifty tons. The roster and payroll, as reported by Diego De Porras, Chief Clerk and Auditor of the Fleet, is the most complete roster of officers and men, and their pay, of any roster that exists for any of Columbus's voyages. Of great interest is not only the name, classification, and pay of each crew member, but also the date of his death if it occurred during the voyage.

Six months' pay was advanced before the voyage to each man. The rest of the money was to be paid when they returned to Spain. There was a great number of young boys aboard, some of them twelve or thirteen years old at the start, including Ferdinand, Columbus's son, who was thirteen. The roster of these grummets, or grommets, lists the names of fifty-six boys—forty percent of the crew. There was an unusual number of Genoese aboard referred to as "Ginoves" for lack of a surname in most instances; the most prominent was Bartolomeo Fieschi, Captain of the Vizcaína.

ROSTER OF THE OFFICERS OF THE FOUR SHIPS

La Capitana
Diego Tristan, *Captain*
(died Thursday, April 6, 1503)
Ambrosyo Sánchez, *Master*
Juan Sánches, *Chief Pilot*
(died May 17, 1504)
Anton Donato, *Quartermaster*

There were also aboard the captains fourteen seamen, five esquires (including a physician), eighteen grommets (boys), and seven chief petty officers. Total complement: forty-eight men.

Santiago De Palos
Francisco de Porras, *Captain*
Diego de Porras, *Chief Clerk and Auditor of the Fleet*
Francisco Bermudes, *Master*
Pedro Gomes, *Quartermaster*

There were also aboard eleven seamen, six esquires (including Diego Méndez, organizer of the famous canal voyage), four chief petty officers, and fourteen grommets. Total complement: thirty-nine men.

La Gallega
Pedro de Terreros, *Captain*
(died Wednesday, May 29, 1504)
Juan Quintero, *Master*
Alonso Ramon, *Quartermaster*

Pedro De Terreros is the only person to have sailed for certain on all four of the Admiral's voyages. He was chosen on the third voyage by Columbus to conduct the formal possession of the Paria Peninsula.

There were also aboard nine seamen, one esquire, and fourteen grommets. Total complement: twenty-seven men.

Vizcaína
Bartolomeo Fieschi, *Captain*
Juan Perez, *Master*
(died Saturday October 7, 1503)

Martín de Fuenterabia, *Quartermaster*
(died September 17, 1502)

Fieschi was a member of a patrician Genoese family. He too sailed a canoe from Jamaica to Hispaniola. After he returned to Genoa he became a commodore of a fleet of warships in the war against France in 1525, and was awarded the title of "Padre del Comune."

There were also aboard eight seamen, four esquires, including a Fray Alexandre, and ten grommets. Total complement: twenty-five men.

Columbus, the Adelantado Bartholomew, and Ferdinand Columbus were not on the roll and drew no pay. The Adelantado sailed on the Santiago and took over the command whenever Captain Porras showed his ineptitude.

Among the grommets' roster of the Capitana we find the name of Diego el Negro (James the Negro), the first black person to ship with Columbus. Among the Genoese sailors we find the names of two grommets, Batista Ginoves on the Vizcaína and Grigorio Ginoves on the Capitana; Guillermo Ginoves, gentleman among the Esquires of the Capitana; and Andrea Ginoves, Esquire on the Santiago. Two Esquires were identified by their full names: Juan Pasan (Giovanni Pasano), gentleman, and Marco Surjano, gentleman, both on the Vizcaína. The latter died on Wednesday, September 11, 1504, the day before Columbus sailed back to Spain. Altogether there were 143 men on this fleet when it left Spain.

Most of the information for the fourth voyage is obtained from the Admiral's writings, including his "Lettera Rarissima," from his son Ferdinand's biography of his father and from the will of Diego Méndez, who accompanied Columbus on the fourth voyage as "escudero" (squire) or gentleman volunteer. During the voyage, Columbus made him his personal secretary, and it is possible that Columbus's "Lettera Rarissima" was dictated to him by the Admiral. This letter originally written in Spanish for the Spanish Sovereigns is available in an Italian translation published in Venice, May 7, 1505, under the lengthy title of "Copia de la lettera per Colombo mandata a li Serenissimi Re e Regina di Spagna; de le insule et luoghi per lui trovate" (Copy of the Letter by Columbus Sent to the Most Serene King and Queen of Spain, Concerning the Islands and Places by him Discovered). It was reprinted in 1810 under the more manageable title of "Lettera Rarissima," by which it is commonly known today. Ferdinand Columbus made use of this letter in writing his father's biography many years later, towards the end of his life, which occurred in 1539.

FROM GRANADA TO HISPANIOLA

The Royal Instructions for the fourth voyage were issued on March 14, 1502, by the Sovereigns from Valencia de la Torre. They consisted of three letters: the Sovereigns' answer to Columbus's most recent letter, their instructions for the voyage, and their letter of introduction to Vasco da Gama just in case the two navigators should meet.

In the first letter, they conceded to most of the Admiral's requests, including permission to take along his son Fernando. In both letters they urged him to leave as soon as possible, and even assured him that the crews had been paid.

Columbus left Granada early in the spring of 1502 and went to Seville to assemble his fleet for the fourth voyage. In a short time, four vessels were made ready. They were caravels with topsails on circular crow's nests mounted on the mastheads. From Seville, they sailed down the Guadalquivir River to Puebla

Vieja, where, no doubt, the vessels were careened for a thorough bottom scraping, caulking, and tarring before proceeding to Sanlucar and Cádiz, where the Admiral, his brother the Adelantado, and young Ferdinand came aboard.

The fleet set sail on May 9, 1502, but due to a lack of wind, it could not put to sea until May 11, when a favorable wind came out of the north. They headed due south towards Azila, the Portuguese possession in Morocco, to lend a hand to the fortress there that Columbus had been told was under siege by the Moors. However, by the time they reached Azila, sixty-five miles away, the Moors had decamped and Columbus paid his respects by sending the Adelantado, his son Fernando, and a group of officers to call on the captain of Azila with expressions of friendship and offers of help from his fleet. The captain, who had been wounded, was very appreciative of the Admiral's concern and immediately sent several cavaliers aboard the Capitana to thank Columbus for his solicitude. Several of these proved to be cousins of Doña Felipa, Columbus's deceased wife. Later that day, they set sail for the Canaries and arrived at the Grand Canary on May 20, anchoring at Isleta, a little islet in the harbor of Las Palmas. They remained there for a few days, then on the twenty-eighth, they proceeded to Maspelomas at the extremely southern end of the Grand Canary to take on wood and water. On the following night, they headed for the Indies.

The trade winds were so favorable that the squadron sailed swiftly on its course, without lowering a sail, arriving at the island of Martinique on the morning of Wednesday, June 15. This twenty-one-day crossing was the fastest transatlantic passage made by Columbus. This is astonishing because he was later to complain that one of his ships performed so badly that it could not keep up with the rest of the fleet, which had to slow down so as not to leave her behind. After stopping at Martinique for three days to take on wood and water and to allow the seamen time to wash their clothes, they sailed to the island of Dominica, ten leagues to the north. Columbus then continued northward along the leeward islands to Santa Cruz and on the twenty-fourth of the same month, sailed along the southern coast of Puerto Rico, then due west to Santo Domingo. This was contrary to the orders specifically given by the Sovereigns directing him not to touch Hispaniola on his outward voyage. The Admiral, however, had been having a lot of trouble with the Santiago, which was sailing extremely badly. She could not carry any sail without putting her gunwale under. He desired to change the troublesome vessel for another, possibly with one of the twenty-eight vessels of the fleet that had carried Ovando to Hispaniola.

This fleet was being made ready to return to Spain taking along Bobadilla, Roldan, and many of the idlers and malcontents together with their belongings and fortunes accumulated in the New World. Bobadilla was returning on the principal ship with a huge amount of gold, which was the revenue collected during his administration—one nugget of virgin gold alone weighed approximately 3,600 castellanos. On the same ship, in irons, was the unfortunate Guarionex, the once-powerful Cacique of Vega, being sent as a captive to Spain. In one of the ships, Alonso Sánchez de Carvajal was shipping back to Columbus four thousand pieces of gold representing his allotted share of gold recovered from Bobadilla. On another vessel, Francisco Roldan was also returning to Spain with a fortune in gold accumulated in Hispaniola.

On Wednesday, June 29, Columbus's squadron arrived at the mouth of the Ozama River as the fleet of Ovando was getting ready to return to Spain. The Admiral immediately sent Pedro de Terreros, Captain of La Gallega, to visit Ovando and explain to him that the purpose of their visit was to procure a vessel in exchange for the Santiago, which was defective. He also requested permission to shelter the squadron in the harbor because he expected a power hurricane to strike the island. Columbus had been through several hurricanes in the past; being an extremely good observer of weather conditions and having an acute sense of smell, Columbus almost literally smelled the coming of the hurricane. The oppressive feeling in the air, the abnormal tides, the cirrus clouds hurrying through the skies as if to run away from the impending storm, and even the odd pain in his arthritic joints were sure signs that a storm was getting energy to strike a powerful blow on land and sea. The haughtily contemptuous Don Nicolas de Ovando, Knight Commander of Lares and Governor of Hispaniola, refused the request. When Columbus learned of Ovando's refusal to allow him shelter, he ordered Pedro de Torreros back to entreat Ovando not to let his fleet leave for Castile for at least another week, as by that time the hurricane should have passed by the area. Ovando scoffed at the Admiral's forecast, ridiculed him as a false prophet, and ignored his warning. This disdainful refusal saddened Columbus to the extent that later, following the storm, he vented his feelings in his "Lettera Rarissima" to the Sovereigns thus:

On reaching the island of Española, I dispatched a packet of letters, by which I begged as a favor that a ship should be supplied me at my own cost in lieu of one of those that I had brought with me, which had become unseaworthy, and could no longer carry sail. The letters were taken and your Highnesses will know if a reply has been given to them. For my part, I was forbidden to go on shore; the hearts of my people failed them lest I should take them further, and they said that if any danger were to befall them, they should receive no succor, but, on the contrary, in all probability have some great affront offered them. Moreover, every man had it in his power to tell me that the new Governor would have the superintendence of the countries that I might acquire.

The tempest was terrible throughout the night, all the ships were separated and each one driven to the last extremity, without hope of anything but death; each of them also looked upon the loss of the rest as a matter of certainty. What man was ever born, not even excepting Job, who would not have been ready to die of despair at finding himself as I then was, in anxious fear for my own safety and that of my son, my brother, and my friends, and yet refused permission either to land or to put into harbor on the shores of which by God's mercy I had gained for Spain sweating blood?[1]

THE VENGEFUL HURRICANE STRIKES

In anticipation of the hurricane, Columbus led his squadron some distance to the west of the Ozama and anchored at the mouth of a river, possibly the Río Jaina. On June 29, the force of the wind began to increase, and by the next day the hurricane struck with full force. All the ships with the exception of the Capitana were torn loose from their anchorage and driven off the coast to the foaming and raging sea. The crank Santiago was almost lost as its Captain Porras was a political appointee and proved to be an inept sailor. Fortunately, the Adelantado, who, according to his nephew Ferdinand, was an excellent sea captain, saved the ship from foundering. Contact between the ships was lost in the black night as each vessel went its own way.

For several days, they were tossed about at the mercy of the storm, fearful of being capsized and giving up each other as lost.

La Gallega lost her boat, which had been in the water when she was driven out to sea. Eventually, Captain Terreros pulled her through the storm. The Vizcaína, under her Genoese Captain Fieschi, managed to avoid disaster owing to his seamanship. Before the storm, Columbus had planned a rendezvous for his ships just in case they should be scattered by the storm. It must have been a heartwarming sight when on Sunday, July 3, each ship in succession sailed in at the appointed landlocked harbor of Puerto Escondido (now Puerto Viejo de Azua) in the Bahía de Ocoa, about fifty miles west of Santo Domingo.

In the meantime, Ovando's fleet of twenty-eight ships was not as lucky. Two days after setting sail, as the fleet was approaching the eastern point of Hispaniola, the hurricane burst over it with tremendous fury, scattering and capsizing nearly all vessels. Some ships foundered, and others were forced ashore and pounded to bits by the raging sea. Twenty-three to twenty-five ships were lost, most with all hands onboard. Among those that went down was the flagship commanded by Columbus's friend Antonio de Torres, carrying as passengers Bobadilla and Guarionex, the captured Cacique. Francisco Roldan, the mutineer, also lost his life. With this ship, nearly 200,000 castellanos worth of gold and the greatest gold nugget ever found in the Indies, weighting 3,600 castellanos, were lost. Three or four ships struggled back to Santo Domingo heavily damaged. In all, over five hundred persons went down with the ships. The city of Santo Domingo itself, built mostly of wood, was nearly leveled. Only one ship, the Aguja, managed to reach Spain. Fortunately, this vessel, assigned by Ovando to Columbus's agent Alonso Sánchez de Carvajal because it was a poor sailor, carried aboard four thousand pounds of gold belonging to Columbus; this safely reached the hands of Don Diego Colón in Spain.

Columbus's friends were certain that this was an act of temporal retribution; his enemies were just as certain that the Admiral had resorted to sorcery.

Columbus remained in Azua for several days to repair his vessels and permit the crews to rest or indulge in recreational activities. Young Ferdinand recalls the fun they had fishing. He states:

I shall describe two remarkable kinds of fish among the many they caught. One I recall with amusement, the other with wonderment. The first was a ray as large as a medium-sized bed, which the men of the Vizcaína stabbed with a harping iron while it slept on the surface…and [the harping iron] being tied to the boat by a long thick rope, it drew the boat through the harbor as swiftly as an arrow…eventually the fish died and was hauled aboard with tacking gear.[2]

The boy was then excited in discovering that some mammals live in the sea and describes his first experience with a manatee—a herbivorous type of sea lion:

The second fish was caught by another means; the Indians call it manatee, and it is not known in Europe. It is big as a calf and resembles one in taste and color, but is better tasting and fatter; and those who believe that all manner of land animals live in the sea argue that the manatee is not a fish but a calf, since it does not look like a fish and feeds only on the green it finds along the shore.[3]

From Azua harbor the squadron sailed westward, rounded Cabo Beata, and headed for a landfall in Jacmel in Xaragua to take shelter from an impending storm. With the threat removed, they left Jacmel on July 14 and set their course due west but could not hold to it as they ran into a flat calm. The ocean currents then carried them to the Morant Cays, Jamaica, sixty miles southeast of the present capital city of Kingston. They landed on an island that Columbus called "Puddles" (Las Pozas) because the men found water by digging in the sands as no springs or rivers could be found. They resumed their course without much delay; once again the powerful equatorial current together with the southeast wind forced them northeast. They passed Jamaica through the Cayman Islands to a little cay east of the Isla de la Juventud (formerly the Isle of Pines), which Columbus named "Avegada," possibly Key Largo. They had been borne away by the currents a distance of 350 miles!

They remained two or three days in this area, the northern end of the Jardínes de la Reina, which Columbus discovered in 1494. On July 27, an energetic northeast wind sprang up, enabling Columbus and the fleet to set a westward course and cross the Caribbean Sea, a distance of 360 miles, in only three days. They landed off the Gulf of Honduras in the Isla de la Bahía group (Bay Islands), possibly the present Isle de Guanaia, sometimes called "Bonacca." Had they been able to maintain a west by west course, which they had set from Cuba, they would have landed on the Yucatan Peninsula and come in contact with the Maya people and their advanced culture. Instead the northeast wind had forced them further south to explore the east coast of Central America and, as it turned out, to confront hostile tribes.

Chapter Forty

SEARCHING FOR A PASSAGE TO INDIA

Once at the island of Guanaja, Columbus sent the Adelantado ashore with two boats filed with seamen. They met Indians who in many ways resembled the Indians from the other islands except that these had narrower foreheads. They also saw many pine trees covering the fertile and verdant island. The Adelantado and his men approached a group of friendly Indians to barter with them but found no takers. However, they did give the Spaniards some ores, which Ferdinand called "calcide," possibly iron pyrite, which the seamen thought was gold and kept concealed for a long time because trading with gold was forbidden. A large dugout canoe, as long as a galley and eight feet wide, made of a single tree trunk like the other Indian canoes, approached. It was paddled by twenty-five men and it was freighted with merchandise and was possibly coming to trade with the Guanaja Indians. Some historians have theorized that this canoe had come from the coast of Honduras, an area of high Indian culture that had been part of the Maya empire of the Cocomes and that they were carrying out regular trade with the island of Guanaja.

Amidships of the canoe was a palm leaf–covered awning similar to those used in Venetian gondolas. Under this awning were the children and women and all the baggage and merchandise. The merchandise they carried interested the Admiral because it was a clue to the Indians' culture. These goods included cotton mantles and sleeveless shirts embroidered and printed in different colors, breechcloths of the same design, and cloth such as the Moorish women of Granada wore. Of particular interest were the long wooden swords with edges implanted with flints; hatchets made of copper, and not with stone as used by other more primitive Indians; and crucibles for melting copper. Their provisions consisted of roots and grains like those of the Indians of Hispaniola; a great amount of cacao beans unknown to the Spaniards but highly prized by the natives as a food and means of monetary exchange; a beverage extracted from maize and resembling beer; and utensils neatly handcrafted from clay, marble, and hard wood. From these articles Columbus selected some specimens to take back to Spain and gave the natives various trinkets that seemed to satisfy them.

Convinced that he was approaching more civilized nations than he had seen before, Columbus sought more information about the surrounding countries. They told him that they had come from a rich and industrious country located to the west. Columbus briefly thought of following their instructions by sailing to the west, but his mind was set on discovering the strait. He could easily make a trip later by sailing downwind from Cuba. In retrospect, we now wonder how the course of history might have changed had Columbus indeed sailed to the west. Sailing westward at the same latitude from Guanaja he would have reached the Gulf of Honduras and a landfall in a couple of days on the Yucatan Peninsula near Monkey River Town in Belize. However, for the present he made plans to sail to the mainland, whose mountains could be seen directly to the south.

SAILING ALONG THE COAST OF HONDURAS TO GRACIAS A DIOS

Before leaving the island of Guanaja, the Admiral detained an elderly native named Yumbe, who seemed to know more than anyone else, to act as a guide along the coast. He served the Admiral willingly and loyally along the coast of Honduras and was released at the limits of the area in which his language was spoken, just before they reached Cape Gracias a Dios.

Columbus made for the mainland, only thirty miles south of the island, at a place that he called "Punta Caxinas" from the name of a tree that grew there. The fleet anchored possibly in a harbor called today Puerto Castilla near the present city of Trujillo. The Indians here wore dyed shirts and breechcloths, like those in the canoe. They also had for protection thick quilted cotton jerkins like breastplates that offered protection against arrows and even blows from Spanish swords. These were Jicaque Indians of the Honduran kingdom of the Mayas.

The fleet beat to the windward and Sunday morning, August 14, 1502, and they anchored off the mouth of a river. Banners flying, the Adelantado went ashore to hear Mass, accompanied by the captains and many mariners. On Wednesday, August 17, the Adelantado went ashore, this time to take formal possession of the land in the name of the Catholic Sovereigns. Columbus named it "Río de la Posesion" (River of Possession). More than one hundred Indians bearing food came down to the shore to witness the ceremony. Consider the paradox! The Indians showered gifts on the Spaniards who were taking possession of their land! They brought food of various kinds: "Chickens that were better tasting than ours, geese, roast fish, red and white beans resembling kidney beans, and other commodities like those of Hispaniola," recalls Ferdinand.[1] The natives of this part of Honduras had higher foreheads than the previous Indians. They spoke a different language and decorated their bodies with tattoos by burning in Moorish-style designs; some displayed painted lions, others deer, turreted castles, and a variety of figures.

For some festivities, some painted their faces black or red, others drew stripes of various colors on their faces, and still others blackened their eyes. The old Indian guide told the Admiral that many of them were cannibals. In certain sections of the coast the natives had their ears bored and distended large enough to contain a hen's egg; this prompted Columbus to call that region "la Costa de la Oreja" (the Coast of the Ear).

From the River of Possession, the fleet proceeded eastward along the coast with great difficulty, beating against contrary winds and continuously tacking all the way. It took them thirty-eight days of sailing to make sixty leagues. The northern coast of Honduras is almost entirely on the 16°N latitude parallel from the Gulf of Honduras to the Cape of Barra Putuca, where it slants southeast for about ninety miles to Cabo Gracias a Dios. Columbus's voyage eastward along this coast proved to be a veritable ordeal. The gale winds ripped at the sails and what they gained through tacking they lost to the currents that, like the rushing waters of a river, seemed to stop the vessels in their tracks. It was like climbing a greased pole. They had some respite at night when the fleet anchored close to shore, for fear of proceeding along an unknown coast in the dark, but in many instances this procedure would cost them the gains made during the day as the current would force them out to sea. As if the winds and currents were not enough punishment, they had to contend with the deluge of tropical storms that drenched them to the bones. The vessels' endurance was sorely tested, the hulls' seams were opened, and the provisions were damaged by the seawater. The mariners had to face continuous duty, manning the sails because of tacking and working the pumps to keep the water out of the hulls.

During those awful storms of long duration, the Admiral had suffered greatly from arthritis. He was also concerned about the Adelantado, whom he had persuaded to join him, and more so for his young son, Ferdinand. As usual, what sustained Columbus was his abiding faith in God and in his own ability to surmount all adversities. On September 14, they finally reached the Cape of Barra Putuca, where the coast trended south so that the wind became favorable and the vessels picked up speed. They all gave thanks to God, and appropriately the Admiral gave the cape where they had arrived the name of "Gracias a Dios," or "Thanks to God." In recounting this frightful experience in the Lettera Rarissima," the Admiral himself stated:

Hence as opportunity affords I pushed on for the mainland, in spite of the wind and a fearful contrary current, against which I contended for sixty days and after all only made seventy leagues. All this time I was unable to get into harbor, nor was there any cessation of this tempest, which was one continuation of rain, thunder, and lightning; indeed it seemed as if it were the end of the world. I at length reached the Cape of Gracias a Dios, and after that the Lord granted me fair wind and tide.

And he then worried about his crew:

My people were very weak and humbled in spirit, many of them promising to lead a religious life, and all making vows and promising to perform pilgrimages, while some of them would frequently *go to their messmates to make confession. Other tempests have been experienced but never for so long a duration or so fearful as this.*²

Columbus's health problems were beginning to sap his strength. He was afflicted with gout, which affected his mobility. He seldom left his flagship, delegating to his brother the responsibility of carrying out all land excursions. But he never gave up any of his nautical duties, which required constant watchfulness. For this purpose, he had a small cabin built on the poop deck of his flagship from which he could observe, even when bedridden, the activities on deck and provide guidance if necessary.

VOYAGE ALONG THE COSTA DE MOSQUITOS OF NICARAGUA

Having rounded Cape Gracias a Dios, the fleet sailed directly southward along the Costa de Mosquitos of Nicaragua.

Compared to the terrible weather they had been through, this was easy sailing on one tack, allowing the crews some deserved rest and peace of mind. In two days they covered almost as much distance as they had covered with the wind against them in the previous thirty-eight days on the northern coast of Honduras. On their way they passed many lagunas, craggy promontories, verdant valleys, and many rivers with tortoises and alligators basking on the banks.

After sailing for about sixty leagues, on September 16, the fleet anchored near the mouth of a river and sent boats ashore to replenish their supplies of wood and water. Unfortunately, as they were returning to their ships a sudden swelling of the sea, caused by its encounter with the rapid current of the river, swamped one boat and two seamen were drowned. The Admiral called the place "Río de los Desastres" (the River of Disasters). They sailed southward along the coast for eighty days, covered about 130 miles, and crossed the existing boundary of Costa Rica. On September 25, they reached a region that the Indians called "Cariai" and spent ten days anchored near a beautiful island that the Indians called "Quiriviri." There they dropped anchor to repair the vessels, take on stores, and rest. Here Columbus found "the best country and people that we had yet seen; because the land was high and abounded with rivers and great trees, and the island itself was very verdant, full of groves of lofty trees, palms, myrobalans, and many other species."[3] So the Admiral named it "La Huerta" (the Garden). This place must have been in the modern Bahía de Moin near the city of Limon.

When the natives, possibly Talamanca Indians, saw the three ships they sounded an alarm and prepared to defend themselves against the invaders with their primitive instruments of war: bows and arrows, war clubs, and palm-tree spears tipped with fish bones. The Spaniards, however, made no attempt to land for a couple of days possibly to avoid trouble, but most likely to repair their ships and air-dry their provisions and living quarters. When the Indians noticed the strange visitors' specific intentions, they became curious and began to wave their mantles, inviting them to land. Still fearing trouble, the Admiral kept his men aboard the ships; thus prompting some bold Indians to swim to the ships taking along the mantles and tunics of cotton and ornaments of guanin pendants that they wore around the neck. These items they offered to the visitors, but Columbus forbade his men from accepting them. Instead, to show the Indians his generosity, without receiving compensation he sent them presents that they in turn refused. Columbus's refusal of the gifts had apparently offended the Indians' pride. To emphasize their refusal, the Indians collected all the visitors' gifts, tied them into a bundle, and left them on the shore, where the Spaniards found them the following day. The impasse was finally resolved when the Indians sent aboard the flagship two young virgins, one about fourteen and the other eight years of age, to be used ostensibly as hostages but more likely for sexual gratification of the crew. The girls were naked but had guanin pendants hanging from their necks.

This stratagem reflected much intelligence by the Indians; and the girls displayed much courage, for though the Christians were completely strange to them in aspect, manners, and race, they showed no fear or grief but always looked pleasant and modest. On this account, the Admiral treated them well and had them clothed and then sent ashore, where the old man who brought them and fifty Indians came out to receive them joyfully.[4]

The next day the Admiral sent the Adelantado ashore with a secretary to record some information about the area. Two leading citizens, possibly greeters, approached the Adelantado eager to have a conversation with the Spaniards. When the secretary displayed paper and pen to record the conversation, the Indians were so terrified they took immediately flight, scattering some power in the air. They regarded writing as a form of sorcery and were afraid of being bewitched. Moreover, because the visitors had refused to accept their gifts, especially the young virgins, they became more convinced that the Spaniards were sorcerers.

The fleet remained in the La Huerta area for several more days, during which time they careened, cleaned, and repaired their vessels and recuperated from the horrible ordeal they had endured along the Costa de las Oreja. Finally, on October 2, the Admiral sent the Adelantado with a strong force to reconnoiter the area and to learn of the Indians' customs and manners. The party was very much impressed with the variety of fauna found in the area—more animals than they had ever seen in the Antilles including wild boar, deer, monkeys, pumas, and even a large wild fowl resembling a turkey. In examining a large house with a cane roof in one village, they found tombs, one of which contained a dried and embalmed corpse; in another there were two other human bodies wrapped in cotton and so preserved that they were free of any disagreeable odor. The tombs were adorned each with a tablet carved with figures of animals and also the likeness of the dead person including beads, guanin objects, and the ornaments precious to the deceased during his lifetime.

When ready to sail, the Admiral detained seven Indians to learn more about their culture and to act as guides and interpreters, but he kept only two of them, the most intelligent, sending the others home with gifts. The Indians were very disturbed by the seizure and the following day sent out emissaries with gifts to ransom the captives. They offered as additional presents two wild boars, but the Admiral assured them that it was not his intention to take the captives to Spain. He needed their help to guide him down the coast. Then he would release them, as he had already done with another Indian guide picked up when he first reached the mainland. He gave various presents to the emissaries and sent them away, disconsolate and apprehensive about the fate of their friends.

Chapter Forty-One

ADVENTURE ALONG THE COAST OF VERAGUA AND PANAMA

Wednesday, October 5, the Admiral set sail from Cariai in a southeasterly direction along the coast. After a journey of fify miles, the fleet came across a channel that, from all appearances, was worthwhile investigating. This channel, presently called Boca del Drago, leads into a large bay now named Almirante in Columbus's honor. Several islands guard the bay, with channels opening between them, so that there are three or four entrances into the bay. The islands appeared very green because they were covered with groves, and the fragrance of fruits and flowers were everywhere. The ships sailed precariously between one island and another as if in canals in the streets of a city; their spars brushed the overhanging branches of the trees.

After anchoring in the bay, the men landed on one island, where they found twenty canoes beached on the shore. Their owners had disappeared among the trees at the sight of the visitors, but encouraged by the two Indians from Cariai, the fleet's new guides, they returned to the shore. The Spaniards saw Indians who were stark naked: some of them with pure gold discs suspended around their necks by cotton cords; others wore ornaments of guanin shaped like eagles. They no longer evinced any fear of the visitors and gladly traded a gold disk weighing ten ducats for three hawks' bells. When asked, through the Cariai interpreters, the source of the gold, the Indians replied that they got it on the mainland not far from there.

The next day, October 7, the boats were sent to the mainland at the far end of the bay that the Admiral called "Bahía de Alburema," which on today's maps is the Laguna de Chiriqui located on the northwestern part of Panama. It is a deep and wide expanse of water at the foot of a green mountain range that rises eleven thousand feet above sea level. They found fifteen canoes filled with Indians there. Their bodies were naked—except for their genitals, which were covered with cotton clouts—and they were all painted in white, black, and red.

Two of the Indians were seized and brought before the Admiral, who was anxious to learn all about the natives of that area. One of them wore a gold disk weighing fourteen ducats and the other a gold eagle weighing twenty-two ducats, and the Admiral asked through his interpreters the source of the gold. The Indians replied that much gold could be found one or two days' journey inland. Columbus also learned from these Guaymis Indians that he was on an isthmus between two seas, and that another province called Ciguare was located across the cordillera—nine days' march away—and that much gold could be found in that area. They also mentioned several other places where gold and gold mines could be found, the last of these being Veragua, about twenty leagues away.

The fleet remained in the beautiful Chiriqui Lagoon for another ten days, giving the men the chance to relax and enjoy the company of the peaceful natives with whom they traded their trinkets for gold and food. On October 17, the fleet put out to sea again, rounded the modern Peninsula Valiente, and headed eastward. They then passed on the lee of the Isla Escudo de Veragua and reached the Golfo de los Mosquitos—a gulf without a single harbor. After a day's run of twelve leagues, they anchored at the mouth of a small river called Guaiga. This was the gold region the Guyamis had mentioned to Columbus. Again, they became infected with gold fever, and the search for the strait to the Indian Ocean was no longer a priority.

SAILING ALONG THE COAST OF VERAGUA

On reaching Guaiga, Columbus entered a harborless coastline that extends to the Bahía de Limon (Lemon Bay), the Caribbean entrance to the Panama Canal, a distance of 125 miles from Chiriqui Lagoon. It is a type of coastline where vessels have no protection against the elements and where they can be anchored with any degree of safety only at a river's mouth or roadstead. Because of this condition, the fleet sailed along the Golfo de Los Mosquitos as fast as the west winds would carry it until a hospitable haven could be reached. There were no villages to be seen along the coast, but the sight of smoke inland along the river valleys indicated the existence of population centers. And it was at these offshore locations that they anchored. The first of these roadsteads, reached after sailing against the trade wind for about twelve leagues, was at the mouth of a river that Ferdinand called "Guaiga." When some boats were sent toward land, about two hundred Indians came out of the woods, armed with spears, clubs, and swords of palm. Their yells were accompanied by the sound of wooden drums and blasts of conch shells. They waded a short distance in the sea toward the boats, brandishing their primitive weapons in defiance, in an attempt to prevent the invaders from landing. The Indians' hostility was mollified by the Indian interpreters to the extent that they willingly began to barter. The Indians again got the short end of the deal by giving away seventeen plates of gold worth 150 ducats for a few toys and trinkets.

The Spaniards returned the following day, October 21, to barter for more gold but again the Indians met them with the same hostility as on the previous day. This time the Indians threatened them with spears if they did not retreat. The Spaniards countered with a display of force of their own. They shot an arrow, wounding an Indian in the arm, and a discharge from a lombard forced the rest to flee in panic. Four Spaniards jumped on shore, caught some Indians, and obliged them to exchange three more gold disks for trinkets.

Columbus was now convinced of two things: there was gold in Veragua and the Guaymi Indians were ferocious; thus, a more cautious approach was needed in dealing with them. His interest now was gold and its source. They continued along the coast of the Golfo de Los Mosquitos, still bucking the trade winds, and anchored at the mouth of a larger river. Again, the Spaniards heard the sound of drums and conchs giving the alarm that invaders were approaching. Two Indians rowed to the flagship and, after being satisfied with the Admiral's peaceful intentions, returned to their Cacique with a favorable report. The Indians allowed the boats to land, and when the Cacique learned of the Spaniards' desire for gold, he promptly bartered a gold disc he wore around his neck, and permitted his subjects to do the same. The Spaniards collected nineteen discs of pure gold in exchange for the usual trinkets.

Ferdinand reports that "this was the first place in the Indies where the Christians saw signs of building; it was a great mass of stucco and appeared to have been made of stone and lime. The Admiral ordered a piece to be taken as a souvenir of that antiquity."[1]

Columbus, however, did not report any such find in his letter. The Mayas used construction of this type, but the Guaymis, considerably further east and south, were not part of their culture and Ferdinand's report has baffled historians for centuries.

The fleet continued eastward to the town of Cobrava in another province. Because no natives could be seen on its river banks and because a favorable wind came up, they held their course as the fleet passed five villages of active trade. One of them was Veragua, which, according to the Indian interpreters, was the source of the gold and the polished disks. On the following day, they arrived at a village called Cubiga, and here the Indian interpreters told the Admiral where gold could be found. This area extended for fifty leagues along the coast from Almirante Bay to Cuba.

They did not stop in Cubiga, but proceeded instead northeastward along the coast as far as the harbor of Puerto Bello (Portobello), a few miles past the eastern entrance to the present Panama Canal. According to Ferdinand:

He gave it that name because it is very large, beautiful, thickly populated, and surrounded by cultivated country. He entered it on November 2, passing between two small islands. Within the harbor vessels may lie close to shore and beat about if they wish. The country about the harbor is well tilled and full of houses only a stone's throw or crossbow shot apart; all is pretty as a picture, the fairest thing one ever saw. During the seven days that we were detained there by rain and foul weather, canoes came from all about to barter all sorts of food and skeins of the fine spun cotton for trifles of brass such as lace points and tags.[2]

During the Spanish colonial days and, of course, several centuries before the building of the Panama Canal, Portobello was a thriving commercial site being selected as the Caribbean terminus of commercial traffic crossing the Isthmus of Panama. It was here that the galleons from Spain exchanged their cargoes for the silver and gold from Peru and commercial products from Darien.

On Wednesday, November 9, the fleet left Portobello and continued sailing eastward for about nine leagues, when a contrary wind sprang up, forcing the fleet back several leagues into a harbor Columbus named "Puerto de Bastimentos" (Harbor of Provisions) because the area was full of maize. Ten years later it was renamed "Nombre de Dios" (Name of God) by Nicuesa. Here they remained until the twenty-third repairing their ships, which leaked excessively due to the multiple piercings by the "teredo" or worm abounding in tropical waters. This pest is the size of a man's finger and, like termites, will bore through the ships planks and timbers not protected with copper sheeting.

The following day, the fleet sailed eastward again to a place called Guiga, probably the mouth of the Río Culebra. When the boats went ashore there, they met a crowd of three hundred Indians and bartered with them for food and some gold pendants that hung from the natives' ears and noses. They did not stay there too long as Saturday, November 26, they sailed in a little harbor that the Admiral named "El Puerto del Retrete" (the Port of the Retreat) because its diminutive size would not hold more than five or six ships. The Admiral was deceived by the mariners, who had previously sounded the harbor and had deliberately lied about its width because it was to their advantage to jump ashore from the vessels to trade with the Indians. Unfortunately, placing the vessels so close to shore made them easy prey to the Indian hordes, a fact of deep concern to the Admiral. The entrance to the harbor was only seventy-five to one hundred feet wide with sharp rocks rising about the surface on each side. It was so deep that anchorage could be obtained only near the land, so that a person could easily jump onshore. And this is exactly what happened. In the darkness of the night the seamen would slip ashore in small groups without permission to trade with the Indians, who with their accustomed hospitality would welcome them in their homes.

The Indians at first traded peacefully, but according to Ferdinand, "The sailors, a greedy and dissolute set of men, committed innumerable outrages. This provoked the Indians to break the peace, and some fights occurred between the two sides."[3] The Admiral, who always treated the Indians with kindness and justice, tried to assuage their wrath and bring peace among the factions but without success. The belligerent Indians gathered in growing numbers around the ships that were close enough to shore to be boarded without much effort. The Admiral tried firing a shot in the air from his lombards, hoping the thunderous explosion would scare them away. This only made the Indians more threatening and they responded with:

Shouts and beating the branches of the trees with staves and uttering great threats to show they did not fear that noise. To temper their pride and teach them not to scorn the Christians, the Admiral ordered a shot fired at a group of Indians on a hilltop, and the ball falling in their midst, let them know that this thunder concealed a thunderbolt. After that they hardly dared peep out from behind the hills.[4]

Despite this account of their provoked hostility, Ferdinand had words of praise for the physical endowments of these Indians.

He thought they were the best-looking Indians the Christians had ever seen. They were tall and handsome—not potbellied. Ferdinand also reported the appearance, for the first time in the Indies, of large crocodiles in the harbor, noticing that they came out in large numbers to sleep on the shore:

And give out an odor as strong as if all the musks in the world were collected together; they are so ravenous and cruel that if they find a man asleep they will drag him into the water to eat him, but they are cowardly and flee when attacked. The lizards are found in many other parts of the mainland; some say they are crocodiles like those of the Nile.[5]

Because of the miserable weather, the fleet remained in the Retrete for nine days to the discouragement of the crews. Stormy weather tends to make men and beasts gloomy and despondent, and these mariners were no exception. They were particularly concerned about their ships, which they considered no longer seaworthy because of the damage done by the worms. The possibility of discovering a strait seemed more elusive as they sailed along. Even if a strait were discovered, it would not put money into the mariners' pockets; trading gold, however, could be more lucrative. Even the Admiral began to doubt the existence of the strait. Some historians have indicated that the explorer decided to turn back because he had reached the end of the unexplored territory without finding the strait. According to them, he had learned that the previous year Rodrigo Bastidas, sailing west from Venezuela, had reached the Gulf of Darien and possibly even the little harbor of Retrete. This, however, is hardly possible. Columbus could not have known about Bastidas's voyage, which had been based on the Admiral's account of the third voyage. This information had been made available to Bishop Fonseca and passed on also to Hojeda and Vincente Yañez Pinzón. After completing his voyage along the coast of Darien, Bastidas had taken off for Hispaniola, where he had been forced to careen his shipworm-riddled ships. Governor Ovando had sent him home on the Aguja, the ship that survived the terrible West Indies hurricane of July 1502, which also struck Columbus's fleet off the Ozama River. More important, the disappointment of not having found a strait and any subsequent ridicule could be easily silenced by bringing to the Sovereigns a good measure of gold.

TEMPESTUOUS VOYAGE ALONG THE COAST OF VERAGUA

On Monday, December 5, instead of following his course to the east as originally planned, the Admiral decided to go back to Veragua to look for gold. On the same evening, he anchored in Portobello, ten leagues westward. On the following day, as he was continuing on his course, the wind suddenly veered to the west again:

But thinking that it would not last, he decided not to alter course but bear up against the wind for a few days. Never was seen more unsettled weather. Now the wind was fair for Veragua; now it whipped about and drove us back to Portobello. And just as we were most hopeful of making port the wind would change again, sometimes with such terrible thunder and lightning, that all the men dared not open their eyes and it seemed the ships were sinking and the heavens coming down.[6]

Ferdinand then continues with his vivid description of the dreadful storm:

Sometimes the thunder lasted so long that we were sure some ship of the fleet was firing signals for help; at other times there fell such a storm of rain that it poured torrents like another deluge. All suffered greatly and were in despair; for they could not get even half an hour's rest, were wet through days on end....In such terrible storms they dread the fire in the lightning flashes, the air for its fury, the water for the waves, and the land for the reefs and rocks of that unknown coast.[7]

As if this constant harassment by the winds and rain was not enough, on Tuesday, December 13, a water spout passed between two ships, prompting the mariners to recite the Gospel to exorcise it:

Had the sailors not dissolved it by reciting the Gospel according to St. John, it would surely have swamped anything it struck for it raises the water up to the clouds in a column thicker than a water butt, twisting it about like a whirlwind.[8]

The Admiral read the passage from John 6:17–20, describing the storm on the Sea of Galilee when Jesus walked on the waters and reassured the terrified sailors, saying, "It is I, do not be afraid."

After the reading, with the Bible in his left hand and with a drawn sword, Columbus traced a cross in the sky and a circle around his whole fleet, according to Ferdinand. The Admiral's own account in his "Lettera Rarissima" is more personal, more alarming, and more passionate. Columbus tells of having reached Nombre de Dios and of having been detained there by a powerful current for fourteen days:

After I had made fifteen leagues with great exertions, the wind and the current drove me back again with great fury, but in again making for the port which I had quitted, I found on the way another port, which I named Retrete, where I put in for shelter with as much risk as regret, the ships being in sad condition, and my crews and myself exceedingly fatigued. I remained there fifteen days, kept in by stress of weather, and when I fancied my troubles were at end, I found them only begun. It was then that I changed my resolution with respect to proceeding to the mines, and proposed doing something in the interim, until the weather should prove more favorable for my voyage. I had already made four leagues when the storm recommenced, and wearied me to such a degree that I absolutely knew not what to do; my wound reopened, and for nine days my life was despaired of; never was the sea seen so high, so terrific, and so covered with foam; not only did the wind oppose our proceeding onward, but it also rendered it highly dangerous to run in for any headland, and kept me in that sea which seemed to me as a sea of blood, seething like a cauldron on a mighty fire. Never did the sky look more fearful; during one day and one night it burned like a furnace, and every instant I looked to see if my masts and my sails were not destroyed; these flashes came with such alarming fury that we all thought the ships must have been consumed. All this time the waters from heaven never ceased, not to say that it rained, for it was like a repetition of the deluge. The men were at this time so crushed in spirit that they longed for death as a deliverance from so many martyrdoms. Twice already had the ships suffered loss in boats, anchors, and rigging, and were now laying bare without sails.

When it pleased our Lord, I returned to Puerto Gordo, where I made repairs as well as I could.[9]

At the height of the storm, the Vizcaína was separated from the other three vessels; but fortunately, after an absence of three days, during which time she lost her boats, she managed to join the other vessels. After enduring such troubles of wind and sea they had two days of calm, a respite that encouraged many sharks to surround the ships, which some of the sailors considered to be a bad omen. Actually, these sharks proved to be a blessing in disguise, for the sailors had been over eight months at sea and had eaten all the meat and fish they had brought from Spain. The sharks were eagerly sought and caught by the crews, providing welcome fresh meals for the hungry, who had been eating spoiled food for survival:

What with the heat and the dampness even the biscuit was so full of worms that, God help me, I saw many wait until nightfall to eat the porridge made of it so as not to see the worms; others were so used to eating them that they did not bother to pick them out, for they might lose their supper by being so fastidious.[10]

On Saturday, December 17, the fleet put in a port that the Indians called "Huiva," probably the modern Lemon Bay, which is situated three leagues east of the rock called Peñon (actually a cliff at the mouth of the Río Chagres). In this channel-like bay they rested for three days. It was strangely prophetic that Ferdinand should describe Lemon Bay as being "a great channel" inasmuch as the northern entrance to the Panama Canal is in the same location. Had they still been interested in looking for a strait, they could have gone with canoes or boats up the Río Chagres and marched fifteen miles overland to the Pacific Ocean. Instead, it remained for Vasco Nuñez de Balboa in 1513 to discover the Pacific Ocean. They ventured ashore and were astonished to discover that the Indians lived in small cabins on the top of trees. On December 20, they set sail toward Veragua again but another storm arose, forcing them into another harbor, which they left three days later when the storm abated:

But the weather, like an enemy that lies in wait for a man, suddenly attacked us with such fury that it drove us almost to the Peñon, when as we were hoping to enter the harbor where we had first taken refuge, the wind whipped about so violently that it blew us into the harbor where we had been on Thursday, December 12. There we stayed from the second day of Christmas until January 3, 1503.[11]

This respite gave them an opportunity to repair the Gallega, take on maize, water, and wood, and steer for Veragua. But alas, foul weather and contrary winds burst upon them again so that again they suffered grievously; the Admiral thus named this section of the coast "La Costa de los Contrastes" (the Coast of Sudden Wind Changes). Because January 6 was the Feast of the Epiphany, they anchored near a river that the Indians called "Yebra" and the Admiral named "Belén" (Bethlehem). In the stormy weather, it took the fleet three days to cover sixty miles.

Chapter Forty-Two

AGONY AND TRAGEDY IN BELÉN

Once he had reached Veragua, Columbus immediately ordered the sounding of the sandbars of the Río Belén and of the Río Veragua directly to its west because both appeared to be too shallow. The Río Belén was about seven feet, and deeper than the Río Veragua; therefore, the Admiral decided to make it his headquarters. To reconnoiter the area, he dispatched several boats up the Río Belén. The men stopped at a village, where the Indians at first tried to prevent them from landing. After noticing the Spaniards' peaceful intentions, the Indians allowed them to approach. They informed them that there were gold mines in Veragua.

The next day the boats took off for Río Veragua, a league to the west of Belén, and proceeded up the river; again, they were met with the same resistance from the natives as on the previous day. It was obvious to the Spaniards that the Indians of that region were of Carib origin and not at all as hospitable as the Indians in Hispaniola. The Indian interpreter on the boat with the Spaniards told the local Indians that they had come to barter with them and would not take anything without payment. Apparently, the Spaniards had finally reached the gold country, for the Indians exchanged twenty disks of gold, some quills of gold dust, and gold nuggets for the usual trinkets of beads and hawks' bells. The Indians said that the gold mines were in distant mountains and that if they desired to extract gold from them they had to practice fasting and abstain from sexual intercourse. Ostensibly, this state of grace and purity was necessary to find gold, which they considered as a sacred and mystic treasure of the earth. This custom of fasting, prayer, and chastity was also practiced by the gold-seekers of Hispaniola.

CROSSING THE BAR OF THE RÍO BELÉN

Based on this favorable report, the Admiral made plans to cross the sandbar of the Río Belén and sail up that river. On Monday, January 9, the Admiral's flagship and the Vizcaína crossed the bar and proceeded up the river. The Gallega and Vizcaína missed the flood tide but managed to cross the bar the following day. The natives were very eager to trade for the fish that in certain seasons of the year swam there in incredible numbers. They also exchanged some gold for pins, strings of beads, and hawks' bells. Having been reassured again that Veragua was the site of the gold ore, the Adelantado left his vessels inside the Río Belén basin and took the boats down the coast, where he went up to Río Veragua to a village. When the Quibián learned of the Adelantado's visit, he went down to the river to meet him, accompanied by his subjects, in several canoes. He was tall and powerfully built, but of warlike demeanor. Nevertheless, they had a friendly meeting and bartered.

On the following day, the Cacique visited the ships and called on the Admiral on the Capitana; Columbus received him hospitably and entertained him. Before parting, the Admiral donated several presents to the Cacique, the mariners exchanged the usual trifles for gold.

On Tuesday, January 24, due to the constant rain they had endured for days, the Río Belén suddenly overflowed and the waters came rushing down precipitously, forcing the ships from their anchors and slamming the flagship against the Gallega, which lay astern; the blow carried away the sail and imperiled the ships. Columbus believed that a sudden heavy rainfall all along the range of distant mountains that he had named "San Cristóbal" had produced the onrushing flood. This casual observation by the Admiral is a meteorological truism. In Central America the mountains gather so much moisture from the trade winds that upon condensation, heavy rains are engendered and freshets rush down the mountainsides. The terrible weather continued unabated for another two weeks, precluding any exploration of the area but allowing the mariners to repair the ships that required re-rigging and caulking.

On Monday, February 6, the fair weather returned and the Adelantado, in command of sixty-eight well-armed, men left the Belén river basin, rowed down the coast to the Río Veragua, and went up to the village where the Quibián, suspicious of his motives, received him with restrained courtesy. So as not to appear openly unfriendly, he acceded to the wishes of the Adelantado to visit the mines and furnished three guides to conduct him.

Two days later, the Adelantado left some of his men to guard the boats and proceeded on foot with the rest. They covered a distance of four and a half leagues and spent the night near a river. The next day they advanced another league and a half, arriving at a dense forest luxuriant with vegetation and trees so tall they seemed to reach the skies. The guides furnished by the Quibián informed them that they had reached the mines and that gold could be found among the roots of the trees. On closer inspection, it seemed the soil was full of gold. In a few hours, each man had collected gold-bearing ore without digging. Their objective had been to locate the mine, for the time being. They had not come prepared with digging tools. They were very pleased with what they saw and were more ecstatic when the guides took them to the top of a hill and showed them the extent of the vast gold-mining territory—as far as the eye could reach, a distance of twenty days' journey westward. The party returned to the ships in high spirits, and Columbus was pleased with the results of the expedition.

To consolidate and protect his find, Columbus decided right then and there to build a town in Veragua and leave his brother in charge while he himself returned to Spain to bring the good news to the Sovereigns and ask them for reinforcements to work the mines. The Admiral already had visions of a Spanish-type settlement similar to the Portuguese São Jorge da Mina built on the Gold Coast of Africa that proved to be very profitable to Portugal. Despite the glad tidings of the gold discovery, Columbus soon learned that the Quibián had deceived the Adelantado by instructing the Indian guides to take him to the mines of a neighboring Cacique with whom he was at war. As Ferdinand explained it:

We later learned that these were not the mines of Veragua, which are nearer, but those of Urira. Because the people of Urira were at war with the Veraguans, the Quibián had guided the Christians thither to annoy his enemies and in the hope that the Christians would go to that country and quit his own.[1]

It might have been for this reason that, on February 16, the enterprising Adelantado and fifty-nine persons set out again overland, followed by a boat with fourteen more men aboard, to explore the coast westward. The next morning, they reached the Río Urira, which is seven leagues west of Río Belén. They received a friendly reception from the Cacique of that region who, accompanied by twenty followers, came to meet the Adelantado and presented him with food. They also had an opportunity to barter among themselves, the Spaniards obtaining many gold disks for the usual trinkets. An interesting observation made by the Christians was the peculiar chewing habit of the Cacique and his leading men. They never stopped chewing a dry herb (possibly the cocoa plant) and occasionally put a powder in their mouths. To Ferdinand this seemed a dirty habit.

The next day, the Adelantado sent most of his men, with many bartered gold discs, overland back to the ships while he continued on foot with thirty men to a village called "Cobreva," where they saw cornfields stretching for many leagues; from there, they proceeded to Cateba. In both villages they received a warm, hospitable reception, food, and gold mirrors by trading. Some of these disks:

Like the paten of a chalice, weighed about twelve ducats... these they wear hanging by a string about their necks, as we do an Agnus Dei or other relic.[2]

This trip convinced the Adelantado that though the people were very hospitable and possibly easier to live with than Quibián, he could not find along the coast a harbor or river comparable in size to the Río Belén with its huge, wide basin at its mouth, over the sandbars. The site for the new settlement had to have a good harbor for commercial purposes, and Belén was the logical choice.

THE NEW SETTLEMENT OF SANTA MARÍA DE BELÉN

Once the Admiral had accepted the Adelantado's report that the mouth of the Río Belén was the best place to establish a new settlement, he gave orders to start the construction immediately. In his letter to the Sovereigns, written later, he stated that he had seen more signs of gold in Veragua in two days than he had seen in Hispaniola in four years. Again, he began to think that these gold mines could have been the source of King Solomon's wealth:

Josephus believes that this gold was found in the Aurea; if it were so, I contend that these mines of Aurea are identical with those of Veragua, which as I have said before, extend westward twenty days' journey, and they at an equal distance from the Pole and the Line. Solomon bought all of it—gold, precious stones, and silver—but your Majesties need only send orders to seek them to have them at your pleasure.[3]

Columbus's plan was simple in scope. He would establish a settlement for exploring and working the gold mines. The Adelantado would remain with about eighty men while he himself would return to Spain for reinforcements and supplies. They chose a spot on high grounds on the banks of the Río Belén.

The eighty men who were to remain were grouped into parties of ten each and soon set about building houses of wood, thatched with leaves of palm trees. One house, much larger than the others, was to be used as a storehouse and arsenal. Most of the foodstuffs such as wine, biscuits, garlic, vinegar, and cheese, all Spanish food, were stored for greater security aboard the Gallega; the Admiral intended to leave this ship for the Adelantado. Because the local waters abounded with fish, all fishing gear such as nets and hooks also would be left behind. There was no danger of famine in the new settlement as long as the settlers maintained a friendly relationship with the Indians. There was plenty to eat for everybody. Fish was abundant and easily caught. Ferdinand related how during the rainy season, schools of fish swam close to shore to escape larger fish pursuing them. All the Indians had to do was to catch them in small nets as they rose to the surface. The Indians also cultivated maize and made good-tasting wine.

THE TRUCULENT CACIQUE

After the settlement of Santa María de Belén had been built and provided with the necessities for sustaining and protecting itself, the Admiral prepared to depart for Spain, but a very serious problem arose. The cessation of the January rains had caused the water level over the bar to drop to only half a fathom, preventing the fleet from reaching the sea. During the rainy season, the sandbar at the mouth of the river was four fathoms deep. But the rains had carried down more sand, nearly choking the mouth of the river. The Spaniards found themselves trapped. Their only hope now was for more rain to raise the water level.

This unforeseen situation turned out to be a blessing, for the Spaniards learned that the Quibián planned to attack the settlement, set fire to the houses, and kill all the Christians. The Cacique had hoped that the Spanish intruders would go away after visiting and surveying the area, but now it was apparent from their construction of the settlement that they were planning to stay. This was an invasion of his lands, and therefore, they must be overwhelmed and destroyed. The Quibián called for all warriors in his area to meet on his ground to make plans to destroy the settlement of Santa María de Belén; however, he pretended instead that his efforts were to make war on Cobrava and other places to the west. Some warriors in military array were seen passing the harbor, thus arousing the suspicion of Diego Méndez, the chief notary on the Santiago. Méndez relayed his fears to the Admiral and offered to row along the coast toward Veragua to search for the encampment. His offer was accepted and he immediately set out to look for it and found it just a couple of miles away around the headland. There on the shore he saw about a thousand warriors howling and yelling, eager for battle.

Landing from the boat alone after instructing the crew of the boat not to leave the landing site, he walked over among the Indians and offered to accompany them with his armed boat. Of course, the offer was rejected, but it had thrown a wrench into their plans, for they dared not move on Belén while Méndez was watching them from a position in the river, ready to sound an alarm if they made a move toward the settlement. In the morning, Méndez reported to the Admiral and expressed the opinion that the Indians had been on the way to spring a surprise attack on the Spaniards, when he had intervened. The Admiral replied that he needed more positive information before he took steps that would destroy a friendly relationship with the Indians.

Méndez then assumed the daring and dangerous mission to visit the Quibián, accompanied by Rodrigo de Escobar. They proceeded on foot alone, along the coast and near the mouth of the Veragua; they found two canoes with Indians who made no bones about telling the Spaniards that the Quibián was getting ready to attack the caravels within two days. With offers of presents, Méndez prevailed on the Indians to escort them to the village of the Cacique where the war group was encamped. There Méndez and his companion learned that the Cacique was nursing a wound in the leg, caused by an arrow. As the two Spaniards approached the Cacique's compound, a loud uproar broke out among the women and children; this prompted the son of the Cacique—a powerful man—to rush out and strike Méndez a blow that made him almost fall to the ground. With complete poise, the Spaniard collected his wits and told the Cacique's son that he had come to cure his father's wound and produced an ointment as proof. In addition, he showed him a barber's kit that he had brought as a present for the ailing Cacique. It was extremely important for the Spaniards, now that they were convinced that the Indians were certain to attack, that they return alive to their fleet. Accordingly, they played their friendship game to the hilt by showing the Indians their method of cutting hair. Méndez allowed his partner, Rodrigo de Escobar, to comb and cut his hair, to the delight of the Quibián, who did not hesitate to have his own hair cut. Méndez then presented the barber's kit to the Quibián, who obliged by sharing dinner with the uninvited guests. The Spaniards then speedily returned to the fleet to inform the Admiral of the portentous news.

CONSPIRACY OF THE NATIVES AND ITS TRAGIC CONSEQUENCES

Méndez's report, which a loyal Indian of that neighborhood confirmed, compelled the Admiral to take immediate action against a surprise attack. The Spaniards' superiority in military equipment and strategy would be no match in conventional open warfare, as they already had proven in previous battles with the Indians.

What worried the Admiral was the possibility of a surprise attack at night, which from all indications was exactly what the Quibián had planned. The Spanish fleet of worm-bored hulls was still landlocked and the settlement built of native wood with palm-thatched roofs could be reduced to ashes in a few hours. It was clear that the Spaniards could not wait for, nor resist, the coming onslaught. Strategy called for them to take the initiative. Both the Adelantado and Diego Méndez recommended the old but bold stratagem of kidnaping the Quibián and some of his lieutenants and holding them as hostages.

On Mach 30, an armed force of seventy-four men, including Diego Méndez, under the command of Bartholomew Columbus, set off in boats and proceeded to the mouth of Veragua. Quickly, without being noticed, they rowed up the river and landed at the foot of the prominence on which the house of the Quibián was situated. Leaving the main body of the force in ambush, with instruction to join him at a given signal, the Adelantado, Diego Méndez, and three other men walked boldly to the house and asked to see the Quibián, ostensibly to look at his wound. When the suspicious Quibián appeared, he asked the Adelantado to approach alone to look at his wound. Once near the Cacique, the Adelantado almost simultaneously took a hasty look at his wound and grabbed him by the arm. Immediately one of Diego Méndez's companions fired a shot from his arquebus as a signal for the rest of the Spaniards to come out of hiding to surround the house and come to their aid if necessary. The Quibián at first put up a struggle, but he was no match against the strong arms of the Adelantado. He was bound hand and foot and carried away with about thirty members of his household, including some of his wives and children.

The Quibián and several of his principal subjects were bound and entrusted to Juan Sánchez, chief pilot of the fleet; he was to carry them on the boat to Belén while the Adelantado remained on the shore with some of his men to finish. Sánchez secured the Cacique with a strong rope to one of the sturdy benches on the boat. In the darkness of the night the Cacique complained piteously that he was in great pain. Touched with compassion, Sánchez loosened the bonds but still held fast to the end of the rope.

The wily Cacique ceased to moan and wail to the great satisfaction of Sánchez. Then suddenly the Indian leaped overboard, forcing Sánchez to let go of the rope so as not to be dragged overboard. He disappeared into the night but Sánchez, who had to worry about the other prisoners, was unable to go after him. Now it was Sánchez's turn to moan and wail, deeply mortified by being outwitted by the savage. Little did he realize that the singular incident would deeply affect the fortunes and safety of their entire enterprise. The rest of the prisoners, delivered without any more trouble, were imprisoned in the Santiago. The Adelantado returned a little later with Diego Méndez, unscathed and loaded with booty. They had remained all night with the hope of pursuing the Indians who had escaped into the countryside, but when morning came and he saw the rugged nature of the terrain, he gave up the search for the Indians and concentrated instead on plundering the Cacique's house. He gathered many gold ornaments including bracelets, anklets, gold disks, and two gold coronets. The whole amount, worth about three hundred ducats, was divided among the party, except for the Crown's share which came to one-fifth of the whole.

The fate of the Quibián was not known. The Spaniards assumed that because he was bound hand and foot he had drowned in the murky waters. At least the interval of peace that followed his disappearance seemed to confirm his death.

It was now spring, and the rains came again; this time they proved to be beneficial because they raised the level of the water, thus allowing the sailors to tow the three ships destined for the homeward voyage over the bar, with a minimum of scraping of their keels. This was accomplished by removing most of their cargoes to lighten the ships and replacing them after crossing the bar. The Gallega was left in the Belén basin for the use of the Adelantado. He was to be left as commander of Santa María de Belén with Diego Méndez as his assistant and an additional seventy men. The homeward-bound fleet, after crossing the bar, was anchored within a league of the shore, awaiting a favorable wind. It was April 6 and the majority of the men were saying farewell aboard the caravels. There were only twenty men and their Irish wolfhound guarding the settlement when four hundred well-armed warriors raided it. The Indians managed to kill one and wounded several Spaniards, including the Adelantado. Diego Méndez, a boastful survivor, describes the Indian attack thus:

The Admiral had hardly put out to sea, leaving me on land with some twenty men, for the rest had gone with the Admiral to help his departure, when suddenly many natives, there must have been more than four hundred men, armed with bows, arrows, and slings, descended upon me and deployed along the mountain in a single file. They uttered a war-whoop, and another and again another; and thus by God's will warned me to battle and to defend myself against them. I was standing on the beach among the huts I had erected and they were on the mountains within the spear's range when they began to shoot arrows and darts as if they were goading a bull. The arrows and darts fell as thick and fast as hail and some of them made a sortie in order to attack us with clubs, but none of them returned; they lay there dead, victims of our swords, with arms and legs cut off. As a result of this fight, all were so terrified that they retired, after having killed seven [sic] of our twenty men in the battle; themselves lost nine or ten of the men who had been the boldest in attacking us. This battle lasted three hours and our Lord miraculously gave us the victory, we being so few and they so many.[4]

While the battle was going on, Captain Diego Tristan of the Capitana was offshore with two boats and twelve men, watching the bloody proceedings. He had left the ships at the roadstead and was on his way up to Río Belén to take freshwater for the long voyage. When the fight was over, Tristan and his two boats continued on his mission, despite a warning from Diego Méndez, who continues with his story:

I advised and warned him not to go up the river; he refused to listen to me and went up with two barges and twelve men. There the people attacked them, did battle with him, and killed him and his whole company except a man who escaped by swimming and brought us the news. And they [the Indians] took the barges and broke them, thus causing us great anxiety, since the Admiral was out to sea with his ships with no boats and we ashore had no means of getting out to him.[5]

The death of Captain Tristan and his men did more to dismay the Spaniards than any other previous calamitous event. From the evidence gathered by the sole survivor, Juan de Noya, a cooper from Seville who saved himself by diving overboard and swimming underwater, the Spaniards had rowed about a league past the village of the Quibián when they were ambushed by the Indians. Spears and arrows rained on them from every side. They came from canoes, which surrounded the boat, from the banks of the river, and even from overhanging branches of trees. The loud yelling, war whoops, and blasts from conch shells added to the confusion of the Spaniards, who, not having any room for action, took cover under their bucklers thus allowing the canoes to close upon the boat to strike their lethal blows. There were only three soldiers among the besieged group, but they never had a chance to use their firearms. Tristan, who fought valiantly, was wounded several times but kept on fighting to spur the entire crew into battle. Finally, a spear pierced his right eye and struck him dead. It was a grossly uneven fight and soon everyone in the boat except Juan de Noya was killed. The bodies were allowed to float down the Río Belén, the bloated, grotesque corpses exhibiting a depressing sight to the comrades as carrion birds fed on them.

THE ADMIRAL'S LAMENT— ABANDONMENT AND DEPARTURE

Columbus had been left alone aboard the Capitana anchored offshore, because Diego Tristan had left to fill the flagships flasks upstream on the Río Belén. He was feverish with malaria and rendered delirious by the sounds of battle in the distance. He wrote in his "Lettera Rarissima":

I was outside very much alone on this rude coast with a high fever and very fatigued. There was no hope of escape. In this state I climbed painfully to the highest part of the ship and cried out for help with a fearful voice, weeping, to Your Highnesses' war cap-

tains, in every direction, but none replied. At length groaning with exhaustion I fell asleep and heard a compassionate voice saying, "O fool, and slow to believe and serve thy God, the God of every man! What more did He do for Moses or for David His servant than for thee? From thy birth He hath ever held thee in special charge. When He saw thee at man's estate, marvelously did He cause thy name to resound over the earth. The Indies, so rich a portion of the World He gave thee for thy own and thou hast divided them as it pleased thee. Of those barriers of the Ocean Sea, which were closed with such mighty chains, He hath given thee the keys. Thou hast obeyed in so many lands, and thou hast won noble fame from Christendom. What more did He do for the people of Israel, when He carried them out of Egypt; or David whom from a shepherd He raised to be king over Judea? Turn then to Him and acknowledge thy faults; His mercy is infinite; thine old age shall not hinder thee from performing mighty deeds, for many and vast heritages He holdeth. Abraham was past one hundred when he begat Isaac, and Sarah was no young maiden. Thou criest out for succor with a doubting heart. Reflect, who has afflicted thee so grievously and so often, God or the world? The privileges and promises which God bestows, He doth not revoke; nor doth He say, after having received service, that was not His intention, and that it is not to be understood differently. Nor doth He mete out suffering to make a show of his might. Whatever He promises He fulfils with interest; that is His way. Thus, I have told thee what thy creator hath done for thee and what He doth for all men. He hath now revealed to me a portion of the rewards for so many toils and dangers thou hast borne in the service of others."

I heard all this as in swoon, but I had to answer to give in definite words; so true, only to weep for my transgressions. Whoever he was he finished by saying, "Fear not, but have trust. All these tribulations are written on tablets of marble and not without cause."[6]

This letter by Columbus has been the subject of controversy among scholars, some of whom have theorized the Admiral suffered from paranoid schizophrenia. Others have spoken of him as a person with a tormented spirit, obsessed by an inflated ego. But Columbus cannot be judged as an ordinary man who operated within ordinary circumstances. Alone in a ship in the middle of an unknown and unexplored continent, with hostile natives threatening from all sides, racked with fever and exhaustion, Columbus lashed out at the Sovereigns for not recognizing the extent of his discoveries and accomplishments, for not understanding the full impact of his prophetic mission, and for denying him the honors and privileges rightfully due him. Again, under these extreme circumstances Columbus showed he was indeed an extraordinary man. In spite of enormous difficulties facing him, with death staring at him, he was still hopeful that he would survive and receive the proper reward for his mission, if not on this earth, certainly in heaven. As for the vision, what is more natural than a religious man running to his God in a moment of despair? If he seems contradictory in his remarks, it is because of his spontaneity of expression, as statements of fact, hope, and observation rapidly follow each other like the waves of a stormy sea.

His style is not classical, but it is passionate, direct, dramatic, imaginative, vivid, and powerfully poetic—the work of a born writer—in spite of his lack of formal education. In this respect, Washington Irving observed:

The artless manner in which, in his letter to the Sovereigns, he mingles up the rhapsodies and dreams of his imagination with simple facts, and sound practical observations pouring them forth with a kind of scriptural solemnity and poetry of language [which] is one of the most striking illustrations of a character richly compounded of extraordinary and apparently contradictory elements.[7]

ABANDONMENT OF SANTA MARÍA DE BELÉN

While these tragic events were taking place, there was a complete breakdown of communication between the vessels anchored offshore, the Adelantado's garrison at Belén, and Tristan's voyage up the Veragua River seeking freshwater for the vessels offshore to depart. Even the Admiral, alone in his flagship, spent ten days in anguish waiting and wondering why Tristan had not returned with the water and most important, with the boat, although he must have suspected what might have happened.

To make matters worse, the Indian hostages held on the Santiago managed to escape. At night these prisoners, including women and children, were confined below deck for safety. The sailors slept on top of the hatch, thus preventing the hostages' escape and securing a comfortable, dry spot for themselves. One night, the captives put together a pile of stones that served as ballast; standing on it they forced open the hatch, thus spilling the sleepy sailors onto the deck. Very quickly, before the sailors could secure help, the most able of the captives leaped overboard. The sailors then secured the hatch shut with a chain and went back to sleep. The next morning when the hatch was opened a ghastly sight greeted the sailors. All the remaining hostages had hanged themselves from the deck beams with pieces of rope from the hold. With some hostages gone and the remainder dead, the Admiral lost all bargaining power for a possible reconciliation and peace with the Indians.

It was obvious now that once the Quibián discovered what had happened to his people he would renew his attacks on the settlement until it was destroyed. It was important to establish communication immediately with the Adelantado, as his situation in the settlement could be desperate. Only the boat of the Santiago was available and the river bar was still blocking the entrance to the lagoon. Pedro de Ledesma volunteered to swim from the bar into the lagoon if the remaining boat would take him to the seaside of the bar. He got his wish and managed to swim from the bar to the settlement and brought back the alarming news that the garrison was near the point of mutiny at the thought they would be left behind. They sent back word begging the Admiral that to leave them behind would mean certain death. Columbus hated to give up Santa María de Belén thus signifying defeat, but there was nothing else to do as he remembered only too well the disaster at Navidad. Besides, this time it was not only the lives of his shipmates that were in jeopardy but that of his brother as well. The problem now was the transfer of men, equipment, and provisions from the settlement to the caravels; the enterprising Diego Méndez had some clever solutions. But again, they were at the mercy of the terrible weather that lasted for eight days. Then:

The weather so improved that the garrison could begin to transport themselves and their gear over the bar, using their single boat and two large canoes lashed together so as not to overturn.[8]

But what a task it was! For fear that the bad weather would be upon them, they planned to complete the operation in two days. Diego Méndez, uncommonly resourceful, cut up the sails of the Gallega, destined to be left behind in the lagoon, to make sacks to receive biscuits and other provisions. He lashed the two Indian canoes with the ship's spars for maximum stability against the waves and made a platform upon which they carried the heavy stuff and equipment such as arms, ammunition, and even dismantled furniture. Then, the well-freighted raft was towed by the only remaining boat to the ships. Almost anything of value was transported by making many trips from the Gallega hulk to the ships. The Admiral was so impressed by the dedicated labors of Diego Méndez that he promoted him to the command of the Capitana, vacated by the unfortunate death of Diego Tristan.

Nothing could equal the joy of the sailors when they found themselves together again onboard their ships. Despite the worm-eaten condition of their vessels, they wanted to get as far away from the coast of Veragua as possible because they had endured so much pain and hardship; that forsaken, storm-battered coast might very well have been their grave site had they not decided to pull up the stakes.[9]

Chapter Forty-Three

HOMEWARD BOUND FROM BELÉN

On April 16, 1503, Easter night, the Admiral sailed from Río Belén with La Capitana, the Santiago, and the Vizcaína. The Gallega was left behind because it had been damaged beyond repair. Destination: Santo Domingo for repair or new ships, thence Spain.

Columbus had correctly estimated that Belén lay on a meridian (coinciding with the central or northern part of Cuba, approximately 80°W longitude). Because Santo Domingo was situated on approximately a 70°W meridian, it was to his advantage to sail eastward along the coast of Central America, where the winds were favorable, and then head north on a single tack if possible. By so doing he would have a much shorter Caribbean passage and the additional advantage of making a landfall in Jamaica, if the westward equatorial currents were unduly active. This was a rational and intelligent plan; it was also a safe one as the early part of the voyage would be made along the coast. But the pilots of the vessels figured it differently. "This decision caused much grumbling among the seamen, for they thought the Admiral intended to sail a direct route to Spain with unfit and ill-provisioned ships," wrote Ferdinand.[1]

Columbus was aware that many adventurers had followed on this track as soon as his navigation plans for the third voyage had been made public. This time he would not share his knowledge of the location of the gold mines in Veragua with any members of his crew. Indeed, he even took the charts away from his pilots, thus incurring the enmity of the Porras Brothers, Francisco, the captain of the Santiago, and Diego, the auditor of the fleet. Despite the complaints, Columbus continued along the "Costa de los Contrastes" and had gone eastward barely one hundred miles when he was forced to abandon the Vizcaína on April 23 at Portobello.

The crew was transferred to the other two caravels, which certainly needed more manpower to pump out the water threatening the damaged Capitana and Santiago. Rounding the cape beyond Portobello, the two-ship fleet sailed past Retrete, then beyond Point Blas, and headed southeast towards the present Golfo de Uraba, passing many islands and cays off one of the most beautiful coasts in the world—known today as San Blas Islands—which Columbus named "Las Barbas" (the Beards or Whiskers). They spent the night on one of the islands, because Columbus was becoming wary of all the cays in his path.

On Monday, May 1, 1503, after sailing 125 miles from Portobello, the fleet reached a headland at the entrance of the Golfo de Uraba, formerly known as the Gulf of Darien; the Admiral called it "Marmóreo" (Marble) possibly because the cliffs were streaked with pale veins. This might have been near the present Panamanian town of Ustupo, located at approximately 78°W meridian and approximately 9°10'N latitude. This is the same meridian that intersects Montego Bay in Jamaica.

Here he held a conference with his captains and pilots, who protested against his insistence on sailing further away from the appointed goal (so they thought) when the ships were in such a deplorable state. Moreover, they were certain the Admiral was already east of the Caribbean Islands, when in actuality the fleet was nine hundred miles west of those islands. Regretfully, he acceded to their demands and set his course due north for Hispaniola. He would have done much better if he had crossed the Golfo de Uraba (Gulf of Danien) and followed the coast of Colombia to the Peninsula de la Guajira before striking northward. They had good sailing helped by a steady easterly wind with a strong current to the west.

By May 10, they had crossed the Caribbean Sea, missing Hispaniola and even Jamaica, and sighting two small islands full of turtles, which Columbus called "Las Tortugas" (Turtles). These were the Cayman Islands—Little Cayman and Cayman Brac—about 110 miles northwest of Jamaica. The fleet did not stop but continued directly north; it arrived on Friday night, May 12, at the Jardíne de la Reina, thirty leagues further north on the south coast of Cuba, which the Admiral had visited on his second voyage. They anchored about ten leagues from Cuba, possibly among the cays. The landfall did not exempt the crews, though already fatigued, from continuing to pump the water out of the hulls of the ships.

The crews were also suffering from hunger. There was nothing to eat but biscuits and a little oil and vinegar. To make matters worse, there came a sudden storm at midnight with such heavy rains and winds that:

The world appeared to be coming to an end, the cables of the other ship broke, and [the weather] came down upon my vessel with such force that it was a wonder we were not dashed to pieces; the single anchor that remained to me was, next to the Lord, our only preser-

vation. After six days, when the weather became calm, I resumed my journey, having already lost all my tackle; my ships were pierced by borers more than a honeycomb and the crew entirely paralyzed with fear and despair.[2]

After struggling against contrary winds and the currents, they anchored at a village on the southern coast of Cuba called Macaca, where the Admiral had touched before in 1494 during his second voyage. With only one anchor left, the ships had to be fastened together to stay put. Fortunately, they found friendly natives there who kindly supplied the hungry crews with cassava bread and refreshments.

Columbus was now in familiar territory. He had the choice of sailing ESE directly to Hispaniola against the wind and current, a distance of two hundred miles across the Windward Passage to the westernmost point of the island, or beat due south to Jamaica, a distance of one hundred miles. The latter was the safer approach, for if the ships were still afloat, he could chance the jump to Hispaniola's western tip, Cabo San Miguel, in Xaragua. Columbus decided on the Jamaica alternative and Ferdinand agreed, as he noted:

We stood over toward Jamaica because the easterly winds and the strong westward-running currents would have never let us make Hispaniola—especially since the ships were so riddled by the shipworm that day and night we never ceased working three pumps in each of them, and if any broke down, we had to supply its place while it was being patched up.[3]

They nearly did not reach Jamaica, for on the eve of St. John's Day (June 23), the water level in the ships had reached almost up to their decks. In this precarious state and by superhuman efforts, they were able to make Puerto Bueno (Montego Bay) by morning. But this harbor had no source of freshwater to sustain them nor any Indians to help them, they sailed eastward; the next day and with the help of a land breeze, they put in a harbor twelve miles away enclosed with reefs. This was the port that Columbus had named "Puerto Santa Gloria" in 1494. Ferdinand's narration continues:

Having got in, since we were no longer able to keep the ships afloat, we ran them ashore as far as we could, grounding them close so they could not budge; and the ships being in this position the tide rode almost to the decks.

Upon these and the fore and stern castles we built cabins where the people could lodge, making our position as strong as possible so the Indians could do us no harm; for at that time the island was not yet inhabited or subdued by the Christians.[4]

And so, on June 25, 1503, they settled down in Puerto Santa Gloria in Jamaica, in a makeshift home with an ocean view. The problem now was how to survive in a hostile territory and how to feed the mouths of 116 hungry sailors and, most importantly, how to get home. They remained there for a whole year.

MAROONED IN JAMAICA

The decision to beach the two caravels in Santa Gloria (Saint Ann's Bay) was an excellent one. A good source of freshwater was available from two local rivers nearby, and the Indian village of Maima was situated less than a mile inland. Columbus, however, was concerned about the misbehavior of the Spanish sailors—

their lust and their inhumane treatment of the Indians had caused so much grief in the past. The natives of Jamaica were of the Taino stock, the same hospitable and docile Indians the Admiral had encountered in the Bahamas and Cuba. But they could be driven to hostility by the wanton deeds of the visitors. Consequently, the Admiral issued the order that no one was to go ashore without permission. With the last rations of biscuits and wine gone, the Admiral ordered Captain Diego Méndez, with three other men, to go into the interior of the island and bargain for food. Once again, this enterprising adventurer was equal to his task. The diplomatic but cunning method he used to obtain a continuous source of victuals is dramatically told in the following passage from his will:

Here I gave out the last ration of wine and biscuits, and taking a sword in my hand went with three men into the interior of the island, since no one had yet dared to search for food for the Admiral and his men. By God's mercy I found the natives so gentle that they did me no harm. On the contrary they welcomed me and willingly gave me food, and in the village of Aguacadiba I arranged with the chief and his men to make cassava bread, hunt and fish, and give a certain amount of food to the Admiral each day, which they were to bring to the ships in exchange for the blue beads, combs and knives, fishhooks, bells, and other articles which we carried for the purposes of barter. After making this agreement, I sent one of the Christians who was with me to the Admiral, asking him to appoint someone who could pay for these provisions and make sure of their dispatch.

…From there I went to another village three leagues away and made a similar agreement with its Cacique and sent another

Christian to the Admiral asking him to appoint someone to act for him in the same way here. From there I went on to visit a great Cacique, whose name was Huareo, at a place now called Melilla, which is thirteen leagues from the ships. This chief received me kindly and gave me a good deal of food and ordered his subjects to bring him a quantity of provisions in three days' time. These were brought and I paid for them in such a way as to leave them content. I arranged that more supplies should be regularly brought and that someone should stay there to pay for them and, having made this arrangement, sent another Christian to the Admiral with the food I had obtained. I also asked the Cacique to give me two Indians who could accompany me to the extreme end of the island, one to carry the hammock in which I slept, the other to carry the food.

Thus, I traveled to the easternmost cape of the island, where I visited a chief, whose name was Ameyro, with whom I swore fraternal friendship, giving him my name and taking his, which is considered a great sign of brotherhood among them. I bought from him a very good canoe, giving him in exchange a very fine brass helmet which I was carrying in a bag, also a coat and one of my two shirts. I embarked in the canoe with the six Indians whom the Cacique had given me to help me row it, and put out to sea in search of the other places I had visited. On arriving at these places where I had gathered food, I found the Christians there whom the Admiral had sent, and entrusted them with the provisions I had brought with me. I then went to the Admiral, who gave me a fine welcome. He was so delighted to see me that he embraced me again and again, asking me about all that had happened on my journey and thanking God for having brought me back safely and delivered me from all these savage people. On the day that I got back to the ships they had no bread left to eat. They were delighted to see me, since they were so short of everything that they were dying of hunger.

From that time onwards, the Indians came every day, carrying provisions to the ships from the villages where I had arranged for the supplies, which were enough for the 230 persons [sic] who were with the Admiral.[5]

Now that an arrangement had been made with the Indians to supply food, the Admiral began to wonder how long it would last. Sooner or later the voracious appetite of the Spaniards—according to Ferdinand, they ate ten times more food than the Indians—would not be satisfied and trouble with the Indians might ensue. One wonders why the Spaniards, so hard-pressed for food, had to rely on the Indians for their supply. With the ocean all around them, why did they not go fishing? Why did they not plant corn or hunt the ratlike hutias? Instead, when their immediate wants were satisfied, Columbus began to plan for the future. Their eventual salvation was to be rescued by the people in Hispaniola. It was useless to repair the vessels as they had neither the tools nor the men capable of redoing the worm-eaten hulls. Both of his caulkers had been killed in Belén and there were no shipwrights in the fleet. The only logical solution was to send a messenger in an Indian canoe to Hispaniola to secure a rescue vessel. It would have been easier to reach Hispaniola on one of their ship's boats, but they had no boats left as the last one had been lost at Cayo Breton during the recent storm. The Admiral approached the intrepid Captain Diego Méndez, a man he deemed capable of making the long trip. The following is Méndez's own account of the conversation:

Ten days later the Admiral called me aside, and told me of the great danger he was in. "Diego Méndez, my lad," he said to me, "none of my people realize the danger of our situation except you and myself. We are very few, these savage Indians are very many, and we cannot be certain that their mood will not change. One day, when the fancy seizes them, they may come and burn us here in these two ships which we have turned into houses. For since the roofs are of straw, they will easily be able to set them alight from the landward side and roast us all alive. It is true that you have made this arrangement with them to bring us food every day, and at present they are doing so willingly. But tomorrow the fancy may seize them to act otherwise, and supplies will cease. If they do not choose to bring us food, we are not in the position to take it by force. I have thought of a remedy, about which I should like your opinion. Suppose that in this canoe you have brought, someone were to risk making the crossing to the island of Hispaniola, he could there buy a ship in which we could escape from our very great danger. Let me hear your opinion about this."[6]

Diego Méndez replied that he was aware of the peril and that it was impossible to traverse the gulf of forty leagues in a rough sea. He also added that he could not think of a single person in the fleet who would venture to do it. The Admiral agreed with Méndez's appraisal but insisted that he was selling himself short, for indeed he would be capable of doing it. To this Méndez replied:

My Lord, I have often put my life in danger to save yours, and those of my companions, and Our Lord has marvelously preserved me.[7]

Then, as gesture of modesty, Méndez mentioned that perhaps other people should be given an opportunity to volunteer and when everyone had begged off, he would risk his life in the Admiral's service, as he had often done before.

The next day the Admiral had all hands brought to the quarterdeck and asked for volunteers for the perilous voyage. However, not only were there no takers, but he was also told most emphatically that the trip was impossible in canoes and that many tall ships had been lost in the channel because of the fury of the currents. Then Méndez arose and, in the spirit of Patrick Henry, said:

My Lord, I have only one life, but I will risk it in your Lordship's service and for the good of all those here present. For I trust the Lord God, that being witness to the purpose from which I act, He will preserve me as He has done many times before.[8]

The Admiral was so moved by Méndez's determination and act of faith that he arose to embrace him and to kiss him on both cheeks.

Méndez lost no time in preparing for the crossing. The following day he pulled his canoe ashore and began to work on it to make it seaworthy. He made a false keel, then pitched and greased it, and finally secured washboards at bow and stern to keep the sea from coming inside. He then rigged a mast and sail and laid in enough provisions for himself, one comrade, and six Indians, who would be required to do the rowing.

In the meantime, Columbus wrote letters to Ovando in Hispaniola, requesting that a ship be sent immediately to pick up the marooned sailors. Columbus also wrote his famous "Lettera Rarissima" to the Sovereigns and a short personal note to his friend Fray Gaspar Garricio of the Monastery of Las Cuevas in Seville. After alerting Ovando to Columbus's plight, Méndez was to proceed to Spain to deliver the other messages to the Sovereigns and Fray Garricio. Apparently, Columbus had abiding faith in Méndez and in the success of his mission.

THE LETTERA RARISSIMA

The letter to the Sovereigns known by historians as the "Lettera Rarissima," from which we have already quoted, is incoherent but powerful; it is interspersed with complaints, pathos, religious mysticism, cosmography, and fantastic conclusions. It reflects the pains and frustrations he had endured and the realization that old age was at hand and that his vaunted "High Voyage" had to come to an inglorious end. But he does not speak about his failure to find the strait and he displays with pride his genius as a navigator and his merits as a discoverer. And it is for this latter reason that he brings to their attention the great importance of the discovery of Veragua. Then, unabashed, he describes his deplorable situation and entreats the Sovereigns to send a ship to bring him and his crew home.

It is hardly conceivable that Columbus wrote this long letter in its entirety in Jamaica. He probably started it much earlier in his voyage and simply wrote it a bit at a time, according to his moods, as he sailed along. This may explain the letter's incoherence. The first part of the letter consists of his narration of sailing from Cádiz to Hispaniola to Panama and highlights his struggles with storms and the deplorable conditions of his ships. While discussing maritime and weather problems, he pauses to reflect on his personal misfortune:

Such is my fate, that the twenty years of service through which I have passed with so much toil and danger have profited me nothing, and at this very day I do not possess a roof in Spain that I can call my own; if I wish to eat or sleep, I have nowhere to go but to the inn or tavern, and most times lack wherewith to pay the bill. Another anxiety wrung my heartstrings, which was the thought of my son Diego, whom I had left an orphan in Spain, and dispossessed of my honor and property, although I had looked upon it as a certainty, that your Majesties, as just and grateful Princes, would restore it to him in all respects with increase.[9]

The second part deals with geographic knowledge and conceits, and winter tempests. The third part describes the passage to Jamaica and includes his request for help. The fifth part, seemingly unrelated, deals with navigation and many miscellaneous events. In the final part, he complains about ships, privileges, and the bad treatment given him. He is especially bitter about the Bobadilla incident:

I was twenty-eight years old when I came into your Highnesses' service, and now I have not a hair upon me that is not gray; my body is infirm, and all that was left to me, as well as to my brothers, has been taken away and sold, even the frock that I wore, to my great dishonor. I cannot but believe that this was done without your royal permission. The restitution of my honor, the reparation of my losses, and the punishment of those who have inflicted them will redound to the honor of your royal character; a similar punishment also is due to those who plundered me of my pearls, and who have brought out a disparagement upon the privileges of my admiralty. Great and unexampled will be the glory and fame of your Highnesses, if you do this; and the memory of your Highnesses, as just and grateful sovereigns, will survive as a broad example to Spain in future ages. The honest devotedness I have always shown to your Majesties' service, and the so unmerited outrage with which it has been repaid, will not allow my soul to keep silence, however much

I may wish it: I implore your Highnesses to forgive my complaints. I am indeed in as ruined a condition as I have related; hitherto I have wept over others—may Heaven now have mercy upon me, and may the earth weep for me. With regard to temporal things, I have not even "blanca" for an offering; and in spiritual things, I have ceased here in the Indies from observing the prescribed forms of religion. Solitary in my trouble, sick, and in daily expectation of death, surrounded by millions of hostile savages full of cruelty, and thus separated from the blessed sacrament of our holy Church, how will my soul be forgotten if it be separated from the body in this foreign land? Weep for me, whoever has charity, truth, and justice! I did not come out on this voyage to gain to myself honor or wealth; this is a certain fact, for at the time all hope of such a thing was dead. I do not lie when I say that I went to your Highnesses with honest purpose of heart, and sincere zeal in your cause. I humbly beseech your Highnesses, that if it please God to rescue me from this place, you will graciously sanction my pilgrimage to Rome and other holy places. May the Holy Trinity protect your Highnesses' lives, and add to the prosperity of your exalted position.

Done in the Indies, on the island of Jamaica, on the seventh of July, in the year one thousand five hundred and three.[10]

This letter was delivered to the Sovereigns, but they hardly took notice of his feelings, nor did they commiserate in any way with his desperate situation.

START OF THE MÉNDEZ–FIESCHI VOYAGE TO HISPANIOLA

Having converted his Indian canoe for an ocean voyage, as already explained, by erecting a mast and sail and storing victuals for himself, a fellow mariner, and six Indians, Diego Méndez departed along the coast eastward. The trip was arduous not only because of the adverse strong currents but because of piratical attacks by roving canoes of Indians. In one instance they were made prisoners, but escaped to reach the easternmost point of the island, thirty-four leagues from where they had left. Then as Méndez was waiting for the sea to become calm before beginning his crossing:

Many Indians gathered with the intention of killing me and taking the canoe and its contents. Once gathered, they drew lots for my life to see who should be fated to carry out their plan. When I saw this, I slipped off to my canoe, which I had beached three leagues away, raised my sail, and returned to the place where I had left the Admiral fifteen days before.[11]

Méndez does not mention the fate of his comrade nor of the Indians. Of course, Columbus was disappointed with the failure of the voyage but extremely happy that Méndez had returned safely. He asked him whether he had the courage to try it again, and Méndez replied that he would if he were given protection from the marauding Indians until he got to the end of the island. The Admiral acceded to his demands and provided seventy armed men under the command of the Adelantado to escort not only Diego Méndez but Bartolomeo Fieschi, the Genoese captain of the Vizcaína, whom Columbus had decided to send along for additional protection and to enhance the chances of at least one boat getting to Hispaniola. It was decided that Méndez and Fieschi would each have his own boat consisting of six Christians and ten Indians. Méndez would be responsible, once he had reached Hispaniola, to charter a ship and then proceed to Spain to deliver Columbus's letter. Fieschi, after reaching Hispaniola, should return as soon as possible with the news that help would be on the way.

After all arrangements had been made, the Indians entered the canoes with their gourds of water and their frugal provisions of cassava bread, water, and biscuits. The Spaniards brought along a fresh supply of hutia meat in addition to their swords and shields.

They pushed eastward along the coast with the Adelantado and his small army keeping pace with them in a fleet of canoes. There was no attempt made to molest them, and they reached the easternmost point of the island without any trouble. Because the sea was very rough, they waited three days for favorable winds before they made a tearful farewell to their comrades. The Adelantado watched the canoes until they disappeared at nightfall in the horizon. The following day he returned to Santa Gloria, stopping along the way to pay visits to friendly Indians, reassuring them of the Admiral's good intentions and friendship.

Chapter Forty-Four

SEEKING HELP IN HISPANIOLA—MUTINY IN JAMAICA

Bidding farewell to the Adelantado on a hot July day in 1503, Méndez and Fieschi took off eastward on a direct course for Hispaniola, urging the Indians in both canoes to make good speed before sunset. The sea was perfectly calm and, because there was no wind to fill their makeshift sails, the canoes' movement was powered totally by the Indians. But the heat was intolerable and, from time to time, the Indians leapt into the ocean to cool and refresh themselves. During the night, half the Indians took their turn at paddling while the other half slept. In like manner, the Spaniards took their turn; half of them would sleep and the other half kept guard with their weapons at hand ready to defend themselves in case of mutiny. They paddled all night and, despite their periodic rest, the Indians were thoroughly fatigued by daybreak.

The captains urged their men to take the paddles, permitting the hard-pressed Indians a deserved respite. Indeed, at times, the captains themselves shared the arduous task. Now another serious problem arose. During the preceding hot day and sultry night, the Indians, heedless of future needs, had drunk all the water. With another hot day, the heat and resulting thirst grew worse, and by noon they were so exhausted they could not row anymore. Apparently, the captains anticipated this and began to dole out mouthfuls of water from a spare keg that each one had secretly stored aboard. By so doing they were able to keep them rowing until the cool of the evening.

They cheered them with the hopes of soon arriving at a small island called Navarra, directly in their path; this was only eight leagues from Hispaniola. Here they could rest and procure water. According to their calculations, they should already have been there, for the captains had estimated that they had covered twenty leagues. But Ferdinand claimed that:

Even with hard paddling, a canoe cannot make more than ten leagues in a day and night on account of the currents turning counter to the course from Jamaica to Española.[1]

That night one of the Indians died of thirst compounded by exhaustion. His body was tossed into the sea. The others lay panting on the bottom of the canoes, but after a short pause, they resumed their rowing albeit very feebly. They attempted to cool their parched mouths with saltwater and they continued until nightfall for a second time without sight of land. They reached the point where the Indian rowers could barely move their paddles, thus necessitating doling out the last few drops of water in their kegs. Now the captains despaired of even finding the tiny island of Navarra. Diego Méndez, constantly on the lookout for the island, was observing the rise of the moon above the distant horizon, when he noticed the outline of a small island covered the lower segment of the satellite like an eclipse. He immediately cried out, "Land! Land!" and joyfully pointed out to the despairing crews their welcome destination. Instilled with new vigor and hope, they were able to reach land by the dawn of the day.

They gave thanks to God and proceeded to look around for water, but the island was devoid of trees and springs and rivers. It was a rocky island only half a league around, and not able to support vegetation; however, rainwater could be found in puddles and in the hollows of the rocks. The Spaniards warned the Indians not to drink freely of that stagnant water, but suffering greatly from thirst, they disregarded their admonition and filled their stomachs and gourds with it. Several died as a result, and others were made dreadfully sick.

Water satisfied their thirst but not their hunger. The men found some shellfish that the enterprising Méndez cooked over driftwood by striking a flame with flint and steel he had brought along. They rested for most of the day on that island and were overjoyed at discerning the mountains of Hispaniola eight leagues away. In the cool of the evening they left Navarra—which, incidentally, is to date the site of a lighthouse maintained by the United States—and arrived safely the next day at the westernmost point of Hispaniola at Cape San Miguel, so named in 1494 because it was sighted by Michele de Cuneo.

SEARCHING FOR HELP IN HISPANIOLA

They rested for two days on the shores of Cape San Miguel (changed by the Spaniards to "Cape Tiburon" and later by the Haitians to "Cap Carcasse"):

Bartolomeo Fieschi, standing on his honor as a hidalgo, proposed to return as the Admiral had ordered. But since his crew were mere Indians and sailors, exhausted and ill from their labors and from drinking seawater, not a man would come with him. The

Christians, for their part, felt they had been delivered from the whale's belly; and their three days and nights corresponded to those of the prophet Jonah.[2]

At this point, Fieschi and Méndez went in different directions. Fieschi remained behind in an effort to find a way of returning to Jamaica. Méndez took six Indians of the island and with his canoe headed eastward along the coast of Hispaniola in an attempt to reach Santo Domingo, 130 leagues away, even though he was suffering from a sickness that Ferdinand attributed to his great privations by land and sea. Méndez himself, however, did not mention being afflicted with any illness. It may very well have been a periodic illness that recurs at seventy-two-hour intervals, like quartan malaria. If that was the case, he must have been a hardy individual to undertake a 130-league voyage against the currents while being subject also to the perils of hostile Indians and the weather. But Méndez had been given orders to find Ovando promptly so that his comrades in Santa Gloria might be saved. He reports laconically:

After traveling eighty leagues along the coast, not without great peril and toil, I reached the province of Azua. Here I was informed by the comendador Gallego that the governor had gone to pacify the province of Xaragua, which was fifty leagues away. On learning this, I left my canoe and set out on foot for Xaragua, where I found the governor, who kept me with him for seven months, during which time he burnt or hanged eighty-four Caciques, among them the lady Anacaona, the greatest chieftain in the island who was obeyed and served by all the others.[3]

Ovando, in contrast to the Columbus brothers, governed with an iron hand, "pacifying" the island by literally exterminating the natives. The reader will recall that the beautiful Anacaona was the widow of Caonabo and sister of the Cacique of Xaragua, after whose death she became the Cacique. She was a virtuous and talented lady. Her wanton execution by Ovando angered Queen Isabella.

The fact that he detained Méndez seven months indicated that he had no wish to rescue Columbus and his men, for fear the Admiral would have his privileges restored. Insofar as he was concerned, he hoped that all would perish. After seven months, Ovando allowed Méndez to go to Hispaniola and attempt to lease a ship to rescue Columbus and his men. But as soon as he had left, Ovando dispatched a caravel under the command of the pardoned rebel Diego de Escobar, on a spying expedition to Jamaica to assess and possibly tantalize the hapless men marooned there. The choice of Escobar was a deliberate attempt on the part of Ovando to embarrass Columbus, because Escobar had been one of the leading rebels under Roldan.

MUTINY OF THE PORRAS BROTHERS

Méndez and Fieschi had been gone but a few weeks when the men at Santa Gloria began to grow restive and sickly after months of activities in which they were constantly on the alert—sailing, exploring, fighting for their lives in the worm-ridden ships on stormy seas, and confronting savage Indians. The marooned men suddenly found themselves in idleness, which, in due time, becomes the most active cause of evil. An old English proverb states that an idle brain is the devil's workshop, for when the devil tempts idle people, trouble is certainly to follow. They began to complain about the food, and many fell sick with the Indian diet. August and September went by without any sign of Fieschi. October, November, and December passed and the ship that Méndez was supposed to have chartered did not show up.

Some men sank into despondency, others began to complain openly, while others let their imaginations get the best of them.

They were sure that Méndez and Fieschi had met with disaster, and their fate was doomed. Something had to be done. They could not go on with a life of confinement in their cold and damp beached ships. They began to talk about mutiny and rallied around the Porras brothers, who had already shown seditious inclinations for several months. Francisco de Porras, captain of the Santiago, and his brother Diego, the royal representative and comptroller, were political appointees who had contributed very little to the success of the voyage. They had powerful friends at court and were confident that they could get away with almost any act of insubordination, for the Porras' sister was the mistress of Don Alonso de Morales, High Treasurer of Castile.

So it was with a great deal of arrogance that on January 2, 1504, nearly six months after Diego Méndez and Fieschi had left in search of help, that Diego de Porras, followed by forty-eight mutineers, confronted the Admiral in the sterncastle of his ship, demanding an explanation for his lack of initiative. Guessing what was afoot, the Admiral calmly replied that he knew no way of getting home until a ship was sent to pick them up, that he was just as anxious of getting home as any one of them, and that if he or his followers had any other plan to propose he would be glad to hold meetings—as many as necessary—to discuss that plan. Porras replied that there was no time for talk. The Admiral must decide either to embark or stay with God. Then turning his back on the Admiral, he cried out, "I'm for Castile, who's with me?" The cry for revolt met with immediate support from his followers, who ran around in great disorder, weapon in hand, and shouting, "To Castile! To Castile!" Ferdinand describes this hostile confrontation as follows:

Although the Admiral was in bed so crippled with gout that he could not stand, he nevertheless got up and hobbled to the scene of the mutiny; but three or four honest fellows, his servants, fearing the mutineers might slay him, forced him with great difficulty to return to bed. Then they ran to the Adelantado, who lance in hand was bravely defying the mutineers, and they took the weapon from his hand by force and shut him up with his brother. They begged Captain Porras to go with God and not be the cause of a murder, which was bound to harm them all and for which he would certainly be punished. They said none would seek to hinder him from going.[4]

On leaving the ships, the mutineers piled into ten canoes that had been tied to them and headed eastward. Many other men, not mutineers but afraid of being left on the island, piled into the canoes, leaving behind a few loyal men but many invalids. Ferdinand remarked that if all men had been in good health hardly twenty would have remained.

Despite his illness, the Admiral came out of his cabin soon after the mutineers had left and entreated his men, even those who were sick, to remain loyal and put their faith in God, who would redeem them from their misfortune and suffering and bring them safely home, where the Sovereigns would reward them for their loyalty to the Admiral and their country.

In the meantime, the mutineers, under the leadership of Francisco de Porras, were paddling their way eastward along the coast of the island, following the route of Méndez and Fieschi to Hispaniola. Wherever they landed they demanded provisions from the Indians and refused to pay for anything, telling them that the Admiral would pay for everything they took, and suggesting that they should kill him if he refused. Having reached the jump-off point—the easternmost point of the island—they paused to wait for good sailing weather and to take on some Indians to do the rowing. On the first calm day they took off and had easy sailing at the start, but when they had scarcely made four leagues, contrary winds arose and the sea began to swell. Unable to cope with rough seas, they became frightened and headed back for the shore.

When the overloaded canoes began to take water, they threw overboard all unnecessary items in order to lighten the load. This, of course, made the canoe more unstable as the wind grew rougher. At swords' point, they forced some Indians overboard to lighten the load even more. The Indians could not make any distance in the rough sea and swam until exhausted, and when they tried to rest by clinging to the gunwales, their hands were hacked off by the mutineers. They killed eighteen in this way, sparing only a few they needed to steer the canoes; this was the Indians' reward for listening to their false promises and their pleas for aid. After returning to shore, they had a meeting to determine what they should do. Some suggested sailing to Cuba, as the voyage would be made easier with the aid of the winds and current, then sailing across the windward passage to Cape Saint Nicolás in Hispaniola. Others suggested returning to the ships, making peace with the Admiral, and taking arms and provisions away from him to replace those thrown overboard. Still others were convinced that they should wait for another period of calm weather and sea before trying again. They decided on another trip and retired to a nearby village, living off the Indians for about a month and waiting for the proper wind and calm sea before making a second and even a third attempt. Both failed due to the contrary winds. They abandoned their canoes and returned westward on foot, robbing food from the Indians and supporting themselves by foul or fair means, depending on whether they were received with kindness or hostility.

COLUMBUS'S CELESTIAL STRATAGEM TO OBTAIN PROVISIONS

With Porras and the mutineers gone, Columbus's loyal followers, about half of the original group, were literally decimated by sickness or despondency. Despite his own infirmity, the Admiral did all he could to hasten the recovery of the sick and lift the spirits of the despondent with words of encouragement and hope. Every one of the healthy men was given a job to do. Some were to take care of the sick, others to mount guard on the wreck and still others to ration provisions, with the sick getting the lion's share of the food. Discipline returned among the group and regulations issued by the Admiral, calmly but firmly enforced, restored loyalty and order once more. Columbus had thus succeeded in preventing against internal dissension, in curing the sick, and in instilling pride and loyalty in his men. Just as everything seemed to go well for the Admiral, his men reported that the provisions supplied by the Indians were falling off gradually and finally ceased to be delivered altogether.

Apparently, the Spaniards' trinkets lost their value as means of bartering as they became more common. Porras's mutinous actions against the Admiral had caused the Indians to lose respect for him; as a result, they stopped bringing food. The Indians were also well aware of the reduced strength of those left on the wrecked ships. It would have been dangerous to try to obtain food from the Indians by force for they ran the risk of being annihilated by superior forces. Columbus at first tried to resolve the problem by offering more trinkets for food, but the Indians kept raising the value of their provisions, in an attempt to force the Admiral and his people off the island.

Confronted with what seemed an unsurmountable problem, the Admiral conceived the idea of playing upon the Indians' superstitious nature to obtain food. From his knowledge of astronomy, and his copy of the Regiomontanus *Ephemerides*, he knew that in three days' time, at midnight on February 19, 1504, to be precise, there would take place a total eclipse of the moon. So, through his Indian messenger, Columbus summoned all the Caciques aboard the Capitana where the Admiral, through his Indian interpreter, made a little speech, which can be paraphrased as follows: All Christians believe in God, who lives in heaven. God rewards those who live a good life and punishes those who are wicked. He had protected Diego Méndez and Bartolomeo Fieschi and permitted them to cross over to Hispaniola despite suffering many trials and tribulations, because they obeyed the orders of their commanders. On the other hand, He had prevented Porras and the mutineers from crossing because they had rebelled against the loyalists. Now this same God was angry against the Indians because they had refused to furnish His faithful worshippers with food for which they were willing to barter, and intended to punish them with famine and pestilence. Furthermore, to convince the non-believers, God would give them a warning from heaven that evening: they would see the moon change its color and gradually plunge the world into darkness, a token of the fearful punishment that God was prepared to visit upon them.

Many of the Indians were greatly alarmed by the predictions, others scoffed at the threats, but all waited patiently for the rising of the moon:

But at the rising of the moon the eclipse began and the higher it rose the more complete the eclipse became, at which the Indians grew so frightened that with great howling and lamentation they came running from all directions to the ships, laden with provisions and praying to the Admiral to intercede with God that He might not vent his wrath upon them and promising they would diligently supply all their needs in the future. The Admiral replied that he wished to speak briefly with his God, and retired to his cabin while the eclipse waxed and the Indians cried all the time for his help. When the Admiral perceived that the crescent phase of the moon was finished and that it would soon shine forth clearly, he issued from his cabin, saying that he had appealed to God and prayed for them and had promised Him in their name that henceforth they would be good and treat the Christians well, bringing provisions and all else they needed. God had now pardoned them, in token of which they would soon see the moon's anger and inflammation pass away. Perceiving that what he said was coming true, they offered many thanks to the Admiral and uttered praises of his God as long as the eclipse continued. From that time forward they were diligent in providing us with all we needed and were loud in praise of the Christian God. [5]

This celestial observation did even more for Columbus than just obtaining provisions from the Indians. It allowed him to calculate the latitude of Santa Gloria Bay in Jamaica with amazing accuracy, considering the crude instruments he had available at the time: the ampolleta (hour glass) and the quadrant. He had noted in the *Book of Prophecies* that the latitude of Santa Gloria was 18°26'N, an error of less than half a degree!

Chapter Forty-Five

HOME AT LAST

It had been eight months since the departure of Diego Méndez and Bartolomeo Fieschi; because no news of their arrival in Hispaniola had been received, the men in Jamaica suspected the worst. Méndez and Fieschi had either drowned or met with foul play at the hands of the Indians. Natives reported seeing a boat adrift down the coast of Jamaica and this heightened the foreboding. It was this news that prompted one Bernal by name, an apothecary from Valencia, and two others, Alonso de Zamora and Pedro de Villatoro, to foment another conspiracy and escape from Jamaica by seizing the remaining canoes.

The mutiny was about to break out when one day, past the noon hour, a small caravel suddenly came in from the sea and anchored near the grounded ships. Her captain, Diego de Escobar, came aboard the Capitana and presented two casks of wine and a slab of salt pork to the Admiral with Ovando's compliments. He also gave the Admiral a message from Diego Méndez to reassure him that he had arrived safely in Hispaniola and would send a rescue ship as soon as he could obtain one. It was obvious that Diego de Escobar had been sent by Ovando not to rescue Columbus but merely to spy on him and report back. Through

Escobar, Ovando apologized for not having sent a vessel large enough to take all the men aboard but hoped to send one along as soon as one was available. Because Escobar indicated that he was prepared to return to Hispaniola that same evening, Columbus hastened to write a letter to Ovando thanking him for his solicitude and reminding him that, because of the dreadful situation existing in Jamaica, it was necessary that a relief ship be sent promptly.

The Admiral and his men were comforted by the coming of the caravel but were puzzled at the aloof and insensitive behavior of Escobar. Columbus sought to dispel their suspicion by reassuring them that another larger vessel would certainly be coming, and by revealing that he himself had declined to depart with Escobar because the vessel was too small to take everybody aboard. He also reassured them that Escobar's haste in departing was at his own request so that no time would be lost in getting a vessel large enough to take everyone to Hispaniola.

THE BATTLE OF SANTA GLORIA

Despite his disappointment at Diego de Escobar's short visit, the Admiral considered the event propitious and favorable in establishing a truce and rapprochement with the Porras faction. He, therefore, sent two of his men to inform them of the recent arrival of Escobar with messages from the Governor of Hispaniola promising prompt deliverance. Columbus also let it be known that he was ready to grant the mutineers free pardon, decent treatment, and a passage in the rescue ships if they returned under his command. To show that he was acting in good faith, he sent them a thick slice of Ovando's pork. The mutineers, however, indicated that they would come back only if they could dictate the terms of surrender. These included preferential space on the ship and a share of all stores and provisions still in the beached ships. Columbus's envoys considered their demands unreasonable and unacceptable, whereupon Porras dismissed the envoys with the threat that the mutineers would take what they had asked for by force. The mutineers lost no time in marching toward Santa Gloria, hoping to seize the ships and take the Admiral prisoner. They marched to an Indian village called Maima, barely a quarter of a league from the ships.

When the Admiral learned of the mutineers' intentions, he sent the Adelantado, backed up by fifty well-armed men, to confront them. Still hoping for a peaceful solution, he sent ahead the two envoys who had previously attempted to negotiate with the mutineers. Porras misconstrued this action as a sign of weakness and dismissed the envoys without giving them an opportunity to state their case. With shouts of "Kill! Kill!" they charged the loyalists with swords drawn and lances in the air. Their strategy was to kill the Adelantado, believing that once he was slain the others would give up the fight. However, the Adelantado did not wait for the onslaught, choosing instead with sword in hand to meet the enemy head on. A pitched battle took place in which the mutineers were severely mauled by the loyalists, four or five of them being killed at the first impact. The Adelantado with his own hand killed Juan Sánchez, the sailor who had carried off the Quibián at Belén, and then Juan Barber, who had threatened the Admiral at the start of the mutiny. Francisco de Porras was taken prisoner and the rest of the mutineers put to flight, leaving behind them the dead and wounded. The Adelantado suffered a wound in the hand, and his chief servant—the only fatality—died from a lance cut on the side. Ferdinand gives a vivid account of the gruesome injuries sustained by Pedro de Ledesma:

As for the rebels, Pedro de Ledesma, the pilot who had gone with Vicente Yañez to Honduras and who swam ashore to Belén, fell over a cliff and was hidden from sight that day and till nightfall of the next, only the Indians knowing where he was. Curious to know how our swords cut, they opened up his wounds with little sticks. He had a cut on the head so deep that one could see his brains; another on the shoulder, which was almost severed, so that his arm hung limp; one thigh was cut to the bone down to the shin; and the sole of one foot was sliced from heel to toe so it resembled a slipper. Despite these wounds, when the Indians annoyed him he would growl at them, "Get away, or I'll do you a mischief," and these words alone caused them to run away in great alarm. When the ship's people learned of his plight, they came and brought him to a palm-thatched hut nearby where the dampness and mosquitos alone should have finished him off. Having no turpentine, the ship's people used oil to cauterize Ledesma's wounds, which were so numerous that during the first eight days of his cure the surgeon swore he was always discovering new ones. Yet he recovered at last; but the chief servant, for whose life none feared, died.[1]

On the next day, May 20, the rebels sent a petition to the Admiral asking forgiveness for their rebellion and promising to return to serve him faithful as before. The Admiral granted them complete pardon but insisted that their ringleader, Francisco de Porras, should remain a prisoner and be put in irons on board. As for the rest of the mutineers, he did not allow them to fraternize with the loyal followers on the wrecked ships. Instead he placed then under the supervision of a captain and allowed them to forage on the island, trading with the Indians whenever possible, until the coming of the rescue vessels.

RESCUE AT LAST

Ovando detained Diego Méndez in Xaragua until March 1504. From Xaragua, Méndez made his way on foot to Santo Domingo, but had to wait another two months before any ships came from Spain. Ovando did not allow him to charter the only caravel available. Finally, a fleet of three ships arrived from Spain; Méndez was able to charter the smallest one. He had it provisioned and sent it to Jamaica under the command of Diego de Salcedo. His mission accomplished, Diego Méndez returned to Spain in one of the other caravels in order to deliver Columbus's letters to the Sovereigns, to Don Diego, and to Pedro Garricio. As news of Columbus's misfortunes reached Hispaniola, Ovando's neglect in not sending a rescue vessel promptly to his aid aroused public indignation. Las Casas, who was then in Hispaniola, reported that Ovando was actually criticized publicly by preachers. Ovando was so embarrassed that at the last minute he ordered another caravel to accompany the ship charter by Diego Méndez.

The arrival of two vessels in Jamaica late in June, under the command of de Salcedo, to whom Columbus incidentally had given the monopoly of soap for the Indies, brought great joy to the marooned mariners. They had been in Jamaica a year and five days. They set sail on June 28, 1504, and they fought contrary winds and currents all the way to Santo Domingo. The crossing of the strait, which had taken Méndez and Fieschi four days, took them three weeks, but they did not go the same route. They made a landfall at Beata Island on August 3, where the Admiral wrote a grateful letter to Ovando. Contrary winds detained the fleet there for a while, but they finally arrived in Santo Domingo on August 13. Ovando received Columbus with great show of honor and reverence, then invited him to his house as a guest, "...but it was a scorpion's kiss, for at the same time he released Captain Porras, the ringleader of the mutiny..." wrote Ferdinand.[2]

Columbus had been forbidden to land in Santo Domingo, a city that his brother had founded, on his outward voyage; now that he arrived in its harbor a sick, broken-down, shipwrecked man, the population welcomed him. But the Admiral was very bitter at the governor's usurpation of his powers and prerogatives. Not only did Ovando set free Porras, but he also talked of punishing the Admiral's men who had killed some of the mutineers. The sly, contemptuous governor then indicated that all the events occurring in Jamaica were within his jurisdiction and that this included all the islands and terra firma. Columbus protested again that he had absolute command, both civil and criminal, over all who sailed in his expedition, but to no avail. Sick at heart and humiliated, the Admiral realized he had no power over the very lands he had discovered.

Thus, he made plans to leave Hispaniola as soon as possible. The majority of his crews remained in Hispaniola rather than chance more seafaring. Because they were destitute, Columbus provided them with money out of his own funds and even paid for the voyage home for those who chose to return. Another ship was chartered especially for the Admiral, the Adelantado, his son, and all his servants and staff—the remainder of the crews that once had manned a proud fleet took passage on the small caravel that had taken them from Jamaica. They set sail for Spain on September 12, 1504, almost eight years from the day Columbus first set eyes on the New World. He was never to see it again.

The passage home was long and stormy. The small caravel that had rescued them in Jamaica broke her mast just outside the Ozama and had to turn back for repair. Columbus went on with his chartered ship, making very little progress. On October 19, the mainmast broke in four pieces during a violent storm that had threatened to capsize the ship:

But the valor of the Adelantado and the ingenuity of the Admiral, who could not rise from bed on account of his gout, contrived a jury mast out of a lateen yard, which we secured firmly about the middle with ropes and planks taken from the stern and forecastles, which we tore down.[3]

Later in the voyage, another storm broke the foremast, but they were able to sail without it a distance of seven hundred leagues until they reached the port of Sanlucar de Barrameda on November 7, 1504, after a passage of fifty-six days from Santo Domingo. Columbus's odyssey was finally over. The sea had tried its best to claim him as its own but to no avail!

No mariner in history had surmounted so many difficulties as the Admiral. He sailed through uncharted seas. He never lost a ship throughout his career, except for the Santa María, for which he cannot really be blamed. On this voyage, he met the challenge of angry seas, adverse tides, violent storms and hurricanes, tropical downpours, and even tornadoes and waterspouts—all with resilience and acceptance, always trusting in God. He suffered with his crew through the suffocating tropical heat, thirst and hunger, and the hostility of the natives. In the end, lowly shipworms, those dreaded teredos, were his undoing. He finally suffered the indignities and bloodshed of a mutiny before being rescued by an unwilling and envious rival.

But he was home now, albeit in very poor health. The hard years of exploration had taken their toll on the once vigorous and hale Admiral. He was disappointed at not finding the strait he sought but heartened by his discoveries of an isthmus and the extensive gold mines in Veragua.

Columbus's homecoming from his fourth voyage was hardly noticed. He had come from his first voyage in triumph, looking like a Roman general, lionized by the public and honored by royalty. After his second voyage, he had returned in the garb of a humble Franciscan friar. His return from the third voyage saw him transfigured into a vanquished king in chains, which had evoked a sympathetic response from the general public. Now, he had come home as a shipwrecked sailor, and hardly anyone noticed or cared. The ailing Admiral with his brother, son, and servants went up the Guadalquivir River from Sanlucar to Seville to rest before reporting to the Sovereigns.

Part IX

THE DEATH OF COLUMBUS
EPILOGUE 1505–1573

Chapter Forty-Six

DEATH OF COLUMBUS

Columbus's return from his fourth voyage was greeted with the proverbial cold shoulder. King Ferdinand at that time was holding court at Medina del Campo, about three hundred miles north of Seville. Queen Isabella was gravely ill. The king's concern for his wife may explain in part his apparent indifference toward Columbus, but Seville was the home office of "La Casas de Contratación de Las Indias," a kind of "India office" whose responsibility was to take notice, investigate, and approve the traffic to and from the Indies. Columbus was also ignored by this agency as well. Francesco Pivello, an Italian financier, who had lately become a naturalized Castilian, was its director. The secretary, Ximeno de Briviesco, a man Columbus had knocked to the ground during preparations for his third voyage, was a bitter enemy of his—which explains the snub.

Columbus had been away two and a half years; his "Alto Viaje," though full of mishaps, made important discoveries, yet nobody seemed to notice his return—at least not the bureaucrats who were busy pleasing the king and the new governor of Hispaniola, Don Nicolás de Ovando. The reader will recall that Ovando had left Cádiz on February 13, 1502, with a magnificent fleet of thirty vessels and 2,500 men for the colonization and exploitation of Hispaniola. From a certain point of view, Ovando had succeeded where Columbus had failed. When Columbus had left Hispaniola in chains in 1500, there were three hundred discontented settlers on the island. Now, four and a half year later, there were ten thousand people, and Santo Domingo was becoming a thriving city. Most important, in the current year it was estimated that eighteen million maravedis of profit were filling the royal coffers.

It did not matter that Ovando was literally exterminating the native population of the Indies; after all, is not gold the lifeblood of a rising empire? To this one might answer: "But must that blood be obtained through the forced bleeding of other human beings?" Queen Isabella's illness notwithstanding, King Ferdinand was not about to go out of his way to receive Columbus. News already had reached him that Columbus had lost his entire fleet, that he had not found the strait, and that he had brought back very little gold. The Admiral was convinced that the gold mines of Veragua were a more productive source of gold than those available in Hispaniola. He felt, however, that the time for exploiting them was not propitious. He did not want to plunder the country but he felt that gold would be collected more easily through peaceful means once the land was settled.

Columbus's conscience was clear. He had served the monarchs of Spain with great diligence. If he had failed in anything, it had not been for want of eagerness on his part.

COLUMBUS SEEKS RESTORATION OF HIS RIGHTS

Columbus's poor physical condition, aggravated by the hardships of his recent voyage, precluded an audience with King Ferdinand. He resorted instead to writing letters, mostly to his son who, living at court, was his logical advocate. Diego had actually been reared under the eyes of the monarchs, had outgrown his position of page, and had become a handsome twenty-four-year-old officer of the queen's bodyguards. He was well liked and admired, particularly by the young ladies of the court, one of whom would eventually make him a kin of the king himself through marriage. Diego had received the letter written by Columbus in Jamaica and given to Diego Méndez for delivery; therefore, he could assume that King Ferdinand had also received the "Letter Rarissima." It was clear then that the king was not inclined to receive the Admiral and be confronted with the same old problems and complaints, especially when the queen was on her deathbed, according to many courtiers.

Broken by infirmities and concerned by the onset of old age, what Columbus wanted most from the king was not an approbation of his voyage but a restoration of his rights and an honest accounting and payment of what was owed him, as he was having a cash-flow problem and wanted prompt restitution. As befitting his rank of Admiral, Columbus leased a house in Seville large enough to accommodate all of his servants and attendants. He was well-off financially but complained continually that he was not getting his fair share of income due him from his properties in Hispaniola, taken by Bobadilla and eventually retained by Ovando. Yet, Ovando handed over to Columbus a chest full of coins to take home with him on his last voyage. Alonso Sánchez de Carvajal, who had been looking after Columbus's affairs in Hispaniola, had safely shipped a large sum of gold due him on the vessel that escaped the dreadful hurricane off Hispaniola in 1502. By his own admission, Columbus claimed that he had left sixty thousand gold pesos in Hispaniola, against which the Genoese merchant-bankers of Seville, Francesco de Ribarol and

Francesco Doria, allowed him to draw. The former, incidentally, had lent the Admiral money that he had invested in the fourth voyage, this being one-eighth of the expenses as required by the Articles of Agreement of 1492. On November 21, he wrote another letter to his son:

I have received your letter by courier. You have done well to stay where you are to remedy and take cognizance of our affairs. The Lord Bishop of Palencia [Diego de Deza] ever since I came to Castile has favored me and desired to honor me. And now is the occasion to ask of him that he be pleased to find a remedy for all my troubles; and that their Highnesses send me the necessary writing and credentials, so that by command all can be set straight and damages awarded.[1]

In this letter, Columbus added a postscript on behalf of his unpaid men and signed it with an often-repeated salutation:

I turn again to write a word for the attention of their Highnesses, begging them that they command pay be given to these men who were with me, for they are poor and it goes on three years since they left their homes. The news which they bring back is more than great. They have passed through infinite perils and labors...Speak of this to the Secretary of the Bishop and to Juan Lopez and to whomsoever you find convenient. Your father who loves you more than himself.[2]

Columbus was more concerned about the payment of his veteran seamen than for himself. They had been advanced six months' pay initially and thereafter were not to draw any more pay until they returned to Spain. Columbus was well aware that some of these persons for whom he was pleading were his enemies, and had even joined Porras's mutiny against him. Yet, his disposition for justice and forgiveness would not permit him to be revengeful.

Several days after the dispatch of his letter to his son, Columbus learned that the Porras brothers were pleading their case in court; without even waiting for a reply, he sent another letter dated November 28:

I should like to have a response from their Highnesses, and that you should procure it for me. I hope in Our Lord to be able to part from here next week. My regards to Diego Méndez. I trust that his veracity and diligence will prevail over the lies of the Porras brothers. Your uncle has been very sick and his malady is in his jaws and teeth.[3]

But there was no answer from the Sovereigns. Queen Isabella was on her deathbed.

THE DEATH OF QUEEN ISABELLA

The happiness that had surrounded Queen Isabella following Columbus's discovery of the Indies, and later the profitable dynastic marriages of all her children, was short-lived. A succession of domestic calamities had fallen upon the noble queen with intermittent regularity since the death of her demented mother, Isabella of Portugal, in 1496.

The Infante Prince Juan, heir to the throne of Castile, died in 1497 after a brief marriage to Princess Margaret, daughter of Emperor Maximilian of Austria. The following year, Isabella, who had married King Manoel I of Portugal, died in childbirth after delivering a boy, Miguel, the heir apparent to the throne of

Castile. Unfortunately, Prince Miguel died one year and seven months after his birth, dashing forever the possibility of uniting Portugal and Spain. After Princess Juana married Archduke Philip of Hapsburg, she began to show signs of mental illness, causing additional grief to her brave mother. Queen Isabella was never to recover from these family misfortunes, which sapped her vitality and strength. In the spring of 1504, Ferdinand fell seriously ill with a fever; the queen contracted the same disease accompanied by more severe symptoms, which because of her weakened condition, she could not fight off. She knew that the end was imminent and on October 12, 1504, she executed her will. She made arrangements for her burial and provided financial assistance to several charities of her choice, to poor maidens without dowries, for example; she also set aside a considerable sum for the redemption of Christian prisoners in Moorish jails. Concerned about the royal succession of Princess Juana because of her mental instability, she prescribed that King Ferdinand be the regent of Castile until her grandson, Charles, should come of legal age. Juana would assume the role of Queen Proprietor with the Archduke Philip as her husband. Then as evidence of her eternal love, she stated:

I beseech the King my Lord, that he will accept all my jewels or such as he shall select so that seeing them, he may be reminded of the singular love I always bore him while living, and that I am now waiting for him in a better world; by which remembrance he may be encouraged to live more justly and holily in this.[4]

On November 23, three days before her death, she added a codicil to the will, prescribing some public measures, particularly the codification of the laws. For this purpose, she appointed a commission to make a study and come up with a new digest of the statutes and "pragmaticas." The second measure was related to her concern for the just treatment and conversion of the Indians to the holy faith, a concern prompted no doubt by Ovando's cruelty toward them.

She died before noon on Wednesday, November 26, 1504, after receiving the sacraments of her faith. She was fifty-four years old and had reigned gloriously for thirty years. Upon hearing of the death of his benefactress, Columbus expressed his sincere bereavement in a letter to his son:

A memory for thee, my dear son Diego, of what is at present to be done. The principal thing is to commend affectionately, and with great devotion, the soul of the Queen our Sovereign to God. Her life was always Catholic and holy, and prompt to all things in His holy service; for this reason, we may rest assured that she is received into His glory, and beyond the cares of this rough and weary world. The next thing is to watch and labor in all matters for the Sovereign, the King, and to endeavor to alleviate his grief. Remember the proverb which says, "When the head suffers all the members suffer." Therefore, all good Christians should pray for his health and long life; and we who are in his employ ought more than others to do this with all study and diligence.[5]

Peter Martyr, the court chronicler, in a letter to the archbishop of Granada, written the same day of the queen's death, mourned the queen's death as did the French and Italian writers of the day, joining in celebrating the memory of a woman who left a mark upon her times.

Isabella is best remembered today as the queen who supported Columbus in his discovery of the New World. But she was a towering figure in her times. She brought Spain from a small feudal state to the rank of a world power. She was intelligent, charitable, pious, and endowed with a strong moral courage, which sustained her in her dark hours.

She was a superb administrator who brought order and stability to her realm by confronting and solving a multitude of problems: the Wars of Succession, the codification of the nation's laws, the lowering of the nobles, the subordination of the church, the elimination of corruption, and the regulation of trade. She was actively involved in the war with Granada and made important military decisions in winning it. With these achievements, in addition to being a loyal wife and dedicated mother of five children, Isabella deserves more from history than simply to be known as the queen who gave Columbus the opportunity to discover a New World. Her accomplishments qualify her as one of the great personalities of her age—certainly a model for the women of the world.

The queen's death was a terrible blow to Columbus. He had lost a sympathetic patron who, more than anybody else, believed and trusted in him and had actually consoled him in his hours of affliction. A week after the queen's death, on December 3, the Adelantado and Ferdinand, who was sixteen at that time, left for Medina del Campo. The primary mission of the Adelantado and his nephew was, of course, to look after the interests of the Admiral. It was known that the queen had made a will that was very favorable to interests of her husband. She knew that at her death he would cease to be King of Castile and that her daughter, Juana (La Loca, or "the demented"), the wife of the fickle Archduke Philip of Burgundy, would succeed her; therefore, she bequeathed to her husband not only her personal income but also half of all the profits accruing from the commerce with the newly discovered Indies. Columbus had hoped that the will would have addressed his contractual problems, but his name was never mentioned in it.

THE LONELY AVID CORRESPONDENT

With the Adelantado and Ferdinand gone to court and with the winter coming on to add pain to his afflictions, the Admiral kept contact with people by writing many letters: in some requesting favors, in others advice; in some giving information, and in others seeking comfort and sympathy.

On December 21, as Columbus intended to travel to court to present his case to King Ferdinand, he wrote to his son Diego to apply for a license to ride a mule. At that time, in an effort to increase the availability of horses in the realm, riding mules was forbidden to everyone, except clergy and women.

On December 29, Columbus wrote to his son again, asking for the mule permit. He received it on February 23, 1505, but due to the cold weather, he postponed his trip until May. By New Year's Day, 1505, Columbus's physical condition had grown worse. It became apparent to him that "la gota," the arthritis that had grown on him with age and the hard life at sea, had made him a permanent invalid—he would never be able to go to sea again. He decided not to seek restoration of his offices in Hispaniola. Because his rights were hereditary, he decided to petition the king to confer the governorship on Don Diego. He was anxious for an audience with King Ferdinand, but the winter weather made it impossible. He would wait for the springtime.

Columbus wrote an account of his voyage to the recently elected Pope Julius II (1503–13) and mailed it unsealed to Diego with instructions that it be looked over by Diego de Deza, the new Archbishop of Seville and by the king. It is doubtful whether the new pope ever saw the report.

Then, hearing a rumor that three bishops were to be appointed for the Indies, Columbus tried to submit the names of two men he held in high esteem: Fray Gaspar and Fray Juan Pérez. But no one consulted him in the affairs of the New World—a rebuke he felt deeply. The only friend of Columbus ever appointed to an episcopal see in the New World was Alessandro Geraldine, fifteen years after the death of the Admiral.

On February 3, Columbus was visited by Amerigo Vespucci, the Florentine explorer who wanted to sail once more for King Ferdinand. Vespucci, as ship chandler, had helped outfit Columbus's fleet for the third voyage in 1498. On February 5, the Admiral wrote Diego:

I have spoken with Amerigo Vespucci, the bearer of this letter. He is going to court, where he has been summoned in connection with points of navigation. He has always been anxious to please me. He is a very honorable man. Fortune has been against him, as against so many others. See what he can do to profit me there and try to have him do it.[6]

We do not know whether Vespucci put in a good word for the Admiral in his meeting with the King; neither do we know the reason for his meeting with the Sovereign. We do know, however, that following his voyage with Alonso de Hojeda to the Pearl Coast, Vespucci had gone to Portugal and made two important voyages along the coast of South America with Coelho, the second one looking for a strait to the Asian Indies as far south as the present San Julian, about four hundred miles north of the southern tip of Tierra del Fuego. He returned to Lisbon on June 28, 1504. The Spanish Sovereigns welcomed Vespucci and eventually planned to have him sail westward, north of the equator, to seek discovery of a strait not found by Columbus. Is it possible that Vespucci's visit had something to do with these plans that never materialized? Vespucci was held in such high favor in Spain that Queen Juana, who succeeded the throne of Isabella, named him to the newly created post of "Pilot-Major" of Spain in March 1508.

COLUMBUS SEEKS HIS REDRESS AT THE KING'S COURT

When the balmy days of May returned to Andalusia, Columbus felt equal to undertaking his long mule-back journey north to Segovia, where King Ferdinand was holding court. In due time he was received by the king with kindness and respect. Columbus, as customary after his voyages, gave a vivid report of his voyage stressing the riches of the province of Veragua, the great tract of terra firma he had explored, the beaching of his vessels in Jamaica, the mutiny of the Porras brothers and their followers, and his eventual rescue by Ovando. His majesty listened with apparent interest but showed no emotion. Obviously, he had heard the same report before and had already formed his own opinion. Later, the Admiral petitioned the king to order restitution of his rights and indemnification for damages suffered.

Columbus's rights were clearly defined in the document known as "The Capitulations of Santa Fé." It granted him the title of Admiral, Viceroy, and Governor of the lands he had discovered, titles to be passed on to his descendants; it granted him the tenth part of the profits from the lands discovered; and it granted him the right to invest one-eighth of the cost of new expedition and to receive one-eighth of the profits from such enterprises. In addition, Columbus demanded a third of all trade conducted in the discovered territories. Columbus discovered that Alonso Enriques, the admiral of Castile, took approximately one-third cut on all trade over his jurisdiction. Thus, he demanded the same right. In letters and arguments, when reference is made to his property rights, Columbus often refers to them as "my tenth, eighth, and third rights."

Like Pontius Pilate, the king was indecisive at the time, and the Admiral took advantage of the situation by suggesting that Don Diego de Deza, his old friend and presently the Archbishop of Seville, be delegated as arbitrator to settle the issue. The king readily approved, as he always held a high opinion of the archbishop as being an upright, honest, fair, and avid supporter of the Spanish exploration of the New World. He had helped Columbus in acquiring three caravels for an earlier voyage. But the approval was contingent on the exclusion of Columbus's rights of Viceroy and Admiral. Columbus insisted that these rights were not negotiable, as they were duly guaranteed by "The Capitulations of Santa Fé." The Admiral would have all or nothing—and he got nothing.

It was obvious that King Ferdinand was not in favor of restoring an infirm Columbus to his post of Viceroy of the Indies, especially after recalling him during his third voyage, through Bobadilla. He eventually proposed that Columbus take a fiefdom in Castile in exchange for his claims. Once again, Columbus would not compromise, but insisted that he and his heirs had a legal right to the offices of Admiral, Viceroy, and Governor and would never renounce them. King Ferdinand then responded that if that was the case, the problem was out of his hands. Because he was no longer the Sovereign of Castile, Ferdinand referred Columbus's claims to the tribunal, the "Junta De Descargas," which had been empowered to execute the will of Queen Isabella and discharge her debts. If Columbus had not been a foreigner or if the Queen had not died, the outcome of the litigation might have been different. "The Capitulations of Santa Fé" had been made in good faith but no one had surmised the immensity of Columbus's discoveries and their financial implications. If the terms of the agreements had been adhered to, Columbus soon would have become the richest man in the world.

King Ferdinand had consulted legal experts on the validity of Columbus's titles. It was hinted that a grant of perpetual authority, especially to a foreigner by a Castilian Sovereign, was a contravention of the Law of Toledo, the Castilian Constitution, enacted in 1480. Thus, King Ferdinand had not been all guile and deception; he really did not know where he stood. Now, following the death of the queen, he was confronted with a more serious problem. He had been ruling her kingdom of Castile as a regent, as provided by the queen's testament, for their daughter the Infanta Juana ("La Loca"), and her husband, the Archduke Philip of Austria.

When, after an attempt to remain in control of Castile, Ferdinand was faced with imminent war, he gave up the crown to Juana and Philip, and withdrew into his hereditary realm of Aragon.

DEATH OF COLUMBUS

With the arrival in Spain of King Philip and Queen Juana, Columbus found a new gleam of hope in the possibility that the new monarchs might look more favorably than Ferdinand on the restitution of his honors and property rights. As a young princess, Juana had been fascinated by the Admiral's tales of his early discoveries; now he hoped that he might find the patroness and friend in her that her mother had been to him.

Columbus wrote a letter to the new Sovereigns apologizing for his present illness, which prevented him from manifesting his respect and devotion; he promised he would be ready and willing to serve them as soon as he recovered from his ailment. The letter was signed:

Admiral and Viceroy and Governor General of the islands, and Terra Firma of the Indies, such as he has discovered and might discover.

Columbus then entrusted the letter to his brother, who was graciously received as his emissary by the new Sovereigns. They listened to his claims with great attention and expressed the hope that they could be quickly resolved.

While the Adelantado was away, Columbus's illness took a turn for the worse. By mid-May Columbus and his friends knew that the end was near. On May 19, 1506, he modified the entails and mayorazgo of 1498 with a codicil, recommending Beatriz Enriquez de Harana to the care of Don Diego and assigning to her an annual payment of ten thousand maravedis. He also left small sums to various people in Genoa and Lisbon, debts of conscience for small favors received many years before. Among them is the payment of half a mark of silver to a poor Jew who lived at the gate of the ghetto in Lisbon. These payments were to be made anonymously.

He then confirmed several clauses from his original entail appointing his son Don Diego heir to all his property and privileges and commending all other surviving members of his immediate family as indicated in the mayorazgo; that is, in the case of Don Diego's death, the entailed inheritance would pass to his brother, Ferdinand, and from him to his uncle, Don Bartholomew, continuing down to the nearest male heir. Six people from Valladolid were summoned as witnesses, including two prominent Genoese: Bartolomeo Fieschi and Giovanni Spinola of the wealthy Genoese trading family

On May 20, 1506, the vigil of the Feast of the Ascension, Columbus suddenly grew worse. A priest was called to administer the last rights in the presence of Don Diego, his son; Don Diego, Columbus's younger brother; Ferdinand; Diego Méndez and Bartolomeo Fieschi, captains of the Capitana and Vizcaína; and a few faithful servants.

Having received the Holy Sacraments of the Catholic Church, Columbus was heard to say: "*In manus tuas Domine, commendo spiritum meum.*" (In thy hands, Lord, I commend by spirit.) And so the Admiral of the Ocean Sea and Viceroy died peacefully and in obscurity despite the fact that the royal court was meeting in Valladolid during that period. There was no general mourning for the man who, in discovering a New World, had brought on the dawn of a continent equal in magnitude to the Old World. Yet, he died not knowing the vastness of his discovery and still believing that Cuba and Hispaniola were remote parts of Asia.

How sad that Peter Martyr, who had alerted the world when Columbus returned from his first voyage enjoining it to "Atollite mentem" (lift up your minds), did not report that Columbus had died.

Chapter Forty-Seven

EPILOGUE

COLUMBUS'S RESTING PLACE

Upon his death, the Admiral's body was laid to rest temporarily in the Church of San Francisco in Valladolid. In 1509, three years after his death, his eldest son, Don Diego, transferred the body to the Carthusian monastery of Las Cuevas in Seville. This must have been a burdensome trip for Don Diego, just as wearisome a journey perhaps as the one taken by his infirm father in 1505. In 1541, or possibly 1542, Columbus's bones were exhumed, along with those of his son Diego, who had been buried alongside his father in 1526, and shipped to Hispaniola by order of Doña María de Toledo, Don Diego's widow. It seems that Doña María had obtained royal permission in 1537 to establish a mausoleum for the Columbus family in the main chapel of the Cathedral of Santo Domingo, which eventually became the resting place, in the sixteenth century, of Doña María herself, Columbus's nephews, and perhaps even the Admiral's brothers, Bartholomew and Diego.

In 1795 at the termination of a war between France and Spain, Hispaniola was ceded to France as part of the peace treaty between the two nations.

The governor of Hispaniola, Joaquin Garcia, with the concurrence and approval of Don Fernando Portillo y Torres, the Archbishop of Cuba, whose archdiocese included Santo Domingo, made elaborate plans for the transfer of the urn containing the remains of the Admiral to Cuba. On December 20, 1795, in the presence of church dignitaries and distinguished civil and military officers, assembled in the cathedral of Santa Domingo, a small vault was opened above the chancel, on the gospel side of the altar. They found fragments of a leaden coffin, a number of bones, and a quantity of mold, evidently the remains of a human body. These remains were placed in a coffin, covered with black velvet and ornamented with lace and a gold fringe. The following day the archbishop celebrated a high Mass for the dead, and at four o'clock in the afternoon the coffin was carried to a brigantine, appropriately called the *Discoverer*, which sailed westward along the coast to the Bahía de Ocoa. There it was transferred to the flagship of the fleet, the *San Lorenzo*, for the long journey to Cuba; it arrived in Havana on the fifteenth of January 1796. The coffin was carried in a grand procession with military honors befitting an Admiral to the cathedral. There, following a high Mass, Columbus's remains were ceremoniously deposited in the wall, on the gospel side of the altar. These elaborate ceremonies and honors, coming nearly three hundred years after his death, offer proof, according to Navarrete, "of the high estimation and respectful remembrance in which they held the hero who had discovered the New World, and had been the first to plant the standard of the cross on the island."[1]

EPILOGUE

In 1898, with the help of the United States, Cuba gained its independence from Spain. Once again, the bones of Columbus were hurriedly exhumed, placed aboard a Spanish destroyer, and carried to Seville, where they were finally sealed in an imposing monument built especially for them in the great transept of the cathedral.

In 1877, when the cathedral in Santo Domingo was undergoing extensive repairs, Dominican workmen discovered on the gospel side of the main altar several coffins of the Columbus family. A small vault about seventeen inches long bore on the outside the initials "CCA," which the Dominicans excitedly decided stood for "Cristóbal Colón, Almirante." On the underside of the lid was inscribed in Gothic lettering, "Illtre y Esdo Varon Dn Criztóval Colón," which could be written out as "Ilustre y Esclarecido Varon Don Cristóbal Colón"; translated as "the Illustrious and Esteemed Nobleman, Don Cristóbal Colón." Inside the coffin there were a few fragments of bones and dust and, of particular interest, a silver plate with the inscription "Ua pte de los rtos del pmer Al t D Cristóval Colón Des r," which could be abbreviations for "Ultima parte de de los restos del Primer Almirante, Don Cristóbal, Descubridor," i.e., "The last part of the remains of the first Admiral, Don Cristóbal Colón, the Discoverer." Some scholars have interpreted the first two Spanish words, "Ua pte," as being "Urna Patente," thus changing the meaning of the sentence to: "The urn of the remains of the First Admiral Don Cristóbal Colón, the Discoverer." If the first interpretation is correct, then we must assume that there may be a sharing of the remains between Seville and Santo Domingo. Of Columbus's remains in Santo Domingo, only a few bones are still intact; there is no skull with the bones—just ashes or dust. It would seem then that not all the bones of Columbus were removed from Santo Domingo in 1795. Is it possible that in 1795, when Archbishop Don Fernando Portillo ordered the bones of Columbus to be exhumed some Dominican helpers might have deliberately left some of his remains in the New World? It may very well be that in the noble struggle between two patriotic factions, the greatness of Columbus justified that his relic be revered in both the New World, which he had discovered, and the Old World, which gave him birth and opportunity to rise to immortality.

REIGN AND DEATH OF PHILIP I
KING FERDINAND RETURNS TO POWER

Having surrendered the sovereignty of Castile to Philip and Juana on June 21, 1506, King Ferdinand returned to his hereditary dominions of Aragon. Philip and Juana as new Sovereigns proceeded to Valladolid to receive the homage of the nobles and to accept the customary oaths of allegiance, which were extended also to their eldest son, Prince Charles, as heir apparent on the eventual death of his mother. Philip assumed complete power and began the process of dismissing old incumbents in office to make room for his own friends and favorites who had come along with him from Flanders. The sudden administrative upheavals, made without due regard to merit or competence, aroused general discontent among the Castilians, who began to resent the thoughtless actions of the foreign ruler. Symptoms of insubordination cropped up throughout the kingdom; in some instances, confederations of nobles were formed in anticipation of open revolt if the young king of Castile did not mend his ways.

In the meantime, King Ferdinand was preparing to visit his new Neapolitan dominions. On September 4, 1506, he and his young bride left Barcelona on board an armed squadron of Catalan galleys and on the twenty-fourth they reached the port of Genoa. After leaving Genoa, the royal squadron was forced into the harbor of Portofino by contrary winds. It was there that he received the sad news of the death of his son-in-law, Philip I. He had died on September 25 in Burgos, following a high fever brought about by a too-violent exertion in a ball game.

Upon his death, Archbishop Ximenes had rallied the old adherents of Ferdinand and dispatched a letter to the Catholic king, apprising him of the situation and urging him to return immediately to Spain. The king, however, determined to continue to Naples; he stopped along the way at several coastal towns until he reached the capital of his dominions in late October. There he was received with great enthusiasm. Following the usual glamorous and elegant social festivities, Ferdinand summoned the parliament of Naples to ratify the treaty he had made with Louis XII of France: the re-establishment of the Angevin proprietors in their ancient estates. This was a very unsatisfactory resolution to an ancient problem and fell short of its promises. The loyal partisans of Aragon were not happy at having to return to their French enemies their own hard-won estates and they demurred. The Neapolitans found themselves burdened with more taxes instead of receiving the expected favors and immunities commonly granted at the onset of a new reign.

King Ferdinand did not leave Naples until June 4, 1507, as he had dedicated himself to putting everything in order prior to his departure. In addition to restoring the Angevins to their estates, he reorganized the interior administration of the kingdom, made reforms in the courts of law, and appeased the Neapolitans by re-establishing their ancient university.

On June 28, the royal fleet entered the port of Savona, where the King of France was waiting for Ferdinand. The subject of their discussions was the possibility of the future of Italy and the establishment of the League of Cambrai.[2] After four days of relaxation, enjoying the great hospitality of the French monarch, Ferdinand and his French Queen of Aragon sailed for Valencia, arriving there on June 20, 1507. The king then went directly to Castile, where at the border he was met by many nobles, including the Dukes of Albuquerque and Medina Celi and the County of Cifuentes.

Ferdinand had left almost in disgrace and now was returning as a conqueror, ready to take command of a country in despair. At Tortoles, Ferdinand was met by Queen Juana and Archbishop Ximenes. Her physical appearance, abnormal manners, and display of childlike affection on meeting her father disturbed and saddened the king, who was now convinced that she was not mentally able to ever rule Castile. He immediately assumed control of Castile without valid authority from the Cortes. This royal transgression was finally resolved constitutionally by the Cortes held at Madrid, October 6, 1510, which approved his role as administrator of Castile in his daughter's name and as guardian of her son Charles.

DON DIEGO'S RISE TO POWER

Following the death of his father, Don Diego succeeded to his rights as Viceroy and Governor and immediately took up the cause that had eluded Columbus—that of the restitution of his rights and privileges. For two years, the young Admiral demanded from the king a settlement of the rights, as expressed in the capitulations, between the king and his father; in all instances, he was rebuffed. This prompted Don Diego to seek redress in a lawsuit against the king, which he initiated before the Council of the Indies. This suit was started in 1508, lasted for several years, and was decided in favor of Don Diego. But the wily monarch found it repugnant to cede such vast powers to the young Admiral and he resorted to the same stalling tactics he had used against Columbus. During this interlude, Cupid's dart came to the rescue. Don Diego fell in love with Doña María de Toledo, cousin to the king, daughter of Fernando de Toledo, Grand Commander of León, and niece to Don Fadrique Toledo, the celebrated Duke of Alba. Doña María responded with mutual affection, and thus, the foreign family of Columbus was united with one of the most aristocratic families of Spain.

By marrying into royalty, Don Diego acquired immense social status. King Ferdinand now looked upon him not as the son of Columbus but as the husband of one of his relatives. It soon followed that with the help of his father-in-law and his wife's uncle, the Duke of Alba, King Ferdinand was influenced in considering Don Diego the logical successor to Ovando in Hispaniola. The king had been perfectly satisfied with Ovando's performance in Hispaniola as his methods, although despotic and cruel, had brought not only stability to the colonies but had enriched the royal coffers as well. However, he had promised Queen Isabella on her deathbed that he would recall Ovando because of his transgressions, especially for his massacre of the Indians and his senseless execution of the remarkable lady Cacique Anacaona. The time had come to make good on that promise. Don Diego was granted all the powers enjoyed by Ovando. The crafty king, however, did not grant him directly the power of Viceroy, but allowed him to use it by courtesy, as his wife Doña María had already been universally acclaimed as the "Vierreina."

The new Admiral left Sanlucar on June 9, 1509, with his wife, his brother Ferdinand, who would stay in Hispaniola for only six months, and his two uncles, Don Bartholomew and Don Diego. They were accompanied by a larger retinue of noblemen with their wives and a number of young ladies of rank, sent out to find suitable wealthy husbands in the colonies. Don Diego started out his rule in truly royal style, and Doña María held court and entertained in a manner befitting a Virreina.

Diego's rule in Hispaniola was a distinguished one. He proved to be an able administrator, despite the constant annoyances and interferences of King Ferdinand, who, at the very outset of his governorship, appointed Alonso de Hojeda, governor of the part of Terra Firma east of the Gulf of Uraba called "New Andalusia," and Diego de Nicuessa, governor of the western province west of the Gulf of Uraba, which included the rich coast of Veragua called by the king "Castilla del Oro." Because both of these provinces had been discovered by Columbus in his third and fourth voyages, the most logical person to govern these lands should have been the Adelantado. It was obvious that Archbishop Fonseca was still exerting his influence on the king. What particularly annoyed Don Diego was the king's unconcern about making such important appointments without consulting the new governor of Hispaniola. Don Diego considered these acts an infringement of the Articles of Capitulation, but he was powerless to act. However, in a later act involving the new governor of Puerto Rico, Ponce de León, Don Diego lodged a complaint with the king. In 1510, Ponce de León had been made governor of Puerto Rico without the knowledge or advice of the Viceroy. In 1512, in his search for Bimini (later called Florida), the land of the "Fountain of Youth," Ponce de León received his orders from the king, who again acted independently of Don Diego. In this particular case, Don Diego's protestations to the king brought a measure of satisfaction, because recommendations by Don Diego for later appointments to that colony were recognized by the Crown.

An important event occurring at about that time, not sanctioned either by the Crown or the Viceroy, was the discovery of the "Southern Sea," later called the Pacific Ocean, by a stowaway, Vasco Nuñez Balboa, in 1513. Attaching himself by devious means to Alonso de Hojeda's colony in New Andalusia (he had stowed away in a ship from Puerto Rico), he showed such remarkable qualities of leadership that he earned the command of an expedition that crossed the Isthmus of Darien. From the summit of the south coast of Cordilleras he laid his eyes on the huge expanse of water that eventually was called the Pacific Ocean. He then marched down into the coastal waters and with due formality claimed for Spain the ocean and all the lands bordering it.

As befitted his stature of Viceroy, Don Diego ordered that a place be built in Santo Domingo, not only to house the royal family but to provide a site for a much-needed seat of government. As structures of such magnitude and decor had never before been built in colonial Santo Domingo, factions inimical to Don Diego began to spread rumors that the Viceroy was not building a home but a fortress to make himself absolute sovereign of the island. It became apparent to Don Diego that the enemies of his late father were also his enemies; that they were bent on undermining his power by magnifying any or all insignificant errors into criminal acts. A faction of the malcontents under Miguel Pasamonte, the king's treasurer, consisting also of some followers of Roldan, began to harass the Viceroy for punishing some petty officers in the colony, obviously a minor act of discipline. But they magnified the incidents and began to write home about unusual virulent messages to the king, who, of course, particularly now in his advanced age, related such matters to Bishop Fonseca. The result of these complaints was the establishment of a royal court in Santo Domingo, which would judge appeals of any of the Viceroy's sentences. Once again Don Diego's authority was being undermined as the role of the Viceroy was one of adjudication without recourse to a court of appeals.

In an attempt to correct a number of abuses in the local government, especially of that branch which dealt with the "repartimientos" (partitionings) of the Indies, Don Diego dismissed those supervisors appointed by Ovando and substituted his own people. This caused a great deal of resentment against him and a great number of complaints to the king, who ordered the Adelantado, who was back in Spain, to return to Hispaniola with important instructions. The Viceroy received the following directives: the labor of the natives should be reduced to one-third; Negro slaves should be procured from Guinea to replace the Indians and the Carib slaves, who were normally more troublesome; they should be branded on the leg to avoid mistaking them for other Indians. Don Diego promised to correct the inequities.

In 1514, while the Adelantado was in Hispaniola, he received a message from the king offering him the governorship of the coast of Veragua. Apparently, Alonso de Hojeda and Diego de Nicuesa had failed in their job of governing those territories peacefully and the king realized that the Adelantado could bring the provinces under control. Don Bartholomew refused the offer, as he felt he was getting too old. Had the offer been made a few years earlier, he might have accepted it. The king's letter stipulated that the governing of Veragua should fall under the jurisdiction of Don Diego—an important change in policy.

EPILOGUE

Seemingly, the king was softening his stance on Don Diego's demands, and the calumnies sent home by the enemies of the latter had not influenced him adversely. Unfortunately, future events would prove otherwise.

Derogatory messages, especially those from the treasurer Pasamonte, continued to arrive in Spain. Additionally, new measures passed by the Crown that Don Diego considered a threat to his privileges prompted him to make a personal appearance in the royal court to explain and vindicate his conduct. He departed on April 9, 1515, leaving the Adelantado to govern along with Virreina Doña María. He was received with great honor by the king and commended for his upright administration, especially for conquering and colonizing the islands of Cuba and Jamaica without bloodshed. Don Diego contended that all accusations against himself had been made because he tried to lessen the oppression of the natives, and the king ordered that all processes against the Viceroy in the court of appeals, or elsewhere for that matter, for damages relating to the regulations of the "repartimientos" should be discontinued and sent to him for consideration. The time being propitious, Don Diego brought up again the subject of favors and privileges, as he now claimed a share of profits made on the coast of Veragua that had been discovered by his father. The king ordered an investigation to be made among the sailors before he would pass judgment on it.

While in court, Don Diego received news from Santo Domingo that his uncle Don Bartholomew had died. The king was very much grieved to hear of the Adelantado's death, for he thought very highly of him as a great seaman, soldier, and statesman. Indeed, he had previously rewarded him with the permanent governorship of the island of Mona with an allocation of two hundred Indians. Don Diego lingered in

King Ferdinand's court in an effort to obtain his vindication. Unfortunately, King Ferdinand died on January 23, 1516.

His grandson Prince Charles succeeded him eventually as Emperor Charles V. Cardinal Ximenes, who became Regent because of Charles's youth did not pursue Don Diego's representations. It was not until 1520 that Emperor Charles V determined Don Diego's innocence and dismissed all charges against him. The Emperor, after due investigation, was convinced that Pasamonte's charges were not justified and that an amicable solution could be obtained by having Pasamonte apologize to the Viceroy. In regard to other acts of indemnifications, the Emperor also ruled that Don Diego had a perfect right to exercise his office of Viceroy in Hispaniola and all other lands discovered by his father—a concession that had eluded him during King Ferdinand's reign. Elated by the good news, Don Diego returned to Hispaniola in September 1520.

He found that considerable changes had been made during his five-year absence. Many of the local officers had abused their powers, and he demanded a thorough accounting of their administrations, resulting in dismissal and punishment of those found guilty. The gold mines had been neglected in favor of the cultivation of sugarcane, which proved to be more rewarding than the mining of gold. This was made possible by the importation of many Negro slaves, who displaced the weaker Indians in the sugarcane fields. The treatment of these slaves was very cruel and barbaric, as they were forced to work long hours in tropical weather, without regard to their health and safety. The result was the first Negro revolt in 1522. A group of about forty slaves working at two neighboring plantations got possession of arms and massacred their supervisors. They then roamed about the country liberating more slaves, their purpose being the formation of a Negro army to subdue their white masters. But it was a hopeless revolt, fired by desperation and doomed to failure. It was Don Diego's unpleasant duty to seek out and punish the rebels. The captured leaders were all hanged in order to discourage further revolts.

The dismissal of the administrators and mistreatment of the Negro slaves once again caused a wide rift between Don Diego and the Pasamonte factions, who proceeded to lodge further complaints with the Emperor. Don Diego was requested to appear in court in 1523. He appeared before the court at Victoria and pleaded his case passionately and with exactitude as to his discharge of duties; he convinced the counsel of his innocence on all charges made by his accusers.

After another favorable reception at court and with his innocence reestablished, Don Diego found the time propitious to renew his claims for adjudication. A commission was appointed by the Emperor, consisting of the President of the Royal Council of the Indies, and a number of other prominent persons; it could not arrive at a decision, however, because of the difficulties in establishing the profits derived from the various provinces, because the amount had escalated with the passing of time. Undaunted, Don Diego remained in Spain, following the royal court from city to city to seek justice.

In the winter of 1525, the court moved from Toledo to Seville; Don Diego, suffering from a fever, left Toledo on a stretcher on February 21, 1526, hoping to follow the court to Seville. There he planned to go to the Church of Our Lady of Guadalupe to offer devotions and seek the intercession of the Mother of God for the restoration of his health and the just termination of his claims. He never made it to Seville. At the end of the day of departure, six leagues away in the town of

Montalban, he became too ill to continue his journey. He died on February 23, 1526, at the age of forty-six.

FALL AND END OF THE DYNASTY

After the death of Don Diego, the enterprising Virreina still residing in Santo Domingo with her five children—two boys, Luis and Christopher, and three girls, María, Juana, and Isabella—took the appropriate steps to maintain the rights of the family. Because the Columbus family had a just claim to the viceroyalty of Veragua by reason of discovery, she conceived the idea of colonizing that province and requested license from the Crown to outfit a fleet for that specific purpose. When her request was refused, she sailed back to Spain to protect the claim of her oldest son, Luis, at the time six years old. The title of "Admiral of the Indies" was conferred upon him and his revenues and other favors upon the family were authorized by the Crown. The title of Viceroy, however, conferred upon his father two years before his death, was held in abeyance and eventually denied the son. By a compromise, Don Luis was declared Captain-Genera of Hispaniola.

His administration of Hispaniola was ruinous and disgraceful—a total disappointment to his mother, who, on behalf of the Emperor, had the good sense to exchange the heritage of Columbus for a dukedom in Veragua and for a marquisate in Jamaica. Don Luis even bargained away the claim of one-tenth of the produce of the Indies for a pension of one thousand doubloons of gold. He was recalled from Hispaniola in 1551 and arrested in 1559 for having three wives. He was prosecuted, imprisoned, and banished to Africa in 1565. He died in Oran (Algeria) in 1572. Don Luis left no legitimate male heirs. He left two daughters by his wife, Doña María de Mosquera—Phillippa and María. He was succeeded, however, by his nephew Diego, son of his brother Christopher. The succession was contested by his cousin Phillippa, daughter of Don Luis. This litigation was settled in a very special manner—Diego married his cousin Phillippa. Their union, a happy one but of short duration, did not produce an heir, and the male line of Columbus became extinct upon the death of Diego in 1578.

Appendix A

Spanish currency, measures, and weights used in the reign of Ferdinand and Isabella and heir modern equivalents.

Currency used:

The maravedi, though no longer coined, was commonly used. Of Moorish origin, common in the twelfth century, it was a small coin made of copper. Coins of higher denominations were made of silver as the real or gold as the mark (marco).

The mark was the largest unit of currency, containing 230 grams of gold. This is the equivalent of 7.412 troy ounces that at market rate of $325 is worth $2,405. The smallest coin was the blanca, made of copper, equivalent to half a maravedi.

> 1 excelente = $\frac{1}{25}$ mark = 870 maravedis = 9.1 grams
> 1 castellano = $\frac{1}{50}$ mark = 435 maravedis = 4.55 grams
> 1 ducat = $\frac{1}{65}$ mark = 375 maravedis = 3.48 grams
> 1 real = $\frac{1}{67}$ mark

Measures used:

> 1 Spanish mile = 8 stadia = 1,000 double paces = 1,619 yards
> 4 Spanish miles = 1 league = 6476 yards = 3.2 nautical miles
> 1 Arabian mile = 2,363 yards
> 1 Roman mile = 4,842 feet
> 1 Italian braccio = 1.92 feet

The nautical mile is based on the length of a minute of arc of a great circle of the earth. An international unit used since 1959 in the United States, it measures 6,076 feet = 1,852 meters, 1.15 US miles.

Weights used:

1 tonelada of wine = 2 bottes = 60 arrobas = 290 US gallons
1 quintal = 4 arrobas = 101 pounds

Appendix B

THE TOSCANELLI LETTERS

I reproduce here the text of the letters as translated by Benjamin Keen in Ferdinand Columbus's *The Life of the Admiral Christopher Columbus*, New Brunswick, Rutgers University Press, 1959.

The Letters of Paolo, a Physician of Florence to the Admiral Concerning the Discovery of the Indies

Paolo the Physician, to Columbus, greetings. I perceive your noble and grand desire to go the places where the spices grow; and in reply to your letter I send you a copy of another letter which some time since I sent to a friend of mine, a gentleman of the household of the most serene King of Portugal, before the wars of Castile, I in reply to another which by command of His Highness he wrote me on this subject; and I send you another sea-chart like the one I sent him, that your demands may be satisfied. A copy of that letter of mine follows:

Paolo the Physician, to Ferñao Martins, canon of Lisbon, greetings. I was glad to hear of your intimacy and friendship with your most serene and magnificent King. I have often before spoken of a sea route from here to the Indies, where the spices grow, a route shorter than the one which you are pursuing by way of Guinea. You tell me that His Highness desires from me some statement or demonstration that would make it easier to understand and take that route. I could do this by using a sphere shaped like the earth, but I decided that it would be easier and make the point clearer if

I showed that route by means of a sea-chart. I therefore send His Majesty a chart drawn by my own hand, upon which is laid out the western coast from Ireland on the north to the end of Guinea, and the islands which lie on that route, in front of which, directly to the west, is shown the beginning of the Indies, with the islands and places at which you are bound to arrive, and how far from the Arctic Pole or the equator you ought to keep away, and how much space or how many leagues intervene before you reach those places most fertile in all sorts of spices, jewels, and precious stones. And do not marvel at my calling "west" the regions where the spices grow, although they are commonly called "east"; because whoever sails westward will always find those lands in the west, which one who goes overland to the east will always find the same lands in the east. The straight lines drawn lengthwise on this map show the distance from east to west; the transverse lines indicate distance from north to south. I have also drawn on the map various places in India to which one could go in case of a storm or contrary winds, or some other mishap.

And that you may be as well informed about all those regions as you desire to be, you must know that none but merchants live and trade in all those islands. There is as great a number of ships and mariners with their merchandise here as in all the rest of the world, especially in a very noble port called Zaiton, where every year they load and unload a hundred large ships laden with pepper, besides many other ships loaded with other spices. This country is very populous, with a multitude of provinces and kingdoms and cities without number, under the rule of a prince who is called the Great Khan, which name in our speech signified King of Kings, who resides most of the time in the province of Cathay. His predecessors greatly desired to have friendship and dealings with the Christians, and about two hundred years ago they sent ambassadors to the Pope, asking for many learned men and teachers to instruct them in our faith; but these ambassadors, encountering obstacles on the way, turned back without reaching Rome. In the time of Pope Eugenius there came to him an ambassador who told of their great feeling of friendship for the Christians, and I had a long talk with him about many things; about the great size of their royal palaces and the marvelous length and breadth of the rivers, and the multitude of cities in their lands, so that on one river alone there are two hundred cities, with marble bridges very long and wide, adorned with many columns. This country is as rich in gold as any that has ever been found; not only could it yield great gain and many costly things, but from it may also be had gold and silver and precious stones and all sorts of spices in great quantity, which at present are not carried to our countries. And it is true that many learned men, philosophers, and astronomers, and many other men skilled in all the arts govern this great province and conduct its wars.

From the city of Lisbon due west there are twenty-six spaces marked on the map, each of which contains 250 miles, as far as the very great and noble city of Quinsay. This city is about one hundred miles in circumference, which is equal to thirty-five leagues and has ten marble bridges. Marvelous things are told of its great buildings, its arts, and its revenues. That city lies in the province of Mangi, near the province of Cathay, in which the king resides the greater part of the time. And from the island of Antillia, which you call the Island of the Seven Cities to the very noble isle of Cipango, there are ten spaces, which make 2,500 miles, that is 225 leagues. This land is most rich in gold, pearls, and precious stones, and the temples and royal palaces are covered with solid gold. But because the way is not known, all these things are hidden and covered, though one can travel thither with all security.

Many other things could I say, but since I have already told them to you by word of mouth, and you are a man of good judgment, I know there remains nothing for me to explain. I have tried to satisfy your demands as well as the pressure of time and my work has permitted, and I remain ready to serve His Highness and answer his questions at greater length if he should order me to do so.

Done in the city of Florence, June 25, 1474.

Master Paolo afterward wrote the Admiral another letter, which read as follows:

Paolo, the Physician, to Christopher Columbus, greetings. I have received your letters together with the things you sent me, and took great pleasure in them. I perceive your grand and noble desire to sail from west to east by the route indicated on the map I sent you, a route which would appear still more plainly upon a sphere. I am much pleased to see that I have been well understood, and that the voyage has become not only possible but certain, fraught with inestimable honor and gain, and most lofty fame among Christians. But you cannot grasp all that it means without actual experience, or without such accurate and copious information as I have had from eminent learned men who have come from those places to the Roman court and from merchants who have traded a long time in those parts and speak with great authority on such matters. When that voyage shall be made, it will be a voyage to powerful kingdoms and noble cities and rich provinces, abounding in all sorts of things that we greatly need, including all manner of spices and jewels in great abundance. It will also be a voyage to kings and princes who are very eager to have friendly dealings and speech with the Christians of our countries, because many of them are Christians; they are also very eager to know and speak with the learned men of our lands concerning religion and all other branches of knowledge, because of the much they have heard of the empires and governments of these parts. For these reasons and many others that might be mentioned, I do not wonder that you, who are of great courage, and the whole Portuguese nation, which has always distinguished itself in all great enterprises, are now inflamed with desire to undertake this voyage.

Appendix C

Points of Sailing

Seafarers of Columbus's era did not think of a course or direction in terms of degrees measured from true north, as we do; nor of compass points, as our forebears did for over three hundred years; but in terms of winds, "los vientos." Of these, eight principal ones were recognized. Each had a name in Italian: *Tramontana* for N, *Greco* for NE, *Levante* for E, *Sirocco* for SE, *Ostro* or *Auster* for S, *Libeccio* or *Africo* for SW, *Ponente* for W, and *Maestro* (*Mistral* in French) for NW. But as most of these names had reference to Mediterranean geography, the Spaniards and Portuguese in ocean navigation adopted the modern system based on eight cardinal points, which we abbreviate N, NE, E, SE, S, SW, W, and NW. The eight intermediate points, NNE, ENE, ESE, SSE, SSW, SWS, WNW, and NNW, they called "los medios vientos," (the half-winds); what we call the "by" points of N by E, NE by N, etc., they called "las cuartas" or "quartas" (the quarter-winds). Hence, "cuarta" (or quarts) became their word for one full compass point, equivalent to $11\frac{1}{4}°$. Thus, if Columbus wished to give the course that we call W by S, he said "Oeste cuarta del Suroeste," literally, "West, one point to the Southwest."

Some Related Facts

    3.18 nautical miles = 3.181-1.6080 feet

Columbus's day on the passage out was calculated from sunrise on the day named, to sunrise the following morning. Thus, the Journal for September 16 begins at sunrise on the sixteenth and continues until sunrise on the seventeenth.

Keeping Time: Columbus used the "ampolleta" or half-hour glass, which he corrected on every fair day by noting when the sun reached the zenith. He expressed time in his journal by the canonical hours. These were: Prime, 6:00 a.m.; Terce, 9:00 a.m.; Sext, noon; Nones, 3:00 p.m.; Vespers, 6:00 p.m.; Compline, 9:00 p.m.; Columbus never mentioned "Sext" and "None."

Observance: He observed Prime at dawn; Terce at 9:00 a.m.; Vespers anywhere from 3:00 p.m. to 7:00 p.m.; and Compline before retiring.

At Vespers all hands were called, a brief service read, the "Salve Regina" sung, and the watch changed.

Notes

PREFACE

1. "The First Booke of the Decades of the Ocean" in Richland Eden, *The First Three Books on America (? 1551)–1555 A.D.*, Birmingham, Turnbull and Spears, 1885. Kraus Reprint 1971, p. 65.
2. Ibid.
3. Ferdinand Columbus, *The Life of the Admiral Christopher Columbus*, edited and translated by Benjamin Keen, New Brunswick, Rutgers University Press, 1959. Hereafter this book will be referred to as *Biography*.
4. *Biography*, p. 33.
5. Samuel Eliot Morison, *Christopher Columbus, Mariner*, New York, Mentor Books, 1956, p. vii.
6. Madariaga, op. cit. (Westport, CT: Greenwood Press, 1967), p. 16.

CHAPTER ONE: THE AMERICAN ABORIGINES

1. *The Log of Christopher Columbus*, translated by Robert H. Fuson, Camden, Maine: International Marine Publishing Company, 1987, p. 76. Hereafter we will refer to this book as *Log*.

CHAPTER THREE: THE PORTUGUESE NAVAL ACTIVITY

1. India or "Las Indias" was a broad term used in the late Middle Ages for the Orient. It was identified further as the Nearer India,

located near the present Ethiopia, and the Farther India, located somewhere in Asia. Eventually, after the discoveries of Columbus and da Gama, the Indies were differentiated further as the West and East Indies, respectively.

CHAPTER FOUR: THE PHYSICAL WORLD OF CHRISTOPHER COLUMBUS

1. Aristotle, *On the Heavens*, Book 11, pp. 4–5.
2. *Biography*, p. 18.
3. Pierre d'Ailly, *Imago Mundi*, Boston: Massachusetts Historical Society, 1927.
4. Lucius Annaeus Seneca (4 B.C.–65 A.D.), Roman philosopher and dramatist born in Córdoba, wrote in the chorus of his tragedy *Medea*: "...*venient annis secula seris, quibus Oceanus Vincula rerum laxet, et ingens Pateat tellus, Tiphysque novos Detegat orbes, nee sit terris Vetima Thule*," which means, "There will come a time in later years when the ocean shall loosen the bonds by which we have been confined when an immense land shall be revealed and Tiphys [pilot of the Argonauts] shall disclose new worlds, and Thule [northernmost part of the ancient world] will no longer be the most remote of countries."
5. II Esdras (Ezra) III, vi 42 (Apocrypha, King James Version): "Upon the third day thou didst command that the waters should be gathered in the seventh part of the earth, six parts hath then dried up and kept them, to the intent that these, some being planted by God, might serve thee."

There is no doubt that Columbus learned more from d'Ailly's *Imago Mundi* than from any other book in his possession, although he takes issue occasionally with the author on certain points.

Because the book was of an encyclopedic nature, he became acquainted with and learned from earlier cosmologists about the physical world. Thus, he learned of Eratosthenes and his method of measuring the circumference of the earth; of Ptolemy, who stated that the known world covered half the globe's circumference allowing 180 degrees from the meridian of Cape St. Vincent to the extreme end of Asia; and of Marinus of Tyre, who stretched it to 225 degrees. He also learned of the Arab cosmographer Alfraganus (Al-Farghani), who on the order of Khalif Almamum (813–832) computed fifty-six and two-thirds miles to the degree as the measurement of the earth. To this reference, Columbus added the marginal note: "...when sailing to Guinea...I took the altitude of the sun with quadrants and found them to agree with Alfraganus which is to say that each degree was equivalent to fifty-six and two-thirds miles, and this measurement is to be trusted."

6. Jacob Burckhardt, *Civilization of the Renaissance in Italy*, translated by S.G.C. Middlemore, London, 1929, Part IV.
7. Ibid.
8. Text of Toscanelli letters in Appendix B.

CHAPTER FIVE: THE PRIMARY CAUSES FOR THE GREAT HISTORICAL EVENTS

1. I believe that the stability of the caravel in roll was due to the broad beam. I had always found it difficult to accept that caravels, shallow of draft, some with a draft as small as six feet, could withstand side wind thrusts on its sails without rolling over. I made calculations on a representative caravel section to determine its "metacentric height," and discovered that it was inherently stable. Inherent stability in ships, or any floating vessel for that matter, is obtained when the center of gravity is below its center of buoyancy. For this condition, if lateral force acts on the ship to cause it to roll, the ship will recover its equilibrium and return to its original position. In the case of a shallow draft sailing ship, with tall mast, the center of gravity may fall above the center of buoyancy, in which case the ship is no longer inherently stable. However, stability may still be obtained, for if a wide beam ship begins to roll a few degrees, one side of the ship will sink in the water more than the other side, which in fact lifts out of the water. The net result is that the center of buoyancy is shifted to the side that is displacing more water. Now, the force vector acting vertically upward through the newly displaced center of buoyancy will generate a restoring couple to force the ship back to its level position. The point of intersection of the vertical vector through the displaced center of buoyancy with the center line of the ship is known as the metacenter. If the metacenter falls above the center of gravity of the ship, stability is achieved. The vertical distance between the center of gravity and the metacenter is the "metacentric height,"

which is a measure of stability; the longer the metacentric height, the more stable the ship.

In addition to having good stability in roll, ships had to maintain level forward movement through the water and a stable platform, not only for the sake of the cargo and armaments, but for the comfort of the crew as well. To prevent pitching, the length of the keel had to be increased as much as possible; more important, the center of gravity had to fall below and in line with the center of buoyancy to maintain the inherent stability of the ship. To accomplish this, the use of ballast sometimes was required to offset the deficiencies of the short-coupled vessel. Yet, despite the low keel to beam ratio of two to two and a half, these ships performed remarkably well on the high seas, thanks to the superior skills of the shipwrights of the period.

2. The earliest known "portolano" to survive is thought to be "Lo Comparso de Navigare," drawn in 1250. This chart shows the coast of the Mediterranean from Cape St. Vincent to the Seville River—a distance of about 150 miles. By the beginning of the fourteenth century, when seafaring in the Mediterranean had begun to expand rapidly, every important Italian port—Amalfi, Pisa, Genoa, and Venice—had shops of cartographers and draftsmen; these produced "portolani" charts of great accuracy and beauty based on log books of returning ships. Coastal outlines, promontories to steer by, harbor plans, islands, shallows, reefs, and nearly every bit of data necessary for navigation was incorporated in the charts. According to experts, the Italian cartographer Petrus Vesconte depicted the coast lines and ports with such fidelity that no alterations were made for the next three centuries. By the middle of the fourteenth century, portolan charts of the Black Sea and the Atlantic coast covering the coasts of Britain, Ireland, and Scandinavia were available. The Laurentian "Portolano" made in 1351 covered almost the entire known world. A composite of eight sheets, it covered the world from Britain to the Canary Islands, and as far east as the middle of India.

CHAPTER SIX: GENOA AND THE COLOMBOS

1. "*Johannes de Colombo de Moconexi, habitator in Villa Quinti, promisit et solemniter convenit Guiermo de Balbante de Alemania, textori pannorum, presenti, facere et curare ita et tauter cum effectu, quod Dominicus eius filius, hic presens et consentiens, etatis annorum XI in circa, stabit et perserverabit cum dicto Guiermo pro famulo et discipulo, causa adiscendi artem, suam, usque ad annos sex proxime venturos.*" Città di Genova, "Colombo" 1932, p. 104, State Notarial Archives, Genoa.
2. "*...dictos Christophorum, Bartolomeum, et Iacobum de Columbis, filios et heredes dicti quondam Dominici eorum patris, iam diu fore a civitate et posse Saonae absentes, ultra Pisas et Niciam, et in partibus Ispaniae commorantes, ut notorium fuit et est.*" Ref. Città di Genova: "Colombo" 1932, p. 176.
3. *Raccolta di documenti e studi pubblicati dalla R. Commissione Columbiana,* ed. by Cesare De Lollis, Rome, 1892–96. This is a monumental work, consisting of nine volumes, published at different times. It contains all the surviving documents pertaining to Columbus and his family. The document pertaining to Columbus's "mayorazgo" is in Part I, Vol I: *Scritti di Cristoforo Colombo,* Rome, 1893, p. 306. Hereafter we shall refer to this collection as the *Raccolta.*
4. *Raccolta,* Part I, Vol II, p. 171.
5. *The Life of the Admiral Christopher Columbus,* p. 4.
6. Martyr, a letter to Queen Isabella, dated May 14, 1493, as quoted by Jean Merrien, *Christopher Columbus: the Mariner and the Man,* London: Odhams Press, 1958, p. 14.
7. For a conclusive refutation of the various places—other than Genoa—advanced as possible birthplaces for Columbus, see Paolo Emilio Taviani, *Christopher Columbus: the Grand Design,* Novara: Istituto Geografico De Agostini, 1974, pp. 85–90.

CHAPTER SEVEN: COLUMBUS'S EARLY YEARS

1. *Biography,* p. 9.
2. A. Giustiniani, *Psalterium,* Genoa, 1515, p. 248.

3. B. Las Casas, *History de las indias*, 3 vols, Mexico: Fondo de Cultura Económica, 1951. On the subject of Columbus's curiosity and learning, see also W. Irving's *Christopher Columbus*, op. cit. vol. II, pp. 360–61.
4. "The Written Language of Christopher Columbus" in *Forum Italicum*, June, 1973.
5. *Biography*, p. 11. This voyage by Columbus, as his son Ferdinand described it, has aroused the interest of scholars for several reasons. First of all, is it possible to change "the point of the compass" so readily in a shipboard magnetic compass? The answer is positive because in a magnetic compass of that period, the instrument was of the aneroid type, i.e., not immersed in a damping fluid. Therefore, it would have been easy to lift the compass card off the pivot and rotate the magnets attached under the card 180°. If a rhumb line is drawn from the island of San Pietro NW by N, which is the approximate course of Marseilles, and if this line is extended linearly SE by S it will intersect the city of Tunis near Carthage. So, it would seem that by the simple expediency of rotating the point in the opposite direction, Columbus was able to reverse the direction of his ship. The island of San Pietro lies off the southwest coast of Sardinia at approximately the same latitude as Cagliari, the capital of Sardinia. The shortest distance from the island of San Pietro to Tunisia's Ghar el Melh (Porto Farina) is approximately 130 nautical miles and to Carthage a little bit longer. An average sailing speed for a ship of that period was five and a half to six knots. In a gale force wind, it could travel at a speed of eight to nine knots. If we assume a comparatively fast rate of seven knots, it would have taken Columbus's ship eighteen and a half hours to reach Tunisia. Therefore, it is unlikely that he could have made the trip from sunset to sunrise as indicated by Ferdinand. If we consider a night's sail to consist of twelve hours, it is reasonable to assume that he could have arrived by noontime. Apparently, Ferdinand, proudly boastful of his father's accomplishments, merely took poetic license with this historical event.
6. *Biography*, p. 13.
7. Ibid, p. 14.

NOTES

CHAPTER EIGHT: THE PORTUGUESE EXPERIENCE

1. *Biography*, p. 11.
2. See C. De Lollis, *Postille alla Historia Rerum di Pio II*, Rome, 1894, pp. 66–80.
3. *Biography*, p. 9.
4. Ibid, p. 14.

CHAPTER NINE: COLUMBUS AND THE KING OF PORTUGAL

1. *Biography*, p. 35.
2. Ibid, p. 35.
3. At his own expense and in exchange for certain royal privileges, Fernão Dulmo had elected to search for the Island of the Seven Cities, also known as Antillia, which supposedly lay west of the Azores in the mid-Atlantic waters. King João acceded to his demands with the stipulation that the expedition be completed within forty days. There is no doubt that, motivated by Columbus's earlier proposal, the monarch was curious about the existence of several mythical islands to the west, in addition, possibly even to the island of Cipango. He had nothing to lose. If Dulmo was bent on gambling on his own for titles of nobility and honor, and possibly a royal grant, he would have no objection. Accordingly, Dulmo, who hailed from Terceira in the Azores, and João Estreito, from Funchal, set sail from Terceira early in 1487 on a western route of discovery, but could not make any headway against the strong westerlies, which prevailed in that latitude. The expedition failed miserably. King João could find no assurance that a westward voyage to Cipango was possible.

CHAPTER TEN: COLUMBUS IN CASTILE

1. Paolo Emilio Taviana, *Christopher Columbus: The Grand Design*, Novara: Istituto Geografico De Agostini, 1985, p. 187.
2. Some scholars believe that Columbus's plan was rejected by the Sovereigns in a meeting held shortly after the Talavera commission had concluded their deliberations in 1487. Notable among these scholars is P. E. Taviani, who offers a different scenario spanning the years of 1487–91 that Columbus spent in Spain trying to

secure approval and financing for his plan of exploration. See Taviani's chapters XL and XLI.
3. *Il Principe, a cura di Luigi Russo*, Firenze: Sansoni, 1959. Machiavelli cited Ferdinand as a perfect example of a politician who achieved his ends by dissembling his aims, a man who always preached peace while waging war.

CHAPTER ELEVEN: YEARS OF AGONY; DAYS OF GLORY

1. *Biography*, p. 37.
2. I am aware that the bridge named after Verrazzano is spelled with one Z, but I prefer Verrazzano because it reflects better the correct pronunciation of the name in modern Italian.
3. Ibid, p. 43.

CHAPTER TWELVE: CAPITULATIONS AND ROYAL DECREES

1. The text of the Capitulations is published in a number of books. The translation I am quoting from is by S. E. Morison, *Admiral of the Ocean Sea*, vol. 1, New York: Time Incorporated, 1962, pp. 96–97.
2. For a discussion of the composition of the crew, see Paolo Emilio Taviani's *Christopher Columbus*, p. 510.

CHAPTER FOURTEEN: BEGINNING OF THE GRAND ENTERPRISE TO THE CANARIES

1. *Biography*, pp. 53.
2. Michele De Cuneo's letter on the second voyage was written to a fellow citizen, Hieronymo Annnari, on October 15, 1495. It was published by Cesare de Lollis in the *Raccolta*, Part III, Vol. 2., pp. 95ff. It was translated into English by S. E. Morison in his *Journals and Other Documents on the Life of C. Columbus*, New York: The Heritage Press, 1963, pp. 210ff.

CHAPTER FIFTEEN: THE DISCOVERY OF THE WEST INDIES

1. *The Log of Christopher Columbus*, translated by Robert H. Fuson, Camden, Maine: International Marine Publishing Co., 1987, p. 53.
2. The gulfweed is a perennial pelagic, that is, it grows right in the ocean from algae, and not on land as originally thought.

3. Without getting too involved in astronomy, we know today that the earth is not a perfect sphere but is a little flattened at the poles and a little thicker at the equator. This causes the axis to wobble the way a slowing-down top does. The axis then describes a funnel-shaped motion once around in about 25,800 years. Stars that are on this circle or close to it become pole stars successively in the course of 25,800 years—the time span of one complete wobble called the Platonic Year.

Polaris today is very close to this thrice, and the celestial pole wandering along the circle is now only 1° away from Polaris. In Columbus's time, Polaris described a radius of about 3°27' about the celestial pole. During the next century, the celestial pole will come even closer to Polaris, but as time goes on, it will draw farther away.

Astronomers tell us that the stars Gamma, Beta, and Alpha in the Cepheus are next in line and will be the pole stars in two thousand, four thousand, and six thousand years, approximately. Unfortunately, these stars do not shine very brightly and will make poor showing—a fact that will not be of much concern to modern navigation.
4. *Log*, pp. 73–77.

CHAPTER SIXTEEN: FROM SAN SALVADOR TO CUBA

1. *Log*, p. 75.
2. The Latin text is from the *Tablas Cronologicas* of Padre Claudio Clemente, quoted by Washington Irving in his *Life and Voyages of C. Columbus*, New York: Putnam's Sons, 1889, p. 193.
3. Although Watling is the choice of a large number of scholars, there is still much disagreement regarding the identity of San Salvador. Many simply do not accept Watling as the first island discovered by Columbus. Grand Turk, Samana Cay, Cat Island, Mayaguana, and Caicos, have all been proposed as sites for the first landing in the New World.
4. Ibid, p. 77.
5. Ibid, p. 78.
6. Ibid, p. 80.
7. Ibid, p. 88.

8. In *Ulisse 2000* "Cristoforo Colombo," Supplement to No. 33/34, October–November 1986, p. 12–19.
9. Ibid, p. 89.
10. Ibid, pp. 91–92.

CHAPTER SEVENTEEN: THE CUBAN EXPERIENCE

1. *Log*, p. 95.
2. Ibid, p. 95.
3. Ibid, p. 98.
4. Ibid, p. 100.
5. S. E. Morison, *Admiral of the Ocean Sea*, op. cit., p. 251. Morison's identification has been questioned by some scholars, primarily because Alfirk is nearly invisible to the naked eye.
6. Ibid, p. 105.
7. Actually, it was a mockingbird.
8. There were no geese in Cuba. It was probably a turkey.
9. Millett. Columbus was referring to corn, which was unknown to Europeans.
10. Ibid, p. 105.
11. Ibid, p. 108.
12. Ibid, p. 113.
13. Ibid, p. 120.
14. Ibid, p. 121.
15. Ibid, p. 123.

CHAPTER EIGHTEEN: HISPANIOLA

1. *Log*, p. 131.
2. Ibid, pp.139–140.
3. Ibid, p. 144.
4. Ibid, p. 144.

CHAPTER NINETEEN: SHIPWRECK—LA NAVIDAD

1. *Log*, p. 153.
2. Ibid, p. 154.
3. Ibid, p. 154.
4. Ibid, p. 163.

5. Ibid, p. 168.
6. Ibid, p. 169.
7. Ibid, p. 173.

CHAPTER TWENTY: RETURN VOYAGE, 1493

1. *Log*, p. 181.
2. Ibid, p. 181.
3. The Azores consist of nine volcanic islands in the mid-Atlantic eight hundred miles west of Portugal between 36°55'N and 39°55'N latitude and between 26°10'W and 31°16'W longitude. They consist of three groups: Santa María and São Miguel in the southeast; Terceira, São Jorge, Pico, Graciosa, and Fayal in the center; and Flores and Corvo in the northwest.
4. The letter is reproduced in its entirety in Chapter 22.
5. Ibid, p. 185.
6. Ibid, p. 186.
7. Ibid, p. 186.
8. Ibid, p. 190.

CHAPTER TWENTY-ONE: INTERLUDE IN PORTUGAL— JOURNEY'S END

1. *Biography*, p. 97.
2. *Log*, p. 192.
3. *Biography*, p. 99.
4. Ibid, p. 100.
5. Rui de Pina, *Cronica d' el Rey D. João II*, Lisbon, 1792. The text in question may be found in *The Northmen, Columbus and Cabot*, ed. by E. G. Bourne, New York: Scribner's Sons, 1906, p. 255.
6. Ibid, p. 255.
7. *Log*, p. 196.

CHAPTER TWENTY-TWO: COLUMBUS'S LETTER— AN ACCOUNT OF HIS DISCOVERY

1. *Veinte*, Probably a misprint for *Treinta*. The actual time was thirty-three days.
2. Misprint for *Isabela*, the name he gave to Crooked Island.
3. i.e., a province of China.

4. Puerto Gibara.
5. 178 is a misprint for 188 leagues, as stated later in the letter.
6. Misprint for Tenerifo.
7. A copper coin worth half a maravedi, about a third of a cent.
8. Columbus meant *Avan*, the Arawak word for a Cuban region from which Havana is derived.
9. Actually, 21° and 20° are correct.
10. Matinino in the Journal for 15 January 1493. The French named it Martinique.
11. The first appearance in print of this name that Columbus gave to the natives of America.
12. The government of Genoa. Columbus as a young man had made a voyage or two to Chios.
13. An oblique reference to the *Pinta*, or to the loss of the *Santa María*.
14. So in both Spanish editions; doubtless a misprint for Azores.
15. Sueste, a misprint for sudoeste.
16. Plural in both Spanish editions.
17. Quatorze. A misprint for cuatro, for the *Niña* entered the Tagus on the fourth.

CHAPTER TWENTY-THREE: THE CONQUERING HERO RETURNS HOME

1. Quoted from Jean Merien, *Christopher Columbus: the Mariner and the Man*, transl. by Maurice Michael, London: Odhams Press Limited, 1958, p. 185.
2. The text of this letter is in John Boyd Thacher, *Christopher Columbus, III*, New York, 1904, pp. 100–113.
3. Salvador de Madariaga, *Christopher Columbus*, New York: Unger 1967. As quoted by Simon Wiesenthal in *Sails of Hope, The Secret Mission of Christopher Columbus*, New York: The Macmillan Company, 1973, p. 133.
4. Björn Landström, *Columbus*, New York: The Macmillan Company, 1966, pp. 104–105.
5. *Biography*, p. 101.

CHAPTER TWENTY-FOUR: THE SECOND VOYAGE OF DISCOVERY

1. *Biography*, p. 58.

2. Ibid, p. 109.
3. The letter of Michele de Cuneo was translated by Samuel Eliot Morison in his *Journals and Other Documents on the Life and Voyages of Christopher Columbus*, New York: Heritage Press, 1963, pp. 210ff. Hereafter, we will refer to this Morison volume as *JOAD*.
4. The text of Dr. Chanca's letter is most accessible in J. M. Cohen's edition of *The Four Voyages of Christopher Columbus*, Maryland: Penguin Books, 1969, pp. 129–157.
5. De Cuneo, Ibid.
6. Niccolò Scillacio's letter was translated by S. E. Morison in his *JAOD*, pp. 229ff. The letter is also reproduced with a different translation facing the Latin text in John Boyd Thacher, Christopher *Columbus, His Life, His Works, His Remains*, Vol. 2, New York: AMS Press, 1967, pp. 223–262.

CHAPTER TWENTY-FIVE: A LITANY OF SAINTS

1. Today about two thousand Carib Indians—descendants of the Caribbean's original inhabitants—still live in the interior of the island. Immediately to the south, less than thirty miles away, lies the island of Martinique, the "Matinino" island that Columbus sought when he left Samana Bay in January. The Admiral came amazingly close to making a landfall on the island of his quest. A keen observer, possessing the skills of a superior mapmaker, Columbus undoubtedly obtained enough information from his Indian captive guides as to rough out a map of the Antilles to guide him on his second voyage.

The Antilles, named after the legendary island of Antillia, is another name for the West Indies. The Greater Antilles includes Cuba, Jamaica, Hispaniola, Puerto Rico, and a few small neighboring islands. These are the larger islands that form the northern limit of the western part of the arc of the Antilles. The Lesser Antilles, which define the eastern border of the Caribbean Sea, complete the arc extending from Puerto Rico to the coast of Venezuela and follow the line of that coast westward almost in a horizontal pattern, on a 120° N latitude parallel to the Gulf of Venezuela.

English geographers have defined the Lesser Antilles further by calling the northern part of the chain the Leeward Islands, extending from south of Puerto Rico to Dominica, and the southern part the Windward Islands, which extend from Martinique south to Grenada.

The Lesser Antilles, though discovered by Columbus for Spain, became later the battle area of the European maritime nations to win supremacy in the New World. The varied languages spoken in these islands are a reminder that they belonged to Great Britain, France, and Holland. These nations have granted some of the islands their independence.

The West Indies were regarded up to the end of the eighteenth century as the most valuable part of America, and these islands were the chief battleground of the rival European powers. With the independence of the United States, the importance of the islands began to wane. Nearly all of them derived their wealth in the past from sugar cultivation, and with the decline in the price of sugar, their income fell so sharply that they have never recovered. Meanwhile, the importation of black slaves from Africa after the Indian populations had been nearly exterminated and the return of whites to their land or origin have changed the racial balance of the islands with blacks outnumbering whites. Lacking industries and relying primarily on agriculture and tourism for income, these islands, some of them oppressed by despotic rulers, have not achieved the expectations of their discoverer.

2. *The Four Voyages of C. Columbus*, ed. & trans. by J. M. Cohen, Baltimore, MD: Penguin Books, 1969, p. 132.
3. Ibid, p. 133.
4. Ibid, p. 136.
5. *Biography*, p. 111.
6. Ibid, p. 112.
7. Both Nevis and St. Kitts are known as the "Planters' Isles" because nearly half of the workforce of these islands is employed in sugar production.
8. Barely five miles long, this island was once a rich port whose freebooters ran supplies for the colonies during the American Revolution.
9. A possession of the Netherlands, half of its population is black and half of Dutch and English ancestry.
10. During the French occupation, it was renamed St. Croix, which is the French translation of Holy Cross, and this is the official name adopted by the geographers on maps. But it is now a possession of

the United States and seamen prefer calling it Santa Cruz possibly because of familiarity, because there are several cities by that name in the United States. This is one of the Virgin Islands bought from Denmark in 1917. Because of its airfoil shape, it parts the trade winds, eliminating any lee shores to provide a haven for ships, except at the unsuited rear of the island. However, on its northern shore near the middle of the island in the present location of Christiansted, there is a natural indentation of the land called Christiansted Harbor.
11. Ibid, p. 136
12. As quoted by Kirkpatrick Sale in his *Conquest of Paradise*, New York, Alfred A. Knopf, 1990, p. 140.
13. They were returning from a pious pilgrimage to Rome when they were attacked by the Huns at Cologne and killed for their faith. These islands are not eleven thousand, only forty-six, owned today by the United States and the United Kingdom. St. Thomas and St. John on the same latitude of 18°20'N, belong to the United States together with St. Croix. Tortola and Virgin Gorda belong to the United Kingdom.
14. Unfortunately, the name "Gratiosa" did not last, as later geographers adopted the name Vieques.

CHAPTER TWENTY-SIX: RETURN TO NAVIDAD

1. John Boyd Thacher, *Christopher Columbus*, Vol. II, p. 255.
2. See Kirkpatrick Sale's *Conquest of Paradise*, pp. 129–31 for a discussion of the controversy over the cannibalism of the Caribs.
3. Thacher, p. 133.
4. J. M. Cohen, *Four Voyages*, p. 150.
5. Thacher, p. 256.
6. Thacher, p. 256.

CHAPTER TWENTY-SEVEN: ISABELA AND CIBAO

1. *Biography*, p. 122.
2. Morison, *JAOD*, p. 210ff.
3. Ibid.
4. Martín Fernández Navarrete, *Obras de F. Navarrete*, p. 368.

CHAPTER TWENTY-EIGHT: IN SEARCH OF TERRA FIRMA— THE EXPLORATIONS OF CUBA, 1494

1. Morison, *JAOD*, p. 210ff.

CHAPTER TWENTY-NINE: RETURN TO ISABELA— JUNE 13–SEPTEMBER 19

1. *Biography*, p. 141.
2. Ibid, p. 142.
3. Andrés Bernáldez, *Historia de los Reyes Católicos*, II vols, Seville, 1870. Quoted by Morison, *Admiral of the Ocean Sea*, vol. II, p. 469.
4. *Biography*, p. 145.
5. Ibid, p. 145.

CHAPTER THIRTY: DISCORD IN ISABELA— TROUBLE WITH THE INDIANS

1. B. Las Casas, *Historia de las Indias*, Lib. 1, Chapter 29, transl. by W. Irving, *The Life and Voyages of C. Columbus*, vol. 1, pp. 22–23.
2. Irving, vol. 1, p. 31.
3. De Cuneo, in Morison, *JAOD*, p. 226.
4. Ibid.

CHAPTER THIRTY-ONE: A PERIOD OF DISCONTENT

1. *Biography*, p. 150.
2. It is very difficult to give an accurate estimate of the number of people who inhabited the Caribbean. Recent scholarship, however, indicates that the population was much larger than estimated—some suggesting that it was close to eight million souls. For a detailed discussion of the population question, see Kirkpatrick Sale's *Conquest of Paradise*, pp. 159–61. Mr. Sale offers even more chilling estimates of the number of deaths caused by disease and Spanish violence.
3. Original Spanish in M. F. Navarrete, *Obras de F. Navarrete*, p. 396.

CHAPTER THIRTY-TWO: COLUMBUS RETURNS TO SPAIN— MARCH 10–JUNE 11, 1496

1. *Biography*, p. 169.

2. *Recipe for making cassava bread:*
The large turnip-like roots of the yucca from which cassava bread is made are very poisonous. After the skin is removed, the roots are rubbed against a rasp, which is a flat piece of wood embedded with many small sharp stones. The white grated cassava is then mixed with water to make a paste. The water and the poison (hydrocyanic acid) is leached out in a clever but primitive manner. A long stocking-like sleeve made of intermeshed straw is filled with cassava paste. A heavy stone is tied to the bottom of the stocking, which is closed to prevent the escape of the paste, and the open end is attached and held firmly to a cantilevered support. The weight stretches the sleeve (thus reducing the diameter), squeezing the paste and leaching out the poison, which the Caribs used in the tip of their arrows. In effect, they utilized the effects of gravity. The dry cassava mass is removed from the stocking-like sleeve and sifted to a fine flour, which can be kept for a long time just like wheat flour. To make cassava bread this flour is mixed with water, kneading it into dough; it is then patted into thin cakes and baked over a griddle made of earthenware. Because cassava bread retains its flavor and freshness for a long time, it was much used by the early navigators.

Cassava is a South American shrub, manioc or yucca, found also in the Caribbean (*manihot utilissima*). There are two forms popularly known as bitter and sweet, both of which are highly cultivated in tropical America for their fleshy, cylindrical, starchy roots, which form a large part of the natives' food and from which tapioca is made. The plant attains a height and breadth of four feet and more. In about seven months after planting, the white, soft roots, which may weigh as much as thirty pounds and are sometimes three feet long and three inches thick, are dug up by hand, washed, and grated or ground to a pulp as already stated. The juice or poisonous part is carefully pressed out, and the flour that remains after pressure is formed into their round cakes and baked. Poisoning from the bitter cassava is due to the presence of minute quantities of hydrocyanic acid, which is driven off in the general process of manufacture. From the pure flour of cassava tapioca is formed, which is frequently used for jelly, puddings, and other culinary purposes. Cassava was the main source of food for the South American and Caribbean Indians, and together with maize (corn), was used on the mainland as the primary source

of carbohydrates. Las Casas wrote that in many cases about two acres of land cultivated with it would yield 150 to 175 loads of cassava bread and that single load could last a person for a month. Agriculture in the Americas was based primarily on maize, with the roots of plants such as the cassava and potato providing a supplementary source of high-energy food.
3. Ibid, p. 173.

CHAPTER THIRTY-THREE: APPROVAL AND PREPARATIONS FOR THE THIRD VOYAGE

1. M. F. Navarette, *Obras*, p. 422.
2. The complete text of the "Mayorazgo" is published in Washington Irving's *The Life and Voyages of C. Columbus*, Vol. III, New York, 1889, pp. 522–33.

CHAPTER THIRTY-FOUR: THIRD VOYAGE OF DISCOVERY— LANDFALL IN TRINIDAD

1. *Biography*, p. 176.
2. Ibid, p. 178.
3. Ibid, p. 178.
4. B. Las Casas, transl. by R. H. Major in *Northmen, Columbus and Cabot*, op., cit., p. 327–28.
5. Ibid, p. 330.
6. Ibid, p. 331.
7. Ibid, p. 339.

CHAPTER THIRTY-FIVE: DISCOVERY OF THE GULF OF PARIA AND THE NEW CONTINENT

1. Las Casas, in *Northmen*, p. 341.
2. Ibid, p. 342.
3. The reference to the Indians wearing "gold leaf" around their necks had been erroneously translated as "golden eyes." The translator had mistaken "hojas" (leaves) for "ojos" (eyes). Las Casas, p. 344.
4. Las Casas, p. 345.
5. Ibid, p. 354.
6. Ibid, p. 355.
7. R. H. Major, *Select Letters of Christopher Columbus*, op. cit., p. 148.

CHAPTER THIRTY-SIX: REBELLION IN HISPANIOLA

1. *Biography*, p. 209–10.
2. Ibid, p. 209–11.

CHAPTER THIRTY-SEVEN: COLUMBUS IN DISGRACE

1. *Biography*, p. 220.
2. Ibid, p. 220.
3. Ibid, p. 221.
4. "Letter to the Nurse of Prince John,' in *Northmen*, p. 381.
5. Ibid, p. 382.
6. Ibid, p. 382.

CHAPTER THIRTY-EIGHT: PREPARATIONS FOR A FOURTH VOYAGE

1. *Biography*, p. 225.

CHAPTER THIRTY-NINE: START OF FOURTH VOYAGE— FRIGHTFUL HURRICANE

1. The "Lettera Rarissima" can be read in its entirety in a number of publications. I am quoting from the translation by R. H. Major, published in *Northmen, Columbus and Cabot*, ed. by E. G. Bourne, New York: Scribner's Sons, 1906, pp. 387–88.
2. *Biography*, p. 230.
3. Ibid, p. 340.

CHAPTER FORTY: SEARCHING FOR A PASSAGE TO INDIA

1. *Biography*, p. 214.
2. Major in *Northmen*, p. 391.
3. Ibid, p. 236.
4. Ibid, p. 237.

CHAPTER FORTY-ONE: ADVENTURE ALONG THE COAST OF VERAGUA AND PANAMA

1. *Biography*, p. 243.

2. Ibid, p. 243.
3. Ibid, p. 245.
4. Ibid, p. 245.
5. Ibid, p. 245.
6. Ibid, p. 246.
7. Ibid, p. 246.
8. Ibid, p. 246.
9. Major in *Northmen*, p. 399.
10. Ibid, p. 249.
11. Ibid, p. 249.

CHAPTER FORTY-TWO: AGONY AND TRAGEDY IN BELÉN

1. *Biography*, p. 252.
2. Ibid, p. 253.
3. Major in *Northmen*, p. 413.
4. The quotations of Michele de Cuneo's colorful account are from *The Four Voyages of Christopher Columbus*, ed. and transl. by M. Cohen, London: The Cresset Library, 1969, pp. 308–9.
5. Ibid, p. 309.
6. *Northmen*, pp. 403–5.
7. *The Life and Voyages of Christopher Columbus*, Vol. III, New York: Putnam's Sons, 1889, p. 405.
8. *Biography*, p. 263.
9. The coast of Veragua is as beautiful and pristine now as when Columbus landed there. The constant rainstorms have prevented any further European settlements. The descendants of the Guaymis still live in the hills. Gold can still be found there, but no one except the Indians is willing or capable to get it out of the earth economically. Because of the extremely heavy rainfalls, mining gold is very difficult.

CHAPTER FORTY-THREE: HOMEWARD BOUND FROM BELÉN

1. *Biography*, p. 263.
2. "Lettera Rarissima," in *Northmen*, p. 406.
3. *Biography*, p. 264.
4. Ibid, p. 265.
5. Cohen, *Four Voyages*. pp. 310–12.
6. Cohen, pp. 312–13.
7. Cohen, p. 313.

8. Cohen, p. 313.
9. *Northmen*, p. 393.
10. *Northmen*, pp. 417–18.
11. Cohen, p. 314.

CHAPTER FORTY-FOUR: SEEKING HELP IN HISPANIOLA—
MUTINY IN JAMAICA

1. *Biography*, p. 263.
2. Ibid, p. 277.
3. Cohen, *Four Voyages*, p. 315.
4. *Biography*, p. 270.
5. Ibid, p. 273.

CHAPTER FORTY-FIVE: HOME AT LAST

1. *Biography*, p. 281.
2. Ibid, p. 282.
3. Ibid, p. 284.

CHAPTER FORTY-SIX: DEATH OF COLUMBUS

1. The letters of Columbus were collected and published in Spanish by Martín Fernández Navarrete in *Colección de los viajes y descubrimientos que hicieron por mar los Españoles*, Madrid, 1823–37. I am quoting from W. Irving's translation appearing in his *Life and Voyages of C. Columbus*.
2. Irving, vol. II, p. 558.
3. Ibid, p. 561.
4. William Heckling Prescott, *History of Ferdinand and Isabella*, New York: The Heritage Press, 1962, p. 242.
5. Irving, p. 565.
6. Ibid, Vol. III, p. 401.

CHAPTER FORTY-SEVEN: EPILOGUE

1. Martín Fernandez de Navarrete, *Obras de Navarrette*, Madrid, 1954.
2. The League of Cambrai, between Maximilian, Louis XII, Pope Julius II, and Ferdinand was formed to break the power of Venice.

Maximilian took possession of a part of the Venetian territory but the besieged Padua in vain (1509). Pope Julius II (Giuliano della Rovere) had hoped to acquire the Venetian possession in the Romanga region.

About the Author

Christopher Columbus: His Life and Discoveries is the fruit of a lifelong love and admiration for the legendary feats of the great Genoese navigator. Dr. Di Giovanni, a researcher, a humanist and a man of faith, always felt a special affinity to Columbus, a man of the Renaissance, who sought, with his discoveries, to expand the boundaries of knowledge and Christianity.

Mario was born December 20, 1911 in a small town near the city of Avellino, some 30 miles east of Naples. In 1921, at age 10, he migrated with his family to the United States, settled in New Jersey, and attended Barringer High School in Newark, excelling in academics as well as track and field. He attended New York University graduating with a B.A. in Mechanical Engineering and later earned a Doctorate in Science. (In 1980, as an alumnus of NYU, he received the "Lifetime Achievement Award" in the field of science for the class of 1935.)

The first years of his professional life were spent in teaching, a vocation to which Dr. Di Giovanni always felt drawn. In 1969, after retiring from his scientific research, he resumed teaching with courses at Loyola-Marymount and Pepperdine Universities.

In 1938, he married his sweetheart Mary Cordasco, also a New Jerseyan. Their union was a model of total and lasting love which was blessed by the birth of a son, Martin, and a daughter, Ann Marie Calabro.

Dr. Di Giovanni's intense and productive career in scientific research began during World War II when he taught Helicopter

Design at a New York trade school. In 1952 he accepted a position with Statham Instruments in California where he worked on research and development in the aeronautical field, particularly with pressure transducers for instrumentation. Later, and with more personal satisfaction, he did biomedical research for application to the human heart, contributing effectively to the development of the first artificial heart. In all, he filed and obtained over 30 patents.

Dr. Di Giovanni was a man of considerable public involvement, taking an active part in humanitarian, cultural and social activities. With Angelo Lupo and Santino Vasquez, he was instrumental in bringing to the west coast "UNICO National," the largest Italian-American service club to the United States. In 1962, he became national president; the first from a western state.

Proud of his Catholic faith, for many years he was a lector at his local parish in Pacific Palisades. In the 1970's, he was among the first to join Father Luigi Donanzan in the campaign to erect Casa Italiana Cultural Center and Villa Scalabrini Retirement Center. In 1979, he became the first elected president of the Villa Scalabrini Council. He was also active within the Federated Italo-Americans of Southern California, the confederation of all Italian organizations in Los Angeles, becoming its president in 1981. In 1982 he received the "Federated Man of the Year Award." Other public recognitions include the UNICO "Vastola Award" in 1972 and the "Commander Award" from the Republic of Italy in 1982.

In January 1980, while conducting a meeting of the Villa Scalabrini Council, he suffered his first heart attack. It was after such a shocking event, forced as he was to further reduce his work, that Dr. Mario Di Giovanni began, in earnest, to write his book on Columbus. He methodically organized the material he had been collecting throughout the years. It was as if he sensed that he had very little time left. Thus this book is truly a work of love and sacrifice. But for the sad event of January 1980 and his decision to hurry on with his elected task, the world might not have known that Dr. Mario Di Giovanni was "an expert on Columbus," as the *Book of Buffs, World Almanac* lists him.

Dr. Di Giovanni died on July 21, 1986, his last task not quite complete.

Christopher Columbus—His Life and Discoveries first saw the light of day in 1991, thanks to the initiative of Columbus Explorers, Inc. It was a fitting tribute to a great navigator, Columbus, on the occasion of the 500th anniversary of his discovery. It is also a deserved memorial to Dr. Mario Di Giovanni, a dedicated scientist and researcher. The Mentoris Project is proud to re-release *Christopher Columbus—His Life and Discoveries* as a paperback and ebook.

NOW AVAILABLE FROM THE MENTORIS PROJECT

America's Forgotten Founding Father
A Novel Based on the Life of Filippo Mazzei
by Rosanne Welch

A. P. Giannini—The People's Banker
by Francesca Valente

Fermi's Gifts
A Novel Based on the Life of Enrico Fermi
by Kate Fuglei

God's Messenger
The Astounding Achievements of Mother Cabrini
A Novel Based on the Life of Mother Frances X. Cabrini
by Nicole Gregory

Harvesting the American Dream
A Novel Based on the Life of Ernest Gallo
by Karen Richardson

Marconi and His Muses
A Novel Based on the Life of Guglielmo Marconi
by Pamela Winfrey

Saving the Republic
A Novel Based on the Life of Marcus Cicero
by Eric D. Martin

Soldier, Diplomat, Archaeologist
A Novel Based on the Bold Life of Louis Palma di Cesnola
by Peg A. Lamphier

COMING SOON FROM THE MENTORIS PROJECT

A Novel Based on the Life of Alessandro Volta
A Novel Based on the Life of Amerigo Vespucci
A Novel Based on the Life of Andrea Palladio
A Novel Based on the Life of Angelo Dundee
A Novel Based on the Life of Antonin Scalia
A Novel Based on the Life of Antonio Meucci
A Novel Based on the Life of Buzzie Bavasi
A Novel Based on the Life of Cesare Becaria
A Novel Based on the Life of Federico Fellini
A Novel Based on the Life of Filippo Brunelleschi
A Novel Based on the Life of Frank Capra
A Novel Based on the Life of Galileo Galilei
A Novel Based on the Life of Giovanni Andrea Doria
A Novel Based on the Life of Giovanni di Bicci de' Medici
A Novel Based on the Life of Giuseppe Garibaldi
A Novel Based on the Life of Giuseppe Verdi
A Novel Based on the Life of Guido Monaco
A Novel Based on the Life of Harry Warren
A Novel Based on the Life of Henry Mancini
A Novel Based on the Life of John Cabot
A Novel Based on the Life of Judge John Sirica
A Novel Based on the Life of Lenonardo Covello
A Novel Based on the Life of Leonardo de Vinci
A Novel Based on the Life of Luca Pacioli
A Novel Based on the Life of Maria Montessori
A Novel Based on the Life of Mario Andretti
A Novel Based on the Life of Mario Cuomo
A Novel Based on the Life of Niccolo Machiavelli
A Novel Based on the Life of Peter Rodino
A Novel Based on the Life of Pietro Belluschi
A Novel Based on the Life of Publius Cornelius Scipio
A Novel Based on the Life of Robert Barbera
A Novel Based on the Life of Saint Augustine of Hippo
A Novel Based on the Life of Saint Francis of Assisi
A Novel Based on the Life of Saint Thomas Aquinas
A Novel Based on the Life of Vince Lombardi

For more information on these titles and
The Mentoris Project, please visit
www.mentorisproject.org.

www.ingramcontent.com/pod-product-compliance
Lightning Source LLC
Chambersburg PA
CBHW020033120526
44588CB00030B/85